HARLEM'S
Hell Fighters

Also by Stephen L. Harris

Duty, Honor, Privilege:
New York's Silk Stocking Regiment
and the Breaking of the Hindenburg Line

100 Golden Olympians

HARLEM'S
Hell Fighters

THE AFRICAN-AMERICAN 369TH INFANTRY IN WORLD WAR I

STEPHEN L. HARRIS
FOREWORD BY ROD PASCHALL

POTOMAC BOOKS
An imprint of the University of Nebraska Press

Published in the United States by Potomac Books, Inc. (formerly
Brassey's, Inc.). All rights reserved. No part of this book may be repro-
duced in any manner whatsoever without written permission from the
publisher, except in the case of brief quotations embodied in critical
articles and reviews.

Maps by Molly O'Halloran

Library of Congress Cataloging-in-Publication Data

Harris, Stephen L.
  Harlem's hell fighters : the African-American 369th Infantry in
World War I / Stephen L. Harris ; foreward by Rod Paschall.— 1st ed.
      p. cm.
Includes bibliographical references and index.
    ISBN 1-57488-386-0 (hardcover : alk. paper)
  1. United States. Army. Infantry Regiment, 369th—History. 2. World
War, 1914–1918—Regimental histories—United States. 3. World War,
1914–1918—African Americans. 4. United States. Army—African
American troops—History—20th century. 5. France. Armâee—African
American troops—History—20th century. 6. World War, 1914–1918—
Campaigns—Western Front. I. Title.

D570.33369th .H37 2003
940.4'1273—dc21

                                                    2002156003

ISBN 1-57488-635-5   (paper)

First Edition

To Connor Lamar
Everyone should have a grandson like Connor

and to
Sergeants Henry Johnson and William Butler
who were denied the Medal of Honor
because of the color of their skin

CONTENTS

ILLUSTRATIONS

PHOTOGRAPHS

MAPS

FOREWORD

This is a regimental history. But also much more. It is a story of bravery, bigotry—and *jazz*. That's right, America's signature music. It is an important book because it not only addresses the tale of a National Guard infantry regiment in battle, it delves into the most persistent and tragic flaw in America's social fabric. And it touches on the rapid internationalization of a special facet of American culture. The author, Stephen Harris, is likely the only writer who could have taken the task of recording and explaining the birth and the initial bloody employment of the 369th U.S. Infantry (created as the 15th New York Infantry Regiment) in the trenches and killing grounds of the Great War's western front. Harris, fresh from the publication of his *Duty, Honor, Privilege,* the story of New York's Seventh Infantry Regiment in World War I, had acquired the research experience and expertise to deal with John "Blackjack" Pershing's citizen soldiers. However, that fine book was about the absolute upper crust of New York City's social elite. This book is about the city's blacks fighting in a faraway land under French, not U.S., command. The contrasts between the "silk stocking" set in combat and Harlem's battling heroes cannot be more dramatic.

A grasp of the times is essential. In 1917 the United States was far removed from the nation's current globe-straddling and dominating status. It was not then a worldwide recognized military power. It was not considered to be the most important financial center in the world. And it could hardly be described as a culturally influential country. Thanks to Henry Ford and vast stretches of rich earth, it did have the reputation for industrial might and agricultural abundance. But many of its industrial facilities and much of its factory output had been underwritten by London's banks. In the third year of World War I, this was just beginning to change as the British were reaching ever deeper into their diminished treasury. Culturally, the United States was important but hardly preponderant. The American film industry was burgeoning but so were European movie companies. In letters, art, and music, America was clearly a second- or third-tier attraction. The nation was, however, famous throughout the world for a brutal practice and a demeaning institution. Lynching and humiliating racial segregation had become prevalent throughout the American South, and due to an aggressive and vigilant Northeastern press, these shameful subjects were being widely reported. Militarily, the United States was not a serious contender. True, the U.S. Navy was world class, but Washington commanded a pitifully small ground force, one that could not even catch a murderous invader, the Mexican bandit Pancho Villa. To battle-wise European military leaders, America might be able to supply infantrymen to flesh out loss-laden British, French, and Italian ranks, but the U.S. Army did not have officers knowledgeable enough about modern warfare to contribute leadership, planning, or the administration of large bodies of troops. European generals would have to lead the Americans, and since U.S. war industries were insignificant and inexperienced, Europe would also have to arm the American foot soldiers. Thus in 1917, the sophisticated and lofty Old World looked down on the culturally inferior and socially primitive New World and saw little more than a ready source of cannon fodder for its trenches.

Gen. John J. Pershing, the commander of the American Expeditionary Force (AEF), was not about to let his troops be used as cannon fodder for European generals—except a few. Two 28,000-man U.S. divisions were placed under British command, and two divisions composed of black soldiers were put under French command. The 369th Infantry was in the latter category. This book explains in some detail the discrimination and wretched treatment soldiers of the 369th had to suffer to obtain the honor of fighting for their country under the control of generals of another country. The author has an interesting idea on why the U.S. commander turned over black American combat units to the French. The reader might keep in mind that Pershing was probably the most experienced American military leader in commanding or accompanying troops of races or religions that differed from those of white America. He had commanded U.S. African-American troops, Apache, and later, Sioux scouts, and he was with Japanese forces during the Russo-Japanese War of 1904–1905. Additionally, Pershing trained, armed, and commanded Muslim soldiers of the southern Philippines. However, being shunned by Pershing might have had some advantages, as the author points out. Oddly enough, many American troops who fought under the French and British would later consider themselves better off than the men who were in the AEF.

These years, the first two decades of the twentieth century, may have been one of the most virulent and poisonous periods of American racism. The rising incidence of lynching was accompanied by the formal institution of segregation laws in the South, many of which were based on legal models taken from Illinois, Indiana, and Ohio. Thus, racism was not confined to states below the Mason-Dixon Line. The author aptly describes the slaughter of New York City blacks during the Civil War and accurately points out the stimulus: poor whites fearing to lose jobs to their black neighbors who were accepting lower wages. This phenomenon reached new heights throughout the United States just before and during the first years of the Great War. This was a time when there was a steady march of southern blacks to factory towns in the North, while parts of American industry were displacing some industrial plants southward to avoid unionized white labor. Working-class whites became at first resentful, then angry, and, finally—particularly in the South— violent. Harris depicts several forms of bigotry. It was often subtle in the North, openly cruel in the South, and as the author shows—in existence among the officer class in France.

Psychologically debilitating racial attitudes were not the only obstacles the 369th had to overcome in preparing to fight in France. Like other American infantry regiments, it had to be equipped and trained for a war that American military leaders had never experienced. In many respects, the European generals were right. The U.S. Army entered the war with a strength of about 310,000 men—less than the number of Britain's *casualties* during the Battle of the Somme or the French losses at Verdun. France, Britain, and Germany were each manufacturing, maintaining, and employing hundreds of combat aircraft. America, the nation that created powered flight, managed to field only six obsolete "Jennies" to support Pershing's punitive expedition in Mexico—and managed to crash them all. Modern machine guns (another American invention) were virtually nonexistent in America's army. Just before

Congress declared war, the Army had scheduled trials to choose a suitable, up-to-date model. The U.S. Army had a three-inch light artillery piece, but facing a lengthy time of setting up mass manufacture, Washington selected the French 75mm howitzer, a gun already available in great numbers. It was the same story with the U.S. Springfield '03 rifle. With the British Enfield in large-scale production, waiting for the American rifle to be mass-produced was out of the question. The Europeans also had a sound point about the inexperience of the U.S. Army's officer corps. In the spring of 1917, only twenty-three American officers had been through the new Army education system to include the Army War College. Because of all these shortcomings, the 369th was as ill-equipped and ill-prepared for a World War I battlefield as any other American infantry regiment.

There was a clear superiority possessed by the regiment. The reader will discover the reasons why the regiment had a military band that apparently put all other such American and European units in the shade. And that seemingly superfluous fact likely had an important impact. The first few years of the twentieth century was an era when dance and popular music was rapidly emerging into an international rage. In America, youth had recently been wildly enthusiastic about ragtime music and was just experiencing the first wave of jazz. At considerable expense and effort, the 369th assembled what was probably the best American jazz ensemble that Europe had ever heard. And the unit was given the opportunity to play before European audiences. While concrete proof is impossible to produce in these sorts of social movements, it is likely that the regiment's band performances in 1917 and 1918 had much to do with creating or accelerating the French tastes for American jazz—a phenomenon that has persisted until this day.

The following story of Harlem's Hell Fighters is an important piece of history, both for America and the world. It is important to remember that attitudes, conditions, and circumstances during the first two decades of the twentieth century were radically different than in today's world. Much has changed—some for the better. In several ways, this tale of bravery, bigotry, and music had something to do with that change.

Rod Paschall

The idea for "Harlem's Hell Fighters" leaped out of the pages of my first book about New York City's citizen soldiers in World War I, *Duty, Honor, Privilege: New York's Silk Stocking Regiment and the Breaking of the Hindenburg Line*. While researching and writing that book, which chronicles the experiences of the Seventh Regiment, I found myself gripped by the story of the Fifteenth Regiment—the 369th Infantry. Although the obstacles that African-American troops had to overcome just to fight for their country in the Great War is known, I felt their story had yet to be told in a way that made them come alive once again. If I could, I wanted to recount the struggles, heartbreak, disappointment, courage, and triumph these soldiers went through to give New York State its first black regiment of National Guardsmen. I wanted to use their voices to tell their story. And to do this I needed the help of a lot of people.

The first, of course, is my wife, Sue. Her encouragement, support, and suggestions, and the fact that while I wrote, she put food on the table, paid the bills, and, in effect, kept the wolf from the door made it a whole lot easier for me to produce this book.

William Miles, the independent film producer, supported me in a way I can never repay. I'm sure he was skeptical at first when I called him from Vermont about my idea for the book. He'd already produced the highly regarded film about Harlem's Hell Fighters, *Men of Bronze*. He'd already run into too many people who said they were writing a book about the regiment—for which he is the historian—but who'd never finished what they started. He says they're from the "Gonna Tribe." As he told me, "The world's full of them—folks who say 'I'm gonna do this, I'm gonna do that,' but they never do anything." Bill is a wealth of information, a great traveling companion and, with his wonderful sense of humor, a joy to be around.

Of course, every writer needs an editor. I'm indebted to Don McKeon, Brassey's publisher, who has now been my guide through two books. His insights are invaluable. And always right.

For reading my manuscript, correcting errors of fact, and offering insightful comments I am grateful to Mitchell Yockelson, reference archivist at the National Archives and Records Administration in College Park, Maryland; and Michael Knapp, who had worked with Mitch at the National Archives, but lately can be found among rare books and manuscripts at Middlebury College's special collections department or in the classroom during winter months teaching a course about African Americans in the Great War.

Two Middlebury College students, Timothy Dybvig and Michael Silberman, were my secret weapons in Paris. While studying in France for a semester, they ransacked archives over there, collecting material for me in French.

I am also indebted to family members of officers and men of the 369th. Gillard Thompson Jr., whose father was a sergeant and drum major, spent hours on the phone with me, telling me stories of the old days. He sent photographs, newspaper clippings, vital information. He believes that when the 369th returned from France in 1919 and was the first American fighting force to march up Fifth Avenue, his father led the Hell Fighters under the Victory Arch and on up into Harlem. Stephen Spencer, son of Maj. Lorillard Spencer, was the first family member to pitch in, and he provided me with a recruiting poster that, I'm sure, has not been seen since 1916. Nathalie Compton Logan dug out a thick diary kept by her grandfather, Capt. Ranulf Compton. Unfortunately, he transferred out of the 369th just when the regiment's adventures overseas were getting exciting. Frederick H. Clark, son of Lt. John Holley Clark Jr., also produced a diary and letters filled with some of the most thrilling descriptions of battle. Other family members included Hamilton Fish, grandson of Capt. Hamilton Fish Jr.; Richardson Pratt Jr., son of 1st Lt. Richardson Pratt; Reid Poles, nephew of Cpl.

Spottswood Poles; and Harry Welty, grandson of Lt. George Robb, Medal of Honor winner.

Librarians are always a godsend to any writer. If I wrote down every librarian who helped me, I'd have another book on my hands. But I want to single out a few. Middlebury College's Starr Library was my home-away-from-home, and the people there did everything to make sure I got what I needed—except lunch. Most particularly helpful were Fleur Laslocky, Shirley Merrifield, and Joanne Stewart.

Far from Middlebury, but every bit as helpful, were Ida E. Jones, senior manuscript librarian at the Moorland Spingarn Research Center at Howard University in Washington, D.C.; Diana Lachatanere, director of the Manuscripts, Archives and Rare Books Division at the Schomburg Center for Research; and Eva Slezak, specialist for the African American Department at the Enoch Pratt Free Library in Baltimore.

Other librarians, curators, and researchers were Michael Aikey, director of New York State Military Museum and Veterans Research Center in Saratoga Springs; Betty Allen at the Union College Library in Schenectady; Fred Bassett of the New York State Museum in Albany; Sheila Biles, library technician for Special Collections and Archives Division at the United States Military Academy; Jacqueline Brown, associate librarian at Wilberforce (Ohio) University Archives and Special Collections, Rembert E. Stokes Learning Resources Center; and Carol Donick, director of the Alice Curtis Desmond and Hamilton Fish Library in Garrison, New York.

Also Gino Francesconi, archivist and museum director for New York's Carnegie Hall; Steven Fullwood, another of the Schomburg Research Center's terrific staff; Linda Hall, archives assistant at the Williams College archives and special collections; Leslie Kaplan at the Smithtown Library's Richard H. Handley Long Island History Collection; John Lancaster, curator of archives and special collections at the Amherst College Library; David V. Lewis at the Indiana State Library; Judy Lilly at Salina (Kansas) Public Library; and Suzanne Eggleston Lovejoy, assistant music librarian at the Yale University Library.

And Dawn Mullin of the South Carolina State Library in Columbia; Antonia Petrash, librarian/archivist at the Robert R. Coles Long Island History Collection housed at the Glen Cove Public Library; Monika Rhue, associate archivist at Johnson C. Smith University in Charlotte, N.C.; Ann Roche at the Goshen, N.Y., Library; Susan Thoms, local history assistant, in the Kennedy Room of the Spartanburg County (S.C.) Public Libraries; Caroline Weaver at the Archives of American Art, Smithsonian Institution; and Patricia C. Willis, curator of the Yale

Collection of American Literature, Beinecke Rare Book and Manuscript Library, Yale University.

Special help was offered by John Howe of Albany, N.Y., who is leading a personal crusade, and rightfully so, to get Sgt. Henry Johnson the Medal of Honor owed him by this country.

Also, Carolyn Lackey, for her knowledge of the holdings at the U.S. Army Military History Institute in Carlisle, Pa.; Peter J. Linder, for his expertise on World War I casualties; Linda Stevens Crissinger for her help in obtaining material about the Camp Wadsworth incident; and Katie Junget at the Bonner County (Idaho) Historical Society.

Hell Fighters has been used two different ways. Either as one word or two. I prefer two words, "Hell Fighters." Jim Europe's band was called the "Hell Fighters." Also, drummer Stephen Wright's first name is sometimes spelled "Steven." However, military records at the Albany State Library and the manifest of the USS *Pocohantas* list his name as Stephen, and that's the spelling I went with.

Strength of the Nation

Like two great rivers surging together at the confluence of Seventh Avenue and Fifty-seventh Street, thousands of New Yorkers, dressed to the nines, rushed toward the entrance to America's temple of music, Carnegie Hall. One part of this theater-going crowd was white; the other, black. They came by foot, overflowing the sidewalk for two blocks on either side of Carnegie Hall. Or they disembarked from cabs and private cars that seemed moored along the avenue like so many riverboats. Inside, the seats were quickly filling. Blacks settled down next to whites—a rarity even in New York, a city that prided itself on its cosmopolitan upbringing. In fact, in Gotham's other theaters, blacks were still quarantined as if they were lepers, forced to sit on the far left or up in the balcony while whites got the choice center rows. But on this night all seats were up for grabs. First come, first served.

It was 2 May 1912, a Thursday, and a remarkable concert was soon to begin. Although it was to benefit the Music School Settlement for Colored People, a struggling, one-year-old Harlem institution for artistically gifted children, the political and social vibes from this concert would soon be heard far beyond the musical world of Manhattan. You could argue that it would give legitimacy to African-American music in a white man's world, that it would ignite a dance craze that would sweep across

America, that it would even deliver enough recruits to fill the ranks of New York's original all-black National Guard regiment that was just then struggling for recognition, and that, in doing all these things, it would mean lasting fame to an extraordinary individual who, although better known for his music, would be the first African-American officer in the Great War to come under enemy fire in no-man's-land.

But at the time, all the founder of the Music School Settlement for Colored People hoped the concert would accomplish, besides raising money, was to prove a theory. David Mannes, a violin virtuoso and concertmaster of the New York Symphony Orchestra, believed that because music is the universal language and blacks are "natural-born musicians" it was music that would bring them and whites together in a mutual understanding.[1] And on this special night of music, blacks and whites were indeed together, and it was this fact that made the concert remarkable. It was most likely the first time in New York that so many African-American artists—at least three hundred of them in solo acts, duets, orchestras, choruses, and church choirs—were to perform their own music in the most famous white-owned, white-run theater in the country, and before a mixed audience.

The pressure on them to prove Mannes right while at the same time showcasing their own talent had to be nerve-wracking. Most white Americans didn't understand black music, no matter what Mannes thought, and they were sure that it would never bring the two races together. "Coon" music, they called it. Jungle chants brought over from Africa by ignorant slaves. Vulgar, sexy, primitive. As far as they were concerned, there wasn't a Bach or Beethoven among them. Not even an Irving Berlin. Hadn't Berlin taken the blacks' syncopated style of music known as ragtime and written "Alexander's Ragtime Band"? It was as if this white composer had rubbed the noses of black composers in their own music—showing them that anyone could write their trash.

Most of the whites settling in at Carnegie Hall knew better. Or at least they pretended they did. Outfitted in the best fashions of the day, encased in stiff, high-collared shirts beneath their dark tuxedos or corseted tightly in long evening gowns, the eminent audience included members of the Wanamaker family, who had often hired the best black musicians to play at private parties in Philadelphia, Newport, and New York. Also in the crowd were Lyman Beecher Stowe who had recently finished a biography of his grandmother, Harriet Beecher Stowe, and Elbridge Adams, executive of the American Piano Company, who had provided all fourteen pianos for the concert.

Perhaps the most observant white member of the audience, when it came to understanding black music, was Miss Natalie Curtis. At thirty-seven, she was devoting her life to the study and preservation of African-American and Native American music. She had already built quite a reputation as an ethnomusicologist. Being the daughter of a famous physician who had performed the autopsy on President Lincoln certainly hadn't hurt her career. An in-law was the late Robert Gould Shaw, the white colonel of the all-black Fifty-fourth Massachusetts Infantry Regiment of Civil War fame. Like Mannes, Curtis believed that "if anything can bring harmony from the present clashing of the two races . . . it might well be the peace-giver—music!"[2] She was as anxious as Mannes that the concert go off without a hitch.

Among the African Americans in attendance were at least two of Harlem's leading ministers: The Rev. Hutchens Chew Bishop, who only a year before had moved St. Philip's Episcopal Church from West Twenty-fifth Street up to West 134th Street to be part of the burgeoning growth of black Harlem, and the Rev. William H. Brooks of St. Mark's Methodist Episcopal Church, known as the "people's pastor." Tom Fletcher, a popular African American entertainer, recalled that the ministers, especially Bishop, whose St. Philip's Coleridge-Taylor Choir was on the program, believed choir members would be classified as sinners if they appeared on the same stage as the musicians. "Professional entertainers in those days," Fletcher wrote, "were considered 'imbued with the spirit of the devil'."[3] Only at the last minute had Bishop allowed his choir to be part of the concert. Other black luminaries in the audience, although there is no record they were there, almost certainly were Napoleon Bonaparte Marshall and Charles Fillmore. The Harvard-educated Marshall was among Manhattan's more successful attorneys. Fillmore, a businessman and Republican politician, personal friend of the late Ohio kingmaker Mark Hanna, and veteran of the Spanish-American War, was in the midst of pressing Governor John Dix into establishing for the first time a regiment of National Guardsmen for New York City's African Americans. In January he had sent Dix a roster of his "provisional regiment," one thousand names, many of them prominent Harlem citizens—with himself as colonel. He still awaited a response from the governor.

Meanwhile, Mannes, even with this sympathetic audience, felt edgy. It looked to him as if New Yorkers were unsure about investing time and money to listen to black music. They were reluctant to purchase tickets for the benefit. Two days before the concert barely one thousand had been sold, meaning that Carnegie Hall—which held up to twenty-eight hundred patrons—would be more than half empty. For Mannes and his Music School Settlement for Colored People, that would mean a public relations disaster. He may have even rued the day he had let the president of the Clef Club, an organization of leading black musicians, talk him into giving the concert. Although he knew that some members of the Clef Club Symphony Orchestra were professional jazz musicians, most of them were, as he feared, "barbers, waiters, red caps, bell-hops and such [and] it was possible for them to attend rehearsals only at times when they were free." Watching these so-called musicians at practice, some of them unable to read a single note of music, the famed concertmaster wondered "if this scattered and disorderly rehearsal attendance could produce anything but chaos."[4]

Curtis agreed. She, too, had watched rehearsals of the orchestra and called them "pathetic in their poverty of opportunity!"[5]

Not all of Mannes's skeptics were white. Composer and world-class violinist Will Marion Cook thought the concert an ill-conceived idea. At first, Cook, who, by his own admission, was "moody, quick of temper and ready for anything that comes along," declined to take part. One reason was that years ago he had sworn never again to play the violin after a newspaper reporter had called him the "world's greatest Negro violinist." Standing at the reporter's desk with violin in hand, Cook, who had studied in Germany and performed before England's royal family, smashed the instrument on the desk. "I am not the world's greatest Negro violinist," he snapped. "I am the greatest violinist in the world!"[6] Another reason Cook feared the concert was that if it proved to be a failure it might "set the Negro race back fifty years."[7]

Colonel Fillmore had to be on edge, too. If the concert flopped, then the governor, who held the power to grant New York City a Negro regiment of National Guardsmen, might refuse to sign into law the bill now on his desk that authorized such a regiment. If blacks were not reliable enough to stage a good concert, then how could they be relied upon to be good soldiers? In 1911 the governor had failed to sign a similar bill passed by the state assembly that called for a black regiment.

As Tom Fletcher noted, "The situation got warm, and as the date for the concert drew nearer, the sponsors began to feel nervous."[8]

Still, with all these worries, Mannes was committed as ever to his concert. It had to be a success. Carnegie Hall had to be filled. Anything less would prove his theory wrong—that through music whites and blacks could be brought together in harmony. Then, from almost out of the blue, articles appeared in the daily newspapers. The day before the concert the *Evening Journal* published a report that turned out to be a godsend. In part, its article stated:

> There are in New York more than 90,000 colored men and women. Very little is done for them, and very little for their children. In all directions they are denied, repressed and kept back. Everyone should

gladly help them find expression for their great musical talent, and to find happiness in that expression.

The article added, "The *Evening Journal* hopes that many of its readers will attend the concert, enjoy it, and perhaps find prejudice based on ignorance give place to sympathy and good will."[9]

The response to the *Evening Journal*'s plea floored Mannes and the directors of the Music School Settlement for Colored People. The concert sold out. The next night, as Carnegie Hall filled up, Miss Curtis remarked, "There were in the audience many of New York's best white musicians and also contributors to our Philharmonic and Symphony orchestras; and the musical editors of the New York papers had come in order to give this enterprise serious consideration. Never before had the Negroes had such an opportunity."[10]

From then on, all Mannes had to do was to sit back and hold his breath. For he knew that the success of the concert had now fallen on the shoulders of a single man.

Amid the swirling river of humanity outside Carnegie Hall, where close to a thousand people still sought tickets, a tall, powerfully built, yet graceful, man, smartly dressed in a white tuxedo and matching white shoes that contrasted sharply with his dark skin, pushed his way toward the entrance. Years later, a friend described him as a "big, tall man, very commanding. Stood up straight like a West Point soldier."[11] His round, wire-rimmed glasses hid eyes that seemed to pop from their sockets. With his glasses off he had the look of constant wonder. And at that moment, James Reese Europe, president of the Clef Club, had to be in wonder at the size of the crowd. No one expected it to be so overflowing, not even Europe. But he was running late, and this flood of people was holding him up. And now, towering in front of him, a nightstick gripped in his thick paws, was a police officer. A reserve force had been called out at the last moment to keep order.

The officer held the nightstick across his big chest and growled, "Get back! Get back!"

Pressing closer to the entrance, Europe hollered above the din, "Officer, I've gotta get through."

The officer glared at the dazzlingly dressed dark-hued man. "What do you mean, you gotta get through?" he snapped. It was clear that the officer's nerves were frazzled, and he'd had it with the overflow crowd.

Europe pleaded that he was the conductor of the orchestra, and, without him, the concert could not go on. Several people nearby, recognizing

Europe, stuck up for him. They told the officer that he was, in fact, the conductor. At last, he let Europe through. When the young musician squeezed inside Carnegie Hall, he was, according to a close friend, "out of breath, all disarranged by his battle with the crowd."[12] As he reached the wings of the stage he sensed the impatience of the audience. He was late, and he knew it. But when he was ready to stride on to the stage, what he saw waiting for him had to have stopped him in his tracks. Natalie Curtis called the sight "astonishing." A black orchestra—"a sort of American 'Balalaika' that filled the entire stage with banjos, mandolins, guitars, a few violins, violas, celli, double basses, here and there a wind instrument, some drums, eloquent in syncopation, and the sonorous background of ten upright pianos."[13] It was the Clef Club Symphony Orchestra, 125 pieces, perhaps more, all standing at attention. (Some accounts placed the number at over 140.) Waiting in the string section, violin in hand, was Will Marion Cook, who had vowed never to play again.[14] Also on stage was the Clef Club Chorus, 150 voices that had been especially trained by Cook to sing "old plantation melodies," and the St. Philip's Church Coleridge-Taylor Choir of 40 men and boys, led by its famous baritone, Harry T. Burleigh. Sitting at one of the pianos was the settlement school's musical director, J. Rosamond Johnson, who, with his brother James Weldon, had written and put to music "Lift Every Voice and Sing," recognized universally as the African American national anthem. There was hardly any room on the stage to move. To make it more jam-packed, part of the vast crowd had been provided chairs on stage, and these were filled. Tom Fletcher recollected that "People were offering anything just to get a chair on the stage with the orchestra."[15] There wasn't an empty seat in Carnegie Hall. Hundreds of people stood in the aisles or in the back by the doors to the lobby. David Mannes remembered how "The hall was packed from floor to the roof, thousands being turned away for lack of even standing room."[16]

Mannes sat up front, close to the center of the stage with his brother-in-law Walter Damrosch, who, as a young man, had talked Andrew Carnegie into building his magnificent music hall. Maybe, in a fleeting second, Europe smiled to himself, thinking that Damrosch, who was then the conductor of the New York Symphony Orchestra, would be laughing if he only knew how Europe's own orchestra had been pieced together. Europe admitted, "Day and night for months I sat and rehearsed each one of the individual sets of [instruments] in their parts— half the boys didn't read music, and I would have to take the guitar and mandolin players and place their fingers on the different strings and correct them time and time again, till I finally taught them the entire program, chord by chord, note by note."[17]

It was Europe's dream to someday found a true "National Negro Symphony Orchestra," with himself conducting. Although he didn't know it at the time, this was as close as he would ever get to that dream.

Now, taking a deep breath, he walked out onto the stage. Mannes never forgot that moment. "Big Jim Europe was an amazingly inspiring conductor. Of a statuesquely powerful build, he moved with simple and modest grace, always dominating this strange assemblage before him with quiet control."[18] Europe motioned for his musicians to sit. He raised his baton, and the orchestra started playing one of his own compositions, a military air entitled "The Clef Club March." The audience moved in sync, their heads swaying and feet tapping in time to the "incisive rhythm," Curtis chronicled. She called Europe a "Pied Piper," and wrote that when the "march neared the end, and the whole band burst out singing as well as playing, the novelty of this climax—a novelty to the whites, at least—brought a very storm of tumultuous applause."[19]

Lester Walton, managing editor and drama and sports critic of the New York *Age,* a leading African-American newspaper, spotted one "[white] lady seated in a prominent box [who] began to beat time industriously with her right hand, which was covered with many costly gems."[20]

The concert was a success. David Mannes reported that the receipts for the night netted close to five thousand dollars. "Besides, which," he added, "a wedge in opening the public halls and theatres to colored performers had been made." He and Europe dreamed of building a concert hall of their own in Harlem, with a theatre and library—"In short, a national home for his [the African American's] best interests."[21] In effect, a black Carnegie Hall.

Europe, whose work in organizing and finding "gigs" (a word he coined) for New York's African-American musicians, closed the concert as he had opened it, with a composition of his own. Standing with his back to the audience, in his brilliant white tuxedo, his broad shoulders soldierly erect, he raised his arm, baton in hand, and the Clef Club Symphony Orchestra began to play "Strength of the Nation." All the men in the audience who were members of the all-black "provisional" troop of the National Guard were brought to their feet. As the program indicated, this composition was "dedicated to the proposed Colored Regiment."[22]

Looking back on that concert years later, Natalie Curtis recounted that, in fact, Europe and his orchestra had eaten up New York. "And then New York ate *them.* That first concert of Negro music in Carnegie Hall was an ear-opener. . . . We had seen the racial soul, denied all opportunity, awake, nevertheless, and sing; and the song, ephemeral though it was, seemed a prophecy of the dignity and worth of Negro genius."[23]

Meanwhile, north of Manhattan, in the governor's office in Albany, the state's chief executive had on his desk a bill, passed by the legislature, that authorized New York's first regiment of black National Guardsmen. It needed his signature to become law. The benefit concert for the Music School Settlement for Colored People, a smashing success, might have convinced him that now was the time to take another step forward and give his black constituents the regiment they wanted. But for the moment he stayed his hand, still afraid to commit his signature to the bill—still not believing in the mighty message of Europe's final number honoring the hoped-for African-American guard that the "Strength of a Nation" is in the diversity of its people.

"We Have the Regiment"

They stepped away from Columbus Circle at eleven on the frosty morning of 12 February 1912. Down Broadway they tramped—toward Union Square and the statue there of Abraham Lincoln. In the chill, gray shadows of Manhattan's skyline, their faces wore expressions of resolve. Crowds of curious people, bundled against the sharp cold, gawked at them. Rarely in the annals of New York City, or any American city for that matter, had a band of self-proclaimed soldiers, all of them men of color, marched en masse through the heart of a major metropolis. There were more than six hundred of them, the nucleus of a so-called provisional regiment that had no legal status whatsoever, divvied into three battalions of twelve companies with one signal corps, one hospital corps, and a lone bandmaster. They had no uniforms. Instead, they were dressed in dark suits. Armbands singled them out as soldiers. Officers wore sashes. They carried no rifles, only the hope that they would soon be recognized as a legitimate part of the New York National Guard. Many were leaders of the black community: lawyers, doctors, merchants, ministers, and even musicians. A handful were veterans of the Spanish-American War. Five weeks earlier their names and hundreds of others— one thousand strong—had been sent to Gov. John Dix along with a petition that he create a black regiment. Dix had authority, under the state's

National Guard regulations, to establish such a unit. Perhaps this show of force on the 103rd anniversary of Lincoln's birthday would convince him of the earnestness of the Empire State's African-American community for a regiment of its own.

The energy behind this unauthorized military gathering was Charles W. Fillmore, a dashing, silver-haired, forty-eight-year-old newcomer to the city from Springfield, Ohio. More than any other man, he had taken the lead in the provisional regiment's establishment, recruited many of its esteemed members, appointed himself colonel, and then hounded city and state officials, from mayors to governors, to do the right thing: give New York blacks the regiment they had dreamt about since before the start of the twentieth century.

For Fillmore the task had not been easy, and on Lincoln's birthday it was far from over. Leading his men south along Broadway on one of the coldest days of the winter, with ice coating the Hudson River, he shivered at the work that still had to be done. As the tramp, tramp, tramp of the six hundred men marching behind him echoed off Broadway's hard pavement, he may have thought back to how far they had come. In spite of the backbiting, bickering, and a fistfight or two, it had been mostly through his unifying efforts that there was finally a fully manned regiment. All that was needed to make it official was for him and his fellow marchers to get Dix to act. But thus far in Fillmore's life, persuading governors to act had proven an exasperating and often humiliating struggle. He could recall his first fateful encounter with a governor—how he rode with him up through the political ranks in his native state of Ohio and then, like a wounded bird, he alone had fluttered back to earth. Ironically, it was a lynching that was to blame for his fall. And now, because of it, he was marching through the streets of New York, and not some city in Ohio—stepping along with a stoicism that hid the worry of a colonel of a regiment unwanted by nearly every white man wielding power in Albany and Manhattan.

The lynching that changed Fillmore's life, drove him out of Ohio and, in a perverse way, lit the spark that flamed to life his provisional regiment, took place in October of 1897 in Urbana, a small town west of Columbus. A black man, accused of "ravishing" a white woman, was strung up by infuriated townspeople. When they first forced their way into the jailhouse, a small troop of local militia, reinforcing the town's sheriff, fired at them, killing a citizen. The townspeople turned their fury on the sheriff and militia. A desperate call went out for Gov. Asa Bushnell, who was standing for reelection, to send more troops. For

Charles Fillmore, the "handsome major." Fillmore lobbied city and state officials in New York to authorize the formation of a black National Guard regiment.

FROM *A PICTORIAL HISTORY OF THE NEGRO IN THE GREAT WAR,* 1917–1918

whatever reason, he failed to respond. The sheriff and militia fled town. The citizens then went back after the defenseless man. Later, the editor of Ohio's leading African-American newspaper, the Cleveland *Gazette,* blamed Bushnell for inaction, especially when he, the governor, probably fearing a white backlash if he investigated the lynching before the November elections, did nothing.[1]

It was this governor—the successor to President William McKinley as Ohio's chief executive—to whom Fillmore allied himself early in life.

Both men were from Springfield. At the time of the lynching, Fillmore served in Bushnell's administration in the office of the secretary of state. Perhaps more important to his career was the fact that he was an officer in the Ninth Ohio Battalion, one of only four black military units in the United States commanded by African Americans. After enlisting in the Ninth's A Company, comprised of Springfield citizens, and first known as the Duquesne Blues and later as Bushnell's Guards, Fillmore moved swiftly through the ranks. Because of his good looks, he was dubbed the "handsome major."

In the autumn of 1897, with a nation barreling at breakneck speed toward a war with Spain, events for Fillmore began to move too fast.

First, the lynching in Urbana rocked Ohio. Next, Bushnell was re-elected. And Fillmore, oblivious, it seems, to the turmoil within the black community, stood with his friend by offering the Ninth to the governor as his personal escort during the inauguration ceremony. Blacks, who, after the lynching, had taken to calling Bushnell "Urbana" because they felt he had condoned mob action,[2] railed at Fillmore for siding with him. One editor mocked the "handsome major" as a "good-natured, easy, harmless sort of fellow with about as much backbone as a fly."[3]

Torn between his loyalty to Bushnell and to his own people, Fillmore compromised. He would still let the Ninth serve as escort, but he would not march. This decision angered the governor. He asked for the major's resignation. Fillmore turned to the most powerful black in Ohio for counsel. George Myers was a Cleveland barber whose influence in the Republican Party reached to the highest levels of government. He counted among his friends President McKinley and U.S. Sen. Mark Hanna. He had been a delegate to the 1892 and 1896 Republican national conventions. From his shop at Cleveland's Hollenden House he kept his eyes on what he termed "The Game," namely the political affairs of Ohio. Fillmore had turned to the right man for help.

In a letter to Myers, dated 18 February 1898, three days after the USS *Maine* had blown up in Havana harbor, he lamented: "I am even in disfavor with a majority of my command and I would resign if it was not for the pleasure it would give the opposition." He went on to say that there was a "movement afoot to either court martial me or discharge me. . . . I am loath to give up my command as my whole ambition is devoted to the military."[4]

He pleaded for Myers to intervene—to get Hanna to land him into the regular army, or at least give him a company of men from Cleveland to command.[5] His request for a commission in the Regular Army was almost impossible to honor. In 1898 there were about twenty-five hundred officers in the Regular Army. Only one was an African American. The odds of adding another was remote. And worse, that one black officer was about to add to the major's woes.

In the meantime, Myers asked Hanna, in effect, if there was any way that, through a presidential order, Fillmore could be commissioned an officer in the Regular Army. But when the request got bogged down in Washington, Fillmore tendered his resignation as a major in the Ninth Battalion.

The resignation did not come soon enough for the editor of the *Gazette*. He wrote, "As for Charley Fillmore all such weak-kneed, backboneless, time-serving white politicians' toadies, of our race, may even worse treatment be accorded them by those they serve at the expense of principles of vital interest and concern to the race. Exit! 'Majah Fillmore: good riddance."[6]

Only days after Fillmore's resignation, on 25 April, Spain declared war on the United States. Three weeks later, Bushnell commissioned Lt. Charles Young, who, it so happened, was that sole black officer in the Regular Army, as commander of the Ninth Battalion, which now, because of the war, had been redesignated the Ninth Ohio Volunteer Infantry. The Kentucky-born Young was the third African American to graduate from the U. S. Military Academy. He spoke Greek, Latin, French, German, and Spanish. His commissioning as colonel of the Ninth crushed any hopes that Fillmore had of regaining command of his old battalion.

Fillmore wrote to Myers. "You was [sic] present when Senator Hanna gave us assurance I would be taken care of upon his return to Washington, and that I should not be at all uneasy as to my commission.

"Now it seems that the authorities are very long winded, especially in my case. I would at least like to get in before the war is over." He complained that Bushnell's influence was holding up any appointments. "If I am to go into the field I would like to go at once and commence getting hardened to the hardships, climate, etc."[7]

Within a few days of posting that letter, Fillmore got his commission as a lieutenant in F Company of the Ninth U.S. Volunteer Infantry. Not to be confused with Fillmore's old unit, the Ninth Infantry was an "immune" regiment of nine companies of black soldiers. (There was a belief that blacks were naturally immune to any tropical disease and thus could fare better in jungle warfare than whites).

When the *Gazette* found out, its editor gloated. "Urbana Bushnell refused to commission him a major of the Ninth battalion just before it was sworn into the U.S. volunteer service because Charley wouldn't march with the battalion when it participated in the Gubernatorial inaugural parade last January. Charley 'swallowed' the Urbana lynching and supported the governor for re-election last fall. For this, it seems, he has received from the individual a good sound kick into a lieutenant's berth from a major's berth."[8]

Fillmore's old battalion never made it to Cuba. But the Ninth Infantry went, one of only three black volunteer regiments to be garrisoned on the island. It landed in Santiago on 24 August and stayed until April 1899. Fillmore did not see combat. Instead, he discovered that, despite what white authorities thought, African Americans were not immune to tropical diseases. Yellow fever struck him down. He survived the virulent disease, and when the war was over he did not go back to Ohio. He took a job in Washington with the U. S. Treasury and later moved to New York City as an operative for the Internal Revenue Department.

Now, as the cold cut through his dark suit and the wind fluttered his officer's sash and the footfalls of another regiment beat a cadence on Broadway, Ohio and its troubles seemed a world away. His immediate concern was how to hold his men together and win over the governor of New York. They were so close to getting what they wanted. But then, they had been close before and had always come away from Albany empty-handed.

It's difficult to trace how far back New York City's African Americans had clamored to be part of the state's National Guard. During the turn-of-the-century administration of Gov. Frank Black, they had tried to get a bill through the legislature authorizing a regiment for them. Because of the hostilities with Spain, the timing seemed perfect. Still they failed. Even Gov. Charles Evans Hughes, who served from 1906 to 1910 before his appointment to the U. S. Supreme Court, turned a deaf ear to their pleas. On the other hand, Hughes's successor, Governor Dix, had, early in his term, consented to an all-black National Guard unit. According to a 6 February 1911 article in the *New York Times,* his pronouncement "caused much rejoicing yesterday in negro circles in this city."[9]

Yet for that entire year Dix did nothing.

The disappointment was great, and throughout 1911, it caused a rift within the black community that nearly tore apart two preeminent civic groups: The Equity Congress, from whose ranks Fillmore had drawn many of his regimental recruits, and the United Colored Democracy, a tribe of Tammany Hall partisans. The president of the Equity Congress was J. Frank Wheaton, a forty-six-year-old attorney and among the most notable African Americans in the city. Before moving to Harlem, he had been Minnesota 's first black state legislator. Chief Edward E. Lee led the United Colored Democracy. A favorite of Tammany Hall boss Charles Murphy, he was a year away from being appointed deputy sheriff for the City of New York. But Lee's leadership was being threatened from within by Robert N. Wood, who had ambitions of his own to be a top Tammany Hall sachem. Lee and Wood were also members of the Equity Congress.

Wanting to take credit for the governor's favorable stance, Wood, whose obituary in city newspapers years later cited him for organizing the state's "first negro regiment,"[10] claimed that on a visit to the capital he had obtained a promise from Dix and, according to the *Times,* the "Governor heartily endorsed the plan proposed by Enwood [the reporter obviously used phonetic spelling for Robert N. Wood]." The article added, "National Guardsmen say they know nothing about the establishment of a negro regiment in the State. They refuse to discuss the matter. The regiment will have the right to go into camp with white troops, and it was said that many of the latter view with disfavor the prospect of such a state of affairs."[11]

Wood's claim that his plan for a regiment was now endorsed by Dix upset members of the Equity Congress.

While they figured out a response to Wood, bad news thundered out of Albany. Adj. Gen. William Verbeck, one of the state's top military officers, said that under no circumstances would there be a black regiment of the National Guard. In rejecting Negro troops for New York City, or anywhere else in the state, he pointed out that it would cost fifty thousand dollars to equip such a regiment and twenty thousand dollars a year to support it. He also declared that in the Guard itself there would be prejudice against a colored regiment.[12]

But on 19 April 1911, Assemblyman Louis Culliver of the Thirtieth Assembly District, which took in a large portion of Harlem and was one of the most heavily populated districts in the state, introduced into the legislature Assembly Bill 1628. It called for the organization and equipment of "a colored regiment of infantry in the city of New York, to become a part of the national guard of the state of New York."

A veteran of the Spanish-American War, officer in the Seventy-first Regiment, and now a budding hero of New York's African-American population, Culliver chaired the Committee on Military Affairs. If and when his bill was passed and then signed into law by the governor, it would direct the adjutant general, in this case, the testy Verbeck, to immediately "organize and equip a colored regiment of infantry" with a minimum of 732 enlisted men. Culliver's regiment, to be headquartered in New York City, would consist of one colonel, a lieutenant colonel, three captains, a chaplain, and a sergeant major. There would be three battalions, twelve companies, and a band. A major, adjutant, two second lieutenants, and a sergeant major would lead each battalion. Each company would comprise a captain, first lieutenant, second lieutenant, a first sergeant, five other sergeants, six corporals, two cooks, two musicians, and forty-two privates. "An infantry band," Culliver wrote, "shall consist of one chief musician, one principal musician, one drum major, four sergeants, eight corporals, one cook and twelve privates."

Culliver's bill also directed the "army board of the city of New York . . . to select, locate and lay out a site for an armory for the regiment."[13]

Fillmore now had his blueprint for a regiment, and it was time to start recruiting members from New York City's five boroughs. And up in Albany, if Governor Dix was honest about his support for a black regiment, he now had been given the opportunity to prove it.

By July, Culliver's bill had passed both houses of the legislature and had been sent to Dix for his signature.

The *Times* editorialized that although Negroes had proven to be good, courageous soldiers and "their moral and legal right as American citizens" to join the National Guard was "perfect," there were "sometimes practical considerations that make injudicious the exercise of rights, and in this case the negro's right to join any militia regiment is a little clearer than his right to have a regiment made specially for him."[14]

The moment the bill passed the legislature, Robert N. Wood took credit for its final shape. And when an upstart Harlem newspaper, the Amsterdam *News*, praised Wood's work, almost the entire Equity Congress membership attacked him and the *News*. Secretary D. E. Tobias asked for a retraction from that "little Negro paper," which he described as an "amateurish publication." He claimed that the newspaper had "done a great injustice to a large body of men in an editorial published in the Amsterdam *News* of July 15, 1911, in which you attempted to ignore the work done by other men and give undue credit for the passage of the Culliver bill . . . to one man."[15] When the Equity Congress met a few weeks later, the session was packed, and members continued to rebuke Wood and the *News*. The state's most influential black newspaper, the New York *Age*, published and edited by Fred R. Moore, reported that "members were in such a warlike frame of mind that they refused to forgive R. N. Wood for trying to convince the public that he was responsible for the passage of the bill at Albany providing for a colored regiment in New York City."[16]

While the Equity Congress and Wood feuded all summer and into the fall, Culliver's bill sat on Dix's desk, unsigned.

To persuade the governor to act, Fillmore quickly recruited the city's most prominent African Americans as officers and enlisted men into what was soon called a "provisional" regiment. Among those joining up, many of them Equity Congress loyalists, was real-estate executive Philip A. Payton, who in the early 1900s had outmaneuvered his white counterparts to open up hundreds of apartment buildings in Harlem to

African Americans. Families then moved en masse, mostly from the Tenderloin District, to these new homes, thus creating the largest black enclave in the world. Another recruit was Virgil H. Parks, Spanish-American War veteran, who had seen action in Cuba and the Philippines.

And on 26 October Fillmore announced that he had mustered in a chief musician, the rank referred to in Culliver's bill, for his regimental band. The new recruit was one of the best-known orchestra conductors in the country and the recent composer of "Strength of a Nation," his anthem to the new black regiment—James Reese Europe. Fillmore then ordered Europe to "recruit a band of forty pieces."[17]

One key name was absent from this illustrious muster roll: Robert N. Wood.

Still, the bill went unsigned. In fact, Moore of the *Age* believed Dix was determined to let it die. Therefore, within the ranks of the United Colored Democracy, upset members were "about as peaceable and loving as two hungry canines after a bone and they appear to be engaged in a contest to see which can bark the loudest."[18] Chief Lee and the scheming Wood fought tooth and nail for the leadership of the Tammany group, each blaming the other for the defeat of the bill. Both had promised Dix that if he signed the bill, blacks—longtime ardent supporters of the party of Lincoln—would vote in droves for the Democratic ticket in November.

In the Equity Congress, when it was official that the bill was dead, two members, attorneys David C. Outlear, a Republican, and Louis A. Lavelle, a Democrat, got into a shouting match over whether to support Culliver for reelection to the assembly. Republicans hurled insults at the Democrats, denouncing them and Culliver for "not giving the Negro voters a colored regiment." Culliver appeared before the group to defend himself. He stated that his bill failed to become law because of the "opposition of Adjutant-General Verbeck, a Republican, who advised Governor Dix not to sign the measure." The Democrats cheered Culliver and moved that the Equity Congress pass a motion thanking him for his effort. Outlear jumped up, objecting to the motion and then went on to condemn Culliver. He charged that the Democrats had no intention of giving blacks their own regiment. He doubted that Verbeck had more power in Albany than either the Democratic-controlled legislature or the governor.

After the raucous meeting, the argument between Lavelle and Outlear spilled out into the street. At 134th Street near Lenox Avenue, they lunged at each other, with Outlear drawing first blood. The *Age* described the fight as a "fast and furious one while it lasted, but was not fought exactly under the Marquis of Queensbury rules, as the contestants, at times, ignored the implements of war usually employed by those who indulge in the manly art, going after each other in mule-like and rat-like fashion."[19]

The newspaper account sided with the Republicans. And when Culliver later eked out a win in the election, the *Age* quipped that the assemblyman owed his victory to the hundreds of blacks in the district who believed that he had been "sincere in his efforts to get a colored regiment for New York City." In a page-one article, the newspaper noted that "Louis Culliver, who introduced a bill in the last Legislature at Albany which provided for a colored regiment in New York City, and who has been posing as a friend of the colored voters, although the measure did not become a law, will have another opportunity to introduce a similar bill."[20]

Culliver never got around to introducing a new bill.

That honor went to Republican and Spanish-American War veteran Dean Nelson of the Twenty-first Assembly District, which included parts of Harlem. On the surface, Nelson seemed an unlikely advocate for a black regiment. He was a Harvard-educated attorney, member of the Sons of the American Revolution, yachtsman, and an ex-member of the Seventh Regiment, the elite Upper East Side National Guard troop that boasted some of the wealthiest New Yorkers as officers and enlisted men. He was new to the legislature, too, having just won his initial venture into state politics by more than a 60 percent margin over his Democratic foe.

However, on 18 January 1912, Nelson introduced Bill 157, an act to amend the military law to establish a "colored regiment of infantry in the city of New York." There were very few specifics in the legislation. It was an abbreviated version of Culliver's bill submitted a year earlier.[21]

For Fillmore, it was another frustrating step in the waiting game.

Meanwhile, in the months before Nelson threw his bill into the hopper, Fillmore vigorously went about recruiting more members for the provisional regiment. With an escort of Boy Scouts and a trumpeter, he traveled as far north as Yonkers to talk men into signing on.

But an importune visit to New York in mid-November by Col. John R. Marshall, commander of the Eighth Illinois, an African-American-led National Guard regiment, set Fillmore and his staff back on their heels. Marshall criticized the way the provisional regiment was being organized. He thought it was top-heavy with officers. "In the first place," he told the *Age*, "the heads are appointing all the officers without first filling the various companies with desirable men." He explained that the "selection of line officers is an easy matter compared with securing men qualified to enlist as privates." He then predicted that New York City would be fortunate if it could muster eight hundred men capable of passing the physical examination that would allow them to serve in the National Guard. Marshall's most damaging statement related to expenses. He claimed costs would reach more than three hundred thousand dollars just to arm and equip the regiment. The building of an armory would be extra.[22]

No doubt, his criticism was read with interest by Albany's decision makers.

Fillmore fired back. His adjutant, J. Albert Jaxon, used the pages of the *Age* to refute Marshall's claim that their provisional regiment was top-heavy with officers. Conceding that Marshall was the most knowledgeable authority in the country concerning the "Negro race on National Guard affairs or militia matters," Jaxon wondered if, perhaps, the Illinois colonel had been misquoted. He pointed out that the Equity Congress had "appointed a committee to recruit a regiment. The committee, consisting of five members, designated Charles W. Fillmore as temporary colonel." He praised Fillmore's past military experience in Ohio, which, he said, ably qualified him to command the regiment. He stated that the regiment had five hundred enlisted men, yet still needed twenty-eight officers—a fact that "in itself refutes the possible charge of over officering." And then, in an offhanded plug for the regiment, he asked the readers of the *Age* if they knew of any "men of proper qualifications, whether they be residents of New York for long years or recent arrivals," and added that there "still exists vacancies from the grade of 'high private' to that of major, inclusive."[23]

Two weeks after Jaxon's rebuttal, Fillmore completed his first full battalion. It consisted of four companies totaling 231 men, 15 of them officers. Maj. Herman Blunt commanded the battalion. Two other battalions were then quickly formed. Maj. George Horton led the Second and Maj. Henry Coles of Brooklyn, former sergeant major of the Twenty-fourth United States Infantry, took charge of the Third. The provisional regiment included companies from Yonkers, Mount Vernon, and Flushing. Among the names missing from the original list of volunteers was James Europe, who a few months earlier had conducted the Clef Club Symphony Orchestra at the benefit concert in Carnegie Hall. In his stead as bandleader was E. E. Thompson. The drum major was Moses Mimms.

On 29 December, Fillmore sent to Dix the muster roll bearing the names of a thousand officers and men. He petitioned him to make this provisional regiment a part of the New York National Guard. In his letter, he reminded the governor that Illinois, Massachusetts, and the District of Columbia had black militias. With the coming of the new year, it was high time for the Empire State to have a black militia of its own, too.

While Fillmore led his "provisional regiment" down Broadway on the anniversary of Lincoln's birthday, north of the city, in and around Bardstown, where his black troops ought to have been on this frigid day, white regiments of New York's National Guard played war games.

The star of these war games was a thirty-eight-year-old major who, in three months, would vault over three ranks and win promotion to major general and command of New York's National Guard. John F. O'Ryan led troops from "New England" in an "attack" against entrenched forces protecting Gotham's water supply and the Harlem branch of the New York Central Railroad. In the mock battle, he had charge of two batteries of the Second Battalion of the New York Field Artillery and a troop of cavalry from Squadron A. They swept into Bardstown, crushed their foe, and blew up an abandoned farmhouse. "Real trenches were dug and real shots were fired by cannon and machine guns," trumpeted the *Times*.[24] Afterwards, both sides retired for a hearty dinner. All and all, it was a glorious day for the white soldiers of New York and especially for O'Ryan. He had apparently caught the admiring eye of Gen. Leonard Wood, U. S. Army Chief of Staff.[25] The ex-Rough Rider felt the young major would make a grand commander of the state's Guard.

O'Ryan was a Tammany Hall man. He had first served in the well-connected Seventh Regiment, and then surged upward. Now with Wood's backing, he had a clear shot to be state commander when the current commander retired in May. Although he later claimed that he had been unaware that he was about to take over the leadership, he asserted that he had "never found that there was anything political with respect to the New York National Guard."[26]

Yet throughout 1912 he found himself embroiled in politics that at first nearly cost him his appointment and then afterward got him momentarily ousted from his newly won role as one of the most powerful military figures in the Empire State. The man he had to face down was none other than Verbeck himself.

In the months after O'Ryan's appointment, Verbeck had his power base in Albany strengthened when Dix established a new office: chief of staff of the military forces of the State of New York—created along the same lines as the chief of staff of the U. S. Army. Although Dix was accused of being in Tammany Hall's pocket—a yes-man for Boss Murphy, if one believed the upstate Democrats who wanted the governor gone—this new office put power into the hands of a Republican, Verbeck, not in those of the Tammany-backed O'Ryan. Among those championing the new position was Assemblyman Culliver, the Democrat who owed his reelection to Harlem's disgruntled black population. He declared that it would allow the general staff to "formulate the policy of the National Guard and recommend laws to the Legislature for the improvement of the Guard."[27]

Dix justified his creation of chief of staff to the "increasing bitterness" between the two men as well as O'Ryan's "disregard of the oft-expressed personal wishes and official directions of the Commander-in Chief [namely, the governor himself]." Dix admitted that he appointed the Tammany Hall minion to the key military post because the "high endorsement of General Wood outweighed those opposed."[28] During the summer of 1912, while the governor vacationed in Europe, O'Ryan, in his new position as Guard commander, requested a salary. When naming O'Ryan, Dix declared there would be no salary for the job. With the governor gone, O'Ryan sent a pay voucher to Verbeck. When Dix returned, his leadership in the Democratic Party crashed down around him and he failed to be renominated. He had, he felt, endured enough. In one of his last acts as governor, he fired O'Ryan.

"I greatly regret that my appointment of an enthusiastic young officer to the highest operative position in the National Guard," the lame-duck governor explained, "should have resulted in so warping his judgment and respect for customary procedure that his relief from duty became an immediate necessity."[29]

O'Ryan's exile from Albany did not last long.

In the November 1912 elections, while the nation voted in Woodrow Wilson, its first Democratic president in twenty years, New Yorkers sent an Upper East Side congressman, William Sulzer, to the governor's mansion. After one term, Dix, the Murphy man, was out. Sulzer, a Democrat from New York City's Fourteenth Assembly District who reveled in his independence from Tammany Hall, was in. The new governor immediately replaced Verbeck with Henry De Witt Hamilton, a direct descendant of Miles Standish and an officer in Brooklyn's Twenty-third National Guard Regiment, as adjutant general. In his first official act, Sulzer reinstated O'Ryan as commander of the National Guard. He felt that the decision to oust the major general was done "without charges and without an opportunity to meet any accusation against him."[30] Sulzer was, at last, the strong leader African Americans had sought for years.

To prove it, all he needed was a new bill calling for a black regiment of the National Guard to sign into law.

It didn't take long for such a bill to reach his office.

Almost as soon as he arrived in Albany for the 1913 legislative session, first-term Assemblyman Thomas Kane introduced Assembly Bill 2100. A Democrat, Kane had in the recent elections recaptured the Twenty-first district by knocking off incumbent Dean Nelson, the same Dean Nelson who, the year before, had introduced his bill for a black regiment—another of the bills Dix had neglected to sign. Kane had been one of Gotham's best athletes in the 1890s, thrice winning the Clipper Athletic Club's all-around championship. His bill, like Dean's, directed the adjutant general to "organize and equip a colored battalion of infantry in New York City [the previous bills, including Culliver's, called for a regiment], the armory board of New York City to provide quarters for said battalion."[31] Kane's bill passed both houses on 2 May and on 7 May was sent to the governor for his signature.

Blacks in New York City collectively held their breath. So many times in the past they had come this far and then no farther. And with another Democrat sitting in the chief executive's chair, a gloomy atmosphere settled over Harlem.

But Sulzer was that rare breed of politician—a man of courage, conviction, and action. In the end it cost him dearly. Within ten months of his being sworn in as New York's forty-first governor, Tammany Hall drove him from office. Yet in that brief span of time he left his mark on the state, and, during his three terms in Congress, on the nation as well. He once said, "An ounce of performance is worth a ton of promise."[32]

Photographs of Sulzer reveal a resolute man. His face is hard, his eyes, described as steel blue, "look straight into yours, and read your innermost thoughts."[33] State Assemblyman Hamilton Fish Jr. remembered Sulzer as a "convulsive tobacco chewer [who] would spit a stream of tobacco juice over my shoulder, aimed at a spittoon located on a floor next to where I sat."[34] Fish claimed Sulzer never missed the spittoon.

While in the state assembly, Sulzer introduced legislation that touched all New Yorkers—even to this day. He fought to abolish sweatshops and to give the working man a prevailing wage, a weekly salary, and a half-day off on Saturday. He opened the Metropolitan Museum of Art on Sunday so that working families could enjoy the city's magnificent art collection. He had the Statue of Liberty lit so that it would shine as a true beacon in New York harbor. In Congress, he helped to establish the Department of Labor. He made certain U.S. senators were elected by popular vote. He introduced a resolution that turned Lincoln's birthday into a national holiday.

In his acceptance speech as the Democratic candidate for governor, he said, "Those who know me best know that I stand firmly for certain fundamental principles—for liberty under law; for civil and religious freedom; for Constitutional government; for old integrities and the new humanities; for equality before the law; for equal rights to all and special privileges for none." He promised that the executive office would always be open so that the "humblest citizen of the State may come to Albany and see the Governor and be treated with as much consideration as the richest and most powerful."[35] That promise included black citizens as well.

Fred Moore, who had been a messenger for five secretaries of the treasury beginning in President Grant's administration, believed that promise. In an editorial, his paper declared that "Gov. Sulzer is a man of the people, approachable, affable, direct in his manner. We feel certain that Negro citizens who have occasion to petition him to muster in a Negro regiment or for other things will receive a more ready and sympathetic hearing than they have had at Albany since Gov. Grover Cleveland left it for the White House some twenty-seven years ago."[36]

There was another, more compelling reason for Moore to believe in Sulzer. Four years earlier, as a congressman, he had stood up in the House of Representatives in defense of the Twenty-fifth United States Infantry. Its African-American soldiers had been charged with shooting up Brownsville, Texas, killing a Mexican bartender, and wounding a white police officer. Their attack on the town had been prompted by threats from the citizens that, because of an alleged attempted rape by one of the soldiers, any blacks would be shot on sight—unless the guilty man was turned over to local authorities. The regiment's commander immediately confined all his troops to Fort Brown, hoping to keep them off the streets and out of danger. Yet between eight and twenty soldiers left the fort and shot up the town. At least, that was the accusation from the Brownsville mayor. He had empty bullet casings fired from military weapons as proof. The War Department upheld the charges against the Twenty-fifth Infantry. President Theodore Roosevelt accepted the War Department's findings. As punishment, soldiers in three companies were dishonorably discharged.

On 27 February 1909, Sulzer rose in their defense, stating that the soldiers had the right to their "day in court." He stated, "They are entitled to this and they never have had this opportunity of proving their innocence." He went on to declare that "I am now and always have been, and I trust always will be, in favor of equal and exact justice to all men—here and everywhere throughout the world—without regard to race or to creed."[37]

Now, on 2 June 1913, Gov. Sulzer signed into law Kane's bill that, after so many years that had seen so many hopes and dreams dashed, provided the Empire State and the City of New York with its first legally constituted troop of black National Guardsmen. After signing the bill, he said: "Justice to the Negro demanded the action."[38]

In an editorial in the *Age,* headlined "We Have The Regiment," Moore praised Sulzer:

> All the previous governors of New York who have passed upon the question from Frank S. Black down . . . have been too weak to overcome the objections, mostly on the social features of the service, of their Adjutant-Generals and staffs, against the authorization of a Negro regiment; Gov. Sulzer had the same objections to overcome, and overcame them, brushing them aside as a strong man should, as having nothing to do with the merits of the case. That is the sort of Governor the State of New York should have all of the time; a Governor disposed to treat all the elements of the citizenship by the same rule of justice and fair play.[39]

Four months later, Sulzer was impeached. Unable to refute charges that he had misused campaign funds—a charge raised by Tammany Hall partisans—he was forced from office in disgrace.

And what would now become of the colonel of the provisional regiment? The passage of Kane's bill certainly meant that Fillmore officially had the command that he had longed for since those hard times in Ohio. Perhaps he thought it was the march of the six hundred men he had led from Columbus Circle down to Union Square to honor the Great Liberator that moved the state to give its largest city its black regiment. Yes, the dashing major who had once fallen from grace now had his command. Or had he?

2

Pancho Villa Rides
to the Rescue

With the impeachment of Governor William Sulzer under way, most work at the state legislature slowed to a crawl. But for the African Americans of New York City, when it came time to breathe actual life into their duly enacted regiment, any action had ground to a dead stop. To their dismay, they discovered that authorizing a black troop on paper was one thing. Giving it real flesh and blood was another.

Perhaps even more distressing was the fact they were about to lose one of the few champions they had in Albany. With Tammany Hall pouring it on, Sulzer was in big trouble.

He had been charged with using campaign funds for personal gain, including speculating with that money in the stock market, and with perjury, bribery of state witnesses, and falsifying receipts. On 15 October he was found guilty on three of the four articles of impeachment against him. As his wife wept, Sulzer claimed that his trial was a Tammany "farce, political lynching, the consummation of a deep-laid political conspiracy to oust me from office." He said that Charles Murphy was behind it, that the Tammany chieftain "ordered" his impeachment and that he controlled most members of the high court who, in the seclusion of their private chambers, impeached him. Murphy went after him, he said, because he refused to call off an investigation into graft.

"The court ruled in everything against me and ruled out everything in my favor. The well-settled rules of evidence were thrown to the winds," Sulzer said. "A horse thief in frontier days would have received a squarer deal."[1]

Hamilton Fish Jr., who would later serve with the black New York regiment, sided with the disgraced governor. He called the charges against Sulzer "trumped up," and swore that the proceedings had been "initiated by the bosses."[2]

Sulzer's loss was a huge blow to the black community. The new governor, Martin H. Glynn, a Tammany-dominated man,[3] ex-newspaper editor, lawyer, and former upstate congressman, had little interest, it appears, in pursuing a regiment for Gotham's African-American minority. And besides, according to the *Times,* Glynn held a "bitter hatred"[4] for ex-Governor Sulzer that had been smoldering almost from the time the two men were sworn in as governor and lieutenant governor.

As long as the Democrats controlled the state, Charles Fillmore's now official regiment would, for all intents and purposes, remain "provisional" and virtually unrecognized by Albany. Therefore, growing anxiety among the city's blacks over their own luckless regiment soon found them squabbling among themselves once again.

On 1 May 1914 C. Franklin Carr, the newest adjutant with ambitions of his own to take over the regiment, sent an unauthorized letter to the state's Adj. Gen. Henry De Witt Hamilton. "The members of the New York provisional regiment of infantry are patiently waiting the dawn of the day when they will be admitted into the National Guard," he reminded him and hinted that they would agree to be officered by whites if only they would be recognized. "They are very desirous of having colored line and field officers, but if the law is construed to mean the latter cannot be awarded them they are perfectly willing to accept such officers as may be designated to take command of the various units just so they are competent and proficient men." If that wasn't enough to raise the hair on the back of Fillmore's neck, Carr added that if most regimental members had "any discretion in the matter Mr. Fillmore, [who styles himself as the Colonel] would receive very little support." It was rumored that Carr had submitted the name of Cornelius Vanderbilt, a great-grandson of the Commodore and a lieutenant colonel in the Twenty-second Engineers, to command the regiment.[5]

The thought of an uprising within his own ranks—that he could be facing another Ohio all over again—must have coursed like chilled blood through Fillmore's veins. And the worse thing, perhaps, was the thought that in the end, when the regiment—his regiment—was, in fact, officered, those officers would be white and not black. That meant no colonelcy for him.

He moved quickly. Stating that Carr's letter had been written without the regiment's authorization, he relieved him as adjutant and replaced him with T. Henry Kearney. He also removed Carr as treasurer of the Officers' School of Instruction, naming in his place Lee Pollard, who earlier had been appointed captain of the signal corps.

While Carr had taken the liberty to throw Vanderbilt's military cap into the ring, two well-known civil rights leaders had been trying for almost a year to get Fillmore's old nemesis from Ohio, Maj. Charles Young, the commander's post—even before Sulzer had signed the bill authorizing the regiment. W. E. B. Du Bois and Oswald Garrison Villard, grandson of the abolitionist William Lloyd Garrison and editor of the New York *Evening Post,* had been in touch with each other and with Young about taking charge of the New York regiment. At the time, Young was a professor of military science at Ohio's Wilberforce University. At first, Villard was unsure that Sulzer would sign the bill. But he assured Du Bois, in a 15 May 1913 memo, that Major General O'Ryan, of all people, had told him "privately that Major Young is his first, second and third choice [to head the regiment]." He added that O'Ryan was "eager to co-operate with him [Young] and is determined that as long as the regiment has been ordered he will do his best to make it a success, and he tells me that he thinks if Young will take the colonelship of this regiment, it will make almost every other regiment in New York sit up and take notice."[6] More than a year dragged by, and nothing became of Villard's efforts to obtain the colonelcy for Young.

In the midst of this latest turmoil, Carr received a letter from an aide to Hamilton in answer to the one he had sent the adjutant general. The message proved devastating and immediately brought back the recent warning of Col. John Marshall of the Eighth Illinois that New York City would not be able to find enough men qualified to be officers. "As not a sufficient number of officers succeeded in passing the prescribed examination to officer one company," communicated the aide, "the organization of the colored regiment has been temporarily postponed, awaiting further development at home and abroad."[7]

Later, Governor Charles S. Whitman's adjutant general, Louis Stotesbury, explained that when he was on the state examining board, there were two reasons for the postponement. The first, he said, was that the "original act of the Legislature, authorizing the organization of a Colored Regiment of Infantry, was hardly treated with sincerity." The second buttressed Colonel Marshall's warning. "We had gone through the form of an examination of Officers for this Regiment. I was on the board. The only officer who passed the Examination was the Chaplain. And, so, the Act had been treated as a dead letter."[8]

This postponement angered Villard. He shot a letter to Major Young, who still waited for any word about the possible appointment to command New York's black troops. Villard reported that "to our sorrow absolutely no headway is being made." He blamed Hamilton for blocking the "whole scheme by letting it die of inanition." He promised Young that he was "writing to Robert Wood and Dr. DuBois calling their attention to the fact that this is the time to make the Governor line up, and that he should be told frankly that if he wants negro votes he must state definitely just what he proposes to do about this regiment. After the campaign, if he is re-elected, I shall take the matter up with him; if Mr. [Charles S.] Whitman, who seems to be the leading Republican candidate, be chosen, I should think the prospects good for achieving something as he is sincerely friendly to the colored people."[9]

With its very existence now being threatened by inaction, the African Americans of New York City needed a new champion to rescue their regiment from the rag pile of broken dreams.

Pancho Villa was hardly a knight in shining armor. Legends that surrounded the revolutionary leader painted him as the Robin Hood of northern Mexico or a bloodthirsty bandit. There was a time when President Woodrow Wilson believed him Robin Hood incarnate.[10] But when his bandits raided the United States, it set off a chain of events that, for all intents and purposes, forced New York State to muster a black regiment of the National Guard.

Villa had been an outlaw on the run early in his life. After the overthrow of the dictator Gen. Porfirio Díaz in 1911 that unleashed a decade of bloody unrest and civil war throughout the country, Villa rose to power as a leader, along with Venustiano Carranza of the Constitutionalists. But when he and Carranza, like thieves fighting over their spoils, had a falling out in 1914, Villa tried to take control of the country by capturing Mexico City. In bitter fighting that waged back and forth for more than half a year, Villa was finally driven north in 1915. That year Wilson added to Villa's humiliation when he recognized Carranza as the legitimate leader of Mexico. That was too much for Villa to bear.

On 9 March 1916, Villa's forces crossed into New Mexico and raided the town of Columbus. Seventeen citizens were murdered.

One of Villa's lieutenants justified the raid, confessing: "My master, Don Pancho Villa, was continually telling us that since the gringos had given him the double-cross he meant not only to get back at them, but to try and waken our country to the danger that was very close to it."[11]

Yet there may have been a more ominous reason for the raid. Germany feared that the United States was near to entering the world war on the side of the Allies. A distraction on its southern border might keep the Americans out of the war for a long time. As it happened, the Germans had already offered ten million dollars to the exiled ex-Mexican president, Victoriano Huerta, first to overthrow the current government of his country and then to launch an attack against the United States. Huerta never made it into Mexico, and the plan was scrapped. The next logical conspirator was Villa. Although not as powerful as he once was, he still had a loyal following of veteran troops expert in guerrilla warfare. An arms merchant, Félix Sommerfeld, convinced the Germans he could get Villa to cross into the United States on a hit-and-run mission.[12]

Whether Villa's raid on Columbus was a result of German collusion may never be known. But it certainly had the desired effect. Wilson ordered the Army and National Guard troops, under Gen. John J. Pershing, to the Mexican border to bring the outlaw he had likened to Robin Hood to justice.

A month later, New York Gov. Whitman, who had ousted Glynn in the 1914 elections, mobilized the state's National Guard for service along the Rio Grande, on orders from the United States War Department. "We are asked to send nine regiments, we have thirteen, " he said in a statement to the press. "We will put in the field at once 15,000 men."[13] New York was the only state required to provide a full division. Almost overnight, the energized city transformed itself into a war zone. National Guardsmen were sequestered in their armories. Young men dashed off to get married. Businesses, including the brokerage firms on Wall Street, promised to give their employees full pay while they were in the service. Hundreds of civilians enlisted in the Guard or the regular army. The fired-up citizens of Long Island City and Queens hollered for regiments of their own. The eleven-hundred-acre Van Cortlandt Park in the Bronx was an armed camp. Tents were pitched everywhere. Corrals were erected to hold the more than one thousand horses that were being shipped from Oklahoma. Throughout the city there was a sense of urgency. Everyone was filled with patriotism. But in the African-American neighborhoods there was a sense of gloom. The black regiment that had been created two years earlier by the state assembly and signed into being by Governor Sulzer was not a part of this sweeping patriotic fervor. It still lay dormant—unmanned and unofficered. Its companies were hollow rosters from the old provisional regiment. And so, as usual, the men of color waited.

But the waiting was about to end. If Villa had unwittingly ignited a chain of events that were to lead to a black regiment, it was Republican Governor Whitman and three of his closest officials—Adj. Gen. Louis Stotesbury, Public Service Commissioner William Hayward, and Military Secretary Lorillard Spencer—who would make certain that the events now unfolding in their state would result in manning the regiment.

First, Spencer, as military secretary, found among the piles of papers in his Albany office Kane's bill that had been signed into law by Sulzer calling for a Negro National Guard regiment.[14] Stotesbury advised Whitman that he should either organize the regiment with an "appropriation for making it effective" or repeal the law. When Whitman made up his mind to at last organize the regiment, Stotesbury, New York's chief military officer, recalled that he "selected the designation—'15th INFANTRY'—and we went ahead."[15]

Whitman had been a crusading district attorney for New York County, fighting police corruption with the same fervor that Theodore Roosevelt had shown when he was police commissioner in the 1890s. Whitman won his party's nomination for governor in 1914. With Hayward, his thirty-seven-year-old assistant district attorney, as campaign manager, he dumped Glynn in the elections. In Albany, Hayward, a transplanted Nebraskan where his father, Monroe Leland Hayward, had been the United States senator, first served the new governor as counsel and then as public service commissioner. The two lawyers were inseparable. Perhaps late in his first term, Whitman, Hayward, and Spencer hatched a plan to remake the black regiment.

Looking back on that day, Hayward later confided to several white officers, among them Maj. Arthur Little, how it all came about. Little recollected Hayward's story in his book *From Harlem to the Rhine.*

> We have heard people say that it [the Fifteenth] was conceived in politics, born in ridicule and reared in opposition. Well, the rearing and the borning characterization may be all right, but they're all wrong about the spirit of the conception. Governor Whitman and I up in Albany found the record of the law sponsored by Governor Sulzer, authorizing the building of an infantry regiment of colored soldiers. The making of that law predated Governor Whitman's first term by a number of years. It is not for us to say whether that was conceived in politics or not, but if it was, it was damn poor politics, because after the law was out on the statute books, nothing was done about it.

The Governor and I started to talk about it, and we agreed that either that regiment ought to be built and given a fair chance of proving itself, or the law ought to be repealed. Gradually the details of the program for the building of the regiment were worked out. Governor Whitman was perfectly sincere in his feelings that the great colored population of New York ought to be given an opportunity to shine in the National Guard field without prejudice; and as you know men, I felt very deeply on the subject of the negro problem, and the unfairness with which it was being met. When the Governor invited me to accept the designation as Commanding Officer of a regiment that did not exist . . . I accepted . . . in all seriousness and in full appreciation of the probable difficulties which lay before me. The absurdity of being Colonel of a regiment of which the Colonel was the only member struck me as a necessary absurdity to accept.[16]

In the retelling, Little left out any mention of Spencer. As it turned out, there was no love between the two men.[17] In fact, Spencer's name rarely appears in the book, as if he had never been in the regiment. Little had

Col. William Hayward, a veteran of the Spanish-American War, became commander of the Fifteenth New York Infantry Regiment (incorporated into the Army as the U.S. 369th Infantry Regiment during the war) in 1916. Hayward was closely connected to the governor of New York, Charles Whitman, and used his influence to finally secure the organization of the Fifteenth Regiment with himself as commander. Pancho Villa's raid on Columbus, New Mexico, which resulted in the deployment of some New York National Guard regiments to the U.S.–Mexico border, helped convince officials that the state needed the additional National Guard regiment.

FAMILY OF RANULF COMPTON

Maj. Lorillard Spencer, a scion of one of New York's wealthiest families, assisted Colonel Hayward in organizing the Fifteenth Regiment. STEPHEN SPENCER

failed to mention that it was Spencer who had found the quickly forgotten law and then shared his discovery with Governor Whitman and Hayward.

Hayward, who was already calling himself a colonel, had been a cadet under General Pershing while at the University of Nebraska. He fought in the Philippines during the Spanish-American War. Because of his wartime experience, it was natural that he should run the regiment. His father had been a war veteran as well, serving with the Twenty-second New York Infantry in the Shenandoah Valley during the Civil War. Hayward believed only unmarried men should serve in the military. He also disdained training at summer camps, like the one at Plattsburgh, stating that they were a midsummer's spree for the men attending.[18] Spencer, a scion of one of New York's wealthiest families, would be the number-two man. A former officer in the elite Squadron A, the thirty-three-year-old Spencer was currently a captain in the Eighth Coast Guard Auxiliary. His great-grandfather had been chief justice of the New York Supreme Court. Another relative, John Spencer, had served as secretary of war under President Tyler. A great-uncle had been the only naval officer in United States history to be hung for mutiny. In 1911, Lorillard's mother more or less renounced her wealth, gave up the social life of Manhattan, Newport, and Tuxedo Park, and sailed off to the Philippines to teach underprivileged children. If Spencer had inherited his mother's sympathetic feelings toward minorities, he would soon be putting them to the test.

During the last week of May 1916, while Pancho Villa was loose along the Mexican border, Whitman, accompanied by Spencer, strode into the Manhattan Casino to address the African-American community. Two bands greeted him. The Clef Club and E. E. Thompson's quasi-military band played "America" as the welcoming delegation escorted the governor to the podium. Dr. Adam Clayton Powell introduced him to the cheering audience that included Fillmore, Payton, Vertner Tandy, the Rev. William H. Brooks, soon to be a military chaplain, and the entertainer J. Rosamond Johnson. When the audience hushed, Powell's voice boomed out.

> Permit me to say to the Governor that he has the distinction of addressing an audience without a hyphen. We are not pro-British, or pro-German, or pro-African; we are not even Afro-Americans. We are just simple, thorough-going Americans from the peeling to the core, and from the core to the peeling. We do not know any flag but the Stars and Stripes, and we do not wish to know any other. We have no country but America, and we do not want any other. We have always stood ready, as Boston Common, Bunker Hill, Fort Pillow and San Juan Heights will testify, and we now stand ready to give our blood in defense of the sacred principles enunciated in the Declaration of Independence.[19]

Following Powell's rousing introduction, Whitman, who had primarily come to the Harlem music hall to lend a hand in raising money for the Booker T. Washington Memorial Fund, told the audience that no reward could be won except by proof of merit. "You are here, you are part and parcel of America, and there can be no progress in which you are not considered. The greatest monument that you can erect to Booker T. Washington is the recognition of your duties as citizens and Americans and the whole-souled fulfillment of those obligations in such a manner as not only to prove your worth but to prove the wisdom of the great democratic experiment."[20] To prove they were part and parcel of New York, the governor informed the crowd that he had just issued orders authorizing the organization of a black regiment of the National Guard and that he had already appointed two medical examiners, indicating that recruitment could begin almost immediately.

To Whitman it must have seemed obvious that with thousands of National Guardsmen heading for Texas, New York City would be a military ghost town. That thought alone was reason enough to justify the new regiment—whether it was black or white.

As it turned out, he was right. Almost overnight, New York had indeed turned into a military ghost town.

Within a week of the governor's orders to mobilize, the first of 15,289 Guardsmen were on their way to Texas. On 27 June, regiments from the New York City area, the Seventh, Fourteenth, and Seventy-first Infantries, totaling 142 officers and 2,541 men, rolled out of the Jersey City railroad station. The Twelfth Infantry, with 37 officers and 673 men, followed two days later, and on 11 July the Fighting Sixty-ninth, with 917 officers and men, departed Manhattan. Within a few weeks over five thousand Guardsmen were gone from Gotham.[21] As other militia units also pulled out, New York was left unprotected. Clearly, there was a need for another regiment. On 16 June Whitman made it official: he appointed Hayward colonel and ordered him to organize the Fifteenth New York National Guard Infantry Regiment. The governor then named Spencer to assist Hayward.

Soon after Whitman's appointments, he seemingly hedged his bets with the city's African Americans by requesting from the War Department that it reassign Maj. Charles Young to the Fifteenth. At the time, Young was in Mexico with the Second Squadron of the Tenth U.S. Cavalry, turning himself into a national hero. On 12 April, he led his squadron on a rescue mission to save the Thirteenth U.S. Cavalry from destruction at the hands of Villa's forces at Hacienda Santa Cruz de la Villegas and, in doing so, according to some historians, averted a full-scale war with Mexico. The *Age*'s editorial writer noted: "At last we notice that the Tenth Cavalry is appearing in the news despatches. It did look like as though the censor's biggest job was keeping any mention of the colored soldiers out of the despatches, but we knew that couldn't be kept up after our boys really got down to work."[22] Mexican citizens, who saw these boys at work, called them "devils." A black trooper overheard one of them say, "They are not Americans. They are devils."[23] Two years later, the French would call them fighters from hell.

Meanwhile, with Hayward as the colonel, the odd man out in this gubernatorial arrangement to run the Fifteenth New York, just as he had been the odd man out in Ohio, was Charles W. Fillmore.

3

"The Color Line Will Not Be Drawn in This Regiment"

With a heartbroken Fillmore now out as commander of the newly established Fifteenth Infantry, it seemed a sure bet that New York City's all-black regiment would be officered by whites, although Whitman had insisted that blacks would be offered commissions. African Americans would more than likely serve only as noncommissioned officers and enlisted men.

That would be true unless Charles Young, promoted to lieutenant colonel for his valor in Mexico and with the right charisma, credentials, and experience to be second in command under William Hayward, was reassigned to New York. His West Point background had more substance than Hayward's education as a cadet at the University of Nebraska—even though Hayward's instructor had been John J. Pershing. But Young's role with the Fifteenth, if, in fact, there might have been one, never materialized. The fifty-two-year-old officer was needed in the southwest, and there he stayed until 1917 when he was medically retired from the Army for high blood pressure and Bright's disease.

His so-called retirement was seen by black leaders as a ruse to get him out of the way so that during the Great War the federal government would not have to deal with such a high-ranking officer of color in the

Regular Army. Of course, that left Fillmore as the next best black candidate for a commission.

But in the summer of 1916 that, too, was not to be—at least not yet. For the moment, two white men had the task of organizing a regiment of African Americans. And although New York's men of color had been clamoring for a regiment of their own for more than twenty years, they had not envisioned that it would be white at the top and black at the bottom. If that was the case, then Colonel Hayward and acting Lieutenant Colonel Spencer had better be the kind of men who could pull it off—raise a regiment and make it work.

According to an officer who had served on his staff during the war, Hayward was a man of "vision" and "imagination."[1] He was also a flamboyant chap of rich taste who, when the war ended, victoriously courted one of the wealthiest widows in the United States. But it was his strong, persuasive personality and flair for the dramatic that in the first year of his colonelcy got the Fifteenth Infantry off to a strong start.

But it wasn't to be easy, and he needed Spencer, who had a more inventive mind. Spencer was always tinkering with things, trying to make something work better. In the coming war, his inventive mind would come up with a gadget to hold shattered bones together before physicians thought of using metal pins. After taking six bullets in the thigh, Spencer would use his own gadget, a kind of coiled spring such as the ones found on screen doors to keep them shut, to hold his smashed leg together.

Among the first acts of the two men was to proclaim that if any recruit passed the officer's examination, he would be given every opportunity to earn a commission. Next they had to convince Vertner Tandy, one of the original members of Fillmore's provisional regiment, to assist them in recruiting men. They promised him that if he passed the officer's exam, he would be placed in charge of A Company, First Battalion. He would become the first official black officer of the Fifteenth Infantry.

But that meant that he had to commit to three years of active service and three years of reserve service.

A well-known citizen of Harlem, Tandy was a reputable architect. He had graduated from Tuskegee Institute in 1904 and then from the Cornell University School of Architecture four years later. When the ninety-eight-year-old St. Philip's Episcopal Church, one of the most venerable African-American churches of New York, moved uptown to West 134th Street in 1911, Tandy designed its new building.

The moment he passed the officer's examination, he joined Hayward and Spencer as the only officers in the Fifteenth. Immediately afterward recruiting posters and advertisements appeared throughout the city:

SOLDIERS, ATTENTION!!
RECRUITS WANTED FOR COLORED
NEW YORK NATIONAL GUARD

HAYWARD, SPENCER and,

to assist me [Hayward] in the work of organizing this regiment,

V. W. TANDY

having passed the required examination and satisfactorily qualified
for commission as 1ST LIEUTENANT in this regiment has been
this day, June 27, assigned as PROVISIONAL COMMANDER
OF THE FIRST COMPANY to be recruited.

The three officers stated they planned to provide for a full regiment of infantry, made up of four companies, a headquarters company, machine-gun company, supply company, and a band. They guaranteed that the "color line will not be drawn in this regiment and as rapidly as COLORED MEN CAN AND DO QUALIFY, and in proportion to the enlisted men secured, they will be COMISSIONED AS OFFICERS." For men of previous military experience, rapid promotion and advancement was also promised. They sought "all able-bodied men of good character, 5 ft. 4 in. (5 ft. 5 or 6 in. in shoes)."[2] Recruiting station Number One was set up in a small cigar store in a corner of the Lafayette Theater at Seventh Avenue and 131st Street. Hayward commandeered the dance hall on the Lafayette's second floor for use as a temporary armory, hoping that a permanent place would soon be found, or built. The basement he used as storage. Hamilton Fish scoffed at the armory when he later joined the regiment. "Of course, we didn't have an armory like the Seventh or Sixty-ninth New York," he wrote, "so we did our recruiting right in the streets of Harlem. Haw, haw, I remember we even had a cigar store and dance hall that we used."[3]

Hayward, Spencer, and Tandy unlocked the doors to their new, but spare, office at the Lafayette cigar store at 9 P.M. on Tuesday, 27 June. Playing at the theater that night was the drama *Alias Jimmy Valentine*. It started at 8:15, and when it was over, the crowd wandered past the recruiting office and perhaps a few curious men stopped in. At least it was a start.

It was slow that first night, if the *Age*'s account was accurate. Only a handful of men signed on. Or were "received," as the newspaper termed it.[4]

The first man to enlist, according to Hayward, was William Bunting, "a big, strapping young fellow." After he was examined by the surgeon, Dr. George Boling Lee, a grandson of Gen. Robert E. Lee, Hayward swore him in. Lt. Col. George F. Hinton, a fifty-three-year-old theatrical agent for John Philip Sousa, Lillian Russell, and Elsie Janis, stood at attention and cried the whole time. Hinton had been brought to assist in the day-to-day duties of running the regiment. After the emotional swearing-in ceremony, Hayward said, "I shook hands with Private Bunting of the Fifteenth New York Infantry, and allowed as how there were now two of us." He offered Bunting the job of first sergeant. "He said he didn't want to be anything but a private," Hayward said, "that that would be glory enough for him."[5]

Other original members of the Fifteenth were Lee Pollard, a holdover from Fillmore's provisional regiment; Peter Banks, a Spanish-American War veteran who had served with the Sixth Virginia Battalion, Edward Buchanan, Roy Miller, and Leaming Wright. If Fillmore showed up on Tuesday night, there was no record of it.

The *Age* covered the first night of recruitment on its front page. It also ran a lead story about how black troops of the "Gallant Tenth Cavalry," ambushed at Carrizal, Mexico, rode to their death. The article recounted how the cavalrymen made a desperate stand against seven hundred Mexicans armed with machine guns. "The American Negro Troops Faced Almost Certain Death at Carrizal with Smiles and Songs on their Lips." The thrilling article also pointed out that "Major Charles Young, the only Negro line officer in the army, and a graduate of West Point, is in active command of his squadron of the 10th in Mexico, and yet however actively his troops may be engaged in the campaign, his name is studiously omitted from the news stories."[6] A week later it disclosed that N.Y. Gov. Charles Whitman had requested that the War Department assign Charles Young to "New York's Negro Regiment now being mustered."[7]

By running both articles on the same page about the heroics of black soldiers, from raw recruits willing to serve in New York to grizzled veterans fighting to the death for their country and then following it up with the report on Young, the *Age* started an enlistment stampede. Within a week, and in spite of a three-year active-duty commitment, A Company of the First Battalion had been filled. Doors to another recruiting station were thrown open at Lenox Avenue and 135th Street. In Brooklyn, Hayward secured the use of the Twenty-third Regiment Armory as a place of enlistment for the Second Battalion. To supervise recruitment there, Hayward counted on a Long Island real-estate tycoon, Monson Morris. Another white officer, the forty-one-year-old Morris, a native of Columbia, South Carolina, had served in the Spanish-American War as a member of the Twelfth Regiment. When one of the recruits was asked by a reporter for the Brooklyn *Eagle* what he thought of Morris, he replied, "Ah's new man and Ah doan know much about him, but Ah knows he's mah Major and Ah'll go through hell for him."[8]

Spencer remarked that if the pace kept up, the regiment would be "fully recruited in a month's time."[9] Two weeks after Hayward started enlisting men, B, C, and D companies were stocked. The First Battalion was now operative. On 12 July, 110 men were sworn in. One of the new recruits was Charles Fillmore.

Lost in the shuffle that night was another recruit. At first glance, he didn't seem promising. He was short, only five feet, seven inches, and bowlegged. But he moved with athletic grace. Most of the African Americans in the recruiting office recognized him. He was Spottswood Poles, center fielder for the New York Lincoln Giants, a powerhouse team that played its home games at Olympic Field in Harlem. The leadoff man for the Lincolns, he was a switch-hitter, and without a doubt, the fastest man in all of baseball. He had been timed sprinting one hundred yards in less than ten seconds, notwithstanding the fact that he was weighted down by a fifteen-pound woolen baseball uniform and wore clumsy spikes. It had been said that he once leaped five feet straight off the ground to snare a line drive.[10] In a game against the Philadelphia Phillies in 1913 he faced their star right-hander Grover Alexander, a pitcher destined for baseball's Hall of Fame—a place where Poles has yet to be enshrined. That season Alexander had the second highest winning percentage of any pitcher in the major leagues, won twenty-two games, and hurled seven shutouts. Playing in Philadelphia, Poles drilled three straight hits off Alexander and scored a pair of runs as the Lincolns crushed the Phillies, 9–2. In his first four seasons with the Lincolns, he hit .440, .398, .414, and .487, "against all levels of competition."[11] It wasn't long before he was compared to another blistering leadoff-hitting center fielder of the day, the Detroit Tigers' Ty Cobb. His own fans called him the "Black Ty Cobb."

For years, John McGraw, manager of the white New York Giants, a team that played its home games near Olympic Field, had watched Poles. After marveling at his ability, McGraw declared that if blacks were allowed to play in the major leagues, Poles would be one of the first men he'd sign up. In any case, the short, bowlegged Poles, a resident of 36 West 142nd Street, who over the weekend led the Lincolns in a doubleheader sweep of the Brooklyn Royal Giants, signed himself up to be a soldier in the Fifteenth New York.

Cpl. Spottswood Poles (on left) and two unidentified Fifteenth Regiment soldiers. Poles, a center fielder for the New York Lincoln Giants, was one of the great Negro League baseball players of the time.
FAMILY OF SPOTTSWOOD POLES

Maybe he couldn't play in the majors because of his color, but he could still serve his country as a soldier.

With so many potential leaders swelling the ranks of the Fifteenth, a school for noncommissioned officers was started. Also, other men were being examined to see if they qualified for commissions. One of these men was Fillmore, and if he passed, it was expected he would receive his captain's bars. The examining officer was Lt. Col. John J. Byrne, formerly of the Seventh Regiment. To the relief of many, he found the now fifty-two-year-old soldier fit. Fillmore had command of the First Battalion, a command that had eluded him since those miserable days in Ohio when he had been accused of betraying his own race.

Byrne found Virgil H. Parks fit for a captaincy, as well. Parks had also been in the provisional regiment. He brought with him to the Fifteenth battlefield experience from his days with A Troop of the Tenth Cavalry that had charged up San Juan Hill with Teddy Roosevelt's Rough Riders.

The ranks were swelling, and Spencer's prediction that the regiment would be fully manned within a month's time was coming true.

But the speed to which the regiment was gaining strength meant that uniforms were in short supply. Of the original fifty-three recruits that had enlisted in Lieutenant Tandy's A Company, uniforms were available for only thirty-seven.

There were not enough rifles, either. Instead, men shouldered broomsticks during drill and on parade through the streets of Harlem. "We paraded around with broom sticks and what-nots for so long that the people of Harlem commenced to believe that the whole thing was a fake," Hayward complained, "and that we were not going to be soldiers at all."[12]

Watching the Fifteenth drill with broomsticks, a patron in a white-owned saloon chortled at "these darkies playing soldiers."[13]

Because most of the men still held full-time jobs, drilling was done when it matched their hours off from work. Companies were unable to drill as one unit. Recruits showed up when they could, some during the day, others at night. Drills, according to Hayward, held upstairs at the Lafayette Theater, had to be arranged for the men's convenience.

Bert Williams, a popular vaudevillian, remembered the early confusion. Perhaps the most widely known black performer in the country because of his work with the Ziegfeld Follies, Williams, like Tandy, had been singled out by Hayward to boost recruitment. Williams claimed to have been a captain in the Eighth Illinois. He was also reported to have been in a regiment in California. Yet with the Fifteenth, he appeared to have been more of a figurehead than a real soldier in spite of his military experience. But his famous name lent credibility to the brand-new regiment.

Everyone familiar with Broadway and the Ziegfeld Follies knew and loved Williams's comical acts. He was appearing regularly to rave reviews at the New Amsterdam Theater on Forty-second Street in the "Follies of 1916." The New York *World* claimed him as "the real genius among the lot."[14] Only recently, the comedian had signed a contract with the Biograph Company to make a series of two-reel comedies. "He was tall and broad-shouldered," recalled James Weldon Johnson, "and on the whole, a rather handsome figure and entirely unrecognizable as the shambling, shuffling 'darky' he impersonated on the stage; luxury-loving, indolent, but highly intelligent and with a certain reserve which at times exhibited itself as downright snobbishness; talking out of a very slow drawl and getting more satisfaction, it seemed, out of being considered a great raconteur than out of being a great comedian."[15] He was a fine baseball player, too, and organized games between the casts of Broadway shows.

Williams believed that the best way to get a laugh was to poke fun at another person's troubles. In a few months, his own troubles were put on display for most New Yorkers to see, and it drew laughter when he led the Fifteenth downtown to the Union League Club to receive its colors from Governor Whitman.

Hayward also brought in several experienced white officers to instruct his men. Maj. Edwin W. Dayton worked with noncommissioned officers, and Capt. Herman Koehler had charge of all the enlisted men, including those under Dayton's instruction.

The task for Koehler, who held the title of "Master of the Sword" at the U. S. Military Academy, was to whip the new soldiers into shape. Already famous throughout New York, and especially in the city itself, as a physical fitness expert, he had been recognized by Congress for his training methods. In 1901 Congress commissioned him a first lieutenant in the U. S. Army, although he had never served a day in the military. Second, in 1905, it authorized more than $350,000 for the construction of a gymnasium at West Point so that he could better train the cadets there. He coached the academy's football, basketball, and swimming teams, and his fencing team was unbeaten year after year. When New York City's National Guard regiments were required to be physically fit, Koehler came down from West Point and did the job, without getting paid.

Pushing sixty years of age in the summer of 1916, Koehler was again called upon by New York State to shape up its civilian soldiers headed for the Mexican border. For five weeks he worked with the National Guardsmen until they left for Texas. As soon as the last troop train pulled out, Hayward charmed the "Master of the Sword" into training his own men.

Koehler's method was straightforward, but all encompassing, and it is likely that he applied it to the men of the Fifteenth. A student of his at West Point believed it was his German style of gymnastics that was the key to its success because it "sought to promote health, strength and agility as well as discretion, resoluteness, courage of endurance."[16] Each exercise was executed upon command barked out by Koehler while he was astride a table planted in front of his troops.

A reporter for the *Age* figured that Koehler was "to put the men through a course of physical development, giving the sitting-up exercises used at West Point."[17]

Dayton's task was to concentrate on the duties noncommissioned officers had to know to be effective leaders. Although he was an archeologist by profession and an author, Dayton had plenty of military experience and was another of the decorated heroes of the Spanish-American War.

Meanwhile, Hayward kept hounding the state quartermaster for rifles, but each time he pleaded his case, he was turned away. Finally, workers at the state arsenal confided that there were hundreds of brand-new rifles that had been set aside for civilians in case of a national emergency. They were stored there under the guise of a so-called civilian shooting club. As Hayward figured, "This civilian shooting club idea, I believe, was an offshoot of some of Gen. Leonard Wood's military preparedness program. He couldn't get any action from the government in the line of military preparedness, but he applied his resourcefulness to seeing what he could do about getting preparedness under camouflage. So he got either a law or a regulation put on the books, encouraging the formation of civilian shooting clubs, or rifle clubs, with the right to draw rifles from the Ordnance Department of the United States Army.

"Well, I started the darndest set of rifle or civilian shooting clubs that you ever heard of. There was regular boom. Practically everybody in the regiment in the early days became the president or the secretary of a civilian shooting club, and we put in a requisition and got the rifles delivered to us."[18]

By the end of July the regiment boasted more than five hundred recruits. A number of them had been part of the original provisional regiment under Fillmore, but the majority, like the baseball player Spottswood Poles, were first-timers, fresh off the city streets. Lt. Col. Hinton called them the "cleanest cut group of men yet received in the National Guard."[19] A member of the four-man examining board, of which all were officers from the Regular Army, claimed the new soldiers represented as "high a type of manhood as they have come in contact with."[20]

The *Age* reported that Hayward, despite the arrival of Dayton, Hinton, and Koehler, wanted black officers. But he was not about to compromise military standards to get them. According to the newspaper, the colonel "emphasized that the standards of this regiment will in no particular be any lower than the standards in any other regiment of the National Guard, and, as a matter of fact, the same standards will prevail as . . . in the regular army." Hayward stated that candidates for commission must qualify under "rigorous tests, and this means intellectually, physically, morally." To date, only four men had been found ably fit: Captains Fillmore and Parks and Lieutenants Tandy and Wyatt. The *Age* then pleaded, "It is urgently emphasized that men of necessary qualifications should ally themselves with the regiment at once. Otherwise, it will necessarily follow that many of the officers will be white men."[21]

Out at Fort Huachuca, Arizona, where the Buffalo soldiers were stationed, a sergeant named Presly Holliday watched with keen attention to the developments in New York. He was a friend of Henry Coles, the old first sergeant of the Twenty-fourth Infantry. Holliday asked the readers of the *Age:*

> Why does the regiment fill up so slowly with officers? I would expect to see ambitious Negroes falling over each other to get commissions in it. . . . This regiment should be quickly officered from the most intelligent and most influential Negroes of New York. I understand there are numbers of lawyers, doctors, merchants and other business men in New York and Brooklyn. From these should come the officers, men whose standing at home will demand for them recognition and the confidence of regular army officers. They should, if possible, be men so accustomed to being deferred to that it will be natural for them to enforce discipline. Inability to enforce discipline is one of the most common weaknesses which white officers attribute to Negroes. . . . It will always be unfortunate for any Negro regiment to send it in the field where it will mingle with regulars, or even militia, if it is officered by men of indifferent education and no standing in their home community.[22]

Black or white officers? Or a combination of both? The battle lines had been drawn. Of course, there was no doubt that at this stage Hayward and Spencer would stay as the regiment's overlords, which meant Spencer, a lieutenant colonel on paper, would be commissioned a major. Charles Young was bottled up in bureaucratic red tape, and even the efforts of Governor Whitman to get him to New York had proven fruitless. There were now four qualified African-American officers, with Fillmore and Parks the leading contenders for ranks higher than captain. Would the rest of the ranks, from second lieutenants to lieutenant colonel, be officered by blacks? Were there enough capable citizens willing to step forward for three years to fill up the commissioned ranks of the Fifteenth? Or would Hayward be forced to bring in young, ambitious white men from other National Guard units, who might be eager to use the regiment for rapid promotion—to make names for themselves and then move on?

Sergeant Holliday's questions had to be answered. Where were Gotham's most intelligent and most influential African Americans? And why weren't they falling all over themselves to be commissioned officers in New York State's first black National Guard regiment?

The Man Who Stood
for Something

In the fading days of summer 1916, the officers' roll of the Fifteenth was about to expand beyond four, and to the relief of New York's black community, the soon-to-be officers were African Americans.

Herbert E. Gee, a former investigator for the United Cigar Company, who had arrived in New York in 1911 from his hometown of Gallipolis, Ohio, joined up for three years. Standing only five feet, six inches tall, Gee had plenty of military experience, first as a sergeant major in the Eighth Immunes, then as a sergeant major in the Forty-eighth U.S. Volunteer Infantry, and finally as a second lieutenant, serving in the Philippines during the Spanish-American War. When recommending him for promotion to sergeant major, his commanding officer called him "reliable, capable" and not "showy."

Gee's fellow officers in the Fifteenth found him to be a "live wire" and "one of the best-informed men on military matters in the regiment."[1] In time, because of his experience, Gee took charge of regimental headquarters.

Another of the late summer enlistees was an attorney and former track star for Harvard University with a name that conjured up military genius—Napoleon Bonaparte Marshall.

"When the S. S. Lusitania was torpedoed by a German submarine boat, I was practicing law in the city of New York," he recalled years later. "I wrote to President Wilson, offering my services in the recruiting of a volunteer Negro regiment of infantry. This I believe constituted the first offer of services in the World War of any colored citizen in the United States, as it was over a year before the declaration of war by the United States against Germany."[2]

If his boast was true—that after the *Lusitania* went down on 7 May 1915, he had been the first African American to offer himself to the federal government as a soldier in the coming fight against Germany— then he had taken a curiously long time in joining the regiment. Counting those early years when Fillmore was out raising his provisional regiment, it had taken Marshall at least four years before he acted. He was not on the original roster that had been sent to Governor Dix in 1912, although his law partner J. Frank Wheaton was. One reason might have been that Wheaton and Fillmore were both Republicans and Marshall a Democrat, and a number of black Democrats were in turmoil about how to support the provisional regiment. Another may have been that he spent time shuttling between New York and Washington because of his wife's work in the nation's capital as founder and director of the Washington Conservatory of Music and School of Expression.

Yet, when he made up his mind to enlist, he was determined to serve the Fifteenth as best he could and to become one of its most effective officers. He certainly had the credentials. First of all, his character was impeccable. A friend described him as "gallant, noble minded." Another said he had a "robust personal integrity."[3] Watching him conduct a court martial, Arthur Little was moved to write, "He held court under conditions of great impressiveness."[4]

Born in the District of Columbia on 30 July 1873, Marshall prepared for Harvard at Phillips Exeter Academy in New Hampshire. In the last decade of the 1800s, the private school accepted black students from Washington's M Street High School, where Marshall had first been a student. Although he was far away from home, he distinguished himself at Exeter as editor in chief of its literary magazine and, with his long legs flying, on the track team. When he graduated in 1893 and moved on to Harvard, he ran with grace, a speedster in the 440-yard run. He lettered for four years, posting best times in the quarter mile of fifty seconds flat. Yet he did more than run at Harvard. As a member of the Harvard Union debating club, the multilingual speedster (he spoke French fluently) proved to be a forensic whiz. He graduated in 1897, taught for a year at Florida State College, and stumped for perennial presidential candidate William Jennings Bryan, in his campaign against

William McKinley. He then settled in Boston, where he got more involved in politics, was appointed the city's first black tax collector, and was elected a justice of the peace.

Marshall moved back to Washington, where he taught at the Washington Conservatory of Music and School of Expression, founded in 1903 by Hattie Gibbs. An extraordinary woman, Gibbs, four years older than Marshall, was the daughter of Mifflin Wistar Gibbs, an agent in the Underground Railway who had toured with Frederick Douglass as a colecturer. In 1889 Hattie became the first African American to graduate from the Oberlin College Conservatory of Music.

It didn't take her long to fall in love with the New York attorney. They were married in 1906 and moved to New York where Marshall partnered with attorneys Wheaton and Oscar Garrett to establish Marshall, Wheaton and Garrett, judged the most influential black law firm in the country.

In the fall of 1916, when he was forty-three, Marshall enlisted in the Fifteenth. He passed his officer's examination and was commissioned a captain.

About the time that Gee and Marshall had committed three years of their lives to National Guard service, another District of Columbia resident who had gone to the same high school as Marshall also made the same commitment. On 18 September 1916, James Reese Europe, composer, conductor, and an entrepreneur instrumental in organizing New York's black musicians into a powerful union, decided it was time to be a soldier. That day he enlisted in the Fifteenth. A week later, he got around to telling one of his newest and dearest friends about his decision to enlist, a singer and composer named Noble Sissle.

Sissle, a college-educated Midwesterner, had reached New York that spring with dreams of his own to be a musical star. Lounging in Europe's office on 26 September, as the orchestral summer season wound down, Sissle, delicately smooth, almost too pretty, was just back from the New Jersey shore where he had directed one of Europe's many Clef Club bands. The tall, powerfully built Europe stepped through the doorway.

"Siss, I'm in it now! I did it! I'm real stuff now!" he said. At first Sissle figured Europe had landed a big musical engagement—"a million dollar proposition." "Boy, I just joined the Fifteenth New York National Guards!"

Sissle couldn't believe his ears. He was certain Europe was giving up his career to be a soldier. It didn't add up. He blurted, "Goodness gra-

James Reese Europe (at the piano) and some of his Clef Club Society Orchestra musicians, circa 1916. Noble Sissle (wearing glasses), who would reluctantly join the Fifteenth Regiment with Europe, is in the back row. BALTIMORE HISTORICAL SOCIETY

cious, Jim, what's the idea? What time have you to devote to anybody's army?"

"Don't worry," Europe said, "you're going to join, too!"

Sissle jumped from his chair. "Oh no, you don't get me in anybody's army! There's plenty of men who have time for that. What time do have I to attend drill? I just can't afford to do it. Jim, your work demands our time—my time, anyhow, especially if you're going to give your time. It keeps me busy now, trying to keep people from complaining when you are not in ten different places at the same time."

"That's all right," Europe told him. "You'll have to join now because I have put your name down as having said you will join." Europe then explained why, and Sissle's version of it is worth repeating:

I was like you, last spring when they came to me with the proposition of joining the regiment. I didn't see where I had time, and first one excuse, then another, I offered, but I found I was wrong, and I want you to join this organization also. In the first place, you are practically a stranger in New York, and it will be the means of your forming comradeship with some fine young men. New York is a peculiar city. People are very clannish here, and you have a very small chance, working at night as we do, to meet many of the fine business men in the city of our race. I have been in New York for sixteen years, and there has never been such an organization of Negro men that will bring together all classes of men for a common good. And our race will never amount to anything, politically or economically, in New York or anywhere else unless there are strong organizations of men who stand for something in the community.

Now some of the most influential men of our race in Harlem are going to join the regiment, as they realize the moral effect it will have, being promoted, financially, by the biggest men on Wall Street. It will eventually mean a big armory where the young men can have healthful exercise, swimming pools, and athletic training, and it will build up the moral and physical Negro manhood of Harlem. But to accomplish these results, the best and most sincere energetical men in the community must get in the move, as there will be a lot of money spent. And you know, the wrong type of persons generally get in the front ranks of these kind of organizations. There are always some smart, dishonest fellows, who have plenty—yes, too much time, who hang around and get in some important office where they can graft for money—and those of us would have too much principle for such, stand back and say we haven't time to spare. Consequently, what happens? The wrong class of men, by their dishonesty and misappropriation of funds, will so disgust those who are contributing financially to the organization, that they will withdraw their funds. And then who would be the sufferers? Nobody but the younger generation. The grafters will have the money, the benefactors will be probably turned against ever contributing any more funds, and who will be to blame? Men like you and I, who sit back and say we have not got time. No, New York cannot afford to lose this great chance for such a strong, powerful institution, for the development of the Negro manhood of Harlem.[5]

After this long sermon, Europe marched Sissle to a café for lunch. There, seated around a table, were four men. The most prominent, for his role in helping to ensure that New York's blacks had a regiment of their own, was the silver-haired Charles Fillmore. Also at the table was Charles Anderson, the Internal Revenue Department tax collector for the huge Third District that took in all of Manhattan north of Twenty-third Street. Because it was the most important tax district in the nation, Anderson, now serving under his third president, was a powerful man in the city—white or black. At fifty, he was too old to join the regiment. But he held the title of honorary colonel. Charles Toney, a member of the old provisional regiment, was there, too. He had arrived in New York in 1905 with a doctorate from Syracuse University as well as a law degree. The only non-Charles in the group was Napoleon Marshall. There was a good chance that Sissle, because he was new to the city, had no idea who these men were. None of them were professional musicians.

Listening to them expound on the importance of the new regiment, Sissle felt himself "thrilled by their exalted opinions." That evening he entered the makeshift recruiting station at the Lafayette Theater, took the entrance examination, and Hayward swore him in as a new private in K Company, the same company Europe had joined.[6]

At the time, Europe was thirty-six years old, Sissle, twenty-seven.

Europe had reached New York in the winter of 1902–1903, when he was twenty-two, armed with a violin, a great ear for music, boundless creativity, the extraordinary ability to organize just about anything, and a resoluteness that would carry him through hard times. His mother, Lorraine, a widow, who lived in Washington along with his two sisters and an older brother, rather hoped that if her son were to be a professional musician, he would lean more toward classical than ragtime. When he was growing up, whether in Mobile, Alabama, where he was born, or in the District of Columbia, his mother had always encouraged him to learn classical music. She taught all her children to read music and play the piano and engaged a violin virtuoso, Joseph Douglass, the grandson of Frederick Douglass, to teach Jim and his youngest sister, Mary, how to play the stringed instrument. When Jim was fourteen and Mary nine, they were good enough to perform a duet under the names "Jas. R. Europe and Mary L. Europe."

When they were not studying the violin, brother and sister received more musical instruction from the U. S. Marine Corps Band, which in those days was under the direction of their neighbor John Philip Sousa. The band often took part in the life of Washington's black community. Europe's biographer, Reid Badger, believed that it was "entirely likely that this early training provided the foundation for Europe's later successes as a composer of marches and as a leader of a military band."[7]

Europe also attended the same M Street High School that Marshall had gone to. He joined the school's African-American cadet corps and earned the rank of sergeant. Other than his time with the Marine band, it was his first taste of soldiering.

Henry Europe, Jim's father, a federal government employee, first with the U. S. Postal Service and then with the Internal Revenue Department, died on the first day of summer of 1899. Not wanting to leave his mother,

Jim stayed in Washington until his elder sister, Ida, came home to live. With Ida to watch over Lorraine and Mary, he took off for New York, carrying a violin and a pocketful of dreams.

For a black musician in New York in the first years of the twentieth century, especially a violin-toting musician, work was hard to come by. There were no real booking agencies. The best bet was to show up at a saloon, bar, or café in the city's juicy Tenderloin District, otherwise known as Satan's Circle—a stretch of nightclubs, gambling parlors, dance halls, clip joints, and whorehouses wedged between Fifth and Seventh Avenues from Twenty-fourth Street on the south to Forty-second Street on the north. It supposedly got its name when "Clubber" Williams, a vicious police officer, was transferred out of the poor Fourth Precinct, where he had fattened his city paycheck through graft, to the prosperous Twenty-ninth Precinct. "I have been living on rump steak," he quipped to a *Sun* reporter, "I will have some tenderloin now."[8] In their pre-Harlem days, many of the city's African Americans lived in the Tenderloin or along its fringe streets or a little further to the northwest from Amsterdam Avenue west to the Hudson River, then known as San Juan Hill, most likely for the black veterans who had settled there after the Spanish-American War. Inside the Tenderloin, mostly on West Forty-second Street, was yet another of New York's great drawing cards—Tin Pan Alley, home of composers and publishers of sheet music.

By the time Europe reached the chaotic streets of the Tenderloin in the winter of 1902–1903, Tin Pan Alley, which got its name from the tinny sound of pianos, had moved uptown from West Twenty-eighth Street between Broadway and Sixth Avenue. In fact, the whole city was heading north. Blacks were pulling out of the Tenderloin in droves, migrating to Harlem. But there were still strips of the Tenderloin that bound entertainers of color together like rosin on a bow.

One strip was along West Fifty-third Street. Here stood several hotels that in the storied history of African-American music were legendary landmarks. The most famous was the Marshall, run by Jimmie Marshall. "Indeed, the Marshall for nearly ten years was one of the sights of New York, for it was gay, entertaining, and interesting," wrote James Weldon Johnson. He described how a "good many white actors and musicians also frequented the Marshall, and it was no unusual thing for some among the biggest Broadway stars to run up there for an evening. So there were always present numbers of those who love to be in the light reflected from celebrities."[9] Johnson also pointed out that the "first modern jazz band ever heard on a New York stage [1905], and probably on any other stage, was organized at the Marshall."[10] (The band was the Memphis Students, and Europe was one of its musicians.)

Tom Fletcher, a top performer of the day, concurred. "Known for its wonderful cuisine and its entertainment, the hotel attracted the best people of both races who rubbed elbows there nightly." He added, "Musicians and entertainers without any place to hang out would all come to the hotel. Down stairs in a large room which served as the bar and which had a number of tables we would sit around and wait for calls for private engagements. The hotel was in the heart of the hotel district, and entertainers called there could reach the hotel or restaurant desiring them very quickly."[11]

Sissle, on the other hand, held that "Quite contrary, than most people thought, there were seldom any colored patrons there except musicians. Mainly because the prices charged for wine and food were prohibitive for most colored people."[12]

Another strip, further downtown on West Thirty-fourth Street, was the Savoy Café owned by Barron Wilkins, and from the stories that old-timers told him, Sissle remembered Barron and his place well.

"There was no musicians' club such as the Clef Club of later years, so the musicians hung out in cafés, saloons and poolrooms. . . . Barron, a big jovial personality with a heart as large as his rotund figure, was one of the greatest benefactors the Negro musicians had in New York. He had a great love and respect for talented artists. Although the exclusive clientele coming to his café to hear the Negroes sing and play, at first came on slumming expeditions, soon they found themselves regular patrons of the interesting entertainment that his unique array of talent afforded." One of the keys to the Barron's success was that he kept an open floor. "Anyone who had anything to offer worth while could always get up and do a number," Sissle said. "Barron was especially kind to newcomers. He would lead in the tipping and applaud the loudest."[13] At the time, insisted Sissle, New York was "whirling like a tornado."[14]

And it was this tornado that Europe was sucked into—"penniless and threatened with starvation," according to Sissle, but "armed with his 'Stringed Box'." If Sissle's memory was right, then Europe first found shelter in Barron Wilkins's Savoy Café. "Why little Jim had resorted to the only hope of staying under cover from the cold nights," he wrote, "taking advantage of the warm back room of a saloon where unknown and unobserved by any who knew, he was able to keep going till better times came."[15] Tom Fletcher, who played a vivid part in those tornado-like days, recollected, "When these entertainers couldn't find a job that would pay a fee for an evening, they would get together in barrooms or any other place where crowds gathered and pass the hat."[16]

Europe struck out with his violin, playing solos in dingy cafés and saloons. He was applauded lustily by the customers because he was good. But he rarely picked up a paying job. Violin music was pretty, but it didn't grab the syncopated soul of the times. Most folks, especially those ready to fork over money, wanted to hear the banjo or the mandolin or the piano more than the violin. For a while, Europe tried to scratch out a living with his violin. No one told him to change instruments. Instead, they allowed him to "sleep." As Sissle explained it, people in show business let newcomers "sleep" if they were unaware of their shortcomings, "believing 'hard times' would finally 'wake you up.'" It was the instrument Europe played that kept him from the big money or even, as Sissle put it, "that smallest of coins, the Indian Head Copper." Europe finally woke up "heartbroken and hungry," put down the violin, and picked up the mandolin.[17]

His life was now about to change drastically, and with it the entire fortunes of hundreds of African-American musicians.

John Wanamaker had made a fortune in the retail business in Philadelphia after opening a clothing store there in 1861. He established a second store in New York City in 1896 when he purchased A. T. Stewart's famous cast-iron building on Broadway. That store, soon Manhattan's leading department store, drew the Wanamakers to the city on many occasions, particularly John's son Rodman, who was learning the ins and outs of running the family business.

Rodman lived in plush mansions that were splashed across the Atlantic seaboard, from Philadelphia to New York to Newport, Rhode Island. He had a home in London and another in Paris. He loved art and convinced his father of its commercial value. He then successfully imported art works from overseas that were offered to Wanamaker's customers at reasonable prices. As the *New York Times* stated, "He showed that art paid." The *Times* also credited him "with helping to change American tastes in fashions of dress and home decorations."[18] Rodman had a good ear for music, too. In the winter of 1903 he probably sent his father's personal secretary, John Love, into the Tenderloin to find musicians to play at his upcoming gala fortieth birthday party—a three-day affair to be held at "Buck Hill," his cottage on the New Jersey shore.

An African American, Love knew where to go—the Marshall Hotel. There, for the first time, he laid eyes on "a mere boy, a piano player."[19] Europe was in the midst of forming a string quartet and its first engagement, according to Love, was for Rodman's birthday celebration. Love and Europe hit off, forming a lifelong friendship. When the quartet made a big hit at Rodman's seaside cottage in mid-February, that friendship spilled over into the Wanamaker family.

After his triumph at "Buck Hill," Europe was in hot demand among the Marshall's more wealthy white patrons for their private dance parties. "Things happened so fast," Sissle wrote, remembering the days soon after he had hooked up with Europe, "and we were snatched from all walks of life, from all environments, and suddenly found ourselves playing and singing at the homes of the Vanderbilts, the Goulds, the Wanamakers in Philadelphia one day, in Pittsburgh for Mrs. Stotesbury the next, then the day after that in Washington for Mrs. Evelyn McLean, or on the private yacht for a cruise, with our small organ and drums, with the Astors, sailing beneath the moon and stars and the drone of the ship's engine punctuated by the popping of champagne corks. . . . We were the only musicians who could play jazz music to satisfy the society people. It was our music, and the wealthy people who had money would not take a substitute when they could buy the original."[20]

It was in the midst of these halcyon times that Europe's organizational genius asserted itself. And it happened at the Marshall Hotel.

"Early one evening," Tom Fletcher reminisced, "when a number of musicians were sitting around or standing around at the bar, Jim Marshall . . . dropped a hint that maybe the fellows ought to be getting a place of their own to hang out. The hint was taken seriously."[21] The date was 1910 and over meal of cooked "opossum," Europe, according to James Weldon Johnson, "carried out an idea he had, an idea that had a business as well as an artistic reason behind it, and organized the Clef Club. He gathered all the coloured [sic] professional instrumental musicians into a chartered organization and systemized the whole business of 'entertaining.'"[22]

Following Marshall's hint, the group moved next door and "fitted it up as a club and also booking offices," said Johnson. "Bands of from three to thirty men could be furnished at any time, day or night." Europe felt better about the move out of the Marshall because it bothered him that when clients had called before to book an engagement, they reached a bar or a saloon. Now they contacted a legitimate office with a legitimate address. Johnson reported that in "one year the amount of business done amounted to $120,000."[23] Europe was elected the Clef Club's first president. He also was appointed conductor of the Clef Club Symphony Orchestra.

While he was booking bands and conducting the orchestra, Europe also learned everything he could about music. As he once confessed to

Sissle, he dreamed of conducting a "National Negro Symphony Orchestra." "It's my life's dream," he said to his friend, explaining that the orchestra would comprise "trained" musicians specializing in the "rendition of Negro music, written by Negro composers." He emphasized that only "skilled Negro musicians [and Negro composers] can do it, because like in the Russian symphonies, all the sufferings and emotions of an oppressed people [are] stored up." In his inner ear, Europe plainly heard the "cry of their soul's harmony."[24] For his dream to come true, Europe knew he had to be a genuine maestro. Fletcher remembered seeing Europe at the piano during a gig at the old Brevoort Hotel near Washington Square, playing and, at the very same time, studying a set of lessons he had fashioned for himself. "He was a good piano player," Fletcher wrote, "but he wasn't satisfied just to be a good piano player, so he began to study all phases of music, theory, harmony, and how to be a conductor."[25]

Organizing gigs for small combos or big bands, and conducting a number of them himself in the homes of the East Coast elite, certainly gave him more confidence in his abilities, but it also exposed black musicians to white audiences and, in a way, seemed to break down racial barriers.

Yet there was always a catch, always some damn thing to let the African American know his place.

For one thing, Europe's musicians were shunted into Fifth Avenue mansions through the service entrances. There was no way they would be let in the front door along with white guests.

Once a black butler for old John Wanamaker fed Europe and his starving musicians dishwater when Jim asked him for a little soup because they were tired and hungry. As band member Eubie Blake saw it, the butler "thinks he ain't like other Negroes. He don't like it when Jim complains." The dishwater arrived in a large china soup tureen. As he ladled the gray liquid into smaller bowls, Blake recalled, "I can't wait . . . we're all dyin' from hunger. Now we grab our spoons and as soon as I tasted this stuff, I had to spit it out. And I see everybody else is doin' the same thing." Not only was the dishwater dirty, it tasted of soap. "But Europe—I see Europe is eatin' the stuff just like it's soup, he don't pay it no mind, just keeps eatin'. My God, I thought, that Europe will eat anything. Now everybody else is watchin' too, see. It ain't just me."

"I realize Jim Europe didn't get where he is with the white folks by complainin'."[26]

In some instances, Europe's musicians were not allowed to play pianos owned by their white benefactors because that meant black fingers might soil pristine ivory keys. The only instruments they fingered were their own—banjos, guitars, mandolins, and the like. Even brass instruments in those early days were rare in a Negro band. William Pettus, a charter member of the Clef Club, recalled the only trumpet player was a man named Thompson. "He hid the trumpet under his coat when he came into the house," Pettus stated, "and we sat him in the back of the orchestra, and he played so soft and sweetly that when the host finally saw him, he would demand that he come out front so they could see and hear him better."[27]

Blake was certain that the white people who hired Clef Club bands believed blacks had no idea how to read music. He recalled how the bands never used sheet music so they could perpetuate that myth. "Now this is the truth," he recalled. "Europe's orchestra was filled with readin' *sharks*. That cornet player, Russell Smith! If a fly landed on the music, he'd *play* it, see, like *that*. But we weren't supposed to read music!

"I'd get all the latest Broadway music from the publisher, and we'd learn the tunes and rehearse 'em until we had 'em all down pat. Never made no mistakes. Of course, I'd always leave the room for a *little* fakin', and them guys that *could* fake, they did it. Then we'd go on a job and naturally we'd play all those tunes perfectly.

"All the high-tone, big-time folks would say, 'Isn't it wonderful how these untrained, primitive musicians can pick up all the latest songs instantly without being able to read music?'"[28]

The Clef Club's successes, its sold-out concerts at the Manhattan Casino and other musical hot spots, and eventually, its groundbreaking performance at Carnegie Hall in May of 1912 led Europe to a surprising partnership with a white couple whose restless feet carried them all on a whirlwind ride through the golden age of American ballroom dancing.

For almost the entire second decade of the twentieth century, you could not pick up a newspaper without reading advertisements for dance instruction. A typical page in the *New York Times,* for example, looked like an alphabet soup of small notices, each one crying out for attention:

"Modern Dances. Trot, Tango, Hesitation Waltz, Boston Glide, Dip and One-Step. Correctly Interpreted, Properly Taught—Quickly Learned by the REMEY Method."

"The Roth Studio. Refined Dancing. Private lessons in modern society dances. Lady and Gentleman instructors."

"Vincent Studios: Refinement is the Keynote of Our Methods."

"MLLE. MINDERE'S STUDIO. Modern Dancing taught privately, correctly."

"Miss Molyneaux Studio. The charm of the One-Step, Hesitation, Tango and Maxie comes from a gracefully poised body exhilarated by syncopated music to make a complete poem of each movement."

"HALLAM STUDIOS: Class and private lessons in all the new Dances. Originated and taught only at our studios under the personal supervision of MR. ALBERT VAN SANDS, formerly with Mr. Vernon Castle. Chaperone in attendance."[29]

The United States was dance crazy. The reason, very probably, was the wiry Vernon Castle, birdlike in his thinness and great beak of a nose, and his tomboyishly pretty wife, Irene. And always in the background, glasses fixed studiously upon the bridge of his nose, baton poised in his hand, was their musical director, the seemingly omnipresent Europe. There was something about dance music that Europe found refreshing. "I have found that dancing keeps husbands and wives together and eliminates drinking, as no one can dance and drink to excess."[30]

In the years 1913 and 1914, the Castles had spun their way on to the American dance scene like whirling dervishes joined at the hips. Before teaming up with Europe, they had hastened the emergence of ballroom dancing from the private homes and salons of the rich, made it popular and, despite the hand-wringing of religious puritans, given it legitimacy. At first, the Castles spent most of their time dancing privately in the parlors of the wealthy, the same parlors in which Europe and his orchestra also played. It was only a matter of time before their paths crossed.

Europe's biographer believes they most likely met for the first time on 22 August 1913 at "Crossways," the Newport mansion of Mrs. Stuyvesant Fish.[31] Described by Irene Castle as a "tyrant in the world in which she moved . . . so militant—like the early suffragettes,"[32] Mrs. Fish had married into a powerful New York family, and it gave her a certain cachet of her own. And because it was the Fish family, she inherited from Mrs. William Astor the role of entertaining society's rich and famous. The *New York Times* said she was "independent and outspoken, warm-hearted and generous."[33] Her husband, at one time a director and president of the Illinois Central Railroad, was the youngest son of Hamilton Fish, former New York governor and U. S. senator, secretary of state in the Grant administration, and direct descendant of Peter Stuyvesant. Named after Alexander Hamilton, the elder Fish had two other sons, Hamilton Jr. and Nicholas, whose son had been the first Rough Rider to fall in the Spanish-American War. Hamilton Jr. had been assistant treasurer for President Roosevelt, and then U.S. congressman in New York's Twenty-first District. His son, also Hamilton and later entwined in Europe's military life, was an ardent supporter of former President Theodore Roosevelt and his Bull Moose Party. He was about to start his first term as a Progressive assemblyman from Putnam County. Mrs. Stuyvesant Fish was his aunt.

Irene Castle vividly recalled the Fish mansion in Garrison, New York, overlooking the Hudson River where she and Vernon were invited to teach the assembled guests the latest dances. "The house was fantastically costly and far too dressy with its masses of gilt and old rose and paintings and velvet portieres. It bustled with manservants in striped pants and short pea jackets covered with braid."[34] The mansion in Newport, where the Castles and Europe were introduced, was similarly ostentatious. Europe's orchestra played both at Crossways in Newport and Glenclyffe in Garrison, while the Castles dutifully performed the latest dances that debuted weekly and read "like a table of contents for a zoo," cracked Irene, "with the Turkey-Trot, the Grizzly Bear, the Bunny Hug, the Camel Walk, and the Lame Duck."[35]

Soon after, Europe and the Castles were always together, devising new steps to keep pace with the dance-crazy nation. "Occasionally Vernon would come up with a new dance like the Half and Half or the Innovation," Irene recalled. "The Half and Half was completely new in that it required a tempo not yet used—5/4 time. James Europe and Ford Dabney created the music for us." It was in Mrs. Stuyvesant Fish's New York mansion on a cold January evening in 1914 that the Castles and Europe introduced the Half and Half, although Irene later swore that there was not the slightest variation from their old routines. "The next day's papers announced the creation of a brand-new dance by the Castles especially for Mrs. Stuyvesant Fish's party.

"Nobody knew the difference, absolutely nobody."[36]

While interviewed for a 12 March 1914 article for the New York *Evening Post,* Europe let it be known that "I furnish Vernon Castle's music, and I have also composed most of the pieces for his dances— among others 'The Castle House Rag,' 'The Innovation Trot,' 'Congratulations,' and 'The Castle Walk.' I have just concluded a contract with him to lead a dance orchestra of forty Negro musicians, all members of my staff, that will accompany him to Europe next summer. We shall play most of the time in Paris."[37]

It was about this time, early in 1914, that Europe startled the black music world by resigning from the Clef Club. His move did not mean that he was relinquishing his leadership. Instead, he and several colleagues created the Tempo Club, almost identical to the Clef Club. Europe was still in business and still a force to reckon with in music in general.

In the spring of 1916, while Europe and his partnership with the Castles was going great guns, Sissle reached New York, seeking fame and fortune. Then twenty-six years old, Sissle stood on the lower deck of a ferry boat that was taking him across the Hudson River from Jersey City to the Twenty-third Street docks in lower Manhattan. As the boat pulled away from the Jersey shore in the early morning, with a misty, gray haze hanging over the waterfront, he felt a "rhythm in his soul, a song in his heart." But when the massive New York skyline loomed through the mist, he was overcome with a sinking feeling.

"Oh, why did I leave home?" he fretted. He felt his body grow weaker by the moment.[38] Yet it was not the first time he had set foot in New York. In 1913, after he had graduated from high school, he had come to the city as a member of the Thomas Jubilee Singers. There he met Dr. William H. Brooks, pastor of St. Mark's M. E. Church. One of the most charismatic men of the cloth, Brooks, who within a few years would be chaplain of the Fifteenth Regiment, almost changed Sissle's life. In a postcard to his father, also a Methodist Episcopal minister, Sissle informed him: "Am going into evangelistic work. I sang for Dr. Brooks in New York City last Sunday. I have a fine letter from him. I think I'll attend the Moody School in Chicago. Yours Noble."[39]

Now, three years later, Sissle was shaken out of his reverie when the engines of the huge boat roared into reverse as the ferry swung into the slip at the Twenty-third Street pier. "Our erstwhile Soldier of Fortune was caught in the maelstrom of surging humanity and literally carried up the gang plank with the surging tide of Jerseyites amid the dangling of the Big Wheels that tightened the guide ropes and banging gates that released the rushing office workers.

"In this moment of near distraction suddenly he was grasped by a stern hand and pulled from the line of hurrying passengers and just as suddenly his sunken spirits flamed into a flood of joy as his buddy, who was waiting for him, grabbed him by the arm. The buddy whom for a moment he had forgotten all about, when, that New York sky line hit him in the face."[40]

Sissle's arrival in New York was, as he claimed, a chapter all by itself:

One day I was a waiter in the Rathskeler [sic] of the Severin Hotel in my home-town of Indianapolis. The next day I was a member of a fifteen piece entertaining orchestra on the bandstand of the Severin. Ten weeks afterward I was in Baltimore, Md.; six months after that a member of Bob Young's Royal Poinciana Sextet at the world-renowned Society Rendezvous at Palm Beach, Fla.; then three months later with Jim Europe in New York City, sitting in a twenty-five piece orchestra in the Grand Ball room of the exclusive Vanderbilt Hotel on Park Ave., playing for a debutante party for one of New York's '100.' In fact, I was floating until Uncle Sam brought me down to earth in 1917 and let me hear some machine guns popping instead of champagne corks.[41]

In the brief time he spent in Baltimore before coming to New York, Sissle ran into another struggling musician. Together they would put their own distinctive stamp on what Sissle felt was "The Golden Age of Jazz."

Eubie Blake, a Baltimore native, was a young composer and piano player almost six years older than Sissle. Since the age of fifteen, he had been playing professionally. He had an engagement at Baltimore's Riverview Park on 16 May 1915, when he was introduced to Sissle.

"Do you write lyrics?" Blake asked. "I need a lyricist. I've been looking for one."

Probably the only songs Sissle had written at the time were for Butler University in Indianapolis, where he had been a student. His compositions were called "Butler Parodies" and included the Butler fight song. That was enough for Blake. He and Sissle collaborated on their first song, "It's All Your Fault." Blake wanted to show it to the vaudeville singer Sophie Tucker, who at the time was at the Maryland Theater in downtown Baltimore.

"Who do we know that can bring it to Sophie Tucker?" he wondered.

Sissle, who, according to Blake, was "all brass," replied, "We don't need anybody. It's a good song. Let's take it down ourselves."

At the Maryland Theater they worked their way backstage. Sissle marched up to Tucker. "I don't remember what he said, but I hear her say, 'Yes, yes,' in her very harsh voice, and the first thing I know I'm sittin' at the piano and playin' and Sissle is singin' 'It's All Your Fault.'" Blake discovered that Sissle "could put a song over" because Tucker liked it enough to sing it at her next matinee.

"It was an instant hit," Blake bragged, "at least in Baltimore. Everybody whistled it in the street. But after that it didn't go nowhere."[42]

Sissle and Blake promised to get out of Baltimore and make their musical fortune in New York. But first Sissle headed for Palm Beach to join Bob Young's sextet as a vocalist at the Royal Poinciana Hotel. It was there that he met Europe. And in the spring of 1916 he crossed the Hudson to be swept up in the dizzying world of Vernon and Irene Castle—a world, according to one newspaper, in which Europe had "all but secured complete control of the cabaret and dance field in the city."[43]

The Honor of the State

By the end of September, Col. Bill Hayward felt the time had come for the state's newest regiment to receive its colors from Governor Whitman. The event would serve as a coming-out ceremony for New York City's African-American soldiers. For Hayward there was no better symbolic place for the colors to be presented than at the opulent headquarters of the Union League Club at Fifth Avenue and Thirty-ninth Street. As a member of the club, the colonel knew its history well and how it had always supported African-American causes, even if those causes brought danger to its own members. A case in point took place in 1863, during the Civil War, when the club had raised the all-black Twentieth New York Regiment in the aftermath of the city's murderous draft riots.

Boasting a membership of Manhattan's leading Republicans, the Union League Club had been created to support the Union cause in the Civil War—a counterbalance to the Northern Copperheads, mostly Democrats sympathetic to the Southern cause. One of its founders was Frederick Law Olmsted, the landscape architect who designed Central Park. Olmsted believed the club would "bring the prestige and social influence of a national business and cultural elite to the work of cultivating loyal opinion among the middle and upper classes."[1] He envisioned a "club of true American aristocracy."[2] Among its first members were former New York Governor Hamilton Fish; philanthropist Theodore Roosevelt; and George Lorillard, one of the city's wealthiest landowners. More than fifty years later, the sons of Fish and Roosevelt and a cousin of Lorillard would be clubmates and fellow officers of Colonel Hayward.

Meanwhile, in the midst of the bloodiest civil unrest in United States history, the raising of a black regiment in New York City took some daring. In a weeklong spree of violence that erupted ten days after the Battle of Gettysburg, more than one hundred people were killed and hundreds more maimed for life. The state militia battled Irish laborers, who believed the passage of the National Conscription Act was unfair because it hit the poor the hardest while leaving the wealthy, who could afford to pay their way out or hire substitutes to take their places, virtually unscathed. A number of Union Leaguers took advantage of the loophole and avoided the war. Theodore Roosevelt paid a substitute, a decision that his eldest son could never reconcile.

Mobs of men who did not have the same means as a Roosevelt torched homes and businesses and tore up railroad tracks. While the heavy loss of life included Union Leaguers, the worst butchery was brought against the city's defenseless African Americans. Not only was the Colored Orphan Asylum on Fifth Avenue and Forty-third Street, which 237 children called home, set ablaze with the cry, "Burn the niggers' nest,"[3] at least eleven blacks were slaughtered—lynched, knifed, shot, or burned and, in one case, dragged through the streets by the genitals.

One of the more heartbreaking ironies of the riot struck the Simmons family. Sgt. Robert J. Simmons of the Fifty-fourth Massachusetts Infantry was about to take part in his regiment's attack on Fort Wagner, South Carolina, while back in New York, his mother, sister and seven-year-old nephew fought for their lives. Rioters terrorized the women and beat the nephew to death with clubs. On 18 July, as Simmons charged over the sand dunes toward the Rebel bulwarks of Fort Wagner, a minié ball shattered his arm. The wounded sergeant was carried to a Charleston hospital, where doctors amputated his arm but were unable to save his life.[4]

When the rioting subsided, attorney George Templeton Strong, one of the founders of the Union League Club, declared, "I would like to see war made on Irish scum."[5]

For the Union League Club the sweetest revenge, one historian wrote, was for them to give blacks "not alms but guns." When its members and the defenseless Negroes were under assault, well-to-do businessmen vowed that if "they escaped alive they would send a regiment of black troops to the front, first marching them through the very streets then ruled by the rioters."[6]

It was astonishing that the Union League and the city's battered black leaders even contemplated a regiment of color, since many of the blacks had just suffered through barbarous attacks upon family and friends. Yet throughout the rest of that uneasy year and into the first months of 1864, the Twentieth New York rose up through the smoldering ashes left by the draft riots.

Two groups of prominent businessmen lobbied Washington and Albany for the right to field a regiment of black New Yorkers—not a unit of National Guardsmen, but an actual troop of federal soldiers. There was little difference between the two rival factions because members of the Union League Club dominated both groups. The first was the New York Association for Colored Volunteers, headed by Peter Cooper, the founder of Cooper Union. The other, of course, was the Union League Club. Foremost among the Union Leaguers in trying to secure a black regiment was George William Curtis, editor of *Harper's Weekly,* whose brother-in-law was the recently slain Col. Robert Gould Shaw of the Fifty-fourth Massachusetts. Another proponent of the regiment was LeGrand Cannon, a banker who had, in April 1861, days after the bombardment of Fort Sumter, held a rally at Union Square of leading New Yorkers as they declared their loyalty to the Republican Party.

For Cannon, it was imperative that New York field a regiment. It meant redemption. "It's greater significance was the raising from their degradation and bringing into the service of the nation the colored citizens of the State of New York, and by that act purging the City from the taint of that wicked, infamous and inhuman riot of July."[7]

Getting a black regiment, however, was as frustrating as when, almost a half-century later, the African-American community sought its own National Guard unit. The groups were stalled on two fronts. President Lincoln did not want to antagonize New York's Democrats and maybe rekindle another riot. And Gov. Horatio Seymour, a Democrat, held the city's Republicans in contempt. It had been his razor-sharp tongue that gave the mob its sense of right. At a Fourth of July rally against the National Conscription Act, he shouted, "Remember this—that the bloody and treasonable and revolutionary doctrine of public necessity can be proclaimed by a mob as well as by a government."[8] A week later, the first lottery was held; the following Sunday, hell broke loose.

In early November, Union Leaguers and Association members joined forces. Letters were sent to Lincoln and Secretary of War Edwin Stanton. Stanton acted. On 3 December he authorized the Union League Club to raise an African-American regiment of one thousand volunteers. Each recruit would receive a payment of $10 a month. Two days later the Union League and the Association began raising twenty thousand dollars. Lt. Col. Nelson Bartram of the Seventeenth New York Volunteers, a vice-principal of a public school in lower Manhattan before the war, was promoted to colonel and sent from the battlefields of Virginia to command the new regiment.

With a commander now appointed, the Republicans sought recruits. A camp was set up on Rikers Island in the East River, and it was soon bustling with new soldiers. Exactly a month later, Stanton was told that the Twentieth New York had reached its quota of one thousand men. By March the regiment was ready to go to war.

Yet, Union Leaguers were unsure of what to do next. If the Twentieth marched through the streets of New York, they feared an Irish uprising—perhaps another bloody riot. They consulted with the thirty-one-year-old former schoolteacher about the perils of such a march.

"Give me room to land my regiment," Colonel Bartram snapped, "and if it cannot march through New York, it is not fit to go into the field."[9]

Parade day was set for 5 March. Led by their young colonel, the Twentieth New York was ferried from Rikers Island to the foot of East Thirty-sixth Street. The muskets the troops carried were loaded. Affixed at the end of each barrel was a bayonet. If there was to be trouble, they were ready. After forming a regimental line, Bartram marched his men to Union Square at Third Avenue and Twenty-first Street. There, on a platform festooned with colorful bunting and made even more festive by the dozens of women who had come to honor the black soldiers, stood some of the city's wealthiest and most influential citizens.

The single flag that fluttered in the cool winter breeze was impressive. On it were a broken yoke and the armed figure of Liberty, and soaring above them both was a conquering eagle.

The honor of presenting the colors went to the president of Columbia College. He told the Twentieth New York, "When you put on the uniform and swear allegiance to the standard of the Union, you stand emancipated, regenerated and disenthralled—the peer of the proudest soldier in the land."[10]

After the presentation, Francis Lieber, the veteran of the Napoleonic Wars, recalled, "There were drawn up in a line over a thousand armed negroes, where but yesterday they were literally hunted down like rats."[11]

The Twentieth then marched south toward the headquarters of the Union League Club. At the clubhouse on Seventeenth Street, the parade was again halted. There Mrs. William B. Astor and a score of women greeted the regiment. Mrs. Astor presented the troops with a parchment scroll, as equally impressive as the regimental flag, and designed by the women of the Union League Club. The scroll had been inscribed by Union Leaguers, and that meant the names of Manhattan's best families were there for all to see—the Astors, the Beekmans, the Van Rensselaers, the Roosevelts, and the Fishes, and none more thrilling to the soldiers than the widow, Mrs. Robert Gould Shaw.

The final leg of departure took the regiment to the Battery, where it then boarded the transport steamer *Ericsson* and journeyed south. Along the route, New Yorkers filled the streets to cheer the city's black soldiers. The scene moved an editorial writer for the *Times* to write the following:

> Eight months ago the African race in this City were literally hunted down like wild beasts. They were shot down in cold blood, or stoned to death, or hung to the trees or to the lamp-posts. . . . How astonishingly has all this been changed! The same men who could not have shown themselves in the most obscure street in the City without peril of instant death, even though in the most supplicant attitude, now march in solid platoons, with shouldered muskets, slung knapsacks, and buckled cartridge boxes down through the gayest avenues and busiest thoroughfares to the pealing strains of martial music. And everywhere are saluted with waving handkerchiefs, with descending flowers, and with the acclimations and plaudits of countless beholders.[12]

Stationed in Louisiana, the Twentieth ran afoul the South's white civilian population. The soldiers were treated badly and, as a result, took matters into their own hands. Their retaliatory action was written off by the district's inspector general, who offered the excuse that they were Northern blacks, New Yorkers, and therefore would not submit to Southern ways—a foreboding comparison to the utterances by South Carolinians in the autumn of 1917 when another regiment of black New Yorkers "invaded" the South. A jumpy War Department moved swiftly and mustered the Twentieth out of federal service. For the black soldiers of New York, the Civil War was over.

Now, a half-century later, Colonel Hayward of the Fifteenth New York, as he prepared to lead his troops through Manhattan to the Union League Club to receive its regimental colors, would soon find that when it came to the treatment of blacks in the South, history had a habit of repeating itself.

Sunday morning, 1 October 1916, brought good news from the western front, as the Great War, seemingly as far away from Harlem and its black citizens as the moon, pushed bloodily into its third year. French and British troops were reported to have made good gains against the entrenched Germans. Yet there was no end in sight to the fighting.

On the home front that Sunday morning, trolley-car drivers on the Third Avenue line were rioting. Rents along West 143rd Street in Harlem had risen to alarmingly high rates, and white and black residents were joining forces to do something about it. Neither group wanted to move, and both agreed that they didn't mind being neighbors.

In Brooklyn, the Dodgers, with outfielder Casey Stengel and a sleight-of-hand pitcher named Leon Cadore, were on the verge of clinching their first National League pennant since 1900. Two years later, Cadore, who, after the war, pitched the longest game in baseball history, would be an officer in the Fifteenth Infantry. On that Sunday, the Boston Red Sox, behind its pitching ace, Babe Ruth, would win its second American League pennant in a row. But in Harlem's Olympic Field, the Lincoln Giants would be forced to win a pair of games without their star center fielder, Spottswood Poles. The "Black Ty Cobb" had other duties to perform on Sunday. Instead of a bat cocked over his shoulder, he now wielded a rifle.

Nine hundred men of the Fifteenth New York rode the subway that morning from their makeshift armory at the Lafayette Theater to the Grand Central Terminal. At Forty-second Street they assembled into companies. Leading the regiment on horseback west to Fifth Avenue and then south toward the Union League Club was Hayward and his staff. The colonel looked every part the soldier. Noble Sissle said he "stood six-two when on his feet." He had a rigid jaw and flashing eyes, and, claimed Sissle, was as "agile as panther, a hundred and eighty pounds of solid humanity."[13] His staff included Lorillard Spencer, George Hinton, and Monson Morris, as well as Capt. Bert Williams, the famous comedian, now inspector of small arms, and Regimental Sgt. Maj. Henry Coles.

Behind Hayward's staff marched E. E. Thompson's rented regimental brass band of sixty-five musicians, none of them actual soldiers and few of them willing to enlist.

Moving with the "precision of veterans," according to the *Age,*[14] stepped ten companies. 1st Lt. Vertner W. Tandy led A Company, the first company formed by the Fifteenth New York. Capt. Charles Fillmore led B Company. Two veterans of the Spanish-American War were out in front of C and D companies, First Lieutenants Virgil Parks and Herbert Gee. Capt. Napoleon Marshall had charge of I Company.

They were a proud, spirited troop as they passed throngs of cheering spectators lined on either side of Fifth Avenue.

Bert Williams, astride a light gray charger, was between commander Hayward and Thompson's band. As the regiment turned on to Fifth Avenue near the New York Public Library, Williams's horse bolted forward, its ears pinned back, and its long tail flared out like a banner in the wind. A reporter for the *Sun* claimed the steed shied away from one of the stone lions guarding the library and "dashed down the avenue."[15] The comedian, who always found humor in the misfortune of others, leaned forward, gripping the saddle to keep his balance. The horse finally stopped, eyed the thousands of people crowded around the front of the Union League Club, waltzed sideways, and then decided to take part in a parade all its own. Waiting on the reviewing stand were Williams's wife and three nieces. "He told us to look for him right behind his close friend Col. William Hayward," recalled one of the nieces, Charlotte Tyler. "He had on his uniform and boots, all dressed up. And we waited, all ready to scream when he'd come past, but he never came. There was the Fifteenth and Colonel Hayward, but no Uncle Eggs."[16]

Several versions of what happened survive. The *Times* reporter described how "Captain Bert's temperamental mount . . . down the avenue . . . rushed, Bert staying in his seat, but apparently his self-confidence had been left with the regiment. He did not even notice that the runaway was dashing straight at four active motion picture cameras set to record the approach of the regiment, and eagerly putting on film every one of the multitudinous movements and expressions registered by himself and the horse." Two police officers stopped the animal, and the crowd applauded. But the horse bolted again. Another police officer got into the act and caught the runaway. Williams "slid from his saddle to the ground and planted the well-known Williams feet on the pavement with more emphasis than he ever waved them over the footlights."[17]

Willliams's family later asked him what had happened. Recounted Charlotte, "On the way down, my horse just turned out of the parade and went down in a subway entrance. I talked to it when it left the parade and I talked to it down there in the subway, but I never did find out why it wanted to go there or why it didn't want to come out."[18]

But Williams told his friend Tom Fletcher that his horse really didn't stop until it "ran into a lady's kitchen. According to Bert, the lady indignantly demanded to know what he meant by bringing a horse into her kitchen, and he told her it wasn't his fault, it was the horse's idea."[19]

Even Hayward had his own version. He believed that if the horse hadn't spied an open doorway to an apartment building, rider and animal "might have been going yet." He told how the "horse entered the apartment house without knocking, clattered right down to the end of the corridor, and halted in front of the bank of elevators. Bert Williams looked helplessly around him, and seeing a nice red plush sofa within reaching distance of one of his feet, dismounted by way of the sofa and reached the ground in safety." Hayward elaborated even more, mimicking Williams's stage act when the doorman charged up to him and ordered the horse out. "Mah friend, if you wants you to take the horse out of here, you jes' take him out yo'self. I'm sure you must know more about that horse than I do." Williams then turned on his heel and marched out of the apartment house, leaving the horse there.[20]

Without further equine high jinks, the Fifteenth halted in front of the Union League Club. Governor Whitman was flanked on the reviewing stand by Adj. Gen. Louis Stotesbury, Maj. F. L. Hopkins, acting military secretary, and other military dignitaries. Missing was Maj. Gen. John F. O'Ryan, who was on the Mexican border with fifteen thousand of New York's citizen-soldiers. Another dignitary standing beside the governor was the commander of the Seventh Regiment, Maj. Gen. Daniel Appleton. Old enough to have witnessed a similar parade more than fifty years earlier that also involved a black regiment, Appleton told Hayward about the similarities. "By their [the men of Fifteenth Regiment] bearing and correct marching, I can see that some of our famous organizations will have to look for laurels when you parade. As you know, I saw the first parade of the Fifty-fourth Massachusetts in 1863, under the command of Col. Shaw, a private of the Seventh, and I can only hope that your regiment may become as famous as that command, which laid down its lives at Fort Wagner with its colonel, although I trust it may be many a year before you are called upon to undertake such a deed."[21]

The governor spoke briefly. Already endeared to the city's African-American population by guaranteeing its first National Guard regiment, he explained that in presenting the regimental colors of the Fifteenth Infantry, along with the standard of New York and the Stars and Stripes, he was committing to them a sacred trust: "There can be no more honorable service than that upon which you are entering—the protection of the Commonwealth, and, should occasion require, the defense of your native land," he said. He explained that "the honor of the State is involved in your daily conduct and in your every act, not only when you are wearing the uniform and following these colors but wherever you are and in whatever activity you may be engaged." Whitman closed, saying, "These colors are yours. Guard them as a sacred possession, protect them, as I know you will, should the necessity arise, even with your lives. God grant that you may never be called upon to make the sacrifice offered by those who have gone before you that the freedom and the civilization and the enlightenment which the flag embodies and represents may abide and remain forever."[22]

The colors were received by Sergeants Homer Butler, Henry Leonard, Harry Trott, Ira Aldrich, and William Cox, a six-footer of "bone and muscle, broad of shoulders, deep of chest, and tapering waist."[23] The regimental flag was emblazoned with a coiled rattlesnake, and the Fifteenth was known thereafter as the "Rattlers."

In the next issue of the *Age,* the lead editorial noted Whitman's speech and mentioned how he had pointed out the "proud record" of the nation's black soldiers. "The Governor spoke truly," the editorial stated. "The colored Americans' record from the Boston massacre down to Carrizal is one to be proud of. The whole record stands out bright and clean, unstained by a single traitorous act. It is a record that silences even the tongues of our enemies." It closed by predicting that "it won't be long before the Fifteenth will be the crack regiment of New York."[24]

When the governor handed the flags to the color guard, he looked the sergeants in the eye and, as Sergeant Cox later recalled, said, "Don't you ever let these flags touch the ground."[25]

"I Will Startle the World"

On a cold December day in 1916, James Europe and Noble Sissle were in their Harlem office, arranging for two orchestras to play in Palm Beach. The telephone jangled. Sissle picked up the receiver. On the other end was Col. William Hayward. Sissle passed the phone over to Europe. He watched his friend's face twist into a comical expression in response to something Hayward had said to him.

"You say you got ten thousand dollars pledged!?" Europe stammered, the eyes behind his glasses looking larger than ever. "Yes sir, I gave you my word, so you can depend on me. Yes sir. I'll see you at the armory tonight."

Sissle knew what was going on, and howled as Europe hung up, grabbed a telephone book, and threw it at him. He ducked and laughed louder. Europe commenced hurling more books at him until, as Sissle recalled, the "divan I was sitting on looked like a wrecked book-case."

When Europe calmed down, Sissle said, "Well, they called your bluff."[1]

The bluff that was called was Europe's promise to Hayward that if he, Hayward, raised ten thousand dollars, then he, Europe, would form one of the best regimental bands in the land. Hayward wanted to use the band to put the Fifteenth Infantry on the map—and to use it as an irresistible recruiting tool. But Europe did not want to be a military bandleader. He had enlisted to be a soldier. When Hayward had approached him about the band, he agreed to put it together and command it, but only if he had ten thousand dollars to work with. According to Sissle, he was certain that even a great arm twister like Hayward, who had managed to get Charles S. Whitman elected governor, would have the devil of a time raising that amount of money.

Europe added other stipulations. First, he told Hayward that the typical military band of twenty-eight pieces was not practical for playing well-balanced music. "He had it all worked out," Hayward recalled, "and he figured that forty-four was the minimum number that a regimental band should have, and that sixty-odd would be better. Well, of course, we couldn't get instruments for forty-four men when the tables of organization only allowed twenty-eight men, and we couldn't get music scores, and we couldn't enlist bandsmen." Europe also said he needed specialists—"a few key men for each of the important instrumental sections of the band, just as we had squad leaders and platoon leaders in line companies. And he knew where he could get such men, but they couldn't afford to serve for the regular army pay, unless we were able to pay them premiums out of our own pockets."[2]

After he had made the proposition to his commanding officer, Europe confided to Sissle that the cost was too high and that Hayward would not bother him anymore about a band.[3]

For some time, Hayward had been troubled about E. E. Thompson and his sixty-five piece military brass band. It wasn't really a military band in the sense that none of its members were in the service—even though Thompson called it the "Fifteenth Infantry Band." When Hayward wanted to use the band, he had to hire it, just as if he was hiring one of Europe's orchestras for a night of music. And although the members of the band were professional musicians, many of them were not good. Hayward described them as "pretty bad." He said Thompson's band "made a noise, and at the time we had twenty-eight bandsmen it made twenty-eight noises all at the same time, mostly not in tune or in rhythm."[4]

After the Fifteenth received its colors, the band put on a concert at the Manhattan Casino. Lucien H. White, a critic for the *Age,* was in the audience, and his review was hardly flattering. He wrote that Thompson's musicians were unfamiliar with the music and with their own instruments. He used the words "crude" and "undeveloped." He warned, "[Thompson] has much to do with his body of men before they are to be called a finished product."[5]

Such a review, published in one of the most influential African-

American newspapers in the country, must have troubled Hayward. He had asked Thompson to recruit musicians into the National Guard so that the Fifteenth's band would be official. But in the end, Thompson had been unable to lure a single man into signing up. In explaining his decision to drop Thompson, Hayward stated: "I do not think the failure to secure enlisted men for the band was through lack of diligent and earnest efforts on Mr. Thompson's part. He had a difficult task. I felt, however, that progress would be made by making a new start from the beginning."[6]

In their defense, the musicians couldn't afford to give up their lucrative nightclub acts for the army life.

The only man who had the kind of sway Hayward was looking for, plus the organizational ability to pull off such a daunting assignment, was Europe. Even if he had agreed, ten thousand dollars was such a whopping sum in those days that the band Hayward envisioned was only a dream. No potential donor would say yes to that kind of money. But then, Hayward was a man who never took no for an answer.

Another man who never took no for answer was Daniel G. Reid, better known as the "Tin Plate King." When he died in 1925, Reid was reportedly worth nearly fifty million dollars.

Reid started his meteoric career at the age of eleven as a bank messenger in Richmond, Indiana. Using part of a meager salary, he bought stock in the bank. Before he was thirty he was vice president. In 1892 he used his stock to purchase a failing tin-plate mill. Welsh-made tin plate dominated the world, so Reid studied Welsh workmanship. He adapted it to American-style production, and within three years, he and several partners had the wherewithal to merge all tin-plate manufacturers in the United States into the American Tin Plate Company, with Reid as president. From there, he moved on as one of the organizers with J. P. Morgan of the US Steel Corporation. He held controlling interest in the Chicago, Rock Island & Pacific Railroad and, as its director, came under government scrutiny for his management methods. A congressional investigation found he had watered down the railroad's stock, looting it of millions of dollars. He claimed that when he took over the railroad, it was nothing but "a streak of rust."[7] He also got involved in the tobacco industry and made millions.

As an industrialist, Reid had the Midas touch; not so in his personal life. He was married three times, twice to dazzling beauties. In a divorce, his third wife nailed him for a lump sum of two hundred thousand dollars in addition to an annual payment of thirty thousand dollars. Even his personal physician sued him. Reid lived on Fifth Avenue with a little brown Pekingese he called Wiggie. The two companions were rarely apart, and Reid was probably petting Wiggie when Hayward dropped in at his downtown office.

The colonel recollected that his trip downtown was done "in a spirit of despair." He laid out his tale of woe and the need for ten thousand dollars. The Tin Plate King then asked, "What do you want me to do?"

All Hayward wanted were letters of introduction to thirty or forty of Reid's richest colleagues, hoping that he, Hayward, could then "touch" each one for five hundred dollars.

"How many of the thirty or forty victims do you expect to land for five hundred dollars a piece?" Reid asked.

At least twenty, Hayward replied.

Reid wrote out a check for ten thousand dollars. Handing it to Hayward, he said: "That's a damn sight easier than writing you forty letters of introduction."[8]

Now that Europe had his marching orders to organize a band, he first had to figure out what instruments he needed.

As Sissle reported, his friend didn't care much for bands. He loved orchestras. Bands were "not flexible enough, they were too brassy and blasting," Sissle wrote. "He loved the mournful cry of the violins, and the soft croon of the celli and the resonant tones of the bass violin, and these things were not to be had in bands according to the regular outline of the instrumentation. Jim hated blasting music and banging cymbals, although there were no bands that did more blasting than his, but that was what the public craved, the world was tuned up to war pitch and Jim wisely went with the world."

Sissle believed that the Fifteenth Infantry Band could be the stepping-stone to Europe's dream of a "National Negro Symphony Orchestra." When he related this belief to Europe, Jim's face brightened. It was at that moment, Sissle sensed, that Europe "turned his whole heart and soul to the formation of what he hoped to be the best military band in the world."[9]

Orders soon came down from Hayward that transferred both Europe and Sissle from K Company to Headquarters Company, with Jim as bandleader and Noble as drum major. The first recruit they went after, but to no avail, was fellow musician Eubie Blake. Although Blake was only a few years younger than Europe, he claimed he was too old to join the National Guard. Afterward, whenever Europe and Sissle were out on the town in their uniforms, with Blake by their side, they'd have fun with him. As Blake reminisced, they'd run into some pretty girls and one or the other would say, "This is Eubie Blake, the slacker." Blake admitted, "I'm no fighter and I didn't enlist.[10]

One of the places that Europe decided to look for band members surprised everybody. It wasn't in Harlem. And it wasn't among African-American musicians. He told Hayward that there was a great scarcity of reed instrumentalists in the United States—clarinetists, flutists, saxophonists, who in a military band serve the same purpose as string instrumentalists do in an orchestra—and that he had to go to Puerto Rico to find and recruit them.

Hayward was astounded. "Europe suggested that if we could give him proper orders to go to Porto Rico [sic] and enlist musicians for his band, that he could get the pick of the crop and build the best band in the army, if I would permit him to pay some bonuses where needed for the key men for each set of instruments."

Europe was fixed with special military orders and special money orders and, according to the colonel, "within less than three weeks we had eighteen of the best reed instrument players in the world, as full-fledged members of the Fifteenth New York Infantry."[11]

The trip to Puerto Rico took some time to set up, and it wasn't until well into 1917, with America already at war with Germany, that Europe finally set off for the Caribbean. In the meantime, there were other musicians that had to be persuaded to enlist. Advertisements were placed in African-American newspapers around the country, offering "AN OPPORTUNITY FOR MUSICIANS—Crack Colored Musicians." Candidates were to "write or wire Lieut. Jas. Reese Europe, 15th Infantry Armory, 2217 7th Av., N.Y."[12]

After the first ad appeared "there came a deluge of answers from everywhere. The very mention that Jim Europe wanted musicians seemed to be all that was necessary," Sissle recalled. He pointed out that most applicants were having a hard time surviving and were barely getting by finding other employment or by playing in local bands. Therefore they had "rushed at the opportunity to make a living at the profession that was their calling." Ex-Army musicians from the Ninth and Tenth Cavalry and the Twenty-fourth and Twenty-fifth Infantry joined, providing Europe with the "most accomplished and valuable men."[13]

There was also a trip to Chicago, where Europe landed a crack cornet player in Frank DeBroit. Hayward thought DeBroit a prima donna and once remarked that the "moustache that he wears in itself marks him as a bit eccentric." Europe confided to his commander that DeBroit liked to "look around the audience and see the girls admiring that moustache."

One of the top cornetists in the country, DeBroit was a huge drawing card, and Hayward didn't want to lose him. So out of the ten-thousand-dollar slush fund, he slipped his prima donna one hundred dollars every month.[14]

Another crack musician was Francis Eugene Mikell. A native of Charleston, South Carolina, Mikell already had a stellar career when he became a member of the Fifteenth Infantry Band. He studied the violin at the Tuskegee Institute and the New York School of Music, and he had led the Jenkins Orphanage Band of Charleston, both as conductor and teacher. Hayward appointed him regimental bandmaster. Because of his close connection to the Jenkins Orphanage Band, Mikell brought in three more recruits. They were trombonist Amos Gilliard and two drummers, Stephen and Herbert Wright.

Europe certainly knew of the reputation of the Jenkins Orphanage Band. The Jenkins Orphanage and Industrial School for Colored Children had been founded in the early 1890s by the Rev. Daniel Jenkins, pastor of the New Tabernacle Fourth Baptist Church in Charleston. He dubbed his young charges his "Black Lambs." To raise funds for his orphanage, he called upon the citizens of Charleston to donate old, unwanted instruments. Although not a musician himself, he hired tutors so the youngsters could learn the various instruments. When they were good enough, he dressed them in brightly colored uniforms, set them on street corners, and had them play. The sight of the forlorn waifs wailing away on cornets or trombones, beating drums, and clanging cymbals emptied many a pocket, and the orphanage survived. By the early 1900s, the band had earned a national reputation. It traveled all over the East Coast, played in New York City, and, in 1909, performed at the inauguration of President William Howard Taft. It went to London and Paris. And one of the men who had a lot to do with its success was Eugene Mikell.

He and his three recruits were soon welcomed into the band. Amos Gilliard was among the first of the orphans to find a home with Rev. Jenkins. It was in the band that he learned how to play the trombone. He had "amazing breath control," according to William "Cat" Anderson, a trumpeter in the band. Anderson, who years later played trumpet for Duke Ellington, recounted how Gilliard had once been hired by a white bandleader, but because he was black he had been hidden from the audience behind a curtain. When the band played "The Rosary," Gilliard hit the last high note and held it "for ages, the crowd went wild with excitement, clapping and cheering, then someone had the idea of opening the curtains, and there stood Amos—the clapping and cheering stopped instantly." After the war, Gilliard went back to the orphanage as an instructor. That's when Anderson first met him. "He would come into band rehearsal and put a brick down on the table, then he'd roar, 'I'll throw this at the first boy who makes a mistake!' It was tough training and no shortcuts." After practice, the orphans begged Gilliard to tell them stories of the old days in New York and of Jim Europe.[15]

Stephen and Herbert Wright, the drummers, were as close as brothers although they weren't related. To show how close they were, they called themselves the Wright brothers. At the time they were recruited into the band, they shared an apartment at 79 West 134th Street. The older of the two Wrights, known as Little Steve, had the most experience as a drummer. But Sissle didn't think much of either as musicians. He denounced them years later as "below the standard educationally" of the rest of the band. They were "practically waifs," he said. "Both of them were of the same height, very dark of color and blessed with a set of pearly white teeth that shone as a flash of ivory against their ebony hue. It was not very long before the Colonel and all of the regiment were wild over them."[16]

Besides his engaging "pearly whites," Herbert Wright had a dark side. A drinker and gambler and a craps player, he had come to New York in 1911 or 1912—he couldn't remember—with the orphanage band. He was only about sixteen, if the date he gave of Christmas Day 1894, as his birthday, was correct. He had no recollection of his mother. His father died when he was six, and he was sent to the orphanage. In Charleston, he had once been arrested for disorderly conduct. In New York, where he worked off and on for several cabarets, he married a streetwalker named Lottie Waddy, who had mothered two illegitimate boys. At first, they had lived in a tenement in the city's Tenderloin District. Twice Lottie spent time in jail: once for larceny, once for solicitation. They separated, and Herbert moved uptown to room with his best friend, Little Steve. When he enlisted in the Fifteenth Infantry Band, he was more than likely suffering through the first stages of syphilis, an illness overlooked by the medical officer.[17]

Little Steve enlisted shortly after Herbert. The men were first placed in H Company. On 15 July they were officially transferred to the band, and promoted to rank of musicians third-class.

In February, Europe entrained to Palm Beach, where, at the posh Royal Poinciana Hotel, he oversaw the work of the orchestras that he and Sissle had been in the midst of hiring out when Hayward called with the news of Reid's ten thousand-dollar check. The trip to Florida was no respite for a tired Europe, who had begun to feel more and more out of sorts. Trying to juggle two full-time jobs—Tempo Club business and a new military band—had to be wear on the conductor. In the ballroom of the Royal Poinciana, a physician noticed how Europe's eyeballs bulged abnormally from their sockets. He asked him if he could take a look at his eyes. Europe agreed and, after the doctor had checked him over, he was warned that his thyroid gland was enlarging and that if it wasn't treated, the result would be strangulation. The physician advised him to see a specialist as soon as he returned to New York.

Europe at first kept the news from Sissle, Blake, and his other close friends. But they knew something was wrong. Jim had been losing weight, he was edgy and tired all the time, and when he took off his glasses his eyes were frightening to look at. Europe refused to see a doctor, as advised. Even Sissle urged him to seek medical treatment. Instead, Europe left for Puerto Rico, promising Sissle, that upon his return, he would go to a doctor.

Sissle remembered getting Europe to the pier in time to catch the ship for Puerto Rico. Jim was "limp as a rag and perspiring in great beads of sweat under the rays of the early morning sun," he wrote. The gangplank had already been lifted away, and so the longshoremen placed Jim and his luggage atop the cargo net and swung the ill soldier aboard. Once on deck, he leaned weakly over the railing and waved good-bye. "The old ship bound for the West Indies slowly pulled off," chronicled Sissle, "carrying the strong hearted but sick form of our One and Only Jim Europe."[18]

The trip to Puerto Rico hardly lasted long enough for Europe to rest up. According to Ruth Glasser in her book, *My Music Is My Flag,* he rounded up eighteen musicians—"clarinentists, valve trombonists, saxophonists and tuba, French horn, bassoon and *bomardino* players in their teens and twenties"—from almost the moment he landed, and "took the next boat back to New York."[19] Sissle claimed he somehow had "bundled them together" and then "all but dragged [them] on board."[20]

Three of the musicians he basically shanghaied turned out to be first rate, and how he ever knew about them remains a mystery. Two were brothers, Raphael and Jesús Hernández; the other was Raphael Duchesne. All three came from musically talented families.

Twenty-six-year-old Raphael Hernández played the cornet, a most dangerous instrument to take up if you believed in the myth that ran through the small town of Aguadilla, where he was raised. According to that myth, anyone who played the cornet would die of tuberculosis. It was no wonder then that, as a child, little Raphael wanted to be a cigar maker, not a cornetist. Described as energetic, unpretentiousness, and with a mischievous sense of humor, he also learned the guitar, trombone, and violin. His brother Jesús was also an accomplished musician, as was his sister Victoria. "In our house," Victoria said, "music was breathed in the morning, it was eaten for breakfast."[21] When Europe found him, he was a violinist in the Orquesta Sinfonica of San Juan as well as a trombonist in the municipal band of Manuel Tizol.

Raphael Duchesne, a clarinentist, was the son of an orchestra leader in the town of Fajardo. An uncle led an orchestra in San Juan. When Duchesne returned with Europe to New York, Europe named him his band sergeant and first clarinetist.

For the eighteen new recruits, New York was as foreign to them as the North Pole. Although they were Hispanic (the Hernández brothers did have some African blood in them), they were treated by white Americans as if they were African Americans. The Puerto Ricans had to adapt within the black community of Harlem, where in some cases they were treated with derisiveness, and at the same time, they had to deal with whites who lumped them all together as if there were not a lick of difference between the two races.

Sissle never saw such a forlorn-looking bunch as when they stepped off the boat. "I'm sure no emigrants ever landed here that looked more picturesque," he recalled. He was struck most by their clothes. "Their Palm Beach suits were not only of many faded colors, but the trousers were too long for short ones and were too short for long ones. The poor little fellows with the East winds whipping around the edges of their sleeve-like clothes, I fear, made their first night in New York far from a comfortable one."[22]

Within a few weeks of his return from Puerto Rico, Europe and his Fifteenth Infantry Band, with Eugene Mikell as bandmaster assisting, got ready for its first concert. An advertisement in the *Age* alerted its readers that a "Great Military Ball & Band Concert Under Auspices of the Officers & Ladies Auxiliary" would take place at the Manhattan Casino at 8 P.M. sharp on 22 June. General admission was set at fifty cents. Loge seats were five dollars, and box seats were five dollars plus general admission. The advertisement also noted, "This is positively the only sanctioned entertainment by the 15th Infantry, before their departure."[23] The entire regiment had been ordered to Camp Whitman for its first intensive training under wartime conditions.

Preparation for the concert was proving hard for Europe. His physical condition was worsening. Still, he went full steam ahead, ensuring that the band would make a memorable debut.

The Manhattan Casino was jammed that tropically hot night with four thousand people. The *Age*'s critic Lester Walton said the "attendance was the biggest of the year."[24] Soldiers guarded the entrances. Nurses in uniform served as usherettes. In the box seats sat Colonel Hayward and his officers and their wives who, noted Walton, "made the occasion a gala one." There were even athletic competitions, and Mrs. Lorillard Spencer, wife of the lieutenant colonel, presented each winner with a prize. Powder was spread on the dance floor to keep the hardwood "from burning up when that four thousand pairs of feet started shuffling over it,"[25] reported Sissle. Walton claimed the dance floor "resembled the Brooklyn Bridge at rush hour."[26]

For the past ten days the band had been rehearsing nonstop. It was now "rarin' to go," and, said Sissle, "Jim Europe did not disappoint the jazz enthusiasts that had gathered there to pay his band homage."[27] Walton found himself impressed with "the dozen or more Porto Ricans who made up the reed section," stating that they "cannot be excelled." He felt the brass section still needed work. But he was quite sure that within a few weeks the "Fifteenth ought to have a well-balanced musical organization and one which should be the pride of New York, irrespective of color."[28]

When the first number was over, a yell thundered from the audience. It was then followed by a "mighty roar." To Sissle the roar meant that "if there was any doubt as to whether the crowd was to adopt the band as its favorite it was dispelled right then and there."[29] According to an old-time employee of the Manhattan Casino, he had never heard such an outburst for a band.

On the powdered-down dance floor, Sissle and his partner were doing everything to set the hardwood on fire. In the sweltering heat, sweat rolled down his face and clotted his khaki uniform. He was lost in the revelry of jazz music and what he believed was the birth of the nation's best military band. Then he overheard a dancer say, "Lieutenant Europe is not directing." On the bandstand stood Sgt. Frank DeBroit, with baton in hand—not Europe. Sissle continued dancing, but scanned the dance floor and the box seat where Europe's wife was sitting. Europe was nowhere to be seen. Sissle hurried off the dance floor. A doorman told him that Europe had gone outside. Sissle slipped out of the Casino into the hot, dark night. He whistled "the call that all musicians around New York use and from the shadow of a darkened doorway I saw Jim's form slowly emerge."

Rushing to his friend's side, Sissle saw rivulets of tears running down Europe's cheeks. His big body trembled. "It was plain that his nerves had at last given away to the strain of his weakening malady. When he realized his time had come to relax, the reaction was more than his once powerful constitution could stand."[30]

Five days later, on 27 June, Europe underwent the first of two operations to repair his thyroid. Sissle sensed the bandleader's military days were now numbered and, without him, "it looked like we were just to be an ordinary Regimental band." In the end there was no reason for Sissle's gloom. The operations proved successful. Europe was back to being a soldier. Yet had he wanted, he could have easily, and without guilt, used his illness as an excuse for an honorable discharge. To his old friend John Love, the private secretary to Rodman Wanamaker, he explained his desire to remain a soldier.

The two were motoring to Newport in early August, where Rodman's son, John Jr., was to marry Pauline Disston of Philadelphia. As usual, the Wanamakers wanted Europe to play at the wedding reception. Love, who long ago had discovered Europe playing at the Marshall Hotel, couldn't understand why, with America at war, he wanted to stay in the Army. "Is there no way you can get out of the army and stay in New York?" asked Love.

"John, if I could, I would not," Europe said. "My country calls me and I must answer; and if I live to come back I will startle the world with my music."[31]

7

"Black Is Not a Color
of the Rainbow"

As each day passed in the early part of 1917, the United States, like one of Vanderbilts' New York Central trains, rattled closer and closer toward the armed conflict in Europe. When winter finally gave way to spring, it was only a matter of time before President Wilson called upon Congress to declare war on Germany. In the meantime, Col. Bill Hayward was desperate for more officers and men. He wanted to fill the ranks of the Fifteenth Infantry so that when war came at last, his regiment, of all the regiments in New York City, would be the most ready. There was a chance—albeit a long shot—that maybe, just maybe, it would be the regiment chosen to represent New York in the proposed Rainbow Division. To be made up of National Guard units from twenty-six states and the District of Columbia, the Rainbow Division, as its name suggests, would be the only authentic all-American division to fight in the war. And how all-American it truly would be if one of its regiments was black!

No wonder Hayward was desperate to bring his regiment up to wartime strength of 2,002 men faster than any other National Guard outfit in New York. In doing so, he also had to make sure that the War Department, which was being bombarded daily by governors and National Guard commanders for a coveted spot in the Rainbow Division, couldn't help but take notice of the black New Yorkers.

Although his troops were now known as the Rattlers because of their regimental flag, the colonel also started calling them the "Fighting Fifteenth," even though the Irish regiment further downtown on Lexington Avenue was already known as the "Fighting Sixty-ninth." The Irish had earned that nickname in the Civil War. The blacks of the Fifteenth had yet to be battle tested. But that didn't bother the colonel one bit. He was certain glory awaited him and his men somewhere on the western front.

But when war was declared on 6 April enlistments stalled while other city regiments seemed to be filling up fast with eager men. In a barbershop, James Weldon Johnson overheard a Harlem citizen's reply when asked why he wasn't joining up with the Fifteenth to fight Germans. "The Germans ain't done nothin' to me, and if they have, I forgive 'em."[1] Noble Sissle noted the slowdown with the band. It still hadn't reached its numerical strength of sixty-plus. "Our applications that had been so readily answered in time of peace were rapidly returned with all kinds of excuses being offered," he recalled. "Among the most desirable men who refused to join were those men right in New York, whom Jim so greatly relied upon."[2]

Hayward dispatched Napoleon Marshall into Harlem to find men. Wearing his uniform, Marshall stood on street corners and tried to corral able-bodied men as they scurried past. In a last-ditch effort, he climbed onto the stage of the Lafayette Theater during the intermission of a show. "The applause when I appeared on stage in my uniform soon chang[ed] into a bedlam of protests and catcalls when I called for volunteers to go fight for their country," he remembered. Above the hooting crowd, he plainly heard someone yell, "What has that uniform ever got you?"

Marshall feared he was starting a riot. Yet, he rebuked the audience. "Any man not willing to fight for his country," he roared, "is not worthy to be one of its citizens!"[3]

Editorials sprung up in the *Age,* supporting the blacks' right to fight. In one of his columns, James Weldon Johnson, wrote:

> The writer has all along held that the Negro, in order to keep his case clean, must perform all the duties of citizenship while he constantly renews his claim to all corresponding rights. Such a course of action does not mean that he should be led by any silly sentimentality in taking up the duty that faces him in the present hour. It does not mean that he should forget his just causes for complaint. It means that guided by hard, common sense and remembering all that this country justly owes him, the Negro will take up and perform the duty that now

falls to him; thereby strengthening his protest for his right and fling-
ing a challenge to the white people of this country to rise to his plane
of magnanimity and do their duty by him.[4]

Another editorial called on blacks to "enlist in the Fifteenth Regiment and thus receive all the honors and credit due those who act at
once for the defense of their country." The editorial concluded, "With all
the power and prestige of the Empire State behind them, they will be
able to score a high mark in elevating the race in public esteem and
maintaining the standard of loyalty hitherto registered in the pages of
history."[5]

But Hayward decided not to wait for blacks to fill up his officer corps.
He went after whites from other National Guard units. In defending his
action, he told the editor of the *Age*, "The leading colored professional
and business men of Greater New York were personally invited by me to
enlist, study and accept a nomination for a commission, but refusal after
refusal was given me on some pretext or another. Two or three with
whom I talked on more than one occasion were about to enlist and work
for promotions when they heard some talk about no 'highbrows' being
wanted in the regiment. Since then they have turned a deaf ear to all
invitations to enlist." It was only when the War Department wanted to
inspect the regiment to see if it met federal standards that Hayward
resorted to officering the Fifteenth with whites. Stating that he only had
twelve commissioned men of color, he claimed, "To me it was a case of
either nominate experienced white men for commissions or be left out
of the service. There was nothing for me to do but to put white officers in
the regiment."[6]

Yet before he commissioned a white officer, he first informed him that
the Fifteenth was a black outfit and, more importantly, it had African-
American officers. He said, "If they can come into the regiment and meet
men according to their rank as soldiers and not as plain Bill or George,
so well and good. However, if [they] intended to take a narrower attitude
[they] had better stay out."[7]

The colonel drew out of the Seventh Regiment a number of men, most
notably his own private secretary in the Public Service Commission,
Cpl. John Holley Clark Jr. A lawyer and son of the principal of Flushing
High School, Clark was a coup. His great uncle, Emmons Clark, had
been a popular commander of the Seventh and had written a history of
the Silk Stocking Regiment. Clark's youngest brother, Arthur, an avia-
tor, had been an ambulance driver in the Middle East and had written
about his experiences in a book entitled *To Baghdad with the British*.

Another brother, Merrell, was also in the Seventh, and he and John had both been with the regiment on the Mexican border. When Clark showed up in Harlem on 3 April as a new captain, he brought with him four friends from the Seventh's B Company. They were Sgts. Harry E. Grant and Herbert J. Slingo and Cpls. Edward R. D. Fox and Frederick W. Cobb. Fox and Cobb were commissioned captains. Grant became a first lieutenant and Slingo, a second lieutenant.

Another Seventh Regiment alumnus was the imposing Capt. Julian Fairfax Scott, a six-foot-three, two-hundred-sixty-five-pound Virginian, who, as the city's second deputy police commissioner, was in charge of detectives. Because he was a resident of Brooklyn, Scott had earlier left the Seventh for a captaincy in the Twelfth Regiment. Now he had switched again.

Also from the Seventh, Hayward landed printing executive, Arthur W. Little, who had joined I Company in 1891, when he was seventeen. A descendant of the pastor of the Mayflower and son of a former U.S. congressman, Little had quit the National Guard and now worked for his father's company, J. J. Little & Ives. But when war was declared he wanted to get back in. Yet there was no place for him, not at his age— forty-three. Already, he had banded with several other Seventh Regiment members to form a skeleton regiment for inclusion into former President Roosevelt's proposed all-volunteer division. Led by Maj. Francis Landon, it included three majors, fifteen captains, fourteen lieutenants, and a chaplain. He sent his list to Roosevelt, and the former Rough Rider was thrilled to get it. He invited the group out to his home in Oyster Bay. Little was part of the group that arrived at Sagamore Hill on 25 April. Roosevelt assured them that when his division was formed, their regiment would be one of its mainstays. But in June, President Wilson quashed the idea. A dejected Roosevelt crowed that if his division had been authorized and sent to France, it would have equaled the record of the Rough Riders a "hundredfold."[8]

"After many discouraging rebuffs, it was General [John F.] O'Ryan who suggested taking advantage of my long militia service," wrote Little. "He urged me to offer myself to Col. Hayward. This I did. On April 23, I was officially advised I had been taken from the Reserve List, detailed for active service with the 15th Infantry, and assigned as Captain commanding F Company of that Regiment."[9]

When Little arrived on his first day of duty, he was assigned to the Second Battalion and ordered to its armory in Brooklyn. Located on 191 Harrison Avenue, the armory was nothing but a "dilapidated old dance hall and beer garden." Little shouldered his way through a "good-natured

Maj. Arthur Little, commander of the First Battalion, U.S. 369th Infantry Regiment, pictured here just after the war, December 1918. A former officer in the old New York Seventh Regiment, Little joined the fledgling Fifteenth Regiment as a forty-three-year-old captain.

U.S. ARMY SIGNAL CORPS

mob of colored men and women," and then spotted an old school friend, the battalion commander, Monson Morris. Other white officers were there, too. Morris was busy giving new recruits physical examinations. When he finished, he introduced Little to the white officers. There were ten of them and, as Little noted, "most of them were graduates of Yale, Harvard or Princeton, and most of them also members of the Union Club, the University, the Racquet, the Knickerbocker, or the Metropolitan, young men to whom 'the easiest way' was open, but in whom there existed no spirit apart from the determination to do their bit, and without hope or expectation of reward except the fullness of their own hearts in the knowledge of a love of country faithfully served."[10]

A number of these men would survive the war and remember Little as a "gallant commander," "unselfish and congenial," one who combined "the strictest sort of discipline with a human understanding and appreciation of the officers and men serving under [his] command."[11]

One of the officers was twenty-two-year-old Richardson Pratt from Glen Cove, Long Island. His grandfather, an organizer along with John D. Rockefeller of the Standard Oil Company, had used his wealth to found Pratt Institute. An Amherst College graduate, Pratt had been working for the Standard Oil Company of New Jersey when war was declared. He brought with him from Glen Cove a dozen or so African-American residents he had recruited there to join the Fifteenth. Among them were Eugene and Howell Hicks, Truman Brewster, Tupper Coffeld, William Denton, Charles Hill, Irving Jones, Harry Simmons, Joseph Tredwell, Adolphus Woodton, Ernest, Frederick, and George Seaman, and what was probably the entire Fowler family. Seven brothers enlisted. Six of them went into G Company, including the youngest, Royal, who was, in fact, underage. His older siblings were Benjamin, the eldest at thirty-five, George, John, almost thirty-four, Howard, Richard, and, in H Company, Barlow, thirty-one.

Some of the other officers that Little met were Hoyt Sherman, a Harvard man and great-grandnephew of Gen. William Tecumseh Sherman; Durant Rice, another Harvard graduate, who, as an ambulance driver in France, had won the Croix de Guerre with Palm; and Yale football and track star William "Buck" Waters, a reporter for the New York *Tribune.* Waters's classmate at Yale, Whitney Kernochan, also signed on as a lieutenant. Whitney's brother was chief justice of the New York Court of Special Sessions. His sweetheart was the daughter of former mayor William Gaynor. A dapper-looking Lewis Edward Shaw, a banker and

First Lt. Lewis Shaw, a banker and insurance broker, was one of the first officers to join Colonel Hayward in the Fifteenth Regiment. WILLIAMS COLLEGE

insurance broker, was one of the earliest officers to ally himself with Hayward. A veteran of the Mexican border with the elite Squadron A, the uptown cavalry unit, the twenty-six-year-old Massachusetts native and ex-Williams College student (he had not graduated) switched military loyalties on 6 April and was commissioned a first lieutenant in the Fifteenth.

Another of the Harvard men was Eric Winston, three-time defending national squash champion. He was noted for his fancy footwork and speed. An observer of the sport ranked him "among the foremost amateurs the game has produced."[12] In 1915 he married Maud Arden Van Rensselaer Kennedy, the daughter of one of the richest families in Hempstead, Long Island.

Winston wasn't the only Hempsteader to serve in the Fifteenth Infantry. Five African Americans enlisted: R. Campbell, Charles Howell, Hammer Jones, Daniel Morgan, and John Tillinghurst.

Hayward later hooked another white officer, this one was from Garrison, New York, who had spent the past two summers training to be an officer at the camp in Plattsburgh. Hamilton Fish Jr., whose father called him the "looked for boy" because out of five children, he was the only son to carry on the family's illustrious name, had been named after the Rough Rider cousin who had been killed at Las Guasimas, Cuba, during the Spanish-American War. Fish was a tall, muscular man, six feet, four inches and two hundred pounds. He was a former all-American and captain of the Harvard football eleven. He was once blamed for the death of a West Point player whose neck was snapped in a game in 1909. After graduating from Harvard he went into the insurance business and served in the state assembly as a Roosevelt Republican. The Roosevelts were all great friends, including the former president's son, young Theodore Jr., and especially his distant cousin, Franklin Delano Roosevelt, who at the time Fish joined the Fifteenth, was assistant secretary of the Navy. Fish and FDR liked each other, but that would later change under Roosevelt's long presidency.

While Fish was at the Plattsburgh officers' training camp, he felt he was entitled to a captain's commission. After all, at the worldly age of twenty-seven, the fact that he was a state legislator, that his father was a former congressman and his grandfather secretary of state in the Grant administration ought to count for something. He had studied hard for his captaincy examination, knew all the drills backward and forward, and marched off to take the test. There he ran into an "elderly" major who had been past fifty before he earned his captain's bars.

Fish recollected how he told the major that "I thought my age, experience, and background were sufficient to make me a qualified candidate."

But the major was not impressed. He refused to let Fish take the examination and, flat out, told him he was too young to be a captain. Fish insisted that he be given the test. The major then said that if he gave him the test, he would ask questions only about cooking, not drill.

The "disgusted" assemblyman returned home without a commission. The next day he was in Manhattan and by chance ran into Hayward. He unburdened his anger about the inept major and his desire to be a captain.

"Ham, if you want to be a captain," a delighted Hayward said, "I'll make you one on the spot." He explained that he was now commanding a Negro regiment, the Rattlers of the Fifteenth New York, and as soon as the chance comes, "I want to be able to take [this] colored outfit to France right off the bat."

To be an officer in a black regiment "appealed" to Fish. He thought of his friend Colonel Roosevelt; he knew how the former president had charged up San Juan Hill in the Spanish-American War alongside the Tenth Cavalry and had "seen how well they had done." Fish accepted Hayward's offer and afterward believed that even "Teddy would have loved to have gone to France with our Fifteenth New York."[13]

Fish recalled how most of the recruiting was done "right on the streets of Harlem," but that he traveled to Dutchess, Putnam, and Orange counties, scouring upstate New York for men.

Before Fish headed north, a Newburgh citizen, John Francis Monroe, conducted a "vigorous recruiting campaign" that, according to the Orange County Times-Press, "resulted in excellent success."[14] Part of Monroe's campaign was a letter addressed to Orange County's young African-American men. Published in the local newspapers, Monroe's letter warned that, because there was no military company for them in the county, they still had the moral obligation to enlist and not wait to be drafted. They should sign up with the Fifteenth Infantry. "By joining this regiment," he wrote, "young colored men will have great chances to become officers, which is done as soon as one is qualified. The only requirements are that they must be responsible, sound health, weigh at least 125 pounds, and measure not less than five feet and four inches in height." He urged them not to be forced into the army. "Don't wait to be drafted. It is no honor in being made to go, so volunteer now and send your name and address to me at once and I will arrange for your examination."[15]

On 8 May, two weeks after Monroe's letter appeared in the local newspapers, Fish, a new captain in his new khaki uniform, rode the train

from Manhattan up to Middletown. He reached the city at nine minutes after four and went straight to the local armory. There, a number
of black men who had heeded the letter awaited him. Seven were sworn
in: William Bailey, William Hasbrouck, Herbert Jarvis, Russell King,
Howard Smith, Elton West, and Henry Williams. Three others were
rejected for various reasons. Fish then ordered the new soldiers to report
to the Fifteenth Infantry armory in Harlem. He told them they would be
sent to the training camp at Peekskill for two weeks of drilling and rifle
practice. Fish left Middletown as quickly as he arrived.

He made similar jaunts up to the towns of Chester, Goshen, Newburgh, Washingtonville, Tavern Rock, and Tuxedo Park. Each time he
was able to enroll a dozen or so men. In the end, more than seventy-five
recruits were gleaned from the county. The ranks of the Fifteenth Infantry were now beginning to swell, and obviously the regiment was no
longer confined to the city limits of New York.

In Goshen, Arthur Decker assisted Fish in his recruiting and was
able to convince twenty-five men to be soldiers. The roster carried the
names of George Adams and Bob Borland, Charlie Crawford, John
DeGroat, Elmer and Nathan Earl, Frank Harden, John and Arthur
Simpson, six men named Smith, and one who dreamt of being an artist.

Horace Pippin, born in West Chester, Pennsylvania, was the grandson of slaves. It was reported that his grandmother had been an eyewitness to the hanging of the firebrand abolitionist John Brown in 1859.
When he was three, Pippin moved with his parents to Goshen. He was
sent to a one-room, segregated school. Because he loved to draw, he had
a habit that irritated one of his teachers. Instead of writing out his
spelling lessons in letters he drew the words in pictures.

"When I was a boy," he wrote in 1920, "I loved to make picturs [sic],
no one paid me any mind."[16]

Horace's mother read the Bible to him and told him stories of Abraham Lincoln and John Brown, stories likely passed down to her from her
mother who had lived at Harper's Ferry—especially the grisly tale of
John Brown's hanging. She sent him to the Goshen M. E. Church, and
from her and his Sunday school teachers, he inherited his strong religious beliefs. When the church held a festival and asked for items from
parishioners to sell, he created his first work of art.

"I went to the store," he recalled, "and got a yard of muslin and cut
it into 6 pieces and fringed them. Then I drew pictures on them such as
Jesus ascending into heaven. They were sold that night."

Pippin used crayons to draw the images on the muslin. A week later a
distraught old lady called on him. She asked if he had made the doilies.
He admitted that he had. She held up one of the doilies. She then said,

"I washed them. This is all that I have of them, and I seen a clean piece of material in her hand. She did not realize that they were made with crayons."[17]

In 1898 Horace's father died. His mother later remarried, but her new husband abandoned the family, and at fourteen, the budding artist had to quit school and get a job. He took a position as a hotel porter. When he was twenty-three, his mother passed on. He left the hotel business and worked for a company that made brakeshoes for railway cars.

When Fish came calling in the spring of 1917, Pippin, who was then residing at 53 West Main Street, Goshen, was twenty-nine. Because of his age and the fact that he had no training, any chance of his ever becoming an artist was rapidly slipping away.

Lorillard Spencer was also out recruiting. Because he spent much of his time commuting between Manhattan and Albany as Governor Whitman's military secretary, he hit the redcaps and trainmen who worked on the New York Central and Hudson River Railroad. He went as far north as Saratoga Springs and talked several waiters and doormen who worked the hotels in the fancy horse-racing resort into being soldiers. There he recruited George and Rouseau Simmons, Martin Briggs, Grant Bannister, Harold and Warren King, and John Jamieson. He likely chatted with Ranulf Compton, a white officer in the Second New York, about switching alliances to become a Rattler. By 14 April Spencer was able to report that he had enlisted sixteen men from Albany. According to a city newspaper, Spencer "wore a broad smile"[18] when he announced that he had the volunteers for the Fifteenth Infantry. But he added that neither he nor his assistant, Sgt. Willard G. Walsh, would be satisfied until they landed fifty men for the regiment.

The first men who "responded to the call to colors" and reported to the Washington Street armory to sign up were Arthur E. Smith, Robert A. DeGroff, George Morris, William M. Freeman, Nelson T. Jones, Daniel Branch, John W. Keen, Martin Klines, Harold G. Caesar, Pleasant J. Rowe, Everest O. Hill, Louis E. Jones, George L. Morgan, William O. Randall, and Clarence O. Sickles. Hill, Jones, Morgan, Randall, and Sickles were among those employed at Albany's Union Railroad Station.

There was no mention in the local Albany newspapers of yet another redcap recruit, a "sweet, unassuming boy"[19] who barely met the physical requirements to be a soldier in the Fifteenth. Henry Johnson, who lived a few blocks from Union Station, was only five feet, four inches tall. His wiry body weighed a mere 130 pounds. A twenty-year-old, he had big, dark innocent eyes. He talked with a slow, ambling southern drawl that marked his North Carolina roots. He had arrived in Albany as a teen-ager, looking for work. He soon settled down in a mixed neighborhood of mostly black and Italian immigrants. Johnson found employment as a baggage handler for the New York Central Railroad and, a few months after he enlisted, the slight soldier married his neighbor, Edna Jackson. She was the daughter of a minister from Schenectady, and her brother Charles was another recruit for the Fifteenth. If the war hadn't in-truded, the newlyweds would have led a quiet, unassuming life. Yet by the end of the summer of 1918, Americans everywhere would know the story of Henry Johnson.

By the middle of May, Spencer had thirty-two volunteers. All of them—Johnson and his brother-in-law Jackson among them—were sent down to Brooklyn, where they were officially mustered into the service.

Needham Roberts, a volunteer from Trenton, New Jersey, enlisted about a week before the Albany group. Within a few months, he would become entwined in the life of Henry Johnson.

Roberts had been a Boy Scout and always loved the organization's military ways and its khaki uniforms. He used to stand in front of a mir-ror and practice his drill. Before the war, Roberts, whose father was pas-tor of the Mount Holly American M. E. Zionist Church, worked as a clerk in a drugstore. He was down in the basement when he heard a newsboy outside yelling, "Extra! Extra! United States Declares War on Germany!" He slipped out of the basement, ran home, gave himself a thorough scrubbing, and donned his best clothes. Then his mother spotted him.

"What are you doing home this hour of the day?" she demanded. As she gave him the once over, she asked, "What are you doing in your good suit?"

Roberts did not miss a beat. "They want me to go down to Border-town to take a package, and I didn't want to go looking ragged," he said.

His mother softened, handed her son a dollar and told him to come home early. Roberts rushed back to the drugstore and told the manager that his sister was gravely ill in Philadelphia and that he just had to see her. He said he needed three days' pay. With a pocketful of cash, he made straight for the railroad station and caught a train for New York, where two of his brothers lived. On the way north, he read his Boy Scout man-ual. Upon arriving in Gotham, he ran to the apartment of his brothers at 157 West Fifty-third Street and explained that he wanted to spend a few days with them. The next morning they showed him around Harlem, and when the trio passed the recruiting station on Seventh Avenue, Roberts vanished into the crowd milling about on the sidewalk. He then worked his way back to the recruiting station, where he enlisted. He was nine-teen years old.[20]

The Fifteenth New York was growing in numbers. The band was very much a part of the recruitment process, itself bolstered by six young musicians from Hampton University in Virginia. According to Noble Sissle, it was common to see all the musicians atop a bus as it rattled into a "colored section" of the city, playing W. C. Handy's "Memphis Blues," or "Army Blues," which happened to be Hayward's favorite jazz tune. "A large crowd would gather," Sissle recalled, "and it was no trouble to get the men and boys of the crowd to get in the bus to take a ride. Once we got the bus crowded we would make a 'bee line' for the recruit-ing office." When the bus screeched to a stop, the band started up again. "As our coup 'two stepped' out of the bus they were danced right into the recruiting office—a pen put in their hands and before they were aware of what was going on, under the spell of jazzettes they had raised their right hand and found themselves jazz-time members of Uncle Samuel's army."[21]

Sometimes the arrival of a surprise recruit startled even the most hard-nosed soldier in the regiment. Such was the case in I Company when a man calling himself Valdo Shita signed on. He claimed to be a Zulu warrior and had spent twelve years in the British Army. A veteran of the Boer War, he had seen action on the western front. His choice of weapon was the bayonet and his taut dark skin bore witness to the fact that he had been in more than two hundred hand-to-hand duels with the Germans. There were "scars all over his body to show for his prowess with the cold steel," a reporter for the Brooklyn *Eagle* wrote. He had also been hit with a gas bomb, noted the reporter, and so his health had finally given out, and he was discharged. He came to the United States and was so moved by what he had heard about the Fifteenth New York that he made up his mind to get back into the war. The moment Shita's fantastic story was verified, he was promoted to sergeant.[22]

Another man who offered his services to the regiment was Charles E. Conick, a homicide stenographer for the U.S. district attorney. A Brook-lyn resident, he was politically connected. He had worked as a private secretary for both Colonel Roosevelt when the former president ran as a Bull Moose and for Roosevelt's cousin Theodore Douglas Robinson. Like Shita, Conick was a noncommissioned officer, and was soon named regi-mental sergeant major. Benedict W. Cheeseman, another stenographer in the district attorney's office, also joined. And like Conick, the Harlem resident was soon a sergeant major.

Hayward welcomed into his regiment the four Davis brothers from Harlem. Recalled Arthur Davis, one of the brothers, "To be a somebody you had to belong to the Fifteenth Infantry. So to be a somebody I joined up." So did brothers Edward, William, and "kid brother" Hannibal, a poet later known as "Spats" because of the way he wore his puttees. When he signed on, "Spats" was barely fifteen years old. Since he could type, he was assigned to Headquarters Company. On the other hand, William, because he was the head of a large family, quickly got an honorable discharge.

"Unknown to me," wrote Arthur, who, at the time he had enlisted, was a checker for the quartermaster department on Governors Island as well as Sunday school superintendent for St. Philip's Church, "I was surprised to learn that each of my sisters had secretly married soldier buddies of ours."[23] His new brothers-in-law were Adolph Lynch, married to his younger sister, Anna, and Edgar Jenkins, wed to Sophie.

All the young Davises had kept the news of their enlisting from their mother. But one day letters arrived at their apartment at West 134th

Sgt. Hannibal "Spats" Davis, the youngest of the Davis brothers, was barely fifteen when he joined the Fifteenth Regiment. He started out as a typist, but he would see combat in France. FROM *HERE AND THERE WITH THE RATTLERS* BY ARTHUR DAVIS, COURTESY OF THE 369TH REGIMENT

Street near Lenox Avenue, each addressed to a Private Davis. "My arrival home on this particular night was really walking into bedlam," Arthur noted. "My mother was now just about cried out, but burst out anew as soon as my key touched the door lock." When he entered the kitchen, his mother and young Anna were in the midst of being consoled by a "kindly gossipy neighbor." The letters ordered the boys, and that also meant the brothers-in-law, to report to regimental headquarters on Sunday morning by eleven o'clock.

When Sunday rolled around, a "most beautiful day," Arthur awoke as usual and marched off to church. He had forgotten about the orders to report to regimental headquarters. When the service ended and he stepped out into the sunshine, two military policemen grabbed him. They "seemed to glory in the act of escorting me down Seventh Avenue to jail" while members of the congregation gaped at their Sunday school superintendent. His students raced to tell the minister about Arthur's arrest. The Reverend Ev Daniels tracked down the officer of the day and talked him into releasing Arthur into his custody, instead of having the young man spend three days in jail. He assured the officer that Arthur would report as ordered.

The next Wednesday Arthur did as ordered. "As I entered the enormous New Star Casino at 100th Street and Third Avenue where many times I had previously gone for big dance affairs in fancy bib and tucker, I was now in olive drab like everybody else in sight."[24]

Of course, no military unit can survive without a chaplain, and who better to serve the Fifteenth New York than the "People's Pastor, "the Rev. Dr. William Henry Brooks of St. Mark's M. E. Church. The day after the United States declared war, Brooks stepped forward as regimental chaplain. The following Sunday was Easter, and his church was so thronged with parishioners to hear his first sermon as chaplain that there was standing room only.

The fifty-seven-year-old Brooks had been the pastor of St. Mark's for more than twenty years when he accepted the chaplaincy. It was claimed that over two thousand people joined the church because of him. Fred Moore called him "one of the most progressive churchmen in Greater New York."[25]

Although he was a true gentle man, and believed you lived life by the Golden Rule, he owned a tongue as sharp as any orator and was not afraid to use it. He once called President Roosevelt a "political trickster" and "prevaricator." He leveled his charges at the Republican leader when he, Roosevelt, failed to exonerate men of the Twenty-fifth United

States Infantry after the shooting incident in Texas—the same incident that had brought Governor Sulzer to his feet in the U.S. House of Representatives to defend the maligned African-American soldiers. Instead, Roosevelt backed the punishment meted against the blacks. In its aftermath, the all-too-familiar race riots broke out in the South, including a bloody episode in Atlanta.

From his own bully pulpit at St Mark's Church, Brooks lashed out at Roosevelt and Americans everywhere who allowed such injustice and murderous happenings. "The innocent men and women in this fair land may be taken from their own doors, maltreated, outraged, humiliated and butchered for no other crime than that they were not born white," he thundered.

It has been a pretense and contention of the South that the shiftless and ignorant Negro was the one she despised; but the real South appeared in her true colors when she took pains to run down, humiliate and outrage most intelligent, thrifty and upright people of the community. This was scarcely over before the Chief Magistrate of the Nation covered himself in eternal shame and disgrace by his unjust, unkind, undemocratic, un-American and Czarcratic, cold, cruel, drastic and infamous order against as brave as heroic as self-sacrificing a set of men as ever wore the blue or bore Old Glory on a field of strife, or battled for liberty beneath the stars of heaven, or tramped in tropic climes or marched in Winter's fiercest storms.

In the same breath, Brooks said, "But we will not be resentful nor revengeful, for we are the children of the sun and of God." He went on, "I pity Roosevelt. I have no word of anger. I forgive him. God bless him. We don't want to be fondled as a race; we simply want to be treated as men, only men. . . . The stars are brightest when the night is darkest, and in the furnace I see the form of One Divine, and walking on the troubled waters I see that same form and hear His voice, 'It is I. Be not afraid.'"[26]

Brooks had all the makings of a great chaplain. A prominent member of his parish recalled that it was the reverend's "grace, gentility, kindliness and courtesy [that] made acquaintance with him a privilege and emulation of his conduct a guarantee of the approval of those who placed a high value upon the things that count most in the cultural development of an individual."[27]

A native of Calvert County, Maryland, Brooks had a passion for education and books. One of his biographers remarked that he had a "scholarly turn of mind and at the same time [was] a student of men and events."[28] He attended Morgan College in Baltimore and Howard University in Washington, D. C. When he came to New York, he entered Union Seminary and also New York University, and later, he studied in France at Dijon University. He served his church in the nation's capital and in the backwoods of West Virginia.

In a letter to his parishioners Brooks once described his hard struggle for an education and the constant sacrifice that he and his family had to endure, and then he urged young men to educate their minds and take advantage of every opportunity for self-improvement, regardless of the effort and personal sacrifice required.[29]

One of the pastor's sons, nineteen-year-old N. Cannon Brooks, was also in the regiment as a sergeant.

Two other chaplains, the Rev. Thomas W. Wallace and the Rev. Benjamin C. Robeson, older brother of Rutgers University football star Paul Robeson, would later bolster the Fifteenth.

Although recruiting had taken a dip soon after Congress declared war on Germany, it rose sharply by the end of April, mainly because of the hectic efforts of Marshall, Fish, Spencer, Rev. Brooks, and others, including a pair of privates. Rexford Williams scoured Yonkers, and William Bunting, the first enlisted man in the regiment, who had turned down an offer to be a noncommissioned officer because being a private was "glory enough," went after the residents of New Rochelle. The family of each new man was encouraged to hang in the window of their home a placard that read: "One boy from this home is serving his country in the 15th N. Y. Infantry."[30]

On 26 April the *Age* reported that thirteen hundred men were now in the ranks of the Fifteenth. At that time, the War Department had set 2,002 men as the fighting strength of a regiment. In the months to come, the official figure would jump to thirty-six hundred men.

There was still room for twenty more officers, and Hayward exhorted the able-bodied African Americans of New York to join up. Already within the ranks of the Fifteenth were twenty-five enlisted men who had qualified as student officers and were assigned to the training camp at Plattsburgh. They were ordered to be in the upstate facility by 19 May and were informed that each candidate would receive one hundred dollars a month from the government. The slate included Thomas Bullock, Russell Braxton, Daniel Cole, William Gee, Stephen Juliet, James McCoy, Lee Pollard, and Leaming Wright. But at the last minute, the trip to Plattsburgh was cancelled.

In early June the men were reassigned to a new camp in Fort Des

Moines, Iowa, specifically designed for black men. It was the brainchild of Joel Spingarn, a leader of the National Association for the Advancement of Colored People (NAACP). Capt. Charles Fillmore was not happy about the creation of such a training camp because he believed it drained officer material from the ranks of the Fifteenth, and he let Spingarn know of his sentiment. "The training is alright for men living outside of New York City," he had written in March, "for here we have the 15th Regt. which is now far short of officers. Persuade men of the calibre of whom you spoke to join our ranks and they will be sure of the best training and commissions. . . . There are more than enough colored men in the community to make desirable and efficient officers, but we cannot get them. We had their word and support before the regiment became a reality, but afterwards many and various excuses were given. I first want to see the 15th Regt, a success."[31]

Yet in June the Fifteenth reached its full strength of 2,002 men and fifty-six officers—making it not only the first of New York City's National Guard regiments to make that boast, but the first National Guard unit in the country to reach war strength. By 20 June, it had 2,010 men.

Other regiments were frustrated that they were not filling up as fast. They all clamored to be fit and ready when the War Department finally made its decision as to which New York City National Guard outfit would be assigned to the Rainbow Division. The Seventh was upset because a number of its men were constantly being pulled out and sent to other units as officers. By mid-June it was still undermanned with 1,860 soldiers. The Sixty-ninth, meanwhile, had a huge waiting list of men eager to serve with the Irishers, but its physicians and examiners couldn't screen these hopeful recruits fast enough to weed out undesirables. To make matters worse, each of the other regiments in the city were ordered to send 350 of their own to the Sixty-ninth—not a welcomed directive.

The race to be the first National Guard outfit ready to go to war, to be part of the Rainbow Division, was heating up. The honor of New York was at stake—or rather, their own honor was. Who among them would get the nod from Washington to be the first of Gotham's regiments to reach the shores of France, to march down the broad boulevards of Paris, to go "over the top" in a glorious charge against the hated Hun?

As spring gave way to summer, it was still anyone's guess. Even Hayward harbored hopes that his troops had a shot.

Then some racist wag drove a stake through the heart of the Rattlers of the Fifteenth New York. He made a comment that, at first, sounded innocent enough, if you were white. And soon everywhere—in armories, in boardrooms, in restaurants, on street corners, or wherever anyone with an interest in the city's military affairs gathered—the comment was repeated. Over and over and over, until it took on a life of its own, became fact and, thus, doomed the Fifteenth.

"Black," the wag opined, "is not a color of the rainbow."

"Color, Blood, and Suffering
Have Made Us One"

The thunderstorms that swept across New York City just before Independence Day, 1917, flashed a warning of the summer to come.

It was 3 July, a Tuesday. City newspapers carried stories of the arrival in Paris of the first American expeditionary troops ready to fight to make the world safe for democracy. Two prominent New Yorkers were with them: Theodore Roosevelt Jr., and his younger brother, Quentin. As thunder rattled overhead like the elevated railroad and sent citizens scurrying for shelter, in Federal District Court in lower Manhattan the anarchist Emma Goldman was on trial for her strident opposition to the United States entry into the war. She later would be convicted and imprisoned on Ellis Island with hundreds of radical immigrants that the government deemed dangerous. There she and the other "undesirables" would be guarded by the machine gun company of the Fifteenth New York Infantry Regiment. Across the Hudson, in Hoboken, the commander of the Department of the East, trying to keep soldiers and sailors sober, ordered sixty-one riverfront salons to shut their doors at ten. At Brooklyn's Ebbets Field, the thunderstorm postponed a game between the Dodgers and their crosstown rivals, the first-place Giants. Up in Harlem's Olympic Field, the Lincoln Giants squeezed in a double-header against the Cuban Stars. Speedy center fielder Spottswood Poles again rattled his own thunder at the plate, banging out hits and scoring runs. In a few weeks he would give up his outfield position when the Fifteenth Infantry went to Camp Whitman for a month of training.

But for the city's black community, the thunderstorm that had rumbled out of the west brought with it the first news of a race riot in East St. Louis, heralding a long, blistering summer of hate. The headline in the *Times* on 3 July shot off the front page—a lightning bolt of fear and frustration, anger and betrayal:

RACE RIOTERS FIRE EAST ST. LOUIS
AND SHOOT OR HANG MANY NEGROES
DEAD ESTIMATED AT FROM 20 TO 75
MANY BODIES IN THE RUINS
Mobs Rage Unchecked
For 24 Hours Till Military
Rule Is Established[1]

The justification for the massacre, according to whites, was the influx of black laborers from the South who took jobs that belonged to whites. The secretary of the Central Trades and Labor Union, affiliated with the American Federation of Labor, in a letter to his delegates had made it clear that something must be done. "The immigration of the Southern Negro into our city for the past eight months has reached the point where drastic action must be taken if we intend to work and live in this community." He described those African Americans as "undesirables" and demanded that the mayor and city council "take some action to retard this growing menace and also devise a way to get rid of a certain portion of those who are already here."[2]

Ten days later the so-called aggrieved laborers, their wives, and even their children, inflaming each others bloodlust with shouts of "Get a Nigger!" took to the streets.

In New York, the *Age* republished an eyewitness account by a reporter from the St. Louis *Post-Dispatch*.

For an hour and half last evening I saw the massacre of helpless Negroes at Broadway and Fourth streets, in downtown St. Louis, where a black skin was a death warrant. . . . I saw man after man, with hands raised, pleading for his life, surrounded by groups of men—men who had never seen him before and knew nothing about him except that he was black—and saw them administer the historic sentence of intolerance, death by stoning. I saw one of these men almost dead from a savage shower of stones, hanged with a clothesline, and when it broke, hanged with a rope which held. Within a few paces of the pole from which he was suspended, four other Negroes lay dead or dying, another having been removed, dead, a short time before. . . . I saw Negro women begging for mercy and pleading that they had harmed no one, set upon by white women of the baser sort, who laughed and answered in coarse sallies of men as they beat their faces and breasts with fists, stones and sticks.[3]

At least 125 African Americans were slaughtered in the East St. Louis riot. A day afterward in New York, as the last thunderstorm swept over the city and out to sea, the sun came out. In the now warm summer afternoon, with puddles glistening in the sidewalks of the San Juan Hill neighborhood, a group of Rattlers from the Fifteenth Infantry gathered in their new uniforms on the corner of Amsterdam Avenue and Sixty-first Street. What was going through their mind? Were they talking about East St. Louis? Had they asked, "Why, for God's sake, should we fight the white man's war?" What is certain—they were minding their own business.

The San Juan Hill neighborhood, described as a "militant warren" by the New York *Tribune*,[4] had been the site of recent riots, including one on 26 May when blacks mixed it up with police and members of the all-white Home Defense Guard with knives, razors, bottles, and bricks. One African American was slain by the police. The riot started when a black man, chased out of a saloon, was stopped by a member of the Home Defense Guard. The *Tribune* reported, "Negroes in incredible numbers poured from the side streets into Amsterdam Avenue and surged northward." When white bystanders saw the fight they jumped in—siding with blacks against the "forces of law and order." A shot rang over the yelling, grunting men, shattering a grocery store window. A black teenaged girl was struck in the thigh.[5]

The fight lasted two hours. When it got dark, a police car patrolled the streets, shining a spotlight at the rooftops where "snipers might be posted with piles of bricks culled from convenient chimneys."[6] Five African Americans were arrested, including National Guardsman Lawrence Joaquin. The police detained no whites. Because of the death of a rioter, charges were dropped "on the ground that the police had already administered sufficient punishment."[7] A day later, two additional officers were assigned to "San Juan's narrowing black belt to reinforce the six ordinarily on post there," reported the *Tribune*. "Possibly because of their presence, but more likely because the 'Hill' no longer is the home of bad men who once made life exciting for the white wanderer, there was no recurrence of the rioting."[8]

Now, five weeks later, twenty-five men of the Fifteenth Infantry lounged on a street corner after the thunderstorm had passed over their troubled neighborhood. The morning newspapers were filled with accounts of the butchery of the day before in East St. Louis. In two weeks the soldiers were to entrain to Camp Whitman.

Already on edge, a patrolman named William Hensen, who had had a finger almost severed in the previous fight, demanded that the soldiers disperse. Joaquin, one of the blacks arrested in the riot, protested Hensen's order. He said that the officer ought to show some respect for the uniform of a soldier. Hensen arrested Joaquin and forced him up the sidewalk toward the police station at West Sixty-eighth Street. After a few blocks, the rest of the soldiers, bolstered by a number of civilians, crowded around Hensen. The police officer pushed Joaquin into a hallway and started clubbing the National Guardsmen with his nightstick. It wasn't long before a patrol car careened down the street with reinforcements. By this time a mob of two thousand blacks had filled the sidewalk and street. Knives flashed in the air and bricks flew at the officers. More police reinforcements poured out of the station house. The blacks were overrun. They scattered down side streets.

Joaquin and fellow Guardsman Vernon Cox were arrested on disorderly conduct charges. Isaac Brown, another soldier, was charged with felonious assault after he slashed a patrolman with a potato knife. Joaquin and Cox were sentenced to ten days in one of the city's worst prisons—a wretched, overcrowded hole on Blackwell's Island (now Roosevelt Island) in the East River. Brown was held on bail of one thousand dollars. His trial was set for the Court of General Sessions.

When word got back to the black community about the harassment and arrest of the National Guardsmen, Fred Moore and the Rev. George Sims of Union Baptist Church, whose three thousand parishioners lived in the San Juan Hill neighborhood, called for an independent investigation. They also appealed to Col. Hayward for help.

"So far as we can ascertain, the men of the Fifteenth were entirely within their rights in standing on a corner," Moore said. "They were in uniform, were perfectly quiet and orderly, and were not interfering with traffic. Most of them moved on when ordered, purely out of a desire to avoid trouble. But we have not found anything indicating that Joaquin was not entirely within his rights in protesting against the order or that he went beyond reasonable bounds in protesting."

Moore added that law-abiding citizens made up the Fifteenth. "There never has been any complaint against the men of this regiment before and if they are being unjustly treated because of their race we propose to find out about it."[9]

Hayward informed Police Commissioner Arthur Woods that he wanted a thorough probe of the incident. He filed a formal complaint against two policemen, including Hensen, for the false arrest of Joaquin. "I cannot find one shadow of justification for this arrest," Hayward told the city's newspapers. "I have not found any one who says Joaquin was doing anything more than standing quietly on the street corner or that he did more than protest verbally when ordered to move on."[10]

For Hayward and his men of the Fifteenth, the incident was closed. Then the colonel motored off to Westchester County to witness the wedding of one of his white officers, Lt. John Holley Clark Jr.

On Sunday, 15 July, ten days after the San Juan Hill incident had been settled and two weeks after the riot in East St. Louis, the Fifteenth and other National Guard troops in the state were mustered into federal service. Rumors and newspaper reports had all but three of New York City's National Guard outfits as part of the Sixth Division to be commanded by Maj. Gen. John F. O'Ryan. Odd units out were the all-white Fourteenth and Forty-seventh Regiments from Brooklyn and the all-black Fifteenth. These three unwanted regiments were to be formed into a new brigade. To what division, if any, this brigade would be attached was not yet known.

Meanwhile, by nine o'clock on Sunday morning, eighteen thousand men throughout the city reported to their various armories. Arthur Little, who on that day received his captain's commission, recalled how the regiment was full of the "spirit of war excitement." Some of the men took that spirit to the extreme and got drunk. One of the reasons they overcelebrated was that on the next day the regiment was off to Camp Whitman for a month—the first National Guard outfit to leave Gotham for training in the field as a federal troop. In May the soldiers had spent eighteen days at camp in Peekskill. There they had learned close-order drill, how to break down their rifles into parts, and how to reassemble them, clean them, and then to hit targets as far away as six hundred yards in rapid fire. At Peekskill, Little boasted that half the regiment, enlisted men and officers, qualified as crack riflemen.

Sgt. Noble Sissle fell in love with his Springfield rifle. "I fondled it; I talked to it. It was my religion; I knew every bolt, every spring; I could take it to pieces and put it together again in the dark and at what speed!" he mused. "I took it on the range and learned the use of its battle sights and when I pointed it and squeezed the trigger and that steel jacket found its mark, what a thrill and comfort to have it by my side."[11]

While Sissle and the others were learning to be riflemen, Lorillard Spencer taught them that, like the "three R's in school—Reading, 'Riting, and 'Rithmetic—in soldiering we learn of the four C's—courage, common-sense, cunning, and cheerfulness." He told the men that when they were ordered to their next training camp, learning "how to execute the different movements of close-order drill well enough to get away with it" was not enough. He wanted them to "know it well enough to teach it to recruits" so that when the time came, there would be an opportunity for promotion into the ranks of noncommissioned officers.[12]

As part of learning the drill, the soldiers also picked up a habit of saluting nearly everything that moved, and their regiment was soon known as "The Saluting Fifteenth." The nickname was the brainstorm of several officers of the Twelfth Regiment, who were at Peekskill to help with the training.

"Our men accepted the principle of a salute to officers more readily than any other principle of a soldier's training," Little wrote. "They seemed to love to salute. They would walk out of their way to approach officers so as to find an excuse to salute." He explained that because many of the Fifteenth's men had been in civilian life porters, red caps, waiters, and doormen, they devised their own way of saluting. "They would first raise the right hand smartly to the visor of the cap over the right eyes, as provided by regulations, but then they would bow very low in the most approved style of cordiality of a Saratoga Springs hotel head waiter, and murmur, 'Mawnin' Sus—mawnin'!'"[13]

Now, on the day they were officially brought into federal service, the men of the "Saluting Fifteenth" readied themselves for another round of intense instruction. This time family and friends sensed that the war in Europe was getting too close and that soon their loved ones would be gone. They crowded around their soldiers—weeping in some cases, afraid to see them go. One woman, the mother of Pvt. Elmer Partridge, begged Captain Little to get him out of the military. After all, she pleaded, he was only sixteen! Little asked her why, at the time of his enlistment, she had sworn he was eighteen. The mother tearfully replied that because he had been so unruly at home, she believed the life of a soldier would teach him discipline. Little did not release the young soldier, and Partridge went overseas with the regiment.

The following morning, the Fifteenth marched to the New York Central railroad station at West 129th Street, escorted by the band, playing "Billy Boy," a tune composed by C. Lucky Roberts with lyrics by drama critic Lester Walton and dedicated to Colonel Hayward. Four thousand people were on hand to see "the boys in brown off," noted Walton's newspaper, the *Age*. A photograph showed soldiers leaning out windows of three trains, holding hands with their sweethearts or wives. "There were many tears shed, kisses given and promises made," continued the *Age*. "Mothers, wives, sweethearts, sisters and fathers participated in the fond farewell. However, even in their leave-taking, crowded with so much doubt and uncertainty, the members of the Fifteenth were in a jubilant mood. The prospect of seeing active service seemed to kindle their enthusiasm."[14]

At about the time the Harlem troops were headed north to Camp Whitman, a much smaller contingent left from Middletown. Led by the Hasbrouck family, with Levi on the fife, Isaac on the bass drum, and William, a veteran of the Civil War, on the snare drum, about a dozen men, including thirty-year-old William Hasbrouck Jr. and the Jarvis brothers, Arthur and Herbert—all who had been recruited three months earlier by Hamilton Fish—marched through town to the James Street train station. There they boarded the Erie Railroad and were on their way to meet the main part of the regiment at Poughkeepsie.

As the entire regiment headed off to camp from all parts of New York, there was still the long-shot hope that the War Department might select the Fifteenth for inclusion into the Forty-second Infantry Division.

Located near Poughkeepsie, about ten miles east of the Hudson River, Camp Whitman was one of three major training camps in the greater New York City area. The other two were on Long Island—Camp Mills near Mineola and Camp Upton, situated far out on the mosquito-invested sand dunes close to a town called Yaphank. Compared to Camp Upton, where the Fifteenth would later be assigned to guard duty, Camp Whitman was, Little recollected, "thick with mid-summer luxuriance." It was almost jungle-like, and one day, sitting on the banks of a stream while black soldiers took their daily bath in the cool, clear water, Little spotted Maj. Edwin Dayton swimming among the men and quipped to another white officer, "With Henry M. Stanley, in Darkest Africa!"[15]

The Fifteenth pitched its tents, dug latrines, and got down to business. The men drilled and drilled, learned the rules of military courtesy, and discovered one of the realities of trench warfare: the cootie. Lice were a fact at Camp Whitman. "We had cootie intrusions right from the start," Little recollected. "True to the traditions of our conservative families, in those early days, we always discussed the appearance of cooties in undertones. Later, over in France, in the trenches, cooties came to be looked upon as a necessary discomfort, upon par with mud, and rats and darkness and cold, and foul air."[16]

And often, when the regimental band marched by some unfortunate soldier who might be delousing himself or peeling potatoes or cleaning out a latrine, and who had been duped into enlisting by jazz music, he would mutter, "If it hadn't been for that damn band I wouldn't be in this army." Yet Sissle recollected that "as soon as the band struck up a tune, that very soldier would be stepping the 'highest'." As far as the band's musicians fared, Sissle noted that when they arrived at camp, they had to set up their own tents. When they were finished, the band's row of tents "looked like a hurricane swept Indian camp." They had to tear the tents down and repitch them. When they were done, the drum major wrote, "They were suffering from everything from calloused [sic] hands and sprained backs to splinters in their fingers. Most of them, especially the Porto Ricans, had never picked up anything heavier than their instruments and as most of them played clarinets, you can judge what their training in weight lifting had consisted of."[17]

War games were played, with companies ambushing each other. Little gloated that his men in F Company had turned the tables on the men under 1st Lt. Lewis Shaw, thwarted an ambush, and captured the "enemy." Shaw, he noted, was "crestfallen."

In the middle of August, training abruptly ended. The Fifteenth was reassigned—broken up into "many parts," Little wrote, "to guard public works and properties."

Hayward was more specific. "The 1st Battalion, commanded by Major Lorillard Spencer, took over and guarded 600 miles of railroad in New York and New Jersey, also took over and guarded the German ships seized by our Government," he informed the U.S. Army's adjutant general.

"The 2nd Battalion, commanded by Major Monson Morris, was ordered for pioneer and guard duty at Camp Upton, and arrived there when it was a wilderness of scrub oak and pine, and the roads were just being built into the site of the future Camp Upton.

"The 3rd Battalion, commanded by Major Edwin Dayton, with the band, went to the site of Camp Dix when it was a corn field and performed this same duty there."[18]

It seemed that the regiment was strewn every which way like unwanted litter on a gusty day. Even the Machine Gun Company had been dispatched on its own—to Ellis Island to watch over so-called German agents and other suspicious persons, such as Emma Goldman, about two thousand of them, who were incarcerated there. The men were also sent to an island in the middle of the Hudson River where ammunition was stored. They were stationed at bridges and the mouths of tunnels along the tracks of the New York Central as well as the Delaware and Hudson railroads between New York City and Albany and even out in Pennsylvania, patrolling railroad lines there. They went to the Brooklyn Navy Yard. Other soldiers found themselves guarding shoe factories on Long Island and clothing manufacturers in New Jersey, whose new business was stitching together military uniforms.

Almost two weeks after the men finished their training at Camp Whitman and were scattered throughout greater New York, an extraordinary parade took place along Fifth Avenue. An estimated five thousand African Americans, half of them women and children, marched in silent protest against the recent race riots that bloodied East St. Louis and several other cities, among them Waco and Memphis.

"We march because by the grace of God and the force of truth, the dangerous, hampering walls of prejudice and inhuman injustices must fall," proclaimed the marchers. "We march in memory of our butchered dead, the massacre of honest toilers."[19]

The only sounds were the tramp of feet on the pavement and the melancholy tap-tap of drums. Children led the silent protest; Boy Scouts in khaki and girls in white dresses, marching first; then women, also gowned in white. Men were outfitted in somber black. One old man, a veteran of the Civil War, proudly marched in his tattered blue uniform with the bronze buttons of the Grand Army of the Republic glittering like gold in the sun. The flags of the United States, Great Britain, Liberia, and Haiti flapped gently as the marchers headed south from Fifty-ninth Street down toward Twenty-third Street, while along their route, twenty thousand more African Americans stood mute. The protesters held banners that stretched halfway across the broad avenue. "Square Deal for Everybody," read one banner. "Your Hands Are Full Of Blood" and "Pray For The Lady Macbeths Of East St. Louis" read two others. One showed a woman on her knees, begging President Wilson to first make *America* safe for democracy—then the world. There were other banners, too: "From Bunker Hill To Carrizal We Have Done Our Duty" and "We Fought For The Liberty Of White Americans In Six Wars And East St. Louis Is Our Reward."[20]

And yet another: "Color, Blood And Suffering Have Made Us One."

In Houston, Texas, a protest a week earlier of a different kind had been hardly silent. Its deafening roar reached all the way to Harlem, and beyond. It shook the bureaucrats at the War Department and forced Woodrow Wilson to mete out punishment in a way unbecoming the president of the United States. And for the black men of the Fifteenth New York, it would later come back to haunt them in the red clay hills outside of Spartanburg, South Carolina.

On 23 August, less than a month after being shipped to southeast Texas from Columbus, New Mexico, to guard the construction of Camp Logan, a military training cantonment, one hundred African Americans of the Third Battalion of the much-storied Twenty-fourth Infantry Regiment mutinied. Seizing rifles, they swept into Houston and shot up the city. Within a few grim hours, twenty people were lying in the streets, dead or dying.

Was the bloodbath a payback for East St. Louis? Or for the more than two thousand blacks lynched or otherwise slaughtered by mobs ever since such records were kept, beginning in 1885?[21] Clearly, those atrocities were in the back of the minds of the soldiers of the Twenty-fourth. Three things triggered their rage, after daily encounters with Houston's Jim Crow laws that kept them butting heads with a brutal city police force, especially regarding continual incidents while trying to board segregated streetcars. Foremost was the growing hostility and utter disrespect shown them by the white construction workers at Camp Logan. Overheard by the soldiers were such comments by the workmen as "Those niggers would look good with coils around their necks." Or "In Texas it cost twenty-five dollars to kill a buzzard and five dollars to kill a nigger."[22] In some cases, white workers quit their jobs rather than be near black soldiers. One of the workers claimed he left because he felt trouble brewing. Next to trigger the riot was the arrival of white regiments. Most troublesome was the Fifth Infantry of the Texas National Guard. The Texans made obvious their deep hatred of the blacks. And in the meantime, police brutality increased. By now, the atmosphere of Houston resembled a boiling pot with the lid about to blow off.

And on the evening of 23 August, it finally blew.

Three soldiers were pistol-whipped in town by the police. One of the whipped soldiers was a corporal of the provost guard whose duty it had been to find out why a civilian had earlier beaten and arrested a soldier. After the police whipped him, he was hauled off to jail. Word got back to camp that he had been killed. It was too much for the men of the Third Battalion. That night they broke into the supply room and grabbed rifles, ammunition, and bayonets. In a light rain, they marched into Houston to shoot up the police force and add streetcar conductors and motormen to the mayhem. Yet, the first victims were teenagers. One boy was struck while standing on the porch of his home. The other was dragged from a car and shot. While gunfire rang through the drizzly night, one thousand whites gathered in front of the police station. Weapons were passed out, and the mob headed toward the rebellious soldiers. Another mob collected at a fire station. Among them were soldiers of the Thirty-third Division from Illinois. Some of these Illinois guardsmen had been rushed into East St. Louis to quell the riot there. Running gun battles raged through downtown. In the end, the Illinois soldiers put down the mutineers.

In the aftermath, seventeen white people and three blacks were killed, although in a few months after a court-martial, thirteen soldiers of the Twenty-fourth would be hung, adding dearly to the total. Within days after the riot, Texans protested against the quartering of Negro troops in the South. By 28 August, a petition signed by the Texas congressional delegation had been sent posthaste to the President, demanding that all black soldiers be removed from their state.

Meanwhile, the apparently feebleminded functionaries in the War Department ordered the Fifteenth, now on guard duty at cantonments around greater New York, to get ready for a trip to Camp Wadsworth in South Carolina. The citizens of Spartanburg then braced themselves for the imminent arrival of two thousand black soldiers.

At about the same time that the War Department made this astonishing lapse in judgment, it made another. After determining that black was not a color of the rainbow, it selected the Sixty-ninth Regiment to represent the New York Guard in the Forty-second Division—a logical enough choice. But it incredibly included the 167th Regiment from Alabama to join the Irish as Rainbow troops.

Manned by boys from the state's rural towns and villages, the 167th traced its roots back to the Seminole Wars and was mustered into the Confederate Army on 4 May 1861 as the Fourth Alabama. During the Civil War it stood with Stonewall Jackson at the first battle of Bull Run. It fought at Gettysburg, Sharpsburg, and Chickamauga before it surrendered at Appomattox Court House. Its hatred for African Americans had kept it out of the fighting in Cuba during the Spanish-American War, where several black units were battling alongside Roosevelt's Rough Riders. They were seen as lacking in discipline, so uncontrollable that Maj. Gen. Joe Wheeler, a Georgia-born former Confederate general who had charge of the volunteer regiments, refused to have the Alabamians shipped to Cuba. On 14 August 1917, the Fourth Alabama became part of the Forty-second Rainbow Division, and was shipped to Camp Mills in Mineola as the 167th. For the first time since the Civil War, southern troops invaded the North. And it wouldn't take long for blood to spill onto the sidewalks of old New York and out in the suburbs of Long Island.

In that uneasy summer of 1917, the soldiers from Alabama and New York were like oil and water. They did not mix. The War Department was hardly a competent chef when it came to tossing together disparate regiments to create a uniquely all-American division—no matter its good intentions. Not only did it bring troops from Alabama to New York, but also Texans, including a company from Houston. But it was the Alabamians who were to cause trouble. Many of them loathed Yankees, and this attitude was obvious the moment their brown-leather boots struck New York soil.

When the men of the 167th Regiment arrived at Camp Mills, they found themselves bivouacked alongside the men of the Sixty-ninth Regiment, now redesignated as the 165th Infantry. After the war, they blamed any troubles they had at Camp Mills on the Irish New Yorkers, especially for circulating "several ugly" and "malicious" rumors that alleged the Alabama boys were "undisciplined and out creating trouble." William Amerine, who did not join the 167th until late in 1918, wrote, "It is said the men of the 165th Infantry (old 69th New York) would tell incoming organizations: 'The Alabamas are coming over and clean you out'." But the truth, according to Amerine, was that when trouble was brewing "the men of the 167th were all in slumberland."[23]

In any case, the Alabamians soon discovered that black troops were stationed nearby. And it seemed that everywhere they went on furlough, blacks abounded. There were black conductors on the trains that took them over to Manhattan, black doormen stationed in front of hotels, and even inside, black elevator men. New York was a sea of black, and they did not like it. In fact, they did not even like the white soldiers who had been plunked down next to them. While caged inside Camp Mills, it didn't take the Alabama regiment long before it went after the 165th Infantry.

The unprovoked assault occurred early on Sunday evening, 2 September. Visitors were just leaving the camp when forty men from two Alabama companies, quarantined because of an outbreak of measles, showed their displeasure with the rigors of camp life. They wanted out. In the shadows of the growing night, they rushed past their own guards and attacked the New York sentries who stood in their way. The 165th had been put in charge of maintaining discipline throughout the camp and were the last obstacle for the Alabamians. The two groups clashed, battling hand to hand. The New Yorkers used the butt end of their rifles to hold off the assailants until reinforcements streamed from their tents and the southerners were routed. The miscreants were rounded up and sent back to their compound where they were put under guard. The two regimental commanders held a hurried peace parley, and Camp Mills returned to normalcy. At least on the surface.

The Alabamians were just getting their blood lust up. They would not clash with the Fifteenth until the end of October, so in the meantime, when out on pass, they roughed up any African-American civilians they spotted.

On a trip to Broadway, three white soldiers spied an African-American doorman in front of a theater. Sauntering by, they hurled racial epithets at him. They bumped into two more blacks and snarled slurs at them. The New Yorkers refused to step aside, and one of them bounced his knuckles off the jaw of an Alabamian, knocking him to the sidewalk. Expecting a melee, a large number of people encircled the five men. At that moment, a taxicab rolled up to the curb, its door swung open, and a white driver yelled for the two blacks to hop in. They jumped into the cab and were driven away. The southern soldiers turned on the crowd, probably wondering how they could put up with such uppity blacks. They vowed to get even and angrily stalked away. A week later, Lester Walton wrote in the *Age* that the "three white soldiers . . . belong to the radical element which tells the North not to 'butt in' on its Negro problem [while they] attempt to 'southernize' a place like New York, having no respect for northern customs."[24]

In another incident near Camp Mills, an Alabama private hurled a rock at a black old-timer named Abraham Jackson who had fought in the Civil War. The missile nearly struck Jackson in the head. The private, named Joe Cruse, was arrested and later given a suspended sentence. "Cruse was one of a gang of Alabama troops that have been making life miserable for all colored people in the vicinity [of Camp Mills]," noted the *Call* newspaper.[25]

Miserable is hardly the way to describe what happened to Charles Farrar, a crippled fifty-two-year-old porter for the Long Island Railroad Company. One night about seventy-five soldiers from the 167th climbed aboard a train at the Borden Street station. Farrar, who was sitting with another black porter, who was not crippled, never had a chance.

"Get off this train!" the Alabamians hollered. Farrar moved toward the exit while his seatmate leaped to the platform. But he was too slow. The soldiers kicked him, beat him with their fists, and tossed him out of the rear of the car to the steel tracks below. Several soldiers jumped after Farrar and beat him senseless. Witnesses were afraid to aid the porter. One Alabamian took out a sharp weapon, a knife or a bayonet, and gouged out Farrar's right eye and then stabbed him in the left eye. Seeing that the soldiers were about to kill Farrar, the other porter signaled the engineer to start the train. The moment the train pulled out of the station, the soldiers jumped on board.[26]

When this incident took place, the men of the Fifteenth had left New York and were in the midst of a different set of troubles at Camp Wadsworth. Thus their own showdown with the 167th Alabama had to wait while they first dealt with the citizens of Spartanburg. And in dealing with them, they had to make sure to avoid another Houston.

The task was not going to be easy.

9

"The Man Has Kicked Us Right to France"

Thursday, 30 August, was a bitter day for the men of the Fifteenth. Col. William Hayward was enraged. "Damn their going-away parade!" he snapped. Tossing back his head in defiance, he laughed a "snarling, cruel, determined laugh."

The colonel had lobbied hard for his regiment to be part of the Forty-second Rainbow Division and had lost out. As he had found out, black was not a color of the rainbow. Now he was on the losing side again. This time his men had been ignored by the military minions in the War Department, and were not to be included in the newly realigned Twenty-seventh Empire Division, led by Maj. Gen. John F. O'Ryan, even though they were New Yorkers.

"We'll have a parade of our own when we come home—those of us who do come home," Hayward assured those officers around him. "And it will be a parade that will make history." His men all held hands and solemnly swore, "Amen!"[1]

The parade that so embittered Hayward and his officers and men was the state's farewell to the more than twenty-five thousand white soldiers who hailed from cities and towns and small farming villages in almost every nook and cranny of New York. These young men had left

families behind in townhouses and isolated farmhouses, in simple sub-
urban cottages and ornate Fifth Avenue mansions, in crowded apart-
ments and tenements in the Bronx, Brooklyn, Manhattan—everywhere
but in the neighborhoods where African Americans lived. They were
headed to Camp Wadsworth in Spartanburg, South Carolina, for what
they hoped to be a few months of fine-tune training and then off to war.
They had hiked "in service trim, these troops—their coats off and khaki
shirts damp in the hot, muggy weather,"[2] down Fifth Avenue from 110th
Street to the Washington Square Arch. That night after the parade, former President Roosevelt, spoke to the men of Division Headquarters.
"No man," he barked, "is fit to be a freeman who is not willing and anxious to be a soldier."[3]

Freemen, indeed!

If the parade had been a bitter pill to swallow, so too were the rumors
that African-American troops from the North would be sent South for
training to Camp Wadsworth or Camp Jackson or other locations far
below the Mason-Dixon Line. Such rumors frightened and infuriated
southern civilians, particularly in the aftermath of the Houston mutiny.

Before the New York parade, the citizens of Spartanburg, who had
embraced the idea of a military training camp in their own backyard,
had been guaranteed that no blacks would be stationed at Wadsworth.
As early as 23 April, Cong. Sam Nicholls, a Spartanburg attorney, raised
the alarm of blacks and whites together in the military. A member of
the House Committee on Military Affairs, Nicholls, whose only brother
had been killed in the war while fighting with the British, was flat-out
opposed to the enactment of the Conscription Act because he believed it
would force whites to serve with blacks. Addressing his fellow representatives, he stated, "You take a white boy from South Carolina and put
him in a negro regiment from Massachusetts or anywhere else, and you
would not have to go to Germany to have war, for you would get war
right at home." That statement brought laughter among the other con-
gressmen.[4] The irony in what he said, perhaps intentional on his part,
was that when illustrating his point, he chose a black Massachusetts
regiment. In the Civil War, it had been the African-American Fifty-
fourth Massachusetts that on the beaches of South Carolina led the
attack on Fort Wagner. After this speech, Nicholls and Gov. Richard
Manning bombarded the War Department about the wisdom of sending
African Americans to South Carolina for training.

By the end of July, Nicholls was convinced that he and Manning—and
for that matter, all South Carolinians—had won. Cocksure of his victory,
he telegraphed the editor of his hometown newspaper, the Spartanburg

Weekly Herald. "Just returned from the War Department. Negro regiments will not be sent to Spartanburg."

The editor of the *Weekly Herald* wrote: "This information coming from Washington should be the source of great relief to our esteemed contemporaries of Greenville, whose sympathies have been so deeply stirred over the prospect of colored troops at the Spartanburg camp."[5] Greenville lay about twenty or so miles west of Spartanburg, yet close enough to Camp Wadsworth for the citizens there to worry about the arrival of soldiers of color. In the meantime, with rumors still being whispered that blacks were on their way, Nicholls kept hammering away at the War Department, a never-ending tirade about how training blacks in South Carolina would be a "grave mistake," a sure way to "kill the war spirit."[6]

To their astonishment, on the day of the farewell parade in New York City, a reporter for the *Times* poked around their city, looking for a story about the camp where, within a few days, the first of thousands of Empire Division troops were to show up. The *Times* man informed city leaders that he knew for a fact that the Fifteenth New York had been assigned to Camp Wadsworth and would follow the rest of the division to Spartanburg. He spilled the beans to the mayor, a funeral director named John F. Floyd, who was up for reelection and could use the information to incite support for his campaign.

Floyd, who once kept a wild bear chained in the town square before he had it shot, exploded. And the *Times* reporter took down every word. The next day all of New York knew what awaited the soldiers of the Fifteenth if their destination was Camp Wadsworth.

"With their Northern ideas about race equality," Floyd, the son of a Confederate soldier, said of the regiment, "they will probably expected [*sic*] to be treated like white men. I can say right here that they will not be treated as anything except negroes. We shall treat them exactly as we treat our resident negroes. This thing is like waving a red flag in the face of a bull, something that can't be done without trouble. We have asked Congressman Nicholls not to send the soldiers here. You remember the trouble a couple of weeks ago in Houston."

The *Times* man visited the local Chamber of Commerce. One of its officials backed up Floyd. "It is a great mistake to send Northern negroes down here," he warned, "for they do not understand our attitude. We wouldn't mind if the Government sent us a regiment of Southern negroes; we understand them and they understand us. But with these Northern fellows it's different."

The chamber official then made a prediction. "I can tell you for certain that if any of those colored soldiers go in any of our soda stores and the like and ask to be served they'll be knocked down. Somebody will throw a bottle. We don't allow negroes to use the same glass that a white man may later have to drink out of. We have our customs down here and we aren't going to alter them."

Under the headline "Fear Negro Troops In Spartanburg," the article ran on page 4 of the Friday edition of the *Times*—the same day the newspaper gave the Twenty-seventh Division's farewell parade front-page coverage.[7]

The War Department immediately denied the report, stating that no decision had yet been made as to where the Fifteenth was to train. In fact, there was widespread fear throughout the South that African Americans were preparing for an insurrection, and the placement of black troops in southern cantonments was not a sure bet. In some cases, it was believed that pro-German agitators were behind the possible uprising, especially at Camp Wadsworth, where it appeared that black laborers were not working hard enough. Camp officers were sure "that sinister influences were at work in the camp" because "numbers of the negroes began to appear at the paymaster's window and demand their pay." Once paid, the blacks left construction sites, not to return. "At the outset this was not regarded seriously because the negroes are constantly on the move from one cantonment to another. But when chance questioning brought out a few of the reasons for the wholesale exodus, an investigation established the need for immediate action." It was obvious, according to one newspaper, that "despite the clumsiness of their [pro-German agitators] work, the trouble makers, playing upon the dense ignorance and credulity of the negroes, have made a great impression."[8]

There were reports, too, of increased holdups, house break-ins, highway robberies, and the rumored revival of voodooism that were making southerners anxious. Gun sales soared. The majority of new gun owners were women. Soon the sound of gunfire echoed on the outskirts of towns as residents took up target practice. In response, the Justice Department dispatched hundreds of special investigators into states where it was believed blacks were most troublesome. In the U.S. Senate, lawmakers charged the German government with fomenting unrest, even as one southern senator claimed the plot had failed "because of the loyalty of our negro citizens in the South."[9]

A letter in the *Herald* on 31 August carried a warning to the Fifteenth. Written by a Spartanburg schoolteacher, the missive at first praised the New Yorkers, saying they were intelligent, that "they know the customs of the South, and they are not going to break over or set at naught these customs." If they acted without causing any strife, then the "strength of the white man will be a wall of protection to the negro soldier while he is training in this city." But if the black man blunders, then the "white man, with all of his superior strength and power, will make war on the negro soldiers."[10]

Another letter struck a hopeful tone. "We claim to be the friend of the negro," it stated. "Upon this momentous occasion, let us prove it. The wise and the brave with the guidance of the Almighty God, rise to the difficulties of any occasion."[11]

In the midst of this turmoil, as the Twenty-seventh Division began its journey south to Camp Wadsworth, it seemed that the Fifteenth had no place to go. It was certainly not wanted in South Carolina. It was not even wanted by the commander of its own state division. Instead, it found itself strewn across New York, New Jersey, and Pennsylvania in loosely connected pockets—guarding a bridge here, a tunnel there, a construction site, an uncompleted camp, a pier, an island, or a dance hall in Harlem.

At one outpost near New Hamburg, New York, the men of B Company found themselves battling a scourge of lice. Capt. Charles W. Fillmore immediately notified Hayward, warning him that the "sanitary man is unable to cope with the situation on account of lack of supplies: and I insist that something be done at once, before the entire detachment becomes infested with the vermin." Hayward then admonished Fillmore for the tone of his letter, telling him it was against Army Regulations and that he expected that his next complaint would be couched in the "proper language."[12]

At the same time lice infected his men, Fillmore received a plaintive letter from "your trusty serg't," H. C. Smith, about the hardships of outpost duty.

> Although I cannot get to bed before 12:30 at night and up before daybreak, I am taking the bitter with the sweet. The reason of my not getting to bed before 12:30 is, because of my midnight guard I have to post at 12 and then its almost 12:30 before I get back. You can understand that if I go to bed in the early evening I may not get up in time to post the guard. I have no alarm clock, my watch is our only time piece.
>
> The rifles are in very good condition, the front yard looks good and the house is clean, excepting the windows and we have no rags to clean the windows, I had some of the men down at the rocks this morning for a bath and clothes were washed this afternoon. If the men

could draw a little money for shaves and haircuts I know they would appreciate it.

I had a little talk with Mr. and Mrs. Hamilton Fish Sunday and they are anxious for the men to use the reading room, which they are learning to do. The town people are getting well acquainted with us, and I might say very fond of us.

If I do not get shoes in the near future I will not be able to post my guard, as my feet are almost on the ground.[13]

In some places, especially along the railroad tracks in upstate New York around where the Fish family lived, local citizens took pity on the men of the Fifteenth, such as Sergeant Smith, and brought them food and hot coffee. Now and then one of the soldiers died out on patrol—either hit by a train or possibly murdered.

"The official records of the Fifteenth New York on guard show fatal casualties to the extent of about one man per week," wrote Capt. Arthur Little. "Most casualties were caused by sentinels being struck by passing trains, although we had drownings, and killings by gunfire and by knife-wounds. One sentinel, apparently, was killed by a Hun working-man at one of the great camps which our men guarded. The soldier's throat was cut as he turned about at one end of his post."[14]

Pvt. Georgia Woodson of B Company was found dead of a fractured skull on a deserted section of track. A resident of 67 West Ninety-ninth Street in New York, Woodson had been guarding a railroad tunnel. The army listed his death as a "railroad accident." Pvt. William Helicous of C Company died while on guard duty in Welleboro, New York. The cause of death, according to the army, was pneumonia. Twenty men from Helicous's company escorted his body to the home of his sister at 17 Second Street, Albany, for burial.

The Fifteenth's first fatal casualty in the war was Pvt. Earnest Miller of K Company, a resident of 2052 Fulton Street, Brooklyn. He died on 25 August of what was termed then as "military tuberculosis."[15]

At Camp Upton in Yaphank, Long Island, there were no deaths reported, but blood was spilled nonetheless. A few skulls were rattled by billy clubs in what had the potential of turning into a full-force race riot.

The construction of Camp Upton, where thousands of New York draftees were to be sent, was slow. The workers were taking their own good time. By the first week of September, it was only a third of the way completed, although ten thousand workers were on the job, along with a special police force assigned to keep an eye on them. The cost overruns were extraordinarily high. What the workers most objected to were black soldiers guarding the camp's entrance who searched them every day as they entered and left the work site.

The guards were Brooklyn men, all in the Fifteenth's Second Battalion under the command of Maj. Monson Morris. On a Thursday night, 12 September, a number of them received passes to attend a dance in Sayville, a small town west of Yaphank. During the evening, Major Morris went to the dance to check up on his men. A reporter for the Brooklyn *Eagle* wrote that "Morris visited the dance hall . . . and found his men in good condition and being held in check by the noncommissioned officers who went along in charge." Morris returned to camp. Apparently, some soldiers got their hands on a bottle or two of liquor and when they arrived back at Upton at around one in the morning, "several were feeling the effects of a joyous evening."[16]

Hungry, the soldiers showed up at a mess hall. A sugar bowl was knocked to the floor. The man in charge of the mess hall, white, allegedly struck a soldier. The white man and the soldier then got into a scuffle. One of the special police officers ran up behind the soldier and clubbed him in the ear. The soldier slumped to the floor while his companions rushed to his defense. They flattened the police officer. They knocked down another police officer. Shots were then fired. Black soldiers awoke in their barracks and came running. Major Morris and 1st Lt. Eric Winston, the national squash champion, sprinted to the mess hall. The fight ended as abruptly as it began.

The *Eagle* noted that there had been numerous fights at the camp in the past between blacks and whites, adding that the "high wages and great demand for labor have resulted in attracting to the camp an undesirable element of whites who have been constantly picking at their guards." It also reported that a nighttime gunfight had recently occurred at the camp's freight yard, with no injuries. It noted that only the African-American soldiers were equipped with side arms and rifles. An inspection of all weapons by Morris, however, proved that none of his men's guns had been fired during the scuffle.[17]

The *Times* reported: "Officers Stop Riot At Camp Upton . . . Shots in Early Morning Cause Great Excitement in Big Long Island Cantonment."[18] The headline in the *Eagle* read: "Negro Troops Clash With White Men: Uproar At Yaphank."[19]

For almost a month afterward, as tensions remained taut as a bowstring at Camp Upton and elsewhere around New York, the fate of the Fifteenth remained a puzzle. It was as if the regiment was an orphan with no place to go, a description that Colonel Hayward was fond of using.

"And then, one afternoon, out of a clear sky," Little recalled, "came to my desk a sheet of flimsy paper carrying a few typewritten lines, ordering the regiment to change of station." The Second and Third Battalions had been ordered to Camp Wadsworth to train with the Twenty-seventh Division. In his book, Little added, "Some thrill!"[20]

One officer of the Fifteenth smelled big trouble brewing if the regiment entrained for South Carolina. When the former state assemblyman from Dutchess County, Capt. Hamilton Fish of K Company, at the time on duty at Camp Dix, got the news he thought it had to have been a mistake. "Those people in that area just weren't ready for a black infantry regiment," he later recalled. "Gangs of toughs would push our men off the sidewalks, call them dirty niggers, just abuse them in every way."[21]

Fish wired his friend Franklin Roosevelt, assistant secretary of the Navy. His thought was to get the Fifteenth over to France right away, out of harm's way, and to a place where it could do the most good. Dated 4 October, his telegram was blunt:

> My brother officers believe with me that sending northern volunteer negro troops south would cause recurrence of race troubles [stop] this battalion could render immediate valuable service in France on line of communications where there is great present need to relieve French troops [stop] when [why?] not solve difficult southern problem by letting these northern negro soldiers go where they can be of immediate use and train for firing line quicker than in the south.
>
> Captain Hamilton Fish Jr.[22]

"Despite my appeal to Roosevelt," Fish wrote, "our orders remained unchanged, and we went to Spartanburg for twelve tension-filled days."[23]

As the Fifteenth New York rolled into Spartanburg on the tenth and eleventh of October aboard special trains, there was one man of significance absent from Camp Wadsworth. Major General O'Ryan, who had never shown much support for a National Guard regiment of African Americans, was in France, inspecting front-line positions with several other U.S. divisional commanders. He was not expected back in America until the end of November. Temporarily, the responsibility for running Camp Wadsworth fell on the shoulders of a graduate of the U. S. Military Academy, Brig. Gen. Charles L. Phillips.

A native of Illinois, but raised in Maine, Phillips had thus far led an undistinguished military career. After graduating from West Point in 1881, he served a few tours of duty on the western frontier. For many years he was an instructor of military tactics. When he had finally been promoted to brigadier general at the age of fifty and assigned to the Twenty-seventh Division's Fifty-second Field Artillery Brigade, he had been in command of the New England Coast Defense. Now he had to

*Capt. Hamilton Fish, Jr.,
at St. Nazaire, France.
Fish was from one of New
York's most prominent
families and served as a
member of the state
assembly before the war.
He tried unsuccessfully to
use his influence to
expedite the Fifteenth
Regiment's departure for
France to avoid having
his black troops stationed
in South Carolina.*

ALICE CURTIS DESMOND AND HAMILTON

FISH LIBRARY, GARRISON, N.Y.

oversee the operation of one of the largest cantonments in the country, a two-thousand-acre tract a few miles west of Spartanburg that was jammed with about forty thousand troops, among them some two thousand unwanted African Americans.

From the get-go, the Fifteenth New York ran into trouble in downtown Spartanburg. On their first night in the city, 11 October, four black soldiers were walking arm in arm with four white soldiers along the main street when they passed a gang of young men lounging on a corner. Racial insults were hurled at the soldiers. The whites reacted quickly. Blows were struck, and, according to the Brooklyn *Eagle,* "there was a lively row for a minute or more." The article pointed out that the "colored soldiers kept out of the fracas." The fight ended when the military police arrived. Observed the *Eagle* reporter, "The feeling against [colored troops] is intense. News of the disorder spread like wild fire, adding fuel to the already hot resentment against the so-called intrusion of the dusky-skinned soldiers. More trouble is expected, and the military police have been given strict orders to be on the lookout for it."[24]

Hayward acted swiftly. The next day he gathered all his officers and men around him in an open field. He leaped atop a bathhouse to make sure they all heard what he had to say. Little made notes of the speech. Hayward, he recalled, "did what he could to offer excuse for the unfriendly attitude of the people of Spartanburg, basing the excuse on the grounds of ignorance and misunderstanding. He explained that the Southern people did not appreciate the fact that the colored man of New York was a different man than the colored man of the South—different in education, different in social, business and community status, different in his bearing of a sense of responsibility and obligation to civilization."

Hayward went after Mayor Floyd. He urged his men to prove their moral worth as citizens "by refusing to meet the white citizens of Spartanburg upon the undignified plane of prejudice and brutality which had been so unfortunately advertised, by Mayor Floyd, as the standard of the community."

Point by point, Hayward argued for his men to act with restraint, even in the face of physical abuse, because they had a "great opportunity to win from the whole world respect for the colored race, with an advance in the elimination of existing prejudices to follow." He told them all that "if violence occurs, if blows are struck, that all of the violence and all of the blows are on one side, and that side is not our side. If wrong by disorder is to occur, make sure and doubly sure that none of the wrong is on our side."

Fred Moore of the *Age* recalled the colonel's remarks. "You are camped in a region hostile to colored people," he quoted Hayward. "I am depending on you to act like the good soldiers you have always been and break the ice in this country for your entire race. We are about to win the regiment's greatest victory."[25]

Hayward beseeched each one of them to raise his right hand and swear "to refrain from violence of any kind under every condition."

As Little described it, "A sea of hands shot up over the sea of heads—and the meeting was dismissed."[26]

Moore remembered how the "Colonel was cheered to the echo."[27]

Fish then dropped in on Mayor Floyd and his cohorts in city government. "I told them that if any of the town's citizens sought by force to interfere with the rights of the black troops under my command, I would demand that swift legal action be taken against the perpetrator. This quieted things down temporarily, but it was a nervous quiet."[28]

Europe's band played a key role in keeping the fragile peace. The day after Hayward made his men swear not to raise a fist in anger or in defense, the band played before Spartanburg's civilian population and camp soldiers at a bandstand in Morgan Square. It was General Phillip's idea that regimental bands perform in town every Wednesday and Saturday evening as an offering of goodwill. The Saturday concert drew a huge crowd, including Hayward and his top officers, who were there to watch for any trouble. They walked among the people in their military overcoats with collars turned up to hide their rank insignias. No one took them for officers. At first, the talk they overheard gave them a start. The townspeople were not happy with a black band. But as Europe led his musicians, a hush settled over the audience. And when the concert was over, the band marched off the stage in crisp military fashion.[29]

James Reese Europe, leader of the 369th Infantry's Regimental Band. When Europe enlisted in the regiment, he wanted to be a "gun-toting soldier," not a musician. Although he organized the band, he served as a lieutenant in the machine-gun company. MILES EDUCATIONAL FILMS

"The colored musicians made such a hit," the *Eagle* reported, "popular request has resulted in their being scheduled to reappear later on."[30] Little pointed out that the program had been "carefully chosen." He also singled out drum major Noble Sissle, "a true artist and our barytone [sic] soloist" who "sang delightfully."[31]

Sissle himself recalled, "In spite of the fact that our band played a concert in the Public Square at which several thousand soldiers and citizens applauded and cheered very vigorously; there was still that feeling of racial prejudice existing." Sissle beheld something else. "In full justice to their southern brothers' hatred, he not only visited it upon the dark skinned soldier from the north but the white boys of the Empire State as well. They were being treated none too cordial and, of course, that being the case you can imagine just how much love they had for the Negro soldiers from the north."[32]

Incidents in Spartanburg kept everyone on edge. Hayward certainly held his breath every time one of his soldiers headed off for town. In one brush with the townies, a black solider, most likely the pint-sized redcap from Albany, Henry Johnson, got knocked into a gutter. When he refused to fight back, he was taunted by the whites. But he held fast, telling them he had promised his commander not to retaliate. At that moment, several soldiers from the Seventh Regiment strolled by. One of them piped up that he had made no such promise to his commander. And the "young, gentlemen soldiers" from New York's Park Avenue commenced to beat the ruffians, knocking them into the gutter so they might get a taste of their own medicine.[33]

Even officers were not immune to insults and threats. Capt. Napoleon Marshall, the Harvard-educated lawyer and former collegiate track star, paid for a ticket to ride a trolley car. Once aboard he was judged a "dirty nigger," and thrown off.[34]

Then disaster nearly struck.

A white truck driver, bouncing along a road, spotted some soldiers from the Fifteenth on the curbside. He pulled up and asked them if they had heard that two of their own had been in a fight in town with a police officer. He probably paused for effect. They were hung, he said next, in the yard outside of police headquarters. When the group of soldiers hurried back to camp, they discovered that two soldiers were absent, that they had missed reveille that morning and then roll call. Moments later, throughout the enlisted ranks, men "whispered"[35] about the lynching, although there had been no corroboration that two men had actually been hanged. The oath the soldiers had given Hayward not to fight back against local citizens was now, in their minds, null and void. They were willing to teach Spartanburg the same lesson that the men of the Twenty-fourth Infantry had taught Houston. Like the Twenty-fourth, they armed themselves with rifles and ammunition and marched into town.

Sgt. Harry Leonard of Headquarters Company got wind of the plan to shoot up Spartanburg. He raced to find Hayward, who was then over-seeing the construction of a footbridge. He said that seventy-five men with loaded rifles were marching on Spartanburg. Hayward grabbed Leonard, and the two jumped into a staff car and sped away. Little, who was nearby, thought that Hayward was off to answer an important telephone call.

As the staff car barreled toward town, with Hayward cursing his driver to go faster and screaming at the military police to get out of the way, he prayed "to get there on time to save our regiment from disgrace—to save the population of that town from destruction! Seventy-five men with service rifles—seventy-five men whom we had taught with such pride how to shoot—seventy-five men with belts full of ammunition—these seventy-five men, with pent up grievance and wrongs (some real, some fancied) bursting their hearts—marching upon that town—to kill!"[36]

The car roared into Spartanburg. The streets were empty. Hayward ordered his driver to the railroad station. No soldiers were there. Getting out of the car, Hayward, suffering from a lame heel, and Sergeant Leonard headed along the main thoroughfare to the edge of town. Standing at ease were barely forty men—not seventy-five. Still, it was a force to reckon with.

As Hayward limped up the street, the leader of the mutineers snapped the soldiers to attention.

"I want an explanation, " demanded the colonel.

The soldier in charge explained that they had heard that two men had been lynched. Therefore, they had marched into town in "perfect discipline." Two men were sent to go to police headquarters to find out if, in fact, there had been a lynching. "If it were so," he told Hayward, "they had come prepared to shoot the police—all of them, if they could find them, and any other people of the town who might interfere or try to assist the police."

They were now waiting for the return of the two men.

Hayward did not wait. He went to police headquarters, where two of his soldiers, with rifles and ammunition belts, stood at attention. Sure enough, they were asking about the missing men of the Fifteenth. The policemen were relieved to see a white officer. They swore that no blacks

had been in trouble or had been arrested, and to prove it, they showed
Hayward the police blotter for the night before and let him and the two
soldiers look inside the jail cells to see that they were empty. Satisfied,
Hayward returned to his soldiers in the street. By that time, the town
had awakened, and a small crowd had collected nearby, wondering what
was going on. Hayward ordered the troops to attention and marched
them back to camp.

"Those men never drilled better in their lives," he told Little. "As they
swung off, and snapped their pieces up to right shoulder, that crowd of
civilians applauded! Can you beat it, Little? Just to think! That town
was, for a half hour or more, just balancing between tragedy and nor-
mality, and they didn't know it. They don't know it; and they mustn't
know it until the war is over and the regiment is mustered out. My, it
was a narrow squeak!"[37]

Hayward reported the incident to General Phillips. Both men knew
that racial tensions would only get worse. The right thing to do was to
get the Fifteenth out of Spartanburg and over to France as quickly as
possible. The only man who could issue such an order was Secretary of
War Newton Baker. Phillips believed that Hayward, and only Hayward,
should meet with Baker, and that the meeting should be done in utmost
secrecy. Phillips then worked on getting the two men together.

Meanwhile, an uneasy peace settled over Spartanburg. The soldiers got
down to actual training. To see how tough they were, Hayward ordered
a forced march of ten miles over rugged countryside. In the middle of
the march, the troops, under the weight of full packs and rifles, were
hit by a raging rainstorm. "The roughest roads possible were chosen,"
reported a writer for the New York *Tribune.* "But the men of the 15th
swung along, singing and enjoying every step of the way. The march in
the rain was a test of their mettle. Directly in the faces the blinding
storm struck the soldiers, but they preserved their alignment as though
passing in review. Back to the camp they came, and as they labored over
wet accouterments they sang."[38]

When the march was over, Sgt. Raymond S. Wright of B Company
defended his title as "Biscuit King" of the regiment. During mess, the
Brooklyn soldier wolfed down twenty biscuits, a daily deed of his that
left the other men shaking their heads.[39]

The Fifteenth also did a stint in the trenches. But, according to the
Tribune, the work there was "lightened for them because of the rag-time
music provided by their band. The men of the 15th were in a seventh
heaven of delight and picks and shovels kept time to the speedy music."

A French instructor was also caught up in this "musical orgy. It was with difficulty that he restrained himself from seizing a shovel and joining the merry entrenchers."[40]

Often, as the troopers sang, they made up their own lyrics. Among their more popular ditties was, according to the Brooklyn *Eagle,* "If You Don't Believe I'm Single, Just Look at the Hole I'm In."[41]

The best voice in the regiment belonged to Sissle, who would rather kill the enemy than sing. "Yes, I had the same feeling all my other Army buddies had," he wrote. "I wanted to shoot myself a German, but like in school where my heart was always set on being a football or baseball star, I ended up a better singer, so it was in my tour of duty in the army—it was always as a Singer of Song and Contributor to the Happiness of My Buddies I invariably ended up doing."[42] Whenever the band staged a concert downtown, and the Fifteenth was by far the most popular band of all the military orchestras stationed at Camp Wadsworth, Sissle was one of its leading attractions. After one of the concerts, the minister of a little church that Lt. James Europe attended when in town asked the bandleader if he would play at one of the evening services—and if Sissle might sing, too.

"We gladly consented," Sissle recollected, not knowing at the time that, as a result, he and Europe would soon find themselves in the center of the most notorious racial confrontation in Spartanburg.

The confrontation began innocently, and on the night after Hayward, fearing for his men, boarded a train to Washington for his secret meeting with Secretary Baker on the regiment's fate. Europe and Sissle honored the request of the minister to perform at a Sunday evening service. Afterward, around ten, the two soldiers headed for a food stand that served black soldiers. As they came down a side street, they saw a number of their men there, as Sissle recalled, "standing around, talking and eating and waiting for the automobiles to carry them back to camp." They joined them. After a bite to eat, Europe looked about him. "Wonder where we can get some New York papers?" he said.

A black civilian, lounging nearby, overheard him. "Why, Lieutenant," he said, "you can get New York papers right over there in the lobby of the hotel."

The building he pointed out was, according to Sissle, an "ordinary-looking family hotel."

"Is it a white hotel?" Europe asked.

"Yes sir, but it is quite all right to go in there," the civilian replied. "The colored people here in town go there for papers."

Europe nudged his drum major. "Go on over Siss," he said, "and get every paper that has the word 'New York' on it. I never knew how sweet New York was 'til I landed here."

Sissle didn't like the idea, and hesitated. The civilian sensed his reluctance and offered to get the papers himself. He said that he worked at the hotel, waiting tables, and that the place was perfectly safe.

Sissle thought, "don't go." But he didn't want to appear cowardly. He crossed the street and peered through a window. Inside were several white officers and the newsstand. Sissle walked into the lobby. An officer reading a newspaper smiled at him. He looked Jewish. Another officer stood at the counter of the newsstand. He stepped aside as Sissle reached the counter. "I asked for the New York papers and was waited on with all the courtesy of a Boston clerk," the drum major recalled. "Receiving my change I turned to leave all flushed with the idea of how ungrounded had been my fears."

He had not gone far when he felt someone from behind grab the collar of his uniform. His hat went spinning to the floor.

"Hey, nigger," barked a gruff voice, "don't you know enough to take your hat off!"

Reaching for his hat and thinking he had made a gaffe in military etiquette, Sissle saw that all the white officers had their hats on. He realized then that he'd been singled out because of his color. As he started to grab his hat, a painful kick landed on his rump. His assailant swore at him.

Sissle stammered, "Do you realize you are abusing a United States soldier and that is a government hat you knocked off?"

"Damn you and the government, too," snarled the man. "No nigger can come into my place without taking off his hat!" The man kept kicking the drum major until he had literally booted him out of the hotel. None of the officers in the lobby had moved to help Sissle. Once outside, he picked up his hat, placed it on his head and adjusted his uniform. He had decided to keep the incident to himself until he got back to camp. Remembering his oath to Colonel Hayward, he did not want to start something.

As he climbed into the car with Europe, he saw soldiers running toward the hotel. Sissle hopped from the car, yelling for Europe to follow him. "I knew he, being an officer, could stop whatever had started." Pressed against the door to the hotel were a number of black soldiers and, ready to lead them into the lobby, was the white officer who had smiled at Sissle. As it turned out, he was Jewish. He had followed Sissle out of the hotel and told the men of the Fifteenth what had happened to their drum major.

In Little's account, the white officers in the lobby wanted to tear down the hotel and were ready to rush the owner when Europe took charge.

A commanding man whether in uniform or not, who stood over six feet, Europe pushed to the front of the mob and barred the door. He ordered the men to be quiet and calm. With Sissle and two sergeants, he entered the lobby, making sure he kept his hat on. Sissle shot a glance back through the window at the men outside. "I will never forget the expression on their faces as I looked through the window at their angry countenances and glaring eyes," he wrote. "Now I can realize why the Germans called us 'Hell Fighters' if that is the way we looked coming over 'the top'."[43]

At that moment, Little and Morris were at the headquarters of the Spartanburg police. They had promised Hayward to remain in town while he was gone. They were using the police station as a communications center. "At about half past eight [Little's time of night does not coincide with Sissle's] we were notified that there was a riot in progress

James Reese Europe (right) and Noble Sissle in the trenches during training. Europe had convinced Sissle that serving in the regiment would help boost the position of African Americans in New York City. Europe would be the first African-American officer to cross into no-man's-land during the war. FROM REMINISCING WITH SISSLE AND BLAKE

at one of the hotels on a side street. We were no more than two or three blocks away, and we reached the scene of the excitement very quickly."

When the two officers reached the hotel, the front doorway was jammed with excited soldiers and civilians, men and women. But there was no riot in progress. Black military police, known as "provost guards," were herding the crowd away from the hotel in an orderly fashion.[44]

Inside, Europe and the owner of the hotel stood face-to-face. Pointing angrily at Sissle, the owner growled that nothing was the matter. "Only that nigger did not take off his hat and no nigger can come into my place without taking off his hat." The owner then shouted at Europe. "And you take off your hat." Sissle felt his heart sink. He knew that Europe would now wreck the place. Instead, the big man obeyed the owner.

"I'll take my hat off just to find out one thing. What did Sergeant Sissle do? Did he commit any offense?"

"No! I told you he did not take his hat off and I knocked it off! Now you get out of here!"[45]

Europe refused to budge. Before anything else could happen, Little and Morris burst into the lobby. The sight of Europe stopped Little in his tracks. "The officer who had quelled that riot by the power and majesty of command was a black man, a full blooded negro," he penned. "1st Lt. James Reese Europe." He saw how Europe's glaring eyes had frozen the owner. "There was no sign of fear in the glance of the negro. Then, with quiet dignity, he turned his back, and walked into the street."[46]

Of course, Little and Morris had to report the incident to General Phillips. They also wired Hayward in Washington. And then they tracked down every newspaper reporter in Spartanburg and begged each one not to report what had happened. No stories appeared in the New York press.

The next day Lt. Lewis Shaw wrote to his mother back in Manhattan. He had been hoping to find a place for her to stay in Spartanburg while he was there training. Now he had news that, in all likelihood, would keep her in New York. "We are all straining every nerve to prevent race trouble, and our men so far, in spite of every insult and provocation, have shown wonderful control. I can not see how it can last indefinitely. Last night one of our most inoffensive and harmless noncoms—Sissle, the one that sings was assaulted by a hotel proprietor for not taking off his hat in the lobby of a dump of a hotel here. We are determined to prosecute the dog for contempt of the U.S. uniform and it will make a big stir you bet even if no further violence comes of it. I expect we will be moved north again."[47]

Shaw did not know how right he was. Almost at the moment he was writing to his mother, in Washington, Hayward and Secretary Baker, along with his assistant, Emmett J. Scott, an African American, were making plans for the Fifteenth to return home to New York.

Hayward had arrived at Baker's office on Monday, 22 October. At the time, Scott was Baker's special assistant in charge of African-American affairs. A shrewd businessman and former educator and journalist, Scott had been Booker T. Washington's alter ego when he served the legendary founder of the Tuskegee Institute as his private secretary. Scott remembered how Hayward "place[d] before the [War Department] the highly inflammable situation existing in Spartanburg."[48] It didn't take Baker long to decide that if he wanted to avoid another Houston tragedy, the Fifteenth had to leave South Carolina. He ordered Scott to accompany the colonel back to Spartanburg to prepare the regiment for its return to New York, where it would be stationed at Camp Mills until a final decision on its fate was made.

"That afternoon I received a telegram from Col. Hayward," Little recalled, "which gave me to understand that he had succeeded in his mission; that he would be with us upon the evening of the second day following the mix-up. We had about two days to clear up our paper work and pack up," Little stated.[49]

Scott saw right away that the atmosphere in Spartanburg was "supercharged." He watched as Hayward collected all his officers together and realized that almost all of them were unaware that he had been to see Baker and that their days at Camp Wadsworth were numbered. After he broke the news to the officers, he had them assemble all the noncommissioned officers, so that Scott, the Secretary of War's emissary, could speak privately to them "face to face and in the frankest way possible." No white officers were to be present when Scott addressed the men.[50]

It was late afternoon, and the sun was low in the October sky when the noncoms gathered around Scott. Facing who he felt were the true leaders of the Fifteenth was a moment he'd "vividly" remember for the rest of his life.

"My address to these men was an appeal and admonition to do nothing that would bring dishonor or stain to the regiment or to the race which they represented." Sounding very much like Hayward when the colonel had spoken to these same men atop a bathhouse, Scott continued,

That whatever of violence they should do in the present difficulty would only react upon their race throughout the country, and that the situation was potentially dangerous, in that it was hardly to be expected that the country would stand for another riot of the Houston character, despite the fact that the men, when visiting the town, had suffered rebuffs and mistreatment which had tried their patience and caused them to wish to visit violence upon the community.

When he had finished, many of the noncommissioned officers came up to him, tears glistening against their dark cheeks. They told him "how bitterly they felt in the face of the insults." But they told him also of "their willingness to listen to the counsel which had been addressed to them for the sake of the Negro race, and for all that was at stake for it and the country during the war."

The only solution in Spartanburg was to get out. As Scott recalled in his official history, *The American Negro in the World War,* there had been three choices. Stay at Camp Wadsworth and "face an eruption and possibly further anger of the white citizens . . . while at the same time inflaming the men of the regiment and many of the white New York guardsmen who were restive under the treatment accorded colored soldiers"; remove the Fifteenth to another training camp; or order the regiment overseas.[51]

The War Department's decision was to ship the Fifteenth to France. The news caught officers and men off guard. Fish wrote his father: "I was directed not to write anyone or telegraph the fact that we are to sail from Hoboken on Sat. Oct. 27th. So you must keep the news in strict confidence. . . . The order reached us to-day from Washington and came like a bombshell and I must say all the officers are delighted. The situation between our soldiers and the poor whites of Spartanburg has been most critical since we arrived, owing to the disgusting treatment the men received: several serious race riots have just been prevented in nick of time, and all of us know that it was only a question of time before our men would retaliate and shoot up or burn up the town."[52]

The decision to ship the Rattlers to France sparked a quip from Europe. "I'm sure sorry I sent you in after those papers in Spartanburg," he said to Sissle. "Here, the man has kicked us right to France!"[53]

Before sailing, the regiment had to be temporarily relocated, and for a few days its new home was to be at the training ground of the Rainbow Division—Camp Mills in Mineola, Long Island.

Breaking camp in Spartanburg was easy. All tents were to be left standing, to be occupied by new trainees. On the morning of 24 October, Hayward ordered his men into parade formation. The Fifteenth passed in review, and as it prepared to march to the railroad siding to board special trains to bring it back to New York, it had to step past two regiments. On one side of the road stood the men of the Seventh New York, the "silk-stocking" soldiers of the exclusive Upper East Side. Across the road, the men of the Twelfth New York, many of them neighbors from the San Juan Hill District, were lined up. Among the troops, thousands of them, there, of course, was not a single black face. Fish recalled that the Seventh, of all the New York regiments, was most "furious" at the treatment the Fifteenth had endured at Spartanburg.[54]

Company after company, the black soldiers marched through this wall of white. And as their feet beat out a martial staccato on the clay soil of Camp Wadsworth, the "brave lads of the 27th Division," Little reported, "sang us through, to the tune of *Over There*."[55] Even Fish was moved. "They lined the company streets singing George M. Cohan's new song, *Over There*. Our boys waved back at them."

"Well, when they got us to Mills," Fish added, "things weren't much better simply because they bivouaced [*sic*] us right next to an Alabama infantry regiment of the Rainbow Division."[56]

The Fifteenth's stay at the camp in Mineola was to be short, and the regiment was to be shipped overseas as soon as possible—ironically, out of harm's way. Yet even the two days sequestered among units of the Rainbow Division turned into an adventure.

The band from the Sixty-ninth was on hand to greet the New Yorkers when they stepped down from the train that had carried them out to Mineola. But Albert Etttinger, a private in the Irish outfit, recalled how his regiment's band paled next to the Fifteenth's band. "Our band was nothing compared with theirs. As they got off the train, they formed up behind forty professional musicians led by Lieutenant Europe, and when they marched into camp, it was a sight to behold, and their music was simply out of this world! Europe had injected syncopated rhythm in his march selections, and we laughed and cheered like crazy." Watching Sissle perform was also a sight to behold. Ettinger remembered him as "a high-stomping drum major, with a twirling baton and a fancy headdress, he was something else!"[57]

The greeting by the Sixty-ninth lifted the spirits of the African Americans. "When we arrived at Camp Mills, I thought we were at last among friends," quoted a private in one company of the Fifteenth. "But good gawd, man, them Alabama fellows called us everything you can think of and then some. There wasn't nothing else to do but fight."[58]

The 167th Infantry from Alabama always felt it got a bad rap when it was training at Camp Mills.

Harking back to its run-in with the 165th Infantry, the historian of the southern regiment stated that it had been a "very insignificant scrap of a personal nature, between small groups of Alabamians and New Yorkers [that] started a lot of baseless criticism against the former [the 167th]." He wrote that it was the Irish soldier boys who always roiled the waters of Camp Mills whenever new troops arrived, warning them that the southern boys from Alabama "are coming over to clean you out." The boys from Dixie were innocent. To prove his point, the historian William Amerine next wrote, "A specific case is cited when the negroes of the 15th New York arrived the whites from the same state ran out and embraced the blacks, repeating to the latter the same old warning. 'The Alabamas are coming over and clean you out,' which caused the 15th that night to have a call to arms, though the men of the 167th at the time were all sleeping soundly."[59]

But in this case, if accounts are right, the Alabamas were hardly snuggled down in their bunks on the night the Fifteenth arrived in camp.

Sgt. Henry Matthews of the Fifteenth remembered the "spirit of antagonism among the Southern portion of the Rainbow Division stationed at Camp Mills." That antagonism was everywhere. The Alabama soldiers nailed up signs throughout the camp. "This Side For Colored." "This Side For White." Because it was an "unusual thing to occur in our State," Matthews wrote, "we thought it our duty to tear down the signs, which we did. The white soldiers then circulated the report that they were going to run us out of Camp, for which we were amply prepared to meet them."[60]

Matthews recalled numerous "fistfights and altercations." He was proud to report that in those fights "The Old Fifteenth [won] out completely."

Even Ettinger commented on the rough treatment the southerners tried to dish out to the black soldiers. "Our boys from the Sixty-ninth received those of the Fifteenth New York as buddies. Not so the Alabamians. They resented Blacks coming into camp. Hell, they resented us! The first thing you know fights erupted all over the place, and the Sixty-ninth guys usually stood up for the Fifteenth men and fought alongside them against the Alabamians."[61]

The Brooklyn *Eagle* ran an editorial about the fights and near race riots, labeling the 167th hotheaded Alabama men.

A popular impression that there is something missing in the way of discipline at Camp Mills is bound to be created by the news of repeated physical encounters between Alabama white soldiers and members of the Fifteenth Negro Infantry, New York National Guard, by the reports of persistent insulting of the colored men, and by the loud-mouthed threats to "run the Negroes out of camp"; followed by a bugled call to arms by the Fifteenth. . . . One thing is clear. Neither a camp nor the environs of a camp should be the scene of race conflict. White men and black men are on absolutely equal footing as United States sol-diers. They are entitled to equal protection against both insult and assault. A little more attention to this basic principle would have been advisable at Camp Mills. The War Department may well find out just why the basic principle was not considered.[62]

Fish recalled, "Trouble started all over again, only this could have been a hell of a lot worse. Rumors started to fly that the southern boys were actually going to attack us—and we didn't have any ammunition. Oh, it would have been horrendous."

There was no doubt in the minds of Fish's men that an armed attack had been planned. At the time, the 167th had guard duty around the camp, and many of its men were allowed to carry rifles and side arms.

Fish, fearing for his men, went to the New Yorkers of the old Fight-ing Sixty-ninth. "I knew several of their officers, as did a lot of our lead-ers," he stated. "So we went over and told them we were going to do everything we could to stop this, but they better give us some ammuni-tion so our men could defend themselves, if they had to. And they did."[63]

According to Ettinger, the fighting between the 167th and the Fif-teenth had gotten so bad that the black troops were ordered to turn in all their ammunition. The Alabamians, he reported, had been allowed to keep their own ammunition. "We thought that was unfair, so a num-ber of us slipped ammunition to our fellow New Yorkers. They never for-got that, and once, when I visited with a unit of the Fifteenth in France, some of the fellows thanked me for it."[64]

The next night, while the Fifteenth was bedded down, but ready, one of its buglers sounded the call to arms. Now armed, they were ready. Fish had gone as far as to tell them not to give an inch of ground. "It would mean casualties," he related years later, "but what else could we do, run?" He posted his men in a skirmish line inside the barracks and then went out, alone, pistol drawn, searching for officers of the 167th. In a few moments he came across several of them. It was dark enough so that they couldn't see his pistol. He held it behind his back, his thumb between the hammer and cylinder because he was afraid the weapon might accidentally go off. He explained to them the tense situation and warned that his men had orders to fight back. "A lot of people will get hurt," he said. An officer replied, "Don't y'all worry, Captain. We're try-ing to round up the ringleaders now. Y'all appreciate that our boys aren't used to seeing colored soldiers, especially as they're living next door. But we'll handle it."[65]

The fight had been averted. Maj. Edwin Dayton played down the incident to the press. "It was true that the Negro soldiers had been called to arms," he was quoted, "but that was merely in the routine of emergency training." According to one newspaper account, the Fifteenth's southern neighbors had asserted that they were only "kidding."[66]

"But that's the way it was," Fish said. "I guess the government started to realize the best thing to do was just send us abroad."[67]

But if Fish, or any of the men of the Fifteenth had thought that their troubles with Alabama soldiers were over, they were dead wrong.

"Landed at Brest, Right Side Up!"

For almost two weeks the men of the Fifteenth had been "locked in" in their armories or camps, awaiting orders to sail away. The time when they were to depart for France was hushed up. The War Department feared German spies and believed they were lurking everywhere. Troopships left from the Hoboken docks in the dead of night. No lights. No fanfare. No families or friends to see the soldiers off. One day they were at an armory or camp, and the next they were on the high seas. New York's black troops were holed up in three separate places. Maj. Lorillard Spencer's First Battalion, which also included the regimental band, found itself inside an armory at Park Avenue and Ninety-fourth Street. Maj. Monson Morris's Second Battalion was encamped at Van Cortlandt Park in the Bronx, freezing in tents. And Maj. Edwin Dayton's Third Battalion cooled its heels at Franklin Avenue and 166th Street.

Every morning a bugle sounded, and each time the men thought it was the call for departure. The waiting had them all on edge. Capt. Arthur Little recalled, "For two weeks we worked under high pressure, first locating and then drawing complete equipment for overseas service." To him, the inoculations and amount of paper work were "staggering."[1]

One of the few times some of the men escaped their confinement was on 8 November when the band gave an open-air concert at Central Park.

Even though, as drum major, Noble Sissle was part of the concert, he found living inside the armory nerve-racking. The daily bugle calls drove him nuts. When would the final blare ring out, ordering them to Europe? He remembered the lament of one soldier: "What kind of army is this here? I got to leave that brown-skinned gal of mine without a last good-bye." Then a retort from another soldier: "Sing them blues, brother."

On Sunday morning, 11 November, the "bugle sounded the call for assembly and though it had been blasted out for several mornings, yet," thought Sissle, "it seemed on this particular morning that there was a different ring to it."

When he heard the bugle, "a cold chill ran up my back and a sinking feeling came over me."

It was time to depart.

Sissle led the Fifteenth Infantry and its band out of the armory and down Ninety-second Street to the East River. There, the regiment climbed aboard an excursion steamer, the *Grand Republic,* for a quick trip around the tip of Manhattan and over to Hoboken. The march went almost unnoticed by New York's citizens. "Sudden and secret were our movements," observed Sissle, "that there was hardly anyone but passersby who saw us off."[2] Those few people already out on the street stood by and watched the soldiers parade by, their Springfield rifles at shoulder arms. Police lines held the onlookers at bay, as if that were necessary. It was the music that had drawn their attention. In the early morning, those lucky enough saw the regiment thump past with Sissle swinging a long, brass-knobbed hickory baton adorned with a blue cord in cadence with the jazz sound of Colonel William Hayward's favorite tune, "Army Blues."

Once aboard the *Grand Republic,* Little noted how the regiment simply "steamed quietly down the river, around the Battery and up the Hudson River to Hoboken, and the Hamburg-American piers."[3]

On the New Jersey side of the Hudson, the men transferred over to a dull, gray-painted troopship, the *Pocahontas.* As he boarded, Capt. Hamilton Fish was glad he had written to his father, telling him "not to worry—the crossing is perfectly safe and we will not go to the firing line before March. I hope we will not be stuck in the line of communications but after four-months training sent with the rest to the front. I honestly believe that I have the best company in the regt and that they will follow me anywheres."[4]

Lt. Lewis Shaw scribbled a note to his mother and mailed it before striding up the gangplank. "Dear Mumsie: This letter will be . . . delivered when the War Dept hears of our safe arrival on the other side. Keep busy and well for we have lots of good times coming."[5]

Originally named the *Princess Irene,* the *Pocahontas,* a German-built vessel seized by the United States in April 1914, had seen better days. If ever a boat had earned the epithet "tub," it was certainly this one. Yet no one questioned her seaworthiness. Built in 1900 at Stettin, Germany, to transport passengers and freight between New York and the ports of Naples and Genoa, she was 564 feet long with a 60-foot beam and a depth of 34.7 feet. Her speed was sixteen knots. After she was seized, she was moored in Hoboken for almost three years. A report found that the ship had been neglected too long and was in a generally run-down condition. "Her bulkheads, tank tops and boilers were in very bad condition. The *Princes Irene* was dirty and corrosion had started in many parts of her." The report also pointed out that just before the United States impounded the ship, her German crew had destroyed as much of the machinery as it could. After being refitted, patched up and renamed the *Pocahontas,* she had made one shaky round-trip to France when troops from the Fifteenth boarded her for their voyage overseas.[6]

The officers and men were too excited to dwell on the condition of their ship. They were anxious to get under way.

Brig. Gen. David C. Shanks, commander of the Port of Embarkation, was also anxious for the ship to set sail. On board were thousands of turkeys he had entrusted to Colonel Hayward. Shanks wanted those turkeys delivered to the American troops in time for Thanksgiving. Another precious cargo being stowed in Hayward's cabin, or so the colonel thought, were about three thousand "choice cigars," a gift of the Union League Club. As it turned out, the container held tent pegs, not cigars. The error was not discovered until long after the Fifteenth had reached France.

As evening closed in around the pier, all lights were extinguished. The sight was eerie, as bodies moved in the darkness and the ship moaned in her moorings, and across the river the pale orange and white lights of the big city reflected off the cold, November surface of the Hudson. The autumn weather was surprisingly calm and gentle. Hayward and his staff stood on the deck as squat tugboats nosed the *Pocahontas* out into the shipping lanes of New York Harbor. They watched as their gray troopship passed below Manhattan, Hayward's adopted home, where he had already made quite a reputation for himself in politics.

At about midnight the *Pocohontas* cruised through the Narrows into the Lower Bay. There a convoy of ships waited, guarded by three "speedy destroyers." The jubilant colonel felt history was being made. He clapped Captain Little on the shoulder. "Well, you old pirate and buccaneer," he beamed, "we're on the way! Isn't it wonderful!"

Hayward and Little felt smug, too. "That night, as we sailed for the battle fields of France, and realized that the Twenty-seventh Division was in winter quarters in Spartanburg," Little wrote, "we chuckled, and I must confess that, in a good-natured, friendly spirit, we even gloated a little."[7]

There was no gloating for Sergeant Sissle. He had been in a funk all day, since the morning bugle had roused him out of his bunk. Lt. James Europe had teased him about getting the regiment "kicked to France," and he failed to find the humor in that remark. After all, it was his hind side that had felt the angry boot of the racist hotel owner and his pride that felt the "whole sting of humiliation." Over the throbbing engines of the *Pocahontas* he thought of the African-American New Yorkers all around him, who had volunteered to fight a war for democracy even though in their own country they were kicked about like any dog and not allowed to fight back. Still, he took pride in the fact that the Fifteenth was the first black fighting unit to sail for Europe. "Under the cover of night," he later recorded, "we stole down the Hudson and out of the harbor and joined our convoy and were off to France."[8]

Capt. C. H. Ranulf Compton of C Company, a four-year veteran of the Second New York National Guard Regiment with service on the Mexican border, found himself surprisingly calm. A Harvard man, father of three children, and resident of Saratoga Springs who had transferred from the Second to the Fifteenth on 18 February 1917, Compton was, at that exact moment, seeing his life as a thrilling novel and, although he was thirty-eight, felt he was just beginning to live it. Standing on deck, he was neither excited nor sad as he "watched Manhattan—that citadel of light—grow smaller, smaller." He felt that perhaps it was the business-like manner in which the ship pulled away from its moorings and cut through the Narrows between Staten Island and Brooklyn that had put a damper on his spirit. He spotted a small boat rocking close by, and a voice cried out in the dark, "Who are you? A foreign or American ship?" And the voice laughed, and the boat bobbed away. Compton smiled at the joke and later that night wrote in his diary, "Family, friends—all left behind as I begin the 1st Chap. of the great adventure."[9]

For most of the soldiers this was the first time they had ever been on the high seas. The only connection to the ocean was that their grandparents or great-grandparents had been brought to America in slave ships. Thus, for the diminutive Henry Johnson and his Albany comrades, the first sight of the dark Atlantic had to have left a deep impression on their minds. The artistic eye of Goshen's Horace Pippin likely filed away for use at a later time the panoramic view of ships at night, the regiment off on an adventure of a lifetime.

Spottswood Poles, now a wagoner in the Supply Company, might have wondered if he'd ever make the trip back across the Atlantic to play baseball once more with his talented teammates on the New York Lincoln Giants. Leaning on the railing, the Fowler brothers, all seven of them, perhaps wondered if they'd all make it back to Katherine, their mother, now waiting for them to return to Glen Cove. Was Pvt. Christopher Wineglass of H Company lonesome for his mother, Susan, most likely asleep in their apartment at 1719 Fulton Street, Brooklyn? Or did Cpl. William Van Dunk of M Company, part Ramapo Indian from Hillburn, New York, have last thoughts of his mother, also Susan? As the *Pocahontas* slipped past the shadowy shore of Staten Island were Pvts. Henry and Tim Quarles straining to see any lights from tiny Tompkinsville, their hometown? Was Miss Chippendale, the girlfriend of Pvt. Douglas Howe of A Company, astir in her apartment at 319 East 121st Street? And was Sgt. Henry Matthews of C Company feeling sad for leaving his wife Nettie behind at their place at 227 West 143rd Street?

Also on deck was Pvt. Henry Plummer Cheatham, a splendid raconteur who always sprinkled his stories with wit and wisdom. The ocean was not new to him. As an ex-sergeant major of the Twenty-fourth Infantry, the thirty-five-year-old "Plum" had spent several years stationed on the Philippine island of Corregidor. He had crossed the Pacific several times. His experience as a noncommissioned officer and the fact that he had a college education and could argue with a barrister's skill would move him up through the ranks. But that extra step of wresting a commission from a white man's army would prove almost impossible until his friend Lieutenant Europe got in touch with Rodman Wanamaker and his own, well-connected father, a former congressman from North Carolina, intervened on his behalf. At the moment, however, Plum's thoughts were probably on his wife and children left behind at 392 Canal Street.

For Sgt. Valdo Shita, the many-scarred Zulu warrior, the ocean was old stuff. He had fought in South Africa and in France, and he had been shot, stabbed, and gassed. To him, the wide Atlantic was one more obstacle on the way back to the killing fields of the western front.

The *Pocahontas* plowed eastward through calm seas, doggedly keeping up with the convoy. Then, more than one hundred miles out, its piston rods snapped. The engines sputtered. The tired troopship slowed. But the convoy kept steaming onward in the night, the hulking shapes of its other ships fading away against the flat horizon. There was nothing for the crew of the *Pocahontas* to do, but swing their broken vessel around and return to New York harbor.

"So we had turned about," Little lamented, "to limp home on one screw."[10]

Twenty-four hours after the men of the Fifteenth had embarked for France, they were back home. Their war had to wait. Now, depressed, discouraged, and downright angry, they trooped off the *Pocahontas,* to be sent to Camp Merritt in New Jersey to await new orders. Their stay at the camp, where once again they were billeted near southern soldiers, was a sour experience for all.

Sgt. Henry Matthews recollected how, when they marched into Camp Merritt, hastily erected signs informed the "colored" soldiers to stay on their side of the streets. The Fifteenth New York ripped up the signs and carried them through the camp. "This action on the part of the regiment must have thrown the fear of God in the heart of the Southern white soldiers," Matthews believed, "and there was no open warfare. Nevertheless, we traveled over the entire Camp as we pleased but since such signs had been put up we decided that we were going to keep the Georgia and Alabama white soldiers off our side of the streets and when any of the boys were met in the street, naturally they would be treated a little rough."[11]

Captain Compton noted in his diary the arrival of a labor battalion from Arkansas. The white laborers resented the black soldiers. "Disturbance in 2nd Bat, 15th due to term of 'nigger' used by off. From Labor Bn. Extra guards established + whole regiment on extra guard with an officer in every street until quiet."[12]

Their pledge to their commander not to fight back kept them in check. "Had it not been for the honor, respect and high esteem held by every member towards our leader, Colonel Hayward, no doubt the boys would have set up a No-Man's Land right there in Camp Merritt," stated Matthews.[13]

When the soldiers were not fending off insults from the Georgians, Alabamians, and Arkansans, some of them snuck away, going home for a visit. The incidences of AWOL ran high. One enterprising private from Pittsburgh rode a series of trains all the way to western Pennsylvania without paying a dime. He would hop a train and ride it until thrown off at the next station. He kept this up until he got home. A soldier was sent to bring him back, at regimental expense.

Defending these men, Little said that they had "no intention of deserting. They just wanted to see their families."[14]

If Sergeant Shita had a family, it was thousands of miles away in Africa. He amused himself with gambling and had picked up extra change. Pvt. Joseph Fagan of I Company, who lived at 12 West 137th Street, wound up owing the Zulu warrior two dollars. Sitting on his cot on a Sunday afternoon, almost two weeks after the regiment had been holed up at Camp Merritt, Shita demanded to know when Fagan would pay off his debt. The private's answer did not sit well with the sergeant. He grabbed his Springfield rifle and shot Fagan dead while the unlucky Harlem resident sat on his own cot.

Two days before the homicide of Private Fagan over a two-dollar IOU and Shita's arrest, the War Department, on 23 November, ordered the creation of the Ninety-third United States Infantry Division, a provisional organization of "colored" troops from National Guard units in New York, Connecticut, Massachusetts, Illinois, Ohio, Maryland, Tennessee, and the District of Columbia. Ironically, with so many states and the nation's capital, the makeup of the new division was close to that of the Forty-second, the Rainbow Division. But it would get no such colorful sobriquet.

On paper, and that's as far as it ever got, this new combat division would eventually have a strength of nearly 1,000 officers and 27,114 men, with 260 machine guns and 16,193 rifles, backed by twenty-four 155-mm howitzers, forty-eight 75-mm guns, and twelve six-inch trench mortars.

The new division, to be commanded by Brig. Gen. Roy Hoffman, comprised two infantry brigades. The Fifteenth New York and the Eighth Illinois were placed in the 185th Brigade, and in the coming months received a change of numerical designation. The Fifteenth New York would become the 369th Infantry, but would not know about that change until after it had moved into the front line. The Eighth Illinois would be the 370th Infantry. The 186th Brigade would be made up of two new regiments, the 371st, to be formed at Camp Jackson in South Carolina from draftees, and the 372nd, made up of National Guardsmen from Connecticut, Massachusetts, Maryland, Ohio, Tennessee, and the District of Columbia.

Selected as commanders of the two new brigades were, for the 185th, Brig. Gen. Albert H. Blanding, and, for the 186th, Brig. Gen. George H.

Harries. Blanding was from Iowa. Before the war he led the Second
Florida Regiment and was instrumental in organizing the Thirty-first
Infantry Division. He was forty-two years old.

At the time, none of this mattered to Colonel Hayward and his staff.
Generals Hoffman and Blanding could go ahead and organize and train
their division and brigade. And while they were doing so, one of their
regiments would already be on the western front. Thus early in December, the Fifteenth marched out of Camp Merritt, bound for Hoboken and
another try for France aboard the mended *Pocahontas*.

As the regiment bid Camp Merritt a bitter good-bye, Captain Compton commented in his diary about the streak of bad luck that had hit
the Fifteenth: "Now perhaps the jinx is broken."[15]

This time the battered troopship had other soldiers assigned to it—40
officers and 337 enlisted men. Quarters were cramped, and officers were
jammed three and four to a cabin. Shaw sent off a letter to his mother.
"It seems like home to be back in the same stateroom again. And we are
much pleased with the prospect of being on our way soon." He closed by
telling her to be brave, "as I know you will and the time will pass quickly.
Your affectionate son, Lewis."[16] He mailed the letter on Monday, 3
December, and then settled down for the trip across the ocean.

The troopships anchored near the *Pocahontas* were abustle with
activity as yet another convoy was being prepared for the long voyage.
When it was time to cast off, these ships were towed from their slips.
All but the *Pocahontas*. A fire had been reported below in the coal-filled
port bunkers. The blaze was bad enough so that all the coal had to
taken off to allow the bunkers to cool. Sergeant Matthews reported that
among the men the talk had been of a plot to sabotage the ship. "It was
claimed that there were some time bombs found in the coal bunkers,
and also spies on board, consequently our ship returned to its moorings
in Hoboken."[17]

The bunkers were repainted before a new coal supply was loaded on.
The job took ten days. The men never left the troopship but stayed in
their tight quarters, wondering if they would ever get to France. Their
families were unaware that they had not left New York.

Compton wrote in his diary: "Every body is grumbling over the delay.
We are absolutely tied up on board + no one may go ashore or communi-
cate off the boat. I hope we make France in time to eat Xmas dinner +
be 'over there' the 1st year of the war."[18]

Brigadier General Shanks, in charge of the Port of Embarkation,
wired Hayward. "Goodness gracious, Colonel, are you ever going to get
those coons and turkeys to France?"[19]

On the eighth day of their confinement, 11 December, unknown to the Fifteenth New York and even unknown to the president of the United States, on a raw, overcast morning just outside of San Antonio, Texas, thirteen black soldiers of the Twenty-fourth United States Infantry were hung for their part in the Houston mutiny. The execution took place in utmost secrecy. Thirteen wooden gallows had been built in a secluded edge of Camp Travis in a grove of mesquite trees on the banks of a creek. Lined in a grim row out of sight of the gallows were thirteen wooden coffins. Next to each coffin a shallow grave had been dug. Bonfires were lit, their spectral light playing off the gallows. As a thin streak of sunlight spread across the eastern sky, an army truck drove up to the scaffolding. Thirteen soldiers, handcuffed and with their ankles shackled, were lifted from the truck and set on thirteen folding chairs. As the hangman's knots were set over the heads of the condemned soldiers, they stood at attention. As if on cue, they started to sing low and mournfully. "I'm coming home, I'm coming home." At seven-seventeen, the trapdoors swung open and the thirteen American soldiers dropped to their death, their necks broken the moment their bodies violently snapped at the end of each rope.[20]

The day after the execution, the Fifteenth was once again ready to set sail for France. Shaw sent another missive to his mother. "This is my third sealed letter to be mailed by the War Dept. This delay so near to home is tedious, but we will be off soon now. I am in best health and comfortably fixed. All the love in this world to you, sweetheart, you are the finest and bravest woman I know. Your loving son, Lewis."[21]

At midafternoon on the 12th, the *Pocahontas* left its slip in Hoboken and eased out into the Lower Bay off Sandy Hook. The ship stayed there throughout the night and the next day, as other ships collected around her.

Compton noted, "There is an air of expectancy on every face." He watched a sailor dance on deck, smiling and blowing his whistle. Officers talked earnestly, yet he felt that everyone still feared for the ship.[22] The men on deck now huddled against the December cold, their collars turned up, knitted helmets, a gift of the American Red Cross, under their campaign hats, pulled low over their frozen ears.

"That night was such a one as a writer of fantastic sea tales would describe in choosing an appropriate setting for running a blockade," Little thought. "Pitch dark, and snowing, with a gale of wind, and very cold."[23] Sissle recollected that when darkness fell, in came a blizzard, "swept by a gale that must have been blowing 85 miles an hour, accompanied by a blinding snow storm."[24] Compton noted the deep blackness of the night and the "howling veil of snow."[25] Cpt. Napoleon Marshall, the regiment's judge advocate, swore that while the troopship picked its way through the Narrows in dense fog, the temperature was thirteen degrees below zero.

Ships were everywhere, some of them so close that Little figured that from where he stood, he could actually lob a baseball onto their decks. The *Pocahontas* bucked in the crashing waves. On deck, small groups of soldiers sang tunes of love and longing. The storm intensified. The snow turned wet and heavy. In New Jersey, telephone wires "broke and fell in such numbers that . . . communication was badly interrupted," reported the *Times*. The Long Branch weather station south of Sandy Hook clocked winds at seventy-five miles an hour. "The wind had produced a raging ocean all along the coast," according to the account in the *Times*. "The danger to shipping was great because of the suddenness of the storm."[26]

On the deck of the *Pocahontas,* officers and men had their eyes riveted on a British oil tanker off the port bow, bobbing perilously close to them in the raging sea. "Not a light to be seen," Little wrote, recalling how the tanker loomed in front of them, "just a dark mountain standing out as an inky spot on a gray dark screen."[27] Sissle was sure he had seen no officers or crew aboard the tanker and believed they were all below deck, asleep.[28] The tanker's anchor line had become entangled with a line from the *Pocahontas.* Snow whipped against the faces of the watchful men, their hearts pounding. Snow and ice crusted the deck of their ship. The ensnarled tanker rose and fell with the huge waves, pitching closer and closer to their troopship.

One of the officers near Hayward wisecracked. "If we don't get rammed tonight, it'll be because we're doomed to be torpedoed, later in the week."[29]

As the night wore on, it appeared that the tanker might ride out the storm without ramming the *Pocahontas.* Most of the officers turned in. Standing on the freezing deck with the wind and snow biting into their faces was folly. Besides, there was nothing they could do.

At around three in the morning the oil tanker lost its battle with the storm. It crashed into the side of the *Pocahontas.* Because of the high seas and the fact that it was chained to the *Pocahontas,* it kept ramming and ramming the troopship. Each time it struck, the *Pocahontas* quivered.

Compton, bunking in with Lts. Robert Ferguson and Edwin R. D. Fox, was awakened by 1st Lt. Charles F. Frothingham Jr. He broke the news; their ship had collided with another. None of the half-awake officers believed him. Fox leaped to the porthole. "My God!" he blurted. "It's right along our wall! A tanker!" Compton and his fellow officers swore. "It was cold enough in the stateroom without the chilling news," he added to his diary. He threw on his great overcoat, grabbed a life preserver, and went up on deck. "It was blowing like one could imagine it was impossible in real life to blow." The tanker looked "black and menacing" to him. A strong light on the forward deck "made everything look distorted and unnatural + it looked as if 'abandon ship' might sound any minute."[30]

The moment the tanker first rammed the *Pocahontas,* Sissle bolted from his bunk. "These 'caresses' made a terrific noise, not unlike that of an exploding, ripping sub-marine torpedo," he remembered.

The entire regiment sprang from its sleeping quarters and, half-clad, raced upstairs to the deck. Many of the soldiers were barefoot. Most of them had grabbed their lifejackets. "I never knew that lifejackets could be worn in so many different ways," Sissle remarked.[31] In some instances, four and five soldiers fought over one lifejacket. A distress signal screamed in the dark, and searchlights from other vessels played against the *Pocahontas* and her unwanted companion—two ships lashed together in a watery dance of death. Compton described how they "groaned and creaked like lost souls."[32]

The hero of the night was the ship's executive officer, a lieutenant commander named Green. He was barely five feet tall, according to Sissle. He had slightly bowed legs, kept his cap far back on his head, sucked on a pipe, and had a "fife-like voice." Wearing rubber boats and a long slicker, Green surveyed the situation and ordered some men on to the other vessel to try and untangle the lines that held the boats together. He then placed bumpers between the ships to stop any more damage. He next tossed a rope ladder over the side of the *Pocahontas,* and scrambled down like "monkey," his slicker a cape in the wind.

"Everyone breathlessly watched the rail for him to reappear," Sissle wrote. "From our position we could not see . . . where he was, but we could see that every time the waves dashed against our boat they must have completely covered him." Green reached the gaping hole and decided it was not a threat. He scrambled back up and, to the cheers of sailors and soldiers alike, gave everyone the good news.[33]

It took another three hours, until 7 A.M., before Green and his crew got the two ships free from each other. The British tanker had ripped away three or four metal plates on the starboard side of the *Pocahontas.* Several lifeboats were also crushed. Captain Marshall remembered how the tanker "remained wedged all night in a six foot hole which it gashed in our starboard bow."[34] At least the damage was well above the waterline. Although there was little danger of the troopship sinking, the mishap threatened to pull the *Pocahontas* out of another convoy. Unless it had been on a torpedoed troopship, no other regiment suffered a harder time getting overseas than the Fifteenth. Bent piston rods, fire in a coal bunker, and now rammed by an oil tanker—three separate incidents. What more could happen?

First of all, the side of the ship had to be patched in a hurry because the convoy was not about to wait for the *Pocahontas* to return to Hoboken for repairs. Second, Hayward had to do some fast talking to convince the commander of the convoy to let the work be done while en route. The commander agreed, but only if repairs were completed by dusk. He did not want to have to worry about a leaky ship halfway across the Atlantic when his mind was on prowling German U-boats. Compounding the problem, there were no destroyers on hand to escort the convoy across the ocean to the mouth of the English Channel. The convoy had to go it alone, a decision that irked Fish. Later he wrote to Franklin Roosevelt. "It was a great surprise to all of us to find out that our convoy was not protected by destroyers until two miles from the French coast," Fish reprimanded the assistant secretary of the Navy. "It now appears that our destroyers are protecting English grain ships to the detriment of the safety of American lives and ships. . . . I have no desire to criticize anyone and only hope to remedy the condition before it results in a disaster, especially as regards transports." He also criticized the lack of space onboard, with no room to exercise and the "closeness of the quarters becomes worst [*sic*] every day spent on board ship."[35]

As the storm subsided, repairs went frantically ahead. Both the ship's commander and Green felt they ought to turn back, yet they allowed the work to be done even as the *Pocahontas* rocked in seas that were now less violent but still menacing. The work crew consisted of navy men and mechanics from the Fifteenth—"a beautiful picture of industrial cooperation," Little called it. "We had in our regiment about every kind of laborer, skilled and unskilled, known to building, mechanical, and engineering industries." The regiment also had on board "complete and absolutely up-to-date machine shop equipment, including drills which could make holes in the great steel plates of the ship structure, as prettily as a dairyman can cut through a hard form of butter."[36]

The cooperative work force toiled in the cold Atlantic, hung over the side of the troopship in slings. With bare hands in the numbing cold, they patched up the hole. They took frequent breaks to keep warm, to thaw out their numb, stiff fingers. Marshall wrote that after patching up the hole, "We took our chances rather than turn back again."[37]

By 6:30 the repairs had been completed. The Fifteenth rejoiced the moment they felt the old engine rumble to life and the *Pocahontas* set its course for France.

Seven troopships made up the convoy, escorted, according to Sissle, by a "big Man of War" that was "leading our winding course."[38]

"Many of the boys rolled in agony from seasickness," Arthur Davis had been told by his younger brother, Hannibal. "Many had not been on the water wagon so long. I have been informed that the answer to 'Fall Out' by a noncom was simply, 'Can't make, it sir. I'm dying.' The comforting reply to that, 'Die and prove it. Fall out!'"[39]

Even Europe suffered from the rolling, pitching troopship. In one episode, while the navy gunners were holding target practice, he staggered up on deck wearing two lifejackets. He moaned to Little that when he got to France, he was going to stay there for the rest of his life in the land of his name.

Compton was not only seasick, he had been fighting a horrible sore throat that had inflicted him ever since the night of the blizzard. His bones ached. He rolled in agony on his bunk while outside his stateroom men vomited. "Hold your head over the railing," he heard one soldier say, followed by derisive laughter. And then another soldier said, "Look at this bugler. Man, he's given up everything but the trip."[40]

Days aboard the *Pocahontas* proved tedious. Bunk making, breakfast, and exercise on deck. Lieutenant Shaw found himself sitting in class from one o'clock until dinner while "in the morning routine duties and studying took all our time."[41] Noon was dinner hour. "By four o'clock we had supper," Sissle recounted, "because all the kitchen mess tables and everything had to be done during daylight as not a light was allowed on the ship after dark, not even a cigarette could be smoked on deck."[42]

Fish complained to his father about the monotonous routine. "Breakfast at eight o'clock, inspection of quarters at 10:30, lunch at twelve, and examinations from 1:15 to 3:15, dinner at 3:30. In the morning we study our musketry bulletins for the afternoon exams which are always written and conducted just as in college under strict surveillance." He pointed out that on one day he took nine exams. "My marks are much higher than any of the Majors," the Harvard graduate bragged, "and my company average is the highest of the outfit." Because the days were cut short for fear of submarine attack, the nights were the worst, he wrote, "tedious and everlasting."[43]

Compton, still sick, found "no pleasure to grope along dark halls, into a dark wash room to find a wash bowl in the dark. The smell from the

engine room, the kitchen, the crowded hatches, the good and bad cigarettes on all sides kept a sick one in a constant state of squeamishness."[44]

The only lights were blue running lights to guide the soldiers and
crew at night. Just after sunset there was always another blue light, a
"hazy blue" that spread, otherworldly, across the ocean and sky when
the sun dipped beyond the horizon. That blue light wrapped the troopships in a ghostly luminescence. The deck was usually crowded at this
time with soldiers promenading around, some arm in arm. If they were
not walking, they leaned against the railing or by the lifeboats. Their
talk was in mysterious murmurs. During the day there was humor
among the men. As night descended, the humor vanished. They turned
serious and somber, and their talk was low, almost in whispers.

Musing on those melancholy moments, Sissle wrote, "I don't believe
that another regiment of men went into battle with such a sentiment as
was ours—we were the Baby National Guard Regiment of New York,
had no armory, no previous military experience. Just a bunch of much
made over boys under the leadership of a politician Colonel. Before any
of us were aware of it, we found ourselves in the middle of the Atlantic
Ocean, going to fight. Only half-equipped and no training in modern
warfare—not even a part of any division. Just a single little regiment.
Even the Colonel did not know what we were going to do after we got to
France."[45]

Sissle didn't know how right he was. The average American soldier
received six months of training at a major camp or cantonment while in
the United States and another two months overseas before he was sent
into the front line. He was trained as part of a division. The soldiers of
the Fifteenth had none of that—no division to train with and less than
two weeks at a cantonment. And no place to go because no one wanted
to deal with the orphaned black regiment.

In the meantime, far below decks, deep down beneath the water line,
groups of men sang spirituals as if they were at camp meetings. One
song struck Sissle. The soldier's voice, a natural lyric tenor, contained a
mellow "celestial sweetness" as he sang, "Steal away, steal away/Steal
away Jesus/Steal away, steal away home." Sissle wrote, "Before he had
gotten two bars with the song there would rise from that hatch a strain
of heavenly harmony that would sweep from one section of the hold to
another and in perfect harmony you could hear the resonant melody
floating up through the hatchways." As Sissle walked on, the singing
grew fainter until he came to another hatchway and heard a different
song or often a prayer, "Asking God to protect the mothers and loved ones
at home, to keep them safe from all harm. That, as the ship rode the

treacherous deep, God would guide us through to safety on the shores of France, that we might be able to give our service so that this world would be a better place to live in."

As night closed tightly around the ship, the officers gathered in the darkened dining room and on the stairs leading up to the main deck. On a landing just outside the dining room a small piano had been placed. Europe sat at the piano. Sissle stood by his side. Next to him, Fish led his own K Company quartette of white and black singers. Whenever a song was finished, silence settled over the homesick audience "choked up with emotion," until Europe began to play. "As lightly as the ship glided through the waves of the gulf stream, came the rippling harmonies that floated from those ivory keys as in the darkness the long slender fingers of Jim so deftly felt their way."[46]

The vivid image of Europe playing his music stayed with the men for years. Compton remembered Christmas Day, how lonesome it was for everyone and how the men sat by themselves or in small groups, and looked off into space—it was "a long look, 2,500 miles." That night he sat next to the piano while Europe played the mandolin and sang. It proved too much for the captain, and, thinking of his family back in Saratoga Springs, he walked alone on the deck and then turned in.[47]

On 27 December the coast of France was at last visible. The first thing the soldiers spotted was a lighthouse. To one officer it looked like a dark broomstick poking.out of the water. The sight of the lighthouse raised a cheer. "Land, Land!" the men yelled. And through a hazy morning sun they saw for the first time the cliffs guarding the port of Brest. Shaw immediately wrote to his mother. "Land certainly looked good to us when we first discovered it and although we have not debarked yet. France as viewed from the ship is certainly an attractive country. There is no snow on the ground."[48]

For most of the other soldiers it was their first sight of a foreign shore. Hunched against the late December cold, Pvt. Bill Bunn of F Company probably couldn't wait to tell the fellows back in his hometown of Babylon about the strange land with a medieval stone fortress atop the hills surrounding the port city. Cpl. Junius Grevious of A Company must have wondered what his sister Britannia in Yonkers might have thought of such an odd-looking place. Cpl. Nathaniel Young, also of A Company, who within a few months would be struck down by disease, may have written one of his last letters home to his young wife, Viola, waiting for him at 68 West 138th Street.

Although there was no snow on the ground, when the *Pocahontas* was escorted into the port of Brest by several French seaplanes, a snow-storm raged around the ship. It obscured the city that surrounded the natural harbor. The storm that greeted the Fifteenth was nearly as intense as the storm that had bid them good-bye almost three weeks earlier in New York.

In a note to Emmett Scott, Hayward reported, "December 27, landed at Brest. Right side up."[49] Fish repeated Hayward's comment about their snowy arrival in his autobiography: "We landed at Brest . . . right side up!"[50]

Peering over the railing, Shaw found the harbor "full of queer French sailing craft with picturesque salmon colored sails. The cliffs of each side of the entrance and the quaint houses and stone villas are all part of the charming picture. In the distance the town on the heights is clus-tered around a cathedral of exceptional beauty."[51]

Little's recollection differed from the others. "France," he wrote more than twenty years later, "was bedecked in Spring-like sunlight." He then described the "Chateaux and well appointed country places—even lawns . . . were passed by, in inspiriting panorama. The sea, or bay, was as calm as the proverbial mill pond."[52]

The Fifteenth was held on board until New Year's Day, 1918. Hay-ward sent a message to all his troops. It read simply: "New Year's greet-ing to every man of the 15th New York Infantry. Put this in your hat and read it three times a day. 1. Keep your eyes and ears open. 2. Keep your mouth shut."

When the soldiers were finally transported from the *Pocahontas* to shore, amid the heavy snows, wailing sirens of the ships in the harbor, and cheering French sailors, they made history. They were members of the first African-American regiment ever to land on French soil. Fish recalled how "bitterly cold" that historic moment was, "with snow and ice covering the ground."[53]

Goshen's Horace Pippin, a private first class in K Company, put down in his diary in his phonetic way, "I never wonted to see land so bad in my life as I did then, and I felt as if I would kiss the dirt, it were not long before we were not rocking like a dronken man for we now were on that teribell grond of sarro [sorrow] and it were New Year's Day of 1918."[54]

One of Hayward's first orders called for the members of the band to carry their instruments with them when they left the troopship. The sight of black soldiers lugging cornets and trombones, clarinets and saxophones, tubas and drums, and then assembling themselves on the quay brought townspeople out of their houses, even in the bitter weather. American troops landing at Brest was still a novelty—particularly black soldiers. In time, the city would become inured to them, and youngsters would march right along side the Americans, begging for cigarettes for "mon père" while singing in perfect English, "Hail, hail, the gang's all here, what the hell do we care!"

But what happened next, the townspeople would never forget, no matter that over the next six or seven months, hundreds of thousands of United States troops would march through their city on the way to the western front.

Hayward ordered Europe to lead his band in a concert on Brest's cobbled quay, crowded with French sailors, soldiers, and civilians as black American soldiers passed through the streets, up the long, winding hill leading out of the city toward the railyard. The first tune the tall lieutenant selected was the French national anthem, the "Marseillaise." Playing it in a jazzy way, Europe was surprised that none of the French people stood at attention when they heard their country's national song. It was as if they were not familiar with the music. Commented Sissle, "But suddenly, as the band had played eight or ten bars, there came over their faces an astonished look, quickly alert, snapping-into-it-attention, and salute by every French soldier and sailor present." Sissle believed the style of Europe's band playing the "Marseillaise" "thrilled them to a far greater extent than their own bands playing it. It was the unaccustomed interpretation of their anthem that caused the French soldiers and sailors to be so tardy in coming to the salute."

Although American jazz had been performed in Paris before the war, this brief concert on the quay at Brest probably marked the first time that the French working class had ever heard this original style of music.

Europe's band performed a few more martial airs in their jazzy way, then fell in behind the last of the regiment to disembark from the *Pocahontas* and followed it up the hill and out of the city. At the railyard, soldiers were piling into small troop trains with the soon-to-be-familiar words scrawled on the side, "Hommes 40, Chevaux 8" ("Men 40, Horses 8").

"So, with bag and baggage," grumbled Sissle, "we tumbled into the little wagons, as they call them, forty men per wagon, and, true to army custom, didn't know where we were going. The Frenchmen gibbering and shouting excitedly at one another finally closed the side doors of each car and the little old shrill whistle of the engine shrieked and we were on our way."[55]

11

"This Pick and Shovel Work"

If the enlisted men of the Fifteenth New York, cold and huddled together on straw-strewn floors, thought they were headed toward the front to battle Germans, they were sorely mistaken. The troop train was not plunging eastward through the night as they supposed. Instead, it rattled southwestward along the French coastline. Its destination was the mouth of the Loire River, where St. Nazaire, a harbor similar to Brest, squatted in military ugliness. The hundreds of thousands of doughboys who eventually passed through the port, officially known as Base Section Number 1, on their way to the western front, would dub it "Stench Nazaire." For more than two months this ever-burgeoning city, with all the noise and atmosphere of a boom town, would serve as home to the New York Rattlers, much to their dismay and anger. Here they would swap their Springfield rifles for picks and shovels and set about transforming St. Nazaire into a formidable port.

Yet when the Fifteenth first stepped off the troop train and marched through the winding streets of St. Nazaire, they had every reason to believe that they were still combat infantrymen. It was only a matter of time before they were battling the "Boche," or as they now called the Germans, the *Bush*.

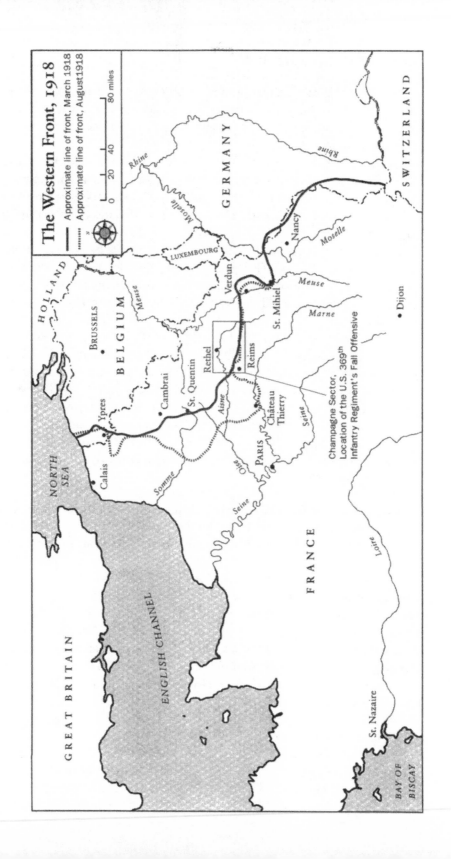

The Western Front, 1918

— Approximate line of front, March 1918
······· Approximate line of front, August 1918

0 20 40 80 miles

SWITZERLAND

GERMANY

Rhine

Rhine

Moselle

Nancy

Moselle

LUXEMBOURG

Verdun

Meuse

St. Mihiel

Marne

Dijon

HOLLAND

BRUSSELS

BELGIUM

Meuse

Rethel

Reims

Champagne Sector,
Location of the U.S. 369th
Infantry Regiment's Fall Offensive

Ypres

Cambrai

St. Quentin

Aisne

Château
Thierry

Seine

NORTH
SEA

Calais

Somme

Oise

Paris

Seine

FRANCE

Loire

GREAT BRITAIN

ENGLISH CHANNEL

St. Nazaire

BAY OF
BISCAY

Still, they had no idea where they were. When they were told, everyone wondered "in his mind," according to Noble Sissle, "what part of France is St Nazaire in? and everyone, for fear of showing some degree of cowardice was afraid to ask if we were near the front."[1]

All that crossed Sergeant Henry Matthews's mind was the biting cold. "After debarking," he grumbled with certain exaggeration, "we were then packed into third-class French passenger coaches, better known in America as 'cattle cars', with atmospheric conditions registering 30 degrees below zero."[2]

In a letter to a friend, Col. William Hayward remarked on the frostiness, too. "Cold, cold, cold. Commodore Peary and Doc Cook would have had chilblains on our sixteen-hour rail journey. But my 2,000 singing, laughing, black, brave children don't mind anything, and are anxious to get at the Huns."[3]

Arthur Little remembered the wee hours of the morning of 2 January when the men finally reached St. Nazaire and poured out of the train. "As we marched through the silent and dimly lighted streets, during the still cold of that night, we looked it over with keen interest. We had seen nothing of Brest. Our trains had been made up down by the water front. The small towns through which we had passed by railroad were mere villages. So, St. Nazaire was, to about ninety-nine percent of the members of our regiment, the first French city, or foreign city of any nation which they had ever seen."[4]

Capt. Ranulf Compton thought the city too deserted, a ghost town. As the newly arrived soldiers came through the city those few hours before dawn, he spotted one lonely, middle-aged woman in a "long black veil." She stepped out of a side street and paid no heed to the marching men.

The troops were greeted by the 316th Labor Battalion with steaming cups of coffee. "A godsend," Compton informed his diary.[5] Still grumbling about the cold, Matthews recalled how the water in their canteens froze and how, when they reached their barracks, they had drill for one hour before turning in. "This was done in order to keep the men from freezing. We were then marched to the parade ground and given hot coffee. And in the midst of it all, a more jolly, happier lot of true American citizens were never witnessed." When the men finally hit the barracks to get some sleep, they had a strong desire to "chloroform every bugler in camp, for we felt as though we would like to sleep for one whole week."[6]

Sissle felt uneasy as the regiment reached the outskirts of St. Nazaire. He had expected the Germans to sweep out of the hills and machine-gun them down. When they reached the city and began marching through its much too narrow and winding streets, he grew more nervous. All he and the band had for weapons were his baton and their instruments. "Although we had been complimented as being a wonderful band," he quipped, "none of us thought we were so great that we could lay down a barrage of jazz music, no matter how jazzy we would be able to play it, that would soothe the bullets and cause them to change their course from the well-directed guns of the enemy."[7]

It did not take the officers and men long to learn why they were at St. Nazaire. They weren't there as combat infantrymen, but rather as common laborers. There was work to be done to turn the city into a deepwater port so it could handle the fleets of ships that would carry the bulk of America's fighting men and materiel to the war in Europe.

The commander of the U.S. forces, Gen. John J. Pershing, chose St. Nazaire as a key port of entry, one of eight bases throughout Europe. When he first laid eyes on the place in the spring of 1917, he liked its two deepwater channels that led to the ocean. "There was a locked, double basin capable of taking ships drawing twenty-eight feet," he recalled in his memoirs. But he also saw the limitations of the harbor. It needed more berths. And the "shore arrangements for handling cargo were almost archaic and storage space was practically confined to the dock sheds. Railway cars in order to be spotted had to be shunted one at a time by means of a turn-table worked by hand. The rail connections with the main lines and the dock yard accommodations were entirely inadequate. Although the facilities were then above the average of French ports, it was evident that radical changes in the system of handling cargo would be necessary to obtain the maximum of efficiency that would eventually be required."[8]

To transform St. Nazaire into a wartime port meant that an army of engineers, mechanics, electricians, construction workers, stevedores, and skilled and unskilled laborers were needed. A quick and easy source were African Americans. Draft them into the army and ship them to France as common hired hands. Two problems would then be solved. First, Pershing would have a source of cheap labor. Second, he wouldn't have to worry about what to do with black soldiers, particularly when he might have to mix them in with white troops. It wasn't just that he feared racial tensions, he simply did not trust their fighting ability.

"It was well known that the time and attention that must be devoted to training colored troops in order to raise their level of efficiency to the average were considerably greater than for white regiments," he argued. "More responsibility rested upon officers of colored regiments owing to the lower capacity and lack of education of the personnel. In the new army, with hastily trained colored officers relatively below white officers in general ability and in previous preparation, the problem of attaining battle efficiency for colored troops was vastly more difficult."[9]

Use them as laborers, and he wouldn't have to worry about them. Muscle and blood, toil and sweat. Strong backs, weak minds. Stevedores, not soldiers. That's all they were good for.

And Base Section Number 1 at St. Nazaire was the spot for them.

As Capt. Hamilton Fish surmised, "They had no place to put the regiment. They weren't going to put us in a white division, not in 1917, anyway; so our troops were . . . sent into the SOS as laborers to lay railroad tracks. This naturally upset our men tremendously." The SOS referred to by Fish was a huge organization of noncombatants called Service of Supply. As Pershing described it, the SOS was responsible for the reception, transportation, storage, and distribution of everything needed by his vast army.

Using the vernacular of his men, Fish recalled how K Company carped when they first heard they'd be part of the SOS. "Ah thought we'se here to fight de Germans. Hell, we'se can do dis back home."[10]

A correspondent for the Brooklyn *Eagle* visited St. Nazaire in June, 1917, more than a half-year before the grudging arrival of the Rattlers. To the reporter, it was "the most American city I have yet found in France." He likened it to Pittsburgh. He described its "important foundry, several steel works, two large ship-building yards, repair shops and a number of industries besides. The city itself has no 'atmosphere' except smoke, and its horizon is lined by tall chimneys and giant cranes. The place is busy, grimy and prosperous." He added that it had "a self-made air. It is a big city in the making."[11]

Almost a year later, a few months after the New Yorkers had left their mark on St. Nazaire, it had turned into a throbbing naval hub. A French journalist, who had frequented the city in the "days of my youth," was astonished by its change. "I found it in a wild and continuous fever," he wrote. "I found its streets packed, its sidewalk jammed with people and altogether too narrow, its harbor panting with the breath of innumerable machines, its docks invaded by strange craft bristling with outlandish rigging, its roadstead crowded with a fleet constantly renewed—it was an unrecognizable town, I tell you."[12]

If it had been like a polluted Pittsburgh before the Americans took over in 1917, then St. Nazaire in the early months of 1918—and throughout the duration of the war—had to be a cesspool.

It was into this cesspool that the New Yorkers found themselves mired, and for how long no one knew. The crude buildings where they lived had earthen floors and, according to Fish, "Fuel is very scarce and the barracks are not even rain proof."[13]

"Here the regiment toiled for weeks," Colonel Hayward grumbled to the adjutant general of the Army, "building docks, erecting hospitals, laying railroad tracks and constructing a great dam. The men never saw their rifles except by candle light."[14]

Captain Little called it "important work to be done." However, like Hayward, he, too, complained. "This pick and shovel work was most destructive of the morale of men who had enlisted to fight. We put up with it, and the incidental indignities, for a long time."[15]

When built, the great dam would control the depth of the water in the harbor at St. Nazaire. Captain Compton jotted in his diary on 26 January, "At Montoir, laying steel, filling, grading, unloading sand, structural steel. Very wet. 250 miles of track, 125 buildings."[16]

In a letter home, Captain Fish wrote, "We are engaged at building a dam and constructing a railroad for American use and will probably stay here until relieved by some newcomers."[17]

Lt. Lewis Shaw told his mother, "Our regiment is making itself most useful now as a work regiment. . . . As we are still at a port our details do everything from stevedoring to railroad and general laboring work. I imagine we will continue this indefinitely, here or elsewhere."[18]

Sergeant Sissle quipped, "It was the policy of the army, quite against our thoughts in the matter, as most of the policies of the army were to the soldiers, to gradually accustom our untrained bodies for the ordeal of trench warfare. To do this they took advantage of a large engineering project, that of building a dam . . . to give our men their first baptism digging in the mud."[19]

Maj. Lorillard Spencer noticed how "amazed" the French were at the speed at which his First Battalion worked while laying miles of railroad tracks. Captain Marshall had charge of four hundred men. They were assigned "to construct the bed of the important railroad," he remembered, "which connected the American debarkation docks at St. Nazaire with the base storehouse of the American Army at Montrois, five kilometers distant."[20]

When the task had been finished, the French marveled at how safe the tracks turned out. "The troops sang all the time," Spencer said. "They had a chantey for track laying and directed much of their recreation to singing Southern melodies and popular songs. All were cheerful, but they were determined and were real soldiers."[21]

The work was backbreaking, and even in the raw, wet cold that ripped through clothing and chilled the men to the bone, they sweated and cursed and worked like slaves. It was soon evident that morale was much lower than the officers, and even Sissle, let on. There seemed to be no end in sight to the humiliation.

And worse. The Rattlers had to put up with Marines stationed nearby. At night certain leathernecks, according to several New Yorkers,[22] slipped past sentries and cold-bloodedly assaulted unwary African Americans. Although military records indicate that only a handful of men of the Fifteenth died while the regiment was stationed at St. Nazaire—all of disease—old veterans, who spoke with anonymity, swore that the Marines had, in fact, murdered a few of their comrades. In retaliation, a squad of daring Rattlers, calling themselves the "Vampire Patrol," exacted an eye for an eye. The Marines quickly stopped their nightly forays into New York turf.

The best way to lift the spirits of the Fifteenth was through music.

Although Lt. James Europe was a line officer and toiling up at the dam, his regimental band was always on hand to keep the men entertained. The bandmaster, Sgt. Francis Eugene Mikell, led the musicians. At first, Drum Major Sissle was unable to take part. Three days after landing in France, he had come down with the mumps. Because the disease, although not life threatening, was contagious, he was confined to the base hospital, along with hundreds of other soldiers similarly afflicted, including a stricken Lieutenant Shaw. The Puerto Ricans in the band, who had been ridiculed by Sissle when they first landed in New York, now ridiculed him for catching a childhood illness and not something more dramatic.

Sissle's replacement as drum major was most likely an ex-Buffalo soldier, Sgt. Gillard Thompson of Headquarters Company. Thompson, a native of Shelbyville, Tennessee, was not a musician and had never played an instrument of any kind. But he possessed a great ear, had a wonderful sense of rhythm, and might have been the handsomest man in the regiment. He had intense, dark eyes, high cheekbones, and a soft moustache. At thirty-two, he was tall—over six feet—and lean like an athlete, and had the bearing of a true soldier, learned from his years with F Troop of the Ninth Cavalry. Gil, as the men called him, rode with the Ninth from 1905 until 1908. He then spent three years with the Twenty-fourth Infantry and another three, until 1914, as a cavalryman stationed at the U.S. Military Academy. From West Point, he moved to New York City and married a pretty girl named Thelma. When he reenlisted, the Buffalo soldier had been out of the army exactly three years to

*This is a postwar
photo of Sgt. Gillard
Thompson, the former
Buffalo soldier who
replaced Noble Sissle
as drum major in the
regimental band when
Sissle became ill.*
GILLARD THOMPSON, JR.

the day. Because he made Harlem his home, he had joined the Fifteenth
New York on 29 March 1917. During his nearly ten years in the service,
Thompson picked up a special skill that came in handy. He could repair
firearms and had even made a living as a gunsmith. In later years he
served the regiment as its armorer.

At the time Thompson first took hold of the drum major's baton, the
morale of the regiment was "very low," according to Sissle, now imprisoned at the base hospital. It was up to the band, under Mikell's direction, to make the soldiers feel better.

"At daybreak every morning," Sissle wrote, "the entire regiment would
be awakened by the martial strains of our band as its members stumbled along the streets in semi-daylight, playing a good ragtime tune to
try to cheer the boys up before they departed for their day's drudgery. In
the evening, if weather conditions permitted, the band would meet the

returning boys from the road and march them back to camp. After supper they would play a concert out on the drill field. In this way, they played a very important part in getting the spirits up and keeping them from waning to the danger point."

In a few days Sissle himself was up and ready to resume his role as drum major. But ten days out of the hospital, he fell "easy prey for the epidemic of terrible Spanish Flu which had begun to sweep through our camp."[23]

Sissle was back in the hospital, stuck in a ward with other victims of the flu. The tragic epidemic that would kill more people than the Great War itself had already begun to claim its first victims among the soldiers of the Fifteenth as Sissle languished in bed, himself sicker than a dog.

Pfc. Horace Pippin wrote about the "rain and wind, it were often cold and some of the boys died there of sickness."[24]

New Jersey resident Dorsey Covington, a private in A Company, died first, on 6 January. Eight days later, Pvt. Howard Streadrick of D Company, died, leaving behind his mother Eunice, at 74 West 148th Street. On 11 February, Pvt. Eddie Robinson of K Company, perished, making Marie, back at 143 West 132nd Street, a young widow. Oscar Fleury went next, on 30 March. A private in H Company, he had lived at 61 Willoughby Street in Brooklyn. On 3 April, Cpl. William Kennedy and Pvt. Stanford Grant, both from Brooklyn and both members of G Company, died. Kennedy had lived at 272 Pulaski Street and Grant at 588 Warren Street. A week later, Richard Woods, another H Company private who resided at 703 North Pine Street in Manhattan, succumbed.

"One of my men [Eddie Robinson] died suddenly in the barracks a few days ago and I went to the funeral yesterday," mourned Fish. "We took the band along and there were two other soldiers buried at the same time. It was imposing as there were different firing squads and the people along the road all stopped and took off their hats, even the German prisoners, as the autos with the bodies went by."[25]

Robinson, Covington, Streadrick, and Woods were buried in France. The bodies of Fleury, Grant, and Kennedy were shipped back to New York. These seven soldiers were hardly the regiment's last victims of the flu.

Meanwhile, the cold weather continued to pester the Fifteenth, and more and more men reported in sick. Shaw called it "beastly."[26] Compton remarked in his diary on 15 January, "We sleep in heavy pajamas— wool caps, heavy stockings and full bedding. Rubber boots are much in vogue. It is cold, raw and rainy. Muck!"

On the fifteenth, the day he had complained about the weather, Compton scribbled down the fact that in the late afternoon the band played "The Star-Spangled Banner" for the first time on French soil. He described that all the men stood at rigid attention. "Our fingers + toes tingled with cold, but we were warmed + enthused by the thought that at last we were in France as part of the AEF and ready to take up our part in the great war. A big star so bright it came out before sunset, shone high up directly in front of the battalion, it seemed, + the old adage 'hitch your wagon to a star,' came into my mind."

To shield a small part of his face from the cold, he grew a "new moustache militaire." Then he came down with a sinus infection that left him "down and out."[27]

Like the awful weather, the manual labor continued unabated.

"We are kept so busy that the time flies and before we know it the summer will be back again," Fish informed Tante, an old family friend. "We know less about the war here than you do. . . . I hope now that I'm over here to get in the front lines before the finish, but I have no idea when that will be." He boasted again about how well K Company was doing, and pointed out that the men "have also developed an excellent quartet which is in demand at all functions, hospitals, YMCA dinners, generals, etc. The K Company Quartet is as notorious as the band. I wish you could hear them."[28]

At about the time Fish was touting his K Company Quartet, a well-respected theatrical producer showed up at St. Nazaire. With the arrival of Winthrop Ames and his companion, E. H. Southern, the regimental band was about to become famous all over France.

Ames, managing director of the influential New Theater in New York and one of the early luminaries of Broadway, and Southern, a prominent Shakespearean actor, were in Europe as representatives of the National War Work Council of the YMCA. They were in the midst of touring France, trying to figure out the best way for American soldiers to be entertained. Also, they were on the lookout for talented doughboys. According to one account of their tour, they were "appraising the talent within the army itself" to "determine just what sort of performance would be best fitted to take up the work of entertaining the troops."[29] They were trying to organize one of the first entertainment centers for soldiers, which would be at a rest station in Aix-les-Bains, a resort town at the foot of the French Alps.

In a talk aimed at recruiting members of America's Over-There Theatre League, made up mostly of actors and actresses, Ames said, "We of the theatre can personally help speed this victory, because our men will fight better if we keep them happy and contented in their exile and because in addition to entertainment we can bring the unspoken message that America is with them and behind them every day and every hour." And he told them that the one thing they should not bring to France is "highbrow" entertainment. "They want cheerfulness and gayety, and clean laughter, and good catchy music, and stirring renditions and little swift plays—oh, anything that's good of its kind, and well done, and made in America."[30]

While he and Southern were scouting doughboy talent, they discovered in St. Nazaire exactly the kind of entertainment they had in mind—and it was indeed made in America.

It was jazz music. They had heard about the Fifteenth Regiment Band from the commander of Base Section Number 1, Gen. Robert Walsh, an ex-cavalry officer who had ridden with the black Ninth Cavalry and knew Thompson. When Walsh mentioned the band to Ames, the theatrical duo had already scouted a "good many American military bands." Walsh said to him, "I don't know much about music myself. But they tell me it's a pretty fair band. Colonel Hayward will have it played for you. You can judge for yourselves."

Ames was skeptical. He later confessed that the bands he and Southern had listened to were just "cheerful adjuncts of camp life; but from any musical standpoint, their performances were mediocre."

As guests of Hayward one evening, they got their first taste of the band at a concert on the parade ground. They sat on wooden chairs on the edge of the muddy field—Ames, his wife, and Southern. Ames was startled at the band's size when it marched onto the parade ground. "No sooner had they began to play," he wrote, "than it become obvious that we were not listening to the ordinary army band at all, but to an organization of the very highest quality, trained and led by a conductor of genius." Ames asked Hayward the name of the conductor. When he was told he was again startled. "He was no less a musician than James Reese Europe—already famous in America, but whom we little expected to find a soldier in France."[31]

Sissle, although still in the hospital with the flu, rightly believed that "Up until the time that Mr. Southern and Mr. Ames came to St. Nazaire they had found very little material." But the ailing drum major was certain that "when they heard our band play, the quartette sing and saw some of the boys dance during the hour and half program that we were able to give them, they immediately said that we were the best entertainment unit that they had seen in France on their tour. It was so typically American that they were immediately going to get in touch with General Pershing, and have our band and entertainers sent to Aix-les-Bains for the opening of the rest center."[32]

Whether Ames and Southern had any influence on Pershing is open to conjecture, but special orders arrived, dated 10 February, directing the band, comprised then of two officers and fifty-six men, and under the command of Captain Little, to the rest station at Aix-les-Bains.

Little immediately had Lieutenant Europe reassigned to the band from the Machine Gun Company. While the officers got the fifty-six men ready to depart by train—a trip that would take four days—Pershing now seemed open to the idea that the Fifteenth was a combat unit and that although it had very little training, there might be a place for it serving with a French army.

Hayward had finally put the bug in Pershing's ear. Before the orders to send the band to Aix-les-Bains, the colonel had written a long letter to Pershing's chief of staff. He knew that not only were his men itching to fight, his officers were itching to get out of the regiment. None of them wanted to be laborers. Compton put in for a transfer to the new Tank Corps. He mentioned that fact emphatically in his diary in thick, bold ink. Fish was mulling over in his mind when it would be the right time for him to seek a transfer. As he told his father as early as 13 January, "I do not know our plans. At present my relations are pleasant with the C. O. and I am waiting developments before trying to get a transfer. The waiting game is best and I am in no hurry for a change."[33]

Hayward was antsy himself, and to Little he declared that "it was time for us to try to do something towards extricating ourselves from the dirty mess of pick-swinging and wheel barrow trundling that we were in. We had come to France as combat troops, and, apparently, we were in danger of becoming labor troops."[34]

The letter to Pershing's headquarters was long, detailing the entire history of the Fifteenth—from its beginning in the summer of 1916 to being the first National Guard regiment in the country to reach wartime strength, to its nearly disastrous stay at Camp Wadsworth and its harrowing voyage over on the shaky *Pocahontas,* to its present rotting to death as a common labor outfit.

As far as Little was concerned, the letter was too short, simply because Hayward had left out a salient fact: St. Nazaire was home to hundreds of prostitutes. In three authorized bawdy houses, there were 150 working women. Another 250 women trolled the streets. Venereal disease among the thousands of troops stationed there was common—

except, according to Little, among the men of the Fifteenth. It wasn't because they were chaste. Far from it. Little had been a champion of prophylactics for years and had been pushing for their use since August, in spite of the grumbling of both men and officers. "The Fifteenth, therefore," he wrote in his memoirs, "had been learning of the advantage of this important feature of the care of soldiers, for more than a third of a year before we landed in France. I had paid the penalty for being a pioneer and a crank, and I was proud of the record which had grown out of my own unpopularity." Little knew that the low rate of venereal disease among his black troops had to impress Pershing.

When Hayward added that point, Little advised him that as soon as the letter was forwarded to Pershing's headquarters, he should report there in person.

As Hayward got ready to visit Pershing, on Lincoln's birthday, 12 February, Little, Europe, and the rest of the Fifteenth Regiment band, the K Company Quartet, and a few other men from Headquarters Company boarded a train bound for a sixteen-day assignment at Aix-les-Bains.

Lieutenant Europe's fame was now about to spread far and wide across France. Along with that fame, almost every French citizen fortunate enough to live along the railroad line that stretched southeastward from St. Nazaire to the Alps would hear for the first time the irresistible syncopated beat of American jazz.

12

Ragtime in France

Aix-les-Bains, the village of the baths, has drawn people to its soothing warm waters since the days of the Romans. Built on the shores of Lake Bourget, with the snow-capped Alps looming to the east, it was, in the early winter of 1918, a whiz-bang of a resort.

Gen. John J. Pershing's Chief of Staff, Col. James G. Harbord, pointed out that Aix-les-Bains was chosen as the first organized "leave area" for soldiers of the AEF "because it was one of the noted play places of the world."[1]

Great hotels and casinos crowded its shoreline. For a hundred years or more the rich and famous had found the place much to their liking. Disguised as the Countess of Balmoral, Queen Victoria often swept in with an entourage of royal guests. She loved the countryside, its climate, and unbounded excitement so much that she wanted to buy a chateau on a hill that overlooked the village. Political exiles found refuge there, too; and celebrated writers such as Alexandre Dumas, George Sand, and Guy de Maupassant plotted their novels, short stories, and romantic trysts there. Perhaps the most notorious visitor of all was the much sought after Mistinguett, the "Queen of Moulin Rouge." She sang often at the theater in the resort's renowned Casino Hotel. Romantically linked to the black prizefighter Jack Johnson, among others, she once cracked, "A kiss can be a comma, a question mark or an exclamation point. That's basic spelling that every woman ought to know." Adding to her allure, Mistinguett insured her shapely legs for five hundred thousand francs.

When Joseph Odell, a special correspondent for *Outlook* magazine, got word that Aix-les-Bains had been chosen as the Army's first leave area, he raced to the mountains to see firsthand what was in store for the doughboys.

"The entire scheme seemed to me to be so reasonable and so necessary," he crooned. "In the first place, Aix is the Mecca in time of peace, of European royalties, big and little, and American millionaires. For situation it is a place beyond description." He then described the high mountains, Lake Bourget's turquoise water and the hotels that were "unsurpassed anywhere in Europe—vast and sumptuous palaces; the Casino (now the headquarters of the YMCA) has long been second only to Monte Carlo for gayety, brilliance and gambling."

Three-quarters of all the hotel accommodations in Aix-les-Bains and neighboring villages had been taken over by the AEF. The YMCA leased the entire Casino Hotel, including its famous theater and assembly hall, as well as its reading, writing, and billiard rooms. The Y also leased several other casinos, hotels, and theaters. For the doughboy, this full-scale takeover meant the daily cost for a room and meals ranged from $2.50 to $3.40. Plus, his government informed him that tipping was forbidden.

The *New York Times* called the place a "great leave centre of the American Army."[2] In the *Outlook,* Odell gushed, "Nothing is too good for the American soldier."[3] Although Aix-les-Bains wasn't Paris, which was then off-limits to the doughboys, it was a close second.

The first order granting soldiers leave was signed in January 1918. Aix-les-Bains officially opened for business on 16 February. In their own sumptuous rooms at the Casino Hotel, Gerry Reynolds, who was in charge of the YMCA's entertainment, Winthrop Ames, who had scouted a lot of the talent, and his companion E. H. Southern, paced in nervous anticipation. They awaited a special train now rumbling toward the resort. Packed with between three and five hundred dirty, tired, battle-hardened, red-blooded doughboys, the train was the first of many that every day would tote thousands of white soldiers to the restaurants, spas, music halls, and gambling dens of the fabled resort.

Reynolds, Ames, and Southern also awaited another train that four days earlier, on 12 February, had begun its four-hundred-mile trip to Aix-les-Bains from the coast at St. Nazaire. It was made up of one first-class coach car, two third-class coach cars, and a freight and baggage car. Stowed on board were eight tons of rations. Carrying the Fifteenth Regiment Band and the K Company Quartet, a paramount part of the YMCA's opening entertainment extravaganza at the Casino Hotel, the train chugged along the Loire River. Its route would take it past Nantes and Tours before it followed the Allier River southeast through Moulins, Bessay, and Varennes and then further east to the Rhone River at Lyons and finally beside the waters of Lake Bourget and into Aix-les-Bains.

Sharing the first-class car all to themselves were Captain Arthur Little and Lieutenant James Europe. The two second-class cars were jammed with more than fifty musicians and singers and a handful of regular soldiers. Wrapped in blankets and still hoping to shake off the flu, huddled Sergeants Noble Sissle and William Holliday. Before the war, Holliday had lived with his mother, Marie Bingham, at 137 West 138th Street, New York, New York. Now the sergeant from the Headquarters Company was as sick as Sissle. It was a wonder that either soldier had been permitted to accompany the band.

As usual, Europe had come to the rescue.

The morning of the train's scheduled departure, Sissle still moped about at the base hospital, a small, cramped building that, unlike the other structures the soldiers slept in, at least had a wooden floor. The sergeant was feeling sorry for himself. He was up and walking, but "far from well." The band was preparing to leave without him. There was a good chance that the tall, gallant-looking Gil Thompson might replace him permanently as drum major. "My morale," he recorded, "was very, very low."

Europe stopped by the base hospital. He knew how important the concert at the Aix-les-Bains Casino Hotel was to the band's reputation. He needed Sissle, especially his wonderful voice.

"Sissle," he said, "pull yourself together. You got to go on this trip with us."

According to the ailing drum major, a doctor warned Europe that it'd be a "dangerous thing to move this boy before he's entirely recovered."

Europe was ready for that argument. He reminded the doctor that the band was headed to a health spa with "natural mineral water." It was in the mountains, he said, where the altitude and climate were perfect for healing sick people. The treatment would be better there than here, he continued. Finally, he said that he could not go off and leave his drum major behind no matter the condition he was in because it was his, Europe's, fault that Sissle had enlisted in the army in the first place. The doctor said that the trip alone might kill Sissle. Europe shot back that if his drum major died, then he'd die with him. He assured the doctor that he'd take along extra blankets, baby him at every moment, and give him "every comfort and protection during the tour." The doctor gave in, and signed an order releasing Sissle to Europe's care.

So in the middle of winter, Sissle packed three sweaters, three overcoats, and four blankets, "bundled" himself up, and rode the hospital ambulance to the train. Europe put him in a compartment in the second-class car with a window. Sissle shared the compartment with Sergeant Holliday. As he described it, "He, too, was bundled up with me and our two old, fever-racked carcasses landed in the same compartment. There were never two patients more tenderly cared for by a bunch of buddies than we were."[4]

The special train had not gone far when, according to Little, it stopped for the night in Nantes, about twenty miles up the Loire River from St. Nazaire. (Sissle, on the other hand, recalled that the first stop was not Nantes, but rather Tours, one hundred miles further up river.) In the evening, in honor of Lincoln's birthday, a concert was scheduled at the city's Opera House. The villagers who did not have tickets to get inside gathered in the huge town square. Here Europe and his band warmed up before going inside for a more formal performance.

As Little reported, the crowd kept silent throughout the first number, a jazzy tune. Sissle was "naturally curious" to see how the French reacted when they first heard a "ragtime number." He felt that whatever "happened can be taken as a test of the success of our music in this country, where all is sadness and sorrow." When the band had finished, the crowd "made up for lost time," Little wrote, "by wild applause." After a few more numbers, Europe and the band entered the Opera House. Inside, what Europe saw must have reminded him of his great, ground-breaking concert at Carnegie Hall in 1912. There wasn't an empty seat. People who couldn't find a place to sit, stood. Everyone crammed into the Opera House was dressed in their finest evening clothes.

"I doubt," wrote Little, "if any first night or special performance at the Metropolitan Opera House in New York ever had, relatively, a more brilliant audience." Little had not attended the Carnegie Hall concert.

The fifty-plus member military orchestra and quartet, each musician and singer in his uniform, knew the importance of the concert. Europe opened with a French march—to the delight of the crowd. The K Company Quartet sang a few numbers. When the band finished John Philip Sousa's "The Stars and Stripes Forever," the Opera House, according to

Sissle, "was ringing with applause." Next, Sissle sang a few plantation melodies. "And then came the fireworks," he said. "The Memphis Blues."

As the band got ready to play its signature number, a tune written almost six years earlier by W. C. Handy and first played by Europe and later adapted by him as a fox trot for the dance team of Vernon and Irene Castle, each musician underwent a sudden transformation. It seemed as if they had forgotten where they were, that perhaps in their mind's eyes they were back in some jazzy Harlem nightclub and not in front of a bunch of non-English-speaking foreigners. The audience had to sense it. On stage, tensed feet shifted. Saliva was blown from brass instruments. The drummers, including the so-called Wright brothers, Herbert and Stephen, tightened their drumheads. Even Europe twitched his broad shoulders. Sissle thought the bandleader "wanted to be sure that his tight-fitting military coat would stand the strain." Then, said the drum major, the "baton came down with a swoop that brought forth a soul-rousing crash." Sissle continued, "Cornet and clarinet players began to manipulate notes in that typical rhythm (that rhythm which no artist has ever been able to put down on paper); as the drummers struck their stride, their shoulders began shaking in time to their syncopated raps." The huge crowd swayed, their feet beat time and Europe himself, according to Sissle, swayed, too, in "willowy motions." He cued the trombone players to let loose a "Jazz spasm" and, as Sissle described it, "they drew their slides out to the extremity and jerked them back with that characteristic crack."

Watching all this—the band, his friend Jim Europe, rocking and bobbing, and the whole audience as if it had an "Eagle Rocking Fit," where muscles went slack and a kind of euphoria swept over body and soul—Sissle thought to himself, "Colonel Hayward has brought his band over here and started ragtime in France; ain't this an awful thing to visit upon a nation with so many burdens?" But when the "Memphis Blues" was over, and the audience roared its approval, he thought again, "This is just what France needs."

Little was also struck by the band's performance. "The spirit of emotional enthusiasm had got into the blood of our men," he wrote, "and they played as I had never heard them play before."[5]

The next day the train rolled on toward Aix-les-Bains. But at almost every large town, it stopped, and the band climbed down with its instruments, marched to the village square, and played for fifteen minutes to a half-hour. When troop trains rattled by, carrying allied soldiers to and

Lieutenant Europe (left) and his 15th Regiment band in France. U.S. ARMY
SIGNAL CORPS

from the front, heads popped out of windows to catch the music, if for
only a moment or two. "Even German prisoners forgot they were prisoners, dropped their work to listen, and pat their feet to the stirring American tunes," Sissle recalled.[6]

In Tours, according to Little's account of the trip, the men got off the
train for a hot meal. While they were at mess, he dropped in at the
provost marshal's office. The officer said that he had heard there was a
band on board the train. "Can they play?" he asked.

Little said that they could, and that if he'd like, they would put on a concert or two, one for the commanding officer and another, a more formal affair, in the biggest theater in town. The officer paused. "Have you got a good band?"

Little, keeping it close to the vest, said, "Pretty good. It's the only one I've heard over here, but I believe it's the best in the army."

The officer was skeptical, informing Little that he had heard about a band back in St. Nazaire that other officers who had listened to it were crazy about. "They say that's the real thing in bands—about double the size of the regulation article, and wonderful to listen to. The leader, I believe, is a chap by name of Europe—Jim Europe, who used to play dance music in New York for Mr. and Mrs. Vernon Castle, when they were all the rage. Ever hear that band?"

Little stifled a smile. He then let him know that his band was the very one, and it was at his barracks right now. The officer muttered, "I'll be damned!"[7]

After two concerts in Tours, the band once again pushed southeast, far enough away from the fighting on the western front. Because of the frequent stops, the train inched along. Late on 15 February, it puffed into the station at Aix-les-Bains. Winthrop Ames sighed. "It was quite a great mental relief when the Fifteenth N.Y. Infantry Band with Lt. 'Jim' Europe at its head with Drum-Major Noble Sissle and his group of singers and dancers rolled into Aix-les-Bains that night before the first contingent of 'dough-boys' were due in town," he recollected two years later. "With the appearance of Europe and his musicians and entertainers we of the committee were sure that we would have a real surprise for our Yanks from their first tour of French duty."[8]

The next day at noon, with the sun shining brilliantly, the other train bearing nearly five hundred soldiers arrived. Thousands of people had packed the square in front of the station. The moment the train hissed to a stop, cheers and shouts of "Vive l'Amérique!" and "Vive la France!" rang out. An official welcoming party was also there to greet them. The party consisted of the YMCA staff, including entertainment chief Gerry Reynolds, army officers, and a citizens committee, as well as the mayor and his subalterns with red sashes at diagonals across their chests and top hats perched upon their heads. The town's pathetic band was on hand, too; pathetic because its members, all twelve of them, were old men, boys, and maimed soldiers—all that was left of a much larger and prouder ensemble. As the doughboys, their uniforms still caked in trench mud, piled out of the train, "this little band," Ames wrote, "set up a thin wail—a brave attempt at the 'Star Spangled Banner.'" It took the battle-grimed soldiers a moment to recognize their country's national anthem. When they did, they grinned and came to attention.

When the last notes "wavered" from the bereft band, the strains of the "Marseillaise" were then heard, loud and clear, "a thrilling burst of sound." At that moment, the Fifteenth's band marched into view.

"The size of the band and the unusual sight of its dark-skinned players surprised the French," Ames recalled, adding that "there is a tradition that no foreign musicians can ever play the 'Marseillaise' properly—and here was a rendering of their national anthem that fairly swept them off their feet." Hats were instantly yanked off heads, and not a soul stirred. When Europe's musicians finished, there was a "sudden and moving burst of cheers." Standing close to Ames, an old Frenchman, tears streaming down his cheeks, cried out, "Mais mon Dieu, c'est magnifique!"[9]

The *New York Times* reported the welcome: "This town is accustomed to entertaining royalty and high military and political personages, but the enthusiasm of the reception today probably surpassed anything in the town's history." The report continued, "Led by an American negro soldiers' band, the men paraded through the main streets."[10] The escort, which was led by Little, with the local dignitaries taking up the rear in carriages, probably marched them to the Casino Hotel, because another huge reception awaited the doughboys there. American women served them light refreshments, and that night they were to be entertained as royally as any bigwig.

The star attraction for the evening's show, the "feature of the bill," as the *Times* described him, was to be E. H. Southern, the masterful stage actor. The excitement of the day had died down. The doughboys had been on the train for twenty-four hours. They were tired, and the dirt that they had been living in for months probably still clung to their skin. They slumped in chairs around tables, drinking hot chocolate. Many of them certainly wanted to be on their own—out seeking adventure and romance in one of the world's great playgrounds.

Then it became time for the Fifteenth Regiment Band to appear on stage. Europe opened the concert with George M. Cohan's "Over There." Ames thought that Europe's rendition "excited those tired boys as I have rarely seen any body of men excited."

When it was over, doughboys jumped on the tables, shouting and waving their caps and cups of chocolate. "Play it again!" they yelled. Europe obliged, again and again and again.

"No other form of entertainment appealed to them quite so much," wrote Ames:

And Lieutenant Europe spared neither himself nor his men. They gave a concert in the casino both morning and afternoon—the programs that ranged from the rag-time tunes that set the crowd a-stamping, to classical pieces that were listened to in silent pleasure. In the evening they played in the theatre as a feature of the vaudeville performance. They played hymn-tunes at the religious services. They even found time to give occasional concerts in the park for the townspeople.[11]

The Fifteenth's sixteen-day tour in Aix-les-Bains was to end on 2 March. But the popularity of the band stretched the tour another two weeks. Ames didn't want Europe and his men to leave. Even the townspeople had grown fond of the black musician. They besieged him with requests to play songs dedicated to a dead soldier or family member, or a snatch of tune that someone in the family had written for a loved one at the front. As Little said, "No such request was ever refused." Europe and the band had to learn some of the tunes, and one day he told Little that he had "written three million notes, representing over twenty different instrumental scores."

When the lieutenant spoke these words, Little noticed in his eyes the "appearance of great fatigue. I inquired if he was well. He said that he was quite well, but that he had been up most of the night, arranging the orchestration for one of those amateur musical compositions."[12]

While Europe was arranging scores of tunes to honor French soldiers and families, Sissle was learning a well-beloved French song, "Joan of Arc." He sang it often at Aix-les-Bains and whenever the band found time to play.

The additional two weeks passed quickly, and on Saturday, 16 March, the band performed its final concerts for the doughboys. The first was at a nearby hospital filled with nearly a thousand patients, nurses, and doctors. The second, of course, was at the Casino Hotel theater. The band had been ordered to report back to the regiment. Hayward had finally won. The men of the Fifteenth New York had been moved out of St. Nazaire as common laborers and into the French Fourth Army as combat infantrymen. On 12 March the regiment had been placed at the disposal of the French Sixteenth Division "for service as a combat unit."[13] The next day, the New Yorkers began packing up and heading for Givry-en-Argonne.

At the hospital, Europe's band stood outside in a small courtyard. Every window, it seemed, was thrown open. Heads craned out in spite of the cold to hear ragtime music one more time. Johnston Le Forest of the American Red Cross, who witnessed the concert, was overcome. He immediately dispatched a letter to Hayward. "I don't want to seem to lay it on too thick. I'm not when I say that I think every one who heard, who hears those boys play, is a better soldier and better able to help win the war."[14]

Later that Saturday evening, the band made its farewell performance at the Casino Hotel. After the final tune was played, the YMCA's Reynolds stepped onto the stage. "It is my sad duty," he said, "to announce that we have listened to our last concert by the Band of the Fifteenth New York Infantry. Orders have been received for them to rejoin their regiment. Tomorrow, these men, who for a month have given us so much pleasure, proceed to the front lines, to serve in the trenches against . . ."[15]

At that moment, the stunned crowd cut off Reynolds. Everyone in the theater rose to their feet. Yelling and whistling made it impossible for Reynolds to continue. Flags draped in front of the balconies were yanked loose by the patrons, who then waved them about in patriotic fervor. Captain Little wrote, "On the stage, the colored soldiers who had been spat upon in Spartanburg, rose and bowed—and grinned."[16]

The biggest irony, of course, was that no black soldier, certainly none in the Fifteenth, would ever set foot in Aix-les-Bains or any other rest area. These places were strictly off-limits to African Americans. In a sharply worded memorandum to General Pershing, dated 9 October, Hayward remarked that he had "attempted since last March to secure leave areas for the men of this regiment, in order that they might have the advantages that soldiers of other regiments have had. The matter has been taken up by correspondence and personal interviews, and by application to military and Y.M.C.A. authorities, but all to no avail."[17]

The next day the band played a last concert in the town square and then marched to the train station. Along the route, the citizens of Aix-les-Bains pressed close to the musicians for one last farewell. At least four to five hundred people were on hand, old men, women, and children. A path had to be cut through the throng by the police. Trainmen pushed folks off the tracks to keep them from getting crushed. After a long delay, the train finally eased out of the fabled resort, and the musicians were off to the front.

"God Damn, Le's Go!"

As far as Col. William Hayward could tell, there were no American troops anywhere near his regiment when it joined the Sixteenth Division, VIII Corps, of the French Fourth Army.

Since 15 March the Rattlers had been rolling into the countryside around Givry-en-Argonne in the Champagne Province, and if anyone had been looking for the regiment, he would not have easily found it, as Capt. Arthur Little and band, en route from Aix-les-Bains, were about to discover. No sooner had Hayward reported to the French command than he was informed by one of its officers that the regiment—the only National Guard unit in the United States to carry its original name, number, and flag to France—was no longer called the Fifteenth New York. It now carried a new numerical designation—the 369th United States Infantry, or *369 ème Régiment d'Infanterie U. S.* At first, that number caused bitterness among the officers and men because any number higher than 200 meant that draftees made up the regiment—a belittlement proclaiming they had been forced to enlist. But in March of 1918, there were no draftees yet assigned to the New York outfit. The soldiers had volunteered. They no doubt deserved a designation bearing out that fact, but, of course, they didn't get it.

The new number also threw off Little, Lt. James Europe, and Sgt.

Noble Sissle, and the rest of the band that had been creeping toward
Givry, stopping and playing in villages along the way. They kept asking
where to find the Fifteenth New York, and no one knew. The regiment, by
that designation, Little recalled, "was unknown, unexpected, unheard of,
undesired, unheralded and unsung; and, if we had been cavalry, no doubt
we should have been unhorsed." Eventually, he learned that it had "died
a peaceful death." When he and the band finally reached Givry and
located the 369th, it was 21 March.[1]

Meanwhile, Hayward's own bitterness was evident in a letter to a
friend and officer in the Twenty-seventh Division, written three days
after the bulk of his troops had arrived at Givry. He wasn't only mad
about the new number, but also that his men, because they were a black
outfit, had been pawned off on the French. Yet, between clenched teeth,
he managed to keep the message upbeat. The reason was simple. The
regiment was no longer a labor troop, but was now ready for battle—
and that meant he could tweak his friend about his lousy predicament
with the Twenty-seventh, which had just spent a disappointing winter
at Camp Wadsworth, South Carolina, awaiting orders about its fate in
the war.

The friend was Reginald L. Foster, commander of the Fifty-second Pioneer Infantry, the old Twelfth New York. As a civilian, Foster was Sunday editor of Gotham's leading newspaper, the New York *World*. In his
letter to him, Hayward's disdain for General Pershing showed through,
censors be damned.

"Our great American general simply put the black orphan in a bas-
ket, set it on the doorstep of the French, pulled the bell, and went away,"
he wrote. He went on to state that when he had told this to a French
colonel, shortly after the New Yorkers had been dumped unceremoni-
ously on the French, the officer, probably Colonel Belheumer who commanded the sector to which Hayward and his men had been assigned,
replied, "Weelcome leetle black babbie."

To Hayward's way of thinking, that particular French doorstep—in
spite of what Gen. John J. Pershing had done—was still "heaven."

"The most wonderful thing in the world has happened to this regiment. A fairy tale has materialized and a beautiful dream has come
true," he went on, knowing Foster or any officer mired in the mud of
Camp Wadsworth who read his letter would be jealous. "We are now a
combat unit—one of the regiments of a French division in the French
Army, assigned to a sector of trenches and it is now a question of days
when we will be holding it."

Hayward then described to Foster how he felt about Gen. John F. O'Ryan.

> You know, I shall never get over my disappointment and chagrin, even if I live through this party, at being left out of the wonderful 27th Division, which I even yet say is the finest body of troops I have ever seen together. However, a quotation from the Holy Writ keeps bobbing into my head away up here. I don't know what book it is in and haven't time to look it up, but it goes something like this—"And the stone which was rejected by the builder has become the corner stone of the temple."[2]

Years later, Capt. Hamilton Fish recalled the orders that landed the regiment in the lap of the French. He felt it was the "perfect solution" for Pershing. "The French were crying for U.S. regiments to go into the French Army. So I guess Pershing figured he could kill two birds with one stone—solve the problem on what to do with us and give something to Foch. From then on we spent our entire service in the French Army. Oh officially we were still the 369th U.S. Infantry, but to all intent and purposes we were *français*."[3]

"Heaven," Hayward called his regiment's new assignment. Heaven because his men were again combat infantrymen and encamped with people who treated them as men—not as second-class soldiers. Sissle took the opposite view. It was hell. But he claimed he was happy there. "Happy in Hell!"[4]

One reason it was heaven was because the French were, for the most part, color-blind. It was especially evident among the lower ranks. They treated their new compatriots as equals, ready to share lice, mud, bread, and wine as if there were no tomorrow, which for some was all too true. Hayward thought so after only a short time with the French and mentioned it in a letter to Emmett Scott, the special assistant to Secretary of War Newton Baker. "The French soldiers have not the slightest prejudice or feeling. The poilus and my boys are great chums, eat, dance, sing, march and fight together in absolute accord."

It was not quite the same among the officers. Hayward noted that, as well, in his letter to Scott. "The French officers have little, if any feeling about Negro officers. What little, if any, is not racial but from skepticism that a colored man (judging of course by those they have known) can have the technical education necessary to make an efficient officer."[5] This was particularly true of the officers who had been stationed in

Colonial French West Africa at the outset of the war. For the most part, the French had looked upon the African troops as fodder to be fed to the German machine gunners. Now with the black Americans, they had more fodder to throw at the hungry enemy.

The French treatment of its own African troops, known as *Tiraileurs,* literally, "skirmishers," had a long history, dating back to the Colonial Wars of the late 1800s. The fierce resistance by the black fighters earned a grudging respect from their French conquerors, and when war was declared in August 1914, recruitment of Moroccans and Senegalese got top priority. It turned most urgent when, in the first year of the war, France lost five hundred thousand men killed, out of a casualty list of two million. More bodies were needed in the trenches to stem the German tide. When he became premier, Georges Clemenceau called for a mass recruitment of Africans. In West Africa, methods of recruiting natives were as bad as when innocent blacks were captured centuries earlier and sold into slavery. As organized manhunts scoured the rural areas, in Senegal, thousands of young men fled the country rather than be pressed into a foreign army to fight a war they knew nothing about. The unfortunate who were being hauled away from their villages were already considered dead men.[6]

By 1918, when the Rattlers were assigned to the Sixteenth Division, Africans serving on the western front had reached more than 150,000. Thirty thousand would fall in combat or die because of the harsh weather. In winter, the men, unable to cope with the terrible cold, died of exposure or suffered from frostbite. Hands and feet were amputated. Finally, the French pulled them out of the trenches in November when the cold set in, sent them south to hibernate for the winter— *hivernage* they called it—but at the first sign of spring, brought them back to the killing ground.

While they were in the trenches, the French used them as shock troops. They made up stories about how savage they were, sending word to the Germans that the wild Africans had earned a bloody reputation back home as "head cutters."[7] Their weapon of choice was a *coupe-coupe,* a large heavy knife.

Yet, when they went screaming across no-man's-land as shock troops, the Germans cut them down. Combat losses among the Africans were 20 percent higher than among the French. In the last two-and-half years of the war, the Senegalese casualty rate was twice that of the French.[8]

Although the French government denied that they used Africans as shock troops in place of their own men, a telling memorandum on 10 April by General Le Gallais, commander of the Sixteenth Division, revealed what he had in store for his new troops—the untested African Americans. Entitled "The Situation of the 369th attached to the 16th," the report was written a month after Hayward's men had been training with the French. The general was impressed with the blacks. He commented on their discipline, their "excellent spirit," and their natural ability with rifle and grenade. He wrote that the regiment "would be especially good as a shock troop."[9]

That meant training would be swift and sweet. Done the French way.

First, almost every bit of American gear—including Springfield rifles and uniforms of olive drab tunics and breeches—had to be turned in. In its place, the newly named 369th Infantry were handed French Lebel rifles, "long rapier-like" bayonets, and French helmets of a dull blue-gray color. Sissle, who had found himself separated from the band on its way to Givry and actually believed he had been the first member of the regiment to come under fire when artillery shells exploded near the train he was on, observed the exchange. "We were fully equipped with French rifles and French helmets. Our wagons, our rations, our machine guns and everything pertaining to the equipment of the regiment for trench warfare was supplied by the French Army."[10]

For Capt. Hamilton Fish, the rifles, which held only three cartridges at a time before they needed to be reloaded, were a big disappointment. "Their Lebels were nowhere near as good as our Springfields," he reminisced sixty years later. "The French, you see, were great believers in the hand grenade—their rifles seemed more or less something to put a bayonet on."[11]

Little's comment: "We felt that a poor exchange had been made."[12]

Yet Sgt. Hannibal "Spats" Davis liked his new weapon. He bragged to his brother Art, who had remained in Harlem, "I myself have got an automatic rifle which shoots two shots per second and have named it Joan of Arc."[13]

In the United States, combat training had been spotty at best: a month at Camp Whitman and two weeks at Camp Wadsworth. There had been guard duty at training camps around New York City, as well as at key factories, seized German ships, prisons holding suspected spies and antiwar agitators, and along five hundred miles of lonesome railroad tracks. In other words, according to a confidential report authored by Hayward on 7 January 1919, the regiment had "practically no training whatsoever."[14]

Now, as one report indicated, the 369th had to learn the fundamentals of French ordnance and equipment—all new to the officers and men. And the U.S. soldiers had to be retrained so that they knew the French "art of war and principles of combat."[15] Fish felt the "French cannot do enough for us and put themselves out in every way to help and instruct our men."[16]

This brief, three-week training period was conducted amid the rumble of artillery fire, both hostile and friendly.

Enemy airplanes constantly buzzed overhead as the Germans scouted out the new American troops, now with the French. In a letter to Scott, Hayward noted, "Brother Boche doesn't know who we are yet, as none of my men have been captured so far, and the boys wear a French blue uniform when they go on raids. I've been thinking that if they capture one of my Porto Ricans (of whom I have a few) in the uniform of a Normandy French regiment and this black man tells them in Spanish that he is an American soldier in a New York National Guard regiment it's going to give the German intelligence department a headache trying to figure it out."[17]

Fish thought the same thing. "I wonder what the Germans will think when they take one of our boys prisoner and find that he cannot speak French and comes from Harlem."[18]

Around this time, two incidents involving Color Bearer, Sgt. William H. Cox, caught both American and French officers off guard.

The first happened when German planes buzzed Maj. Edwin Dayton's Third Battalion. Dayton ordered his men to hit the ground. Soldiers scrambled for cover. Sergeant Cox stood erect, holding the American flag. Dayton snapped at Cox to duck. But he refused. Then the major shouted at the obstinate Cox, asking if he'd heard the order.

"Yassuh Major, Suh! Ah heered d'order."

"Why can't you obey my order!"

"Suh Major Suh . . . Guvnor Whitman, der Guvnor of Noo York State, dun handed me dese colors. An' der Guvner, he saiz ter me, 'Sergean', doan' yoo never let dis flag 'ere touch der ground.' An Suh, Major Suh, so long's mah old laigs is stiff 'nough ter hol' me up straight, and so long's mah han's strong 'nough to hol' dis staff, dis flag, Suh Major Suh, dis 'ere flag ain't ergoan' ter touch der ground!"

After the regiment had spent some time in the trenches, three French generals reviewed the New Yorkers. Among the brass was the colorful commander of the French Fourth Army, Gen. Henri Gouraud. Known as the "Lion of France," Gouraud had lost an arm and almost a leg early in the war. As the generals walked among the rows of America's first black soldiers to fight on French soil, Gouraud saw the U.S. flag for the first

Sgt. William Cox (with standard), the 369th Infantry Regiment's color bearer, and two unidentified soldiers, May 5, 1918. U.S. ARMY SIGNAL CORPS

Gen. Henri Gouraud, the "Lion of France," commander of the French Fourth Army. The U.S. 369th Regiment was assigned to his army during 1918. WILLIAM MILES

time. He and the other generals, including Gallais, approached the flag, held aloft by Sergeant Cox. The generals removed their hats and bowed in front of the flag. After standing at attention for a few moments, Cox was overcome by the emotion of the moment. Then he bowed. The flag dipped, nearly touching the ground. When the review was over, Hayward admonished Cox for dipping the flag. Didn't he know it was against the "Manual of the Color" to dip the national flag? Cox said that he knew the regulations.

"When Ah sees doze French generals er bowin' down and er movin' of dere lips lahk as ef dey wuz er prayen' ter Old Glory, an w'en Ah sees dat Lion O'France General er cryen of love for der Stars and Stripes, Ah jes' saiz ter mahse'f, Suh Kunnel Suh, Ah jes saiz ter mahse'f, Sergeant Cox—'Der man dat done wrote doze re'lations, he never knowed not'en 'bout 'casion as dis!'"[19]

"It is a beautiful sight on a clear night when the big guns are in action," Supply Sgt. William Shepard of L Company wrote to the pastor of the Mount Olivet Baptist Church in Harlem, Dr. William Hayes. "One is reminded of a Fourth of July celebration. They annoyed us very much for a while, but now we are lost when we don't hear them." Shepard, who lived at 248 West 53rd Street, asked Hayes to pray for him and his men and then closed his letter by excusing the look of it. "We have no desk or office, but use stones or anything for writing purposes. It is very cold and rainy, my hands and feet are aching." The pastor's prayers went unanswered. Six months after his letter, Shepard, whose mother Maggie still kept a home in Durham, North Carolina, fell in action.[20]

The villages in which the men were billeted bore the scars of three years of warfare. The New Yorkers were very much aware of the carnage all around them, plain as death, and the steady noise of more destruction a few miles to the northeast of them, where the ominous flash and *whump* of the big guns seemed to call out to them.

The untested soldiers looked toward that horizon, aglow in lethal lightning bolts of reds and oranges, and felt the ground tremble. Like some oath, they kept muttering aloud, "God damn, Le's Go!" until it became the watchword of this "brunette fighting outfit."[21]

On 8 April, the men's prayer was answered. Two battalions of the regiment, with a third battalion held in reserve, began to move into the front lines. Their position was in the Afrique Subsector—part of a five-kilometer stretch along the Aisne River, a meandering stream that drifted southward from Chalons-sur-Marne and then zigzagged through part of the rugged Argonne Forest. The subsector passed over land that had seen some of the heaviest fighting of the war. Once in the trenches, the 369th would spend 191 days in the front lines—the longest tenure of any American regiment in the entire war.

When the men first arrived, the trenches were already occupied by French soldiers and commanded by Colonel Belheumer. Under the plan devised by General Le Gallais, and with the agreement of Hayward, companies of the 369th were to be placed in reserve of French companies and, in case of a German attack, would be ready to move into the first lines of defense. At first, each battalion would spend ten days in the trenches, then be relieved until every company had experienced life in a combat zone. French officers and noncommissioned officers would accompany the Americans as guides and "envoys, each able to speak English."[22]

Before landing in the trenches, the New York soldiers settled down in the villages of Auve, where a base hospital was located, Hans, Herpont, Maffrecourt, and Moulins, where Hayward made his headquarters. Camps were erected. One was in a wooded ravine; another nestled among a stand of poplars. It was named "Camp des Peupliers."

By 13 April the regiment was ready for its ten-day stint in the trenches. On that day, the first African-American troops to ever go into combat on European soil massed for one last review in front of Hayward and his regimental staff.

Little was now in charge of the First Battalion because Maj. Lorillard Spencer was at school. "How those steel helmets did snap in the sun-light," he remembered. He was on horseback, next to his commander. "What a change in a year. What a triumph." When the last of the soldiers filed by, Little and Hayward leaned across their saddles and shook hands. "Good-bye," they both said.[23]

During the move up to the trenches, Ranulf Compton, captain of C Company in Little's First Battalion, his sinus infection cleared up, recalled marching into the small villages, knowing that a few miles away was the front. He sensed a strangeness—how mixed up everything seemed—with "Italian artillery, English ambulances and a few Fr. poilu and Morrocans [sic] all under the French Army." On a late afternoon, as he and his men, including privates Henry Johnson of Albany and Needham Roberts of Trenton, New Jersey, slogged to the crest of a hill, to the west of them, shells flared and burst, and their roar rumbled across the ruined countryside.[24]

Before his company reached the trenches, orders arrived that transferred Compton to the American Tank Corps. Within twenty-four hours,

the Saratoga Springs resident was gone, off to start a new chapter of
his life, where he would find a new friend and officer, George S. Patton.
1st Lt. Seth MacClinton, in civilian life a court stenographer, replaced
him as company commander.

Compton was not the only officer who was soon absent. At least fifteen others, according to Lt. Lewis Shaw, were away at various military
training schools, including himself. That figure rapidly grew, jumping to
twenty-seven in the weeks ahead, while new officers were transferred
into the 369th.

Shaw was attending the American First Corps School, taking an
"advanced course in machine gun and artillery fire." In a letter to his
mother, he confided that "as we always have plenty of good French wine
or Champagne it makes a jolly party." He also found time to have his
portrait painted for only fifty francs. He shipped the finished canvas
home. It was at school that he met officers who had already served time
in the trenches. "From all they say," he assured his mother, "it is no
worse than crossing a crowded street."[25]

Another officer at school was Capt. Napoleon Marshall. Because he
was to be the regiment's gas officer, he was learning about this deadly
weapon. "It was an assignment of the highest importance," he reported,
"for patrolling the forests close to the trenches with an orderly, all night,
it was the duty of the Gas Officer to determine the occasion for giving
the signal for the gongs to clang their warnings to the boys asleep away
back in the reserve, to put on their gas masks."[26]

With so many men at the time away, the officer corps in late April
and early May was as follows:

> *Headquarters*
> Col. William Hayward
> Lt. Col. Woodell A. Pickering
> Adjutant: Capt. George F. Hinton
> Supply Officer: Capt. Edwin R. D. Fox
> Surgeon: Maj. Edward L. Whittemore
> Intelligence Officer: 1st Lt. Durant Rice
> Liaison officer: 1st Lt. Charles F. Frothingham
>
> *First Battalion*
> Commanding: Capt. Arthur W. Little
> B Company: Capt. Charles W. Fillmore
> C Company: 1st Lt. Seth B. MacClinton
> D Company: Capt. Robert F. Ferguson
> Machine Gun Company: Capt. Samuel Shethar

Second Battalion
Commanding: Maj. Monson Morris
F Company: Capt. John Holley Clark Jr.
G Company: Capt. James D. White
H Company: Capt. Eric S. Winston
Machine Gun Company: Capt. Frederick W. Cobb

Third Battalion
Commanding: Capt. Louis B. Chandler
K Company: Capt. Hamilton Fish Jr.
L Company: 1st Lt. John O. Outwater
M Company: Capt. David A. L'Esperance
Machine Gun Company: 1st Lt. James Reese Europe.

When the Americans finally dropped down into the trenches, Capt. Charles Fillmore, who had battled long and hard to establish the Fifteenth New York National Guard Regiment; 1st Lt. James Europe, who had turned down the relatively safe job of regimental bandleader for the dangerous task of machine gun company commander; and 2nd Lts. George Lacy and Lincoln Reid became the first African-American officers in the Great War to enter a combat zone.

Soldiers of the U.S. 369th Infantry Regiment training in the trenches on May 4, 1918. U.S. ARMY SIGNAL CORPS

Soldiers of the U.S. 369th Regiment on the road near Maffrecourt, France, May 5, 1918. U.S. ARMY SIGNAL CORPS

In mid-April that combat zone of nearly five kilometers made up a surprising 20 percent of all the ground held by American troops on the western front. According to Hayward, "Our left rested on the ruins of Ville-sur-Tourbe and our right on the west bank of the Aisne River."[27]

The untested men now shared rat-infested mud holes with two French infantry battalions and several French artillery batteries—in affect a "doubling" up of the troops facing the German line. Entanglements of razor-sharp, rusted barbed wire covered the ground in front of the trenches. The ends of each trench were closed off by thick doors made from more of the menacing barbed wire. One officer believed his men were strongly protected on all sides. The only vulnerable spots, it seemed, were the listening posts, which jutted out into no-man's-land like lonely islands and were manned by only two or three soldiers at a time.

Fish, recently back from gas school, sent word to his father that his K Company was, in some places, "not more than fifty yards" from the German lines. He added that if his company was attacked by the enemy it had orders to resist to the last man. He explained:

The troops under my command were co-operating with an equal number of French troops, and were quartered with them. The condition and morale of my men were excellent and all wanted to remain in the first line trenches when the time for relief came. The food, which was supplied and cooked by the French for our men, was good and there was plenty of it. My men have never had better or more regular meals. The French captain with whom I was quartered, received a menu of the mess daily and ordered any change he deemed necessary. The morale and spirit of the French soldier is wonderful and to a great degree due to their being supplied with regular and well prepared mess. The treatment of the men in the trenches by the French officers is one of comradeship and friendly supervision, especially the non-commissioned officers. The trenches are well constructed and kept in a good state of repair.[28]

What Fish may not have known was that the cooks were Americans from his own regiment. They prepared mess in travelling kitchens that were then hauled to the trenches. The meals were the same as those served French officers and men. After describing the food, Fish described the "innumerable rats" of "all sizes who eat up everything in smelling distance. They eat through the men's pockets and musette bags, climb over them at night and are generally a pest."

Pfc. Horace Pippin complained that sometimes he got fed and sometimes did not.

While K Company was in the trenches, several of its men took part in a raid across no-man's-land. They ran into a squad of Germans. In hand-to-hand fighting, Sgt. Archie Niblack was bayoneted in the abdomen and nearly died. During the fight, an American killed a German and retrieved his helmet as a souvenir. On the way back to the safety of their own dugouts, a German barrage landed in their midst, killing three French soldiers and wounding three others. Fish thought the sound of the incoming "storm of shells sounded exactly like a heavy gale at sea." Perhaps it reminded him of the night aboard the *Pocahontas* when the old troopship bucked against that raging storm off Sandy Hook. "The shriek of the shells," he continued, "was similar to the howling of big waves against the sides of the ship."[29] (To Little the shells "sounded to me like trolley cars coming fast over the Hackensack Meadows, and I knew they were 'arrivals' because the 'departures' were still being fired from points well in advance of us."[30]) One of the wounded Frenchmen was a lieutenant. Shot in the head, the bullet still lodged there, he struggled back to the dugout on his feet, reported on the failure of the raid and showed concern for his dead men. His bravery deeply touched Fish.

After the harrowing episode, both the wounded Niblack and the helmet of the dead German were shipped to New York. Niblack recovered from his wound and was often seen escorting his wife along 135th Street, telling everyone he met how much the men of K Company loved their captain and that when he left France, officers Fillmore and Marshall were in excellent health. The helmet arrived in Albany—a gift for Gov. Charles S. Whitman.

Another souvenir was a hunk from a "large French aerial torpedo" that had landed within a few feet of Fish, but failed to detonate. The enterprising captain turned it into a paperweight. He also took pot shots at a German airplane that circled over his position.

Not all the men in the company escaped unscathed during their ten days in the front-line trenches. Three New Yorkers were asleep in their dugout home thirty feet below the ground when a Frenchman accidentally dropped a grenade. It bounced down the steep steps that led into the earthen hole. When it struck one of the steps the impact ignited the grenade. The explosion sent shrapnel spewing everywhere. Although not killed, the three soldiers were severely wounded and carried back to the hospital at Auve.

Before its ten-day stint in the trenches was up, K Company was pulled back to a rest area. There it stayed for only a short while. It was then moved into another trench system the first week of May. Fish said that his men had "lived up to my highest expectations and by their fearless conduct under heavy fire, showed that they had the willingness and ability to fight." As the company headed back into the line, Fish sensed that there was "no need to pity the boys in the trenches, as they are well fed, comfortable, happy and enjoy the excitement and even the risks."[31]

When Little's First Battalion was relieved after experiencing its first enemy bombardment, he was "delighted with the manner in which the men behaved and with the spirit which they showed. They laughed and screamed in gleeful excitement, as do pleasure seekers at Coney Island when being rushed over one of those great coasting 'Dips of Death.' But they were never the least bit out of hand, or really scared; and they took to their respective covers in good order and promptly."

The moment Little's battalion burrowed into its dugout home, an officer in the French 131st Territorial Infantry Regiment asked him to take the first American shot across no-man's-land toward the entrenched enemy. He obliged. At the same time, the officer, a man named Josse, fired his rifle at the Germans. Then Josse said loud enough for all to hear, "Gentlemen! For many months we have toasted the Americans as our friends. Tonight we may pledge to them our love, and toast them as allies!"

Afterward, late at night, Josse escorted Little into no-man's-land, telling him that as an officer it was an adventure he needed to experience. As they got ready to crawl over the parapet and through a gap in the barbed wire, Josse whispered, "I take the responsibility. But please be very quiet, and crawl very low. If you should be killed, my career would—ah well, who can say? Come, shall we go?"

For the captain, his first trip into no-man's-land proved uneventful, and he returned to his own trenches disappointed.[32]

Yet for another American officer, that first trip across no-man's-land was almost too eventful.

Europe was still riding high from the band's triumphant engagement at Aix-les-Bains when Capt. Louis Chandler's Third Battalion, which included his own Machine Gun Company and Fish's K Company, oozed into the muddy trenches for a short stay. Europe envisioned another musical triumph, this time back in the United States. He said so in a letter to his friend and partner, Eubie Blake—the "slacker" among the trio of Europe, Sissle, and Blake. Europe's letter was prompted by a letter from Blake in which he complained about New York being dull for a musician, that gigs were hard to come by. Europe advised him to "stay on the job and take your medicine. If you think of the comforts you are having over there and think of the hardships we are having over here you'd be happy I'm sure to go on suffering." Europe acknowledged the loss of Vernon Castle, killed in an airplane training accident. He called his old partner "my one real and true friend."

The main thrust of the letter was about the future—when the war ended and he was back in America once again. "I have some wonderful opportunities for you to make all the money you need. Eubie, the thing to do is to build for the future, and build securely and that is what I am doing. When I go up I will take you with me. You can be sure of that."[33]

But if Europe was building for the future, his decision to experience no-man's-land was not only rash, it was risky business. He had heard how fearless his French comrades were in combat. "Dare-devils," he had been told. "Fellows [who] just simply 'fondle' death." And one night this musician-turned-soldier, "like a nut, went frolicking with them, on a raid."

Europe's frolic started innocently enough, over a shared bottle of red wine and the swapping of war stories. He had been visiting three veteran French officers in their dugout. They had been in the war since the beginning. They had fought at Verdun and had survived. The more Europe listened to them recount past battles and embellish their glorious deeds of valor, the more he compared himself and his limited experience in the war to what a "lounge lizard's is to a deep sea diver's." He didn't like the comparison. After all, he had enlisted to be a soldier, not a stay-behind-the-lines bandsman. If he could "witness some of the hair breath thrills of the modern war-fare," well, it would boost his stock.

Maybe it was the wine talking, but Europe said, "One thing I wish to do and that is to go on a raid." He then noticed the odd looks on the officers' faces. "You see," he added, "the General don't think we have been on the line long enough to pull off a raid." Later, thinking back to what he had said, he wondered why he had uttered such a request. An officer jumped up, clapped him on the shoulder and before the American had a chance to recant, snapped, "Bravo! We are going on a raid tonight and you can go with us."

That night Europe prepared for his raid, a raid that marked the first time in the Great War that an African-American officer crossed into no-man's-land. He stripped off his uniform and put on an old French uniform that was bare of any insignia or other marks that identified him as a U.S. officer. His tin hat was exchanged for a cloth cap. Then he and the officers who were to escort him into the danger zone polished off a bottle of wine "just as though they were going to a picnic."

Europe's pulse quickened, his head spun with memories, and, as he recalled that moment to Sissle, "I was thinking of the Band—how sweetly they could play—then I would hear the quartet singing 'Sweet Emelina, My Gal'—then the scenes of dear old Broadway passed by. I could see myself standing before my old favorite orchestra in 'Castles in the Air,' and as I stood there wielding my baton to those jazzing strains of 'The Memphis Blues,' I imagined I once again saw all those old familiar faces tripping by."

At the time Europe set off for no-man's-land, hand-to-hand combat along the French sector had quieted down. The Allies expected a huge German push, but mostly, all they endured was constant artillery bombardment. A war correspondent, assigned to the French armies, reported, "The guns are in full force—a horrid compromise which cannot last very long."[34]

Into a starry night of "intense darkness," with the big guns deathly quiet, and armed with only a small automatic pistol that reminded him more of a cap gun than the real thing, Europe followed his escorts through the maze of twisting, muddy trenches. Dark shapes of soldiers, huddled against slimy dirt walls, made the moment strange. It was like a nightmare. Europe's throat was dry as sand. He longed for human noise, even a simple clearing of the throat, to break the tension. In the sky the stars seemed to mock him with "winking eyes" and he wanted to change places with them.

And then they were at the "jumping off" place, and a French officer whispered for Europe to step to one side. As he did so, silent soldiers moved by him, over the trench wall and into no-man's-land. The officer counted each one—thirty in all. The last two carried a stretcher. In his mind's eye, Europe saw himself on that stretcher, a dying man.

"If only I had the wings of a dove," he confessed to Sissle, "I would have flown away."

He scaled the mucky wall and crawled off toward enemy lines with the French officer next to him, nudging him along. A hole had been cut in the belts of barbed wire and white tape rolled on the ground as a guide. The white tape seemed to be a signal because the French artillery started shelling the German position. The noise from the guns sounded to Europe like a "thousand pheasants." Shells whistled close to their heads, landing forty yards away. As far as he could see, bombs burst "thick and fast" and "how they would scream—and shrapnel was whizzing hither and thither." Europe clung to the ground. The French officer sent up a flare to let the artillery know his position and to allow his men to see the terrain. Then he poked Europe to his knees. A split second later, the American and French soldiers bolted through the gap in the barbed wire and charged the German trench. The land behind the trench was aflame with artillery fire, but the trench itself was deserted. There were no prisoners to be caught that night. Empty-handed, the raiding party scampered back to their own slit in the earth. As Europe dropped down, the German guns roared a response. Dirt flew. As he bolted back through the maze, he kept thinking of a line from his old friend, the comic Bert Williams. "I speck I'm gone before I go." He eyed a dugout and dove in. He stayed in the shelter until the shelling ended.

Later the next day, huddled with his own men and the thrill of a lifetime now behind him, he confided, "I found everything last night that I ever heard existed out there. Next time I go, they will have to read the orders to me with General Pershing's name signed and re-signed to them."[35]

"He Can Go Some!"

By now word was getting back to New York that the old Fifteenth had been in combat. On 11 May a three-column headline across the front page of the *Age* blared: "CRACK COLORED REGIMENT NOW FIGHT-ING WITH FRENCH DIVISION." The article beneath the headline confirmed that the men of the Fifteenth, now known as the 369th, "are fighting in the first line trench with the French to help make this world safe for democracy." The *Age* assured its readers that the New Yorkers, the "first Negro troopers from the United States to meet the Germans on the battle front, have become expert grenade throwers and are masters of the machine gun." It quoted a French general, who, after seeing "these colored fighters while in action," characterized them as "very stout-hearted, but very rash."

The article was based on a letter from Col. William Hayward to editor Fred Moore. Hayward had learned the power of good public relations while running for political office back in Nebraska and campaigning for Governor Charles Whitman in New York. He knew that every bit of publicity the regiment got had to help his men—and himself. In his letter, the former Republican politico brought Moore up to date. "Finished our training and we are now fighting with the French," he wrote. "Today I have two battalions in the trenches of the first line and the third rotating in relief and at rest just a little way behind." The colonel crowed that his men fit in with the French "without a jar or a hitch." He claimed that the "boys have learned so quickly about everything. They can take their machine guns to pieces and put them together in the dark just as easy as they take off their shoes." They have a new song, he added, the lyrics of which go: "We used to use the picks and spades/But now we throw the hand grenades." Hayward said he was proud of them. "They are clean, brave men, fearing nothing—doing everything."[1]

For his part, Moore wanted everyone to know the glorious deeds of New York's black heroes, most specifically the President of the United States. Woodrow Wilson had thus far refused to publicly condemn a rash of lynchings that were spreading across the south like the kudzu vine—choking off life. If Wilson knew that black soldiers were fighting and dying for their country then he might act, say something. *Anything.* As Moore's managing editor, Lester Walton, argued in a letter to Herbert Bayard Swope, one of the most influential newspaper reporters in the United States and a man who had Wilson's ear: "Condemnation of lynching by the President would do more to discourage this National evil than anything else."[2]

To break Wilson's maddening silence, the black community needed its own authentic war heroes. On the night of 13–14 May, in a lonely, isolated listening post out in no-man's-land, it got them. And by a stroke of luck, three war correspondents—one of them a Southerner who admitted that, because he was from the South, he had inherited and acquired prejudices touching on the race question—happened to stumble on to the 369th Infantry and a story that would be wired to newspapers and magazines across America.

How these three scribes found Gotham's soldiers was, in itself, a miracle.

For some time now Thomas M. Johnson of the New York *Evening Sun,* Martin Green of the New York *Evening World,* and the legendary Irvin S. Cobb had been trailing after General Pershing's ever-expanding army. (Captain Little recollected that one of the correspondents was Lincoln Eyre of the *World,* not Johnson of the *Sun.*) The Kentucky-born Cobb was universally despised by African Americans because they viewed him as a racist. A former Manhattan newspaperman, he had made a name for himself writing short stories and articles for the *Saturday Evening Post.* Among his tales was that of Old Judge Priest, a wise character from his hometown of Paducah. Blacks were depicted as ignorant, shuffling darkies. James Weldon Johnson referred to these portrayals as "the traditional mule and the old graveyard joke, and the worn out reference to the watermelon."[3]

Cobb now covered the war for the nationally circulated *Post,* which rushed his stuff into publication the moment it arrived in Philadelphia. Yet as he, Green, and Johnson chronicled the goings on of Pershing's American Expeditionary Force, the only black soldiers they knew about—or at least thought they knew about—were nowhere near the front lines. They were stationed at ports of entry, sweating out the conflict as stevedores.

Hardly material for stirring war stories. And besides, they were "colored."

In early May, the trio got wind that there was already a black regiment fighting. Now, that was different.

"To the three of us word had come, no matter how, that negro troops of ours were in the line," Cobb reported in the *Post.* "No authoritative announcement to that effect having been forth coming, we were at the first hearing of the news skeptical."[4] Green agreed. The fact that there were actual black troops under fire came to him in a *whisper.* "For more than a month they have played a part in the vast theater of war," he wrote of the 369th, "yet save for certain personages at general headquarters nobody in General Pershing's command has been any wiser. Even the war-correspondents, whose duties oblige them to keep in touch with every phase of our military activities, were quite unaware of the newcomers' presence in the line."[5]

They had a story. But first, finding these troops so they could write about them proved as hard as getting their dispatches past the censors.

"So thoroughly camouflaged [the 369th] was," Green reported, "that I roamed the country for over two days before my objective was attained. Being encased in the French Army to a greater degree than any other American contingent—they are the only doughboys supported by French artillery—these chocolate soldiers are temporarily in a state of splendid isolation so far as the remainder of the American expeditionary force is concerned."[6]

Armed with maps, they set off on what they called a "quest," eager to see how soldiers of color would react under fire—especially those trained by an old friend, the ex-state official Bill Hayward.

Cobb recalled how they motored through the countryside in a "high-powered car." They bumped past a black unit of draftees—not the 369th, but an outfit of men from the South. "Tidewater dark[ies]," Cobb explained to his Yankee cohorts. These draftees, or draftees like them, soon would cause problems for Colonel Hayward and his Rattlers. Eventually, the three correspondents rolled into a forested war zone where "sundry French batteries ding-donged away with six-inch shells—shrapnel, high explosives and gas in equal doses—at a German position five miles away." When they drove out of the protection of the woods, they "learned we had landed where we had counted on landing when we started out. It was the regiment we were looking for, sure enough."

Cobb recognized that the black soldiers he spotted were obviously from New York. They were not the draftees they had seen earlier nor were they the shuffling darkies he had so thoughtlessly described in the *Post*. "The negro troopers we encountered now, here in copses, sometimes singly or oftener still in squads and details . . . were sophisticated and townwise in their bearing . . .they were city dwellers." He noticed that they "wore their uniforms with smartened pride; who were jaunty and alert and prompt in their movements' and who expressed, as some did vocally in my hearing, and all did by their attitude, a sincere and heartfelt inclination to get a whack at the foe with the shortest possible delay."

The three correspondents heard something else, too. The soldiers were abuzz about an extraordinary incident that had happened during the night. One private, oiling his three-shot French Lebel rifle, called out to another, "Henry Johnson, he done right well, didn't he?"[7]

The United States's first true hero of the war—at least the first to be honored by the French government with the Croix de Guerre with gold palm—Pvt. Henry Johnson was not bigger than life—the way the American public likes to envision its gallant warriors. At five-four, the Albany redcap had been barely tall enough to pass his military physical. And he weighed a mere 130 pounds, if that. Yet his young wife, Edna, who called her man Bill, once boasted, "Bill ain't big, nor nothin' like that, but oh, boy, he can go some!"[8]

It took a German raiding party, a whole platoon of at least twenty-four men, to find out what Mrs. Johnson meant when she said her Bill *can go some.*

Johnson's first trip into the front line began on the night of 11 May. Under the cover of darkness, so the enemy lurking just behind no-man's-land couldn't see them, Capt. Arthur Little's First Battalion moved into the trenches to relieve Maj. Monson Morris's Second Battalion. Johnson and another private, Needham Roberts, the son of a Trenton, New Jersey, Baptist preacher, were in C Company, now led by 1st Lt. Seth MacClinton because of the departure of Capt. Ranulf Compton. 1st Lt. Richardson Pratt, the Glen Cove banker, had charge of two squads. On

Sgt. Henry Johnson of Albany, N.Y., with his Croix de Guerre. He won the medal by almost single-handedly routing a German raiding party on May 11, 1918, killing four and wounding several more in close-quarters fighting. During the fight, when his rifle ran out of ammunition, he used a bolo knife. CORBIS/BETTMANN-UPI

the 13th, he detailed Cpl. Allen London and four privates, among them Johnson and Roberts, to a remote listening post about fifty to sixty yards out in no-man's-land. Their responsibility was to be the eyes and ears of the battalion—to alert the men back in the main trench of any suspicious activity by the Boche. The Americans and Germans had already clashed several times in no-man's-land, with casualties on both sides. Sgt. Archie Niblack had been bayoneted and survived. F Company's Pvt. James Axxon, a native of Macon, Georgia, and Sgt. Edward Harding, a Brooklyn resident, were also wounded. Their wounds proved fatal. Axxon died on 17 May, the first African American in the AEF to fall at the hands of the enemy in the Great War. Harding's death followed nine days later.

Johnson and Roberts had much to be anxious about. The Germans were cunning. Raiding trenches was an art they had honed to perfection.

The listening post did not offer much protection. It was barely a hole in the marshy ground with duckboards for a floor, tall, heavy grass growing all about, and encircled by barbed wire. But it had been given a grand name: "Combat Group No. 29." Half a football-field length behind it was No. 28. Here Pratt and the rest of the platoon hunkered down for the night. The main trench in which the rest of the First Battalion holed up was another hundred yards distant from Johnson and Roberts.

The Americans were armed with their Lebel rifles and a crate of grenades to repel any attack. Johnson had another weapon: a bolo knife. Brought back from the Philippines by veterans of the Spanish-American War and the Philippine Insurrection, the bolo knife had a blade nine to fourteen inches long, sharpened on one side. It was weighted much like a machete for cutting thick jungle brush—or cleaving skulls. It had been issued to many of the Rattlers as a side arm.

According to Johnson, a French lieutenant came crawling out to inspect their position. Johnson whispered that he thought the Germans were about to attack. The Frenchman ordered Johnson and Roberts back to the main line.

"Lieutenant," said Johnson, "I'm an American and I never retreat."[9]

In the meantime, the three soldiers with Johnson and Roberts, including Corporal London, bedded down in an underground dugout to sleep. The diminutive Albany redcap and the preacher's son stayed awake, peering into the obscurity of the night, their ears like antennas. Around two or three, they heard a strange gnawing noise.

There are several versions as to what happened next.

Johnson whispered to Roberts, "What's that?"

"Rats, I guess," Roberts whispered back.

Roberts then slipped out of the listening post to investigate. He wormed through the tall grass. The gnawing sound, he was sure, was that of wire cutters opening holes in the barbed entanglements. He knew there were Germans somewhere out there. He worked his way back to Johnson to tell him. While he had been gone, Johnson had his eye on a log that seemed to be moving through the grass.

"That's the bush Germans!" he hollered.

At that second, an enemy flare lit up no-man's-land. Twenty-four Germans jumped from their hiding places and charged "Combat Group No. 29." Bullets from their five-shot Mauser rifles zinged through the night. They lobbed stick grenades at Johnson and Roberts. They moved with alarming speed to surround and overwhelm the Americans.

The first rush flattened the two men. Shrapnel ripped into their arms and legs. Roberts pitched backward onto the duckboards that lined the bottom of the listening post. "I'm hit!" he groaned.

Johnson jumped to his feet, emptying his three-shot Lebel into the rushing Germans. His last shot struck a soldier point blank in the chest. Now the rifle was useless. As the Hun dropped in front of him, Johnson eyed another leaping over his fallen comrade with a pistol aimed directly at his face. Johnson swung his rifle like a baseball bat, cracking the enemy on the head. The German toppled.

Roberts, although hurt enough so he couldn't stand, heaved a grenade at the gray-clad forms while stretched on his back. But three Germans still got to him. While one of them tried to strangle Roberts, the others scooped the wounded soldier off his back. They wanted to carry him back behind German lines. Seeing this, Johnson barreled into their midst. He battered the enemy with the butt end of his rifle until it broke. Then he unsheathed his razor-sharp bolo knife. He stuck the first body near him.

In perfect English, the German howled, "The son of bitch got me!"

Johnson growled through gritted teeth, "Yas, an dis little black [bastard] will git you 'gin—ef yer git up!"

Another downward thrust and his bolo knife was "buried to the hilt through the crown of the German's head."

One of the men he had slugged with his rifle wobbled to his feet, yanked out an automatic pistol, and fired away. Johnson felt the sting of bullets and cried out in pain as he was shot in the right forearm, right hip, and left leg. He sank to his knees as the German moved in for the kill. With one last mighty swing of the bolo knife, the runt-sized soldier who "can go some," ripped open the Hun's stomach, disemboweling him.

That act was too much for the enemy, and they gathered their dead and wounded and fled into the night. As the last German faded away, a weakening Johnson pegged a grenade at him.

A few minutes later, Pratt, with reinforcements, reached the outpost. Johnson looked at his lieutenant and said, "Corporal London, turn out the Guard!" and fainted. He and Roberts were carried back to a dressing station and then on to the French hospital at Auve.

The next morning Richardson and Little surveyed the battleground. "We trailed the course of the enemy retreat (a roundabout course of at least a half mile through the woods) to the bank of the river, where they crossed," recalled Little. "We trailed the course with the greatest of ease, by pools of blood, blood-soaked handkerchiefs and first aid bandages, and blood-smeared logs, where the routed party had rested."

Little also found evidence that Johnson's last grenade had hit a man. The German had been "terribly torn by the iron of these explosives."

Little saw a mass of flesh and blood and a hunk of gray cloth caught on a strip of barbed wire. A hole in the ground reminded him of a five-gallon punch bowl "almost filled with thick, sticky blood."

Little discovered there was more to the fight than just human carnage. The Germans had left behind a small, but valuable cache of arms. The inventory included forty stick grenades (potato mashers), three automatic pistols, and seven long-arm wire cutters. He was able to estimate that the number of men in the raiding party had to have been no less than twenty-four.

While the captain was finishing his investigation, Hayward arrived in a mule-drawn wagon with three men. Cobb, Green, and Johnson. To Little, "It was a Heaven-sent opportunity for honorable publicity for our volunteer regiment from Harlem."[10]

Cobb thought so, too. "By chance," he later reckoned, "we had chosen a most auspicious moment for our arrival."[11]

The journalists set about interviewing officers and men and going over the battle scene. Back at the hospital, they were able to talk to Johnson and Roberts, both bearing serious, but not life-threatening wounds. A few days later, stories by Green of the *Evening World* and Johnson of the *Evening Sun* showed up at newsstands. Cobb's article would have to wait until August before the *Post* was able to publish it.

Green was emphatic about the exploits of the two soldiers. "The names of Johnson and Roberts will stand forever on the roll of honor of their race." He described how "Roberts, wounded in three places, stretched out helplessly in the mud, hurled hand grenades, even while the hands of a muscular German were about his throat." Then he turned his attention to the Albany redcap. "Johnson did even more. Having shot one of his foeman down and clubbed another with the butt of his rifle, he sprang to the aid of Roberts with his bolo-knife. As the enemy fell into disorderly retreat, Johnson, three times wounded, sank to the ground, seized a grenade alongside his prostrate body, and literally blew one of the fleeing Germans to fragments."[12]

In the pages of the *Sun,* Johnson narrated the German assault, the first clash, the useless rifle, the grenades exploding, and the "throttling of the helpless Roberts." Then he wrote: "The infuriated Johnson cast about for another weapon, his rifle having jammed just before he felled a second German, but found that the small supply of grenades had been exhausted. He suddenly bethought himself of his 'bolo knife' which he had at his belt, and drawing this brought it down with all his strength, driving the razor-edged blade into the German's head. It must have cleft his skull, for the blade later showed blood to the hilt and the

German's cap, when picked up was found to have been cut almost in half."

He concluded, "The story of their exploit has passed from mouth to mouth, and when [Johnson and Roberts] do return to the trenches, it will be a sort of triumphal return something after the manner of the victorious Roman emperors."[13]

On the front page of the *Age,* editor Moore ran photos of the two heroes and published the *Sun's* account of the battle. Roberts wore a three-piece civilian suit. Johnson, sitting in a chair, had on his doughboy uniform, a campaign hat atop his head. The boldface, two-column headline read: HENRY JOHNSON AND NEEDHAM ROBERTS ROUT 24 GERMANS.[14]

When Cobb's piece finally hit the streets, his account raised some eyebrows and prompted Johnson to pen a lengthy editorial in the *Age.* Cobb detailed the heroics of the two privates under the title "Young Black Joe." Then, admitting that he held racist tendencies, he wrote:

> As a result of what our black soldiers are going to do in this war, a word that has been uttered billions of times in our country, sometimes in derision, sometimes in hate, sometimes in all kindliness—but which I am sure never fell on black ears but it left behind a sting for the heart—is going to have a new meaning for all of us, South and North too, and that hereafter n-i-g-g-e-r will merely be another way of spelling the word American.[15]

Johnson, in his weekly "Views and Reviews" column, warned readers of the *Age* that in Cobb's article "there are things in it which many colored people will object to, or at least feel were unnecessary." Johnson strongly objected to Cobb's description of the soldiers:

> These black boys, but a generation or two removed from slavery, and not yet having full democracy for themselves, yet fighting in France for the democracy of the world, must have a distinct background, but it certainly is not the background of the watermelon and the 'possum and the rest of the worn out "literary color" of Negro stories. Mr. Cobb could see the black boys, but he did not have the genius to discern their new background, so he placed them in the old setting with which he was familiar, the rural districts of Georgia. Some writer will come, perhaps he will be a colored writer, who will see the new background behind these sons of American slaves now fighting for the freedom of European peoples. Mr. Cobb missed it, and missing it, his story would have been better if he had left out "color" and "background" entirely.

Johnson then softened his criticism, noting that Cobb had written the article in a "spirit of sympathy." He mentioned the end of the article, surmising that Cobb had been a user of the word "nigger." But then he noted hopefully, "Anyone who has read some of the things which he has written regarding the race will see by this article that the war has wrought many great changes, even in Irvin S. Cobb."[16]

Two days after Johnson and Roberts had repelled the German attack, General Le Gallais of the French Sixteenth Division signed Order 697. It awarded to them the Croix de Guerre—the first American soldiers to be so honored by the French in World War I. For Johnson, who "can go some," the general added the coveted palm. The *Sun* reporter quoted Le Gallais as stating the account by Little and others was too modest. "As a result of verbal information furnished to me it appears that the blacks were extremely brave and this little combat does honor to the Americans."[17]

In a long letter to Johnson's wife, Hayward described the fight with the German patrol. He told her that her husband was seriously wounded, but not in any danger. "The wounds having been received under such circumstances that everyone of us in the regiment would be pleased and proud to trade places with him." But he cautioned, "It is my hope and prayer to bring him back to you safe and sound, together with as many of his comrades as it is humanely possible by care and caution to conserve. But it must be borne in mind that we cannot all come back; that none of us can come back until this job is done."[18] Hayward's letter was later read into the Congressional Record.

African Americans now had their hero. Within weeks of awarding one of France's highest military medals to a black soldier from Albany, black leaders bombarded the White House, calling on President Wilson to break his maddening silence on the scourge of lynching.

Lester Walton sent a letter to Wilson's personal secretary, Joseph Tumulty. Once again he pleaded for the President to speak out "strongly against what has become a National evil." He added, "As I told Mr. Swope [Herbert Bayard Swope of the New York *World* who, on Walton's behest, had informed Tumulty of the exploits of Henry Johnson], the colored people are depressed on account of the wholesale lynching of Negroes in this country without one word of protest from the chief executive of the Nation. Condemnation of mob law by Mr. Wilson would do more than any other agency to put a stop to this growing evil which puts this country in a none too enviable light before the world."[19]

Only 26 July, President Wilson spoke out at last:

I say plainly that every American who takes part in the action of a
mob or gives any countenance is no true son of this great democracy,
but its betrayer, and does more to discredit her by that single disloy-
alty to her standards of law and right, than the words of her states-
men or the sacrifices of her heroic boys in the trenches can do to make
suffering peoples believe her to be their savior.[20]

Johnson responded in his weekly column.

For the past year The Age has been boldly declaring that it was no
violation of ethics or chivalry nor did it show any lack of patriotism for
the Negro to demand that the nation practice at home the democracy
for which it was fighting abroad, and for which he himself was helping
to fight; for the past year The Age has been pointing out that the tor-
turing and lynching of black Americans by Americans laid the country
liable to the charge of hypocrisy in its pronouncements about democracy; and here President Wilson has said the same things. We hope
the President will not stop at this point but will speak out against
other phases of the denial of common democracy here at home.[21]

Lt. James Europe, in the meantime, had written to Moore, telling him
all about America's newest war heroes.

"The Boches must feel that Johnson and Roberts were some boys," he
wrote, "and if they can get any encouragement out of the fact that we
have three thousand more just like them they are welcome to it."[22]

The Germans were now discovering that these blacks from New York
were not just any run-of-the-mill soldiers.

They were more like fighters from Hell.

"I Wish I Had a Brigade, Yes, a Division"

If all of the blacks of the greater New York City area were "aroused to a high pitch of enthusiasm over the cabled accounts of the glorious and heroic deeds of Henry Johnson and Needham Roberts," as Fred Moore sang in the pages of his newspaper,[1] in France the feeling of euphoria was not so plentiful among the volunteer veterans of the old Fifteenth New York.

When in the late spring Col. William Hayward took over command of the Afrique Subsector from his French counterpart, Colonel Belheumer, including two French infantry battalions as well as two batteries, the chemistry of his regiment was changing, and he didn't like it one bit.

The change was coming at a critical time, too, as the 369th prepared for its first real battle, an expected attack by the Germans in the hilly, wooded Champagne Valley. The War Department, or maybe it was Pershing himself, more than likely looked at the French Fourth Army as a sewer into which it could flush away its African-American draftees, now being shipped by the thousands to Europe. Not all of them could be common laborers. Untrained, many of them ignorant and illiterate, most of them from the rural South, and all of them, it seemed, undisciplined, these draftees went eddying down the chain of command like so much unwanted waste. Hundreds of them kept showing up at the regiment, lacking any history as to what the old Fifteenth meant to the City and State of New York. Three hundred one week, four hundred another. It wasn't their fault. Without any training, they simply did not know any better.

The 369th had begun to balloon from two thousand men and officers to well over three thousand. Eventually, five thousand men would serve in the regiment at one time or another.

General Le Gallais worried about these additions to his American regiment. In an urgent memorandum to the commanding general of the French VIII Corps, he remarked on two hundred new soldiers, commenting that it was too late to properly train them. He said it was impossible to place this large a contingent of soldiers within the Sixteenth Division.[2]

Hayward, too, was beside himself. He kept writing to Gen. John J. Pershing about the problem, but to no avail. He held his anger in check for months, but then finally fired off a letter to the "Commander-in-Chief." Although we're getting ahead of the story, the letter captured the mood of the regiment at the time it was preparing for its first battle. Hayward explained how the replacements arrived "in detachments of several hundreds. They have always come without previous notice to the regiment, some times equipped and some times not equipped, and never trained. No officers have accompanied them, except for the purpose of delivering them to the regiment." He pointed out that the effect on morale was devastating. "The great influx of untrained and illiterate Negroes who came to the regiment from the southern states without any interest in the regiment and no pride in its reputation, and who but poorly could be assimilated." What truly blew Hayward's top was the fact that these raw recruits, for the most part, refused to fight.

> To the disgrace of the regiment, the Negro Race and the American Army, it must be said that large numbers of enlisted men of this regiment conducted themselves in the most cowardly and disgraceful manner. They absented themselves without leave prior to each of the battles sneaking away in the night, throwing away their equipment, lurking and hiding in dugouts, and in some cases traveling many, many kilometers from the battlefield. This result did not come from any condition of general panic, as the regiment was never attacked, but on the contrary itself attacked the enemy each day. The result was that practically all of the heavy casualties were suffered by the older and better men of the regiment, and, of course, among the officers.

Hayward then recommended that those "cowardly offenders" not escape punishment. "Large numbers should be tried for misconduct in the face of the enemy. There should be wholesale executions following convictions." He even threatened that all citations for bravery be revoked.[3]

But months before he had angrily written to Pershing, he had, in a letter to Emmett Scott, assistant to the Secretary of War, felt differently. "I know more about Negro soldiers and how to handle them, especially the problem of Negro and white officers, than any other man living today. Of course, the other regiment I commanded for three years [a troop of the Nebraska National Guard] was a white regiment, so I had a lot to learn, but I've learned it and I wouldn't trade back now."[4]

In early June, Hayward made up his mind about the fighting spirit of his men when he led them on a suicidal charge against entrenched Germans. One of the battalions of the 369th had been advancing through a thickly wooded section of the Champagne sector under artillery fire and withering rounds of machine-gun bullets cracking from the underbrush. A French officer, fearing for the men, ordered the New Yorkers to "retire." Hayward, up front of the battalion with Lt. Col. Woodell Pickering, turned and stared down the officer.

"Turn back!" he growled. "I should say not! We are going through there or we don't come back!" He then tore off the insignia on his uniform that identified him as an American officer, snatched a rifle from one of his men and faced the enemy.

"Retire, Retire!" the Frenchman cried.

Hayward leapt out in front of the battalion, yelling back to the officer. "My men never retire! They go forward or they die!"

Pickering, with his automatic pistol drawn, chased after Hayward. The boys surged with them. Before the stunned Germans turned and ran, Hayward was shot in the leg. Pickering was also wounded. Six Americans were hit, too. But not a doughboy was killed.

Yet a month after this daring assault, bureaucrats in Washington, without once consulting Hayward or anyone on his staff, were issuing smug opinions about the battle-worthiness of black soldiers—especially officers.

Brig. Gen. Lytle Brown, a West Pointer and Tennessee native, opined that officers of color were not in the service to fight but rather "for the advancement of their racial interests." He complained that they "cliqued together and sought at all times to protect members of their own race, no matter whether they were right or wrong." But worse, he judged them as lacking the "mental capacity for command." Even black enlisted men had no confidence in them. Officers were more interested in how they looked and in having a good time, he said, and in a fight they were the first to run for the rear, leaving their own men to shift for themselves. "In general the negro officer was still a negro, with all the faults and weaknesses of character inherent in the negro race, exaggerated by the fact that he wore an officer's uniform."[5]

Brown based his report after hearing from white officers in all the newly formed African-American regiments—except one. Although there were morale problems in the 369th, officers, from Captains Fillmore and Marshall to Lieutenants Europe, Lacy, and Reid, were beyond reproach. However, reports such as Brown's and others would unfairly dog African-American soldiers for the rest of the war and the years following and would serve to keep the army segregated.

In the midst of this controversy and the uncertain mood of the new, untrained enlisted men, a number of white officers in the 369th sought to bail out. Even Capt. Hamilton Fish looked to transfer. In a hurried letter to Gen. Mark Hershey of the Seventy-eighth Division, filled with typographical errors, the scion of New York society who could trace his military ancestors back to the French and Indian War, begged for help.

I have just heard that your Division was over here and I am writing to ask you if you could help me get a transfer from this regiment 369th R. I. U. S. to the 78th Division. . . . I regret to state that there is considerable dissatisfaction among our Officers and about thirty have already requested transfers but with few exceptions they have been disapproved by our Colonel. I have not ask [sic] for a transfer but would like very much to serve with you if it can be arrange [sic]. I am confident that if you could find a place for me and speak to the Adjutant General that I would be transferred immediately.[6]

Already, one of the regiment's most senior officers was gone. Maj. Edwin Dayton, hero of the Spanish-American War who had commanded the Third Battalion, had gotten himself transferred to the 372nd Infantry Regiment. 1st Lt. John Castles was off to the 301st American Tank Battalion that on 29 September, in support of the daring attack by the Twenty-seventh New York Division on the center of the Hindenburg Line, would virtually get wiped out.

Before leaving the regiment, Dayton sent a note to Fish, praising his leadership. "In the many years of my long service I recall no company in an [sic] regiment which was more efficiently and harmoniously built up to the personal standard of its commanding officer than I found your 'K' company in the 3rd Battalion." He singled out Fish's "sterling qualities as an officer and a man in many trying circumstances during the difficult period of organization."[7]

Two other soldiers who wanted out were not officers, but sergeants major. They were Henry Plummer Cheatham and Benedict W. Cheeseman.

It wasn't that they were down on the regiment, with all those southern draftees pouring in. After all, Cheatham was a southerner himself, born in Henderson, North Carolina, in 1892. His father, an ex-slave, had been that state's congressman, serving two terms in the late 1800s, and afterward had settled in the nation's capital as recorder of deeds for the District of Columbia. Cheatham and Cheeseman just wanted commissions, and they knew the only way to get them was to be promoted out of the 369th. Unlike his friend Cheeseman, "Plum" had every reason to believe that he was, in fact, up for promotion. First, he had served in the Twenty-fourth Infantry as its regimental sergeant major while it was stationed in the Philippines. Second, Lt. James Europe had put in a good word for him to Rodman Wanamaker in Philadelphia. And third, he counted on his father, who still had a lot of clout in Washington.

In a letter to his "Dear Papa" in which he asked for help, "Plum" complained that "my usefulness with my present organization is at an end, and this is so because of two reasons: First—I have attained the highest enlisted promotion, and I've fully outgrown it. Second—My Regimental Commander has repeatedly acknowledged my thorough capabilities and stated to others and to me that I am highly deserving of a commission. But he has also stated that nothing could be done for me here because it is not considered good policy to make any more colored officers in this Regiment."

Cheatham also told his father about Cheeseman, "a man and a soldier without reproach, and every thing that I have said about myself, and everything that I'm going to say, will apply to him equally as to me, and I want your action to be inclusive of both of us."

He explained the politics, and although he never mentioned Hayward by name, it was clear that the colonel had frustrated their attempts for a commission:

It is obvious, if we are fitted for promotions that we should be given them. And if we cant [sic] get them here, we just MUST get them elsewhere. We must transfer, and I think you can work it without a hitch. It is a fact that many men in the American Expeditionary Forces— officers, noncommissioned officers and even privates, have been and are being returned to the States for tours of duty as instructors. But not a man from "this dear" regiment has been sent. And it is a fact also that a GENERAL ORDER has been issued over here authorizing the recommendation of qualified noncommissioned officers for appointment to training schools, and for appointments as officers directly from the ranks, as well. A certain colored colonel made FORTY such appointments a few days ago. And yet we are calmly assured that, though there is no question as to our merit, we may not be advanced because the "policy" decrees otherwise. And this "policy" has been devoutly followed that, not long ago, when an increase was authorized, TWENTY-NINE young reservists were requisitioned for and obtained. They were white, of course, and they are here with us now. "It is a laugh."

Cheatham warned that many of the African Americans who were lucky enough to get commissions were, unfortunately, "men whose efficiency is questionable, and they are taking them because they need them. Certainly our military training which we have obtained by the grilling process of actually playing the game, our perfect records and our three months trench-service should equip us to render more real service than a host of such fellows who, in many instances, are as the blind leading the blind, and I believe Mr. Baker [Secretary of War Newton Baker] or any other man of sound common-sense will appreciate the justice of this assertion."

The sergeant major closed the letter: "I know there is no limit to what you are willing to do for me and I hate like the deuce to be always asking favors, but I do want you to see this thing through. And please remember that it is for the good of the service just as much as it is for the good of Cheatham and Cheeseman."[8]

In a letter to his brother, scratched out on the same day he had written to his father, "Plum" complained of the unruliness among the men. "Don't know what we would do if it weren't for the unfailing good humor of our chaps. A regrettable feature is that they love themselves, but they don't love each other as they might. This afternoon the usual 'internal' scrap occurred. One chap introduced a brick to another's head. 'Badly hurt?' I asked a witness. 'Hurt de Frenchman's brick,' he dryly drawled."[9]

But as officers and capable men like Fish, Dayton, and Ranulf Compton scrambled to get out, replacements trickled in, among them the reservists that Cheatham had pointed out to his father.

Five new officers of note, all white but one, were Maj. G. Franklin Shiels, put in charge of the regiment's medical detachment, and lieutenants Leon Cadore, Gorman Jones, Emmett Cochran, and Benjamin Robeson.

The fifty-five-year-old Shiels, a surgeon and former professor at the University of California, gave Hayward's outfit instant prestige. In

1899, as a surgeon of U.S. Volunteers in the Philippines during the Spanish-American War, Shiels had shown extraordinary bravery under fire. Exposing himself to the enemy, he ran more than one hundred yards to aid several wounded Filipinos. He carried one of them back behind the lines. For his gallantry he earned the Medal of Honor.

Lieutenant Cadore was a sleight-of-hand specialist, whether it was with cards, small objects, or baseballs. At twenty-six, he had pitched four years in the major leagues for the Brooklyn Dodgers. After the war, he would gain fame for pitching the longest game in baseball history— a twenty-six-inning affair against the Boston Braves that ended in a 1-1 tie.

Cadore had joined the Dodgers in 1915; in 1917, he posted thirteen wins. But after he had pitched his final game that year, he immediately joined the Army and was sent to Camp Gordon to be an officer. While with the Dodgers, he and Casey Stengel became close friends. The two ballplayers were never apart—until the end of the 1917 season, when

Second Lt. Leon Cadore, a pitcher for the Brooklyn Dodgers, left baseball to enlist in the Army in the fall of 1917. During a two-week furlough in 1918, he pitched in two games for the Dodgers. After the war, he would pitch the longest game, in terms of innings, in major league baseball history, a twenty-six inning 1-1 tie against the Boston Braves.

BASEBALL HALL OF FAME

Cadore enlisted and Stengel was traded to the Pittsburgh Pirates. After earning his commission in the spring of 1918, Cadore was given a two-week furlough before shipping out for France. He went back to New York and pitched two games for Brooklyn. In the first contest he tossed a four-hit shutout against the Cardinals. In the second game he gave up two hits and one run in a no-decision game against the Pirates. In that game, he held Stengel hitless. Afterwards, they sat in the stands and talked over old times. The year before, Stengel and Ed Pfeffer, a twenty-five-game winner for Brooklyn in 1916, had accompanied Cadore to the Brooklyn train station when he was heading off for officer's camp. They gave him a fifty-dollar gold wristwatch. He had been quoted in the New York papers then as saying, "I'm ready to quit baseball and go to war." Now he talked Casey into enlisting. A year later, the two met again on the baseball diamond. Because of his sleight-of-hand tricks, Cadore had captured a bird and was hiding it in his hands when Stengel spotted the feathered creature. He asked Cadore to give it to him. He stuck the bird under his baseball cap and ran out into center field. In front of thousands of Brooklyn fans, Casey doffed his cap. To the delight of everyone, the bird flew off. And one of baseball's great clowns was born.

Two of the new lieutenants, Jones and Cochran, were from Alabama. The son of a deputy sheriff who had been shot and killed by a riverboat gambler, Jones figured he was lucky to have landed anywhere in France, even if it was with troops of color. He was aboard a British armed transport ship, the *Moldavia,* when, on a moonlit night in February, a German U-boat torpedoed it near the entrance to the English Channel. Fifty-three American soldiers lost their lives. Jones struggled into his life jacket as the ship went down. After a few hours he was plucked from the freezing ocean and billeted with an English family in Dover until the United States decided what do with him. Within a few months, he was assigned to the 369th.

Emmett Cochran was the second Alabaman. Actually a native of Georgia who moved to Montgomery before the war, he had been transferred over from the Fifty-fourth Infantry, Sixth Division. It would not be until mid-August that Cochran's presence in the 369th would be felt—and in a most deadly way.

Benjamin C. Robeson, the only African American among these five officers, was one of the replacements for the Rev. William Brooks, as chaplain. The other was the Rev. Thomas W. Wallace. The 369th had sailed to France without a chaplain. Although Brooks was the regiment's first chaplain, he had been too old and physically unfit to go to war. Finding someone to take his place was not a priority of the War Department.

If black troops were to spend time in the war as stevedores, and not in actual combat, there was probably no need for them to have chaplains.

Robeson had followed his father into the ministry. The Rev. William Drew Robeson, a dignified, broad-shouldered man whose youngest son, Paul, recalled as having "rock-like strength," had been the pastor of the Witherspoon Street Presbyterian Church in the tightly knit black community of Princeton, New Jersey. Paul, later a world-famous entertainer remembered for his powerful, electrifying voice, said that his father had "the greatest speaking voice I ever heard. It was a deep, sonorous basso. Richly melodic and refined, vibrant with the love and compassion which filled him." While he was pastor of the Witherspoon Street Church he tried to get his oldest son, William, into Princeton University. The boy's application was denied because of his race, and the family always blamed fellow Presbyterian, Woodrow Wilson, then a professor and administrator at the university, for keeping young William out. The family also blamed the incident for the elder Robeson's curt dismissal by the all-white board of directors as pastor of the Witherspoon Street Church. Unable to get another ministry, Rev. Robeson started life anew as a humble ashman, collecting all the coal ashes from Princeton's townspeople. He conducted that job as he had his ministry, with a quiet dignity that none of his children ever forgot.

Benjamin was every bit his father. "My older brother," wrote Paul, who adored Benjamin, "reminds [me] so much of Pop that his house seems to glow with the pervading spirit of that other Reverend Robeson, my wonderful, beloved father."

Paul also noted Benjamin's natural athleticism, saying that he was such "an outstanding athlete by any standards and had he attended one of the prominent colleges I'm convinced he would have been chosen All-American." He added that Ben was "a remarkable baseball player, fleet of foot and a power at bat; and had Negroes then been permitted to play in the major leagues, I think Ben was one of those who could have the made the grade."[10] When it came to assessing athletic prowess, Paul had the credentials. After the 1918 collegiate football season, while First Lieutenant Robeson was comforting black soldiers on the western front, Walter Camp named Paul, a Rutgers University star, to his All-American football team.

While the new officers were being assigned to the 369th, Lt. Lewis Shaw was just finishing up a machine-gun course and preparing to rejoin the regiment after an absence of almost seven weeks. In a letter to his mother, he mentioned he was anxious to get back to his men. He expected to be assigned to Hayward's staff as a regimental machine-gun officer.

"It is a good and safe job. So I hope I land it for your sake." He warned her, however, that because he had come from the "clubby Third Battalion," he had to overcome a lot of prejudice from the other officers. He confessed that he had found a French girlfriend, only eighteen years old. "She is a great comfort and pleasure to me. I hope to take my weeks permission with her at Nice or some like spot in sunny Southern France. She loves me anyway and adds simply another bit of romance to this worthwhile and exciting life."[11]

He told her of the sudden death of the mother and two sisters of his friend, 2nd Lt. Hal Landon of F Company. In fact, their death enraged the Allies and was more evidence of German butchery. On Good Friday, 1 April, the Germans bombed Paris. Long-range cannons hurled shells into the center of the city. One shell struck a Catholic church. Five women perished inside, and nine others were wounded. Outside the church lay hundreds of mangled corpses. Among the dead buried in the rubble were Mary Landon, wife of New York City lawyer Edward Landon, and their two daughters. The loss was enough to get Landon out of the service, but the New Yorker refused to leave. He now had a personal score to settle with Germans.

As Bastille Day neared, Landon and his fellow officers and men of the 369 ème Régiment d'Infanterie U.S., from the veterans of the old Fifteenth New York to the newly arrived untrained draftees who had never set foot in Gotham and who were to try the patience of Hayward, had their moment against the might of the German Army.

The colonel himself was ripe and ready for that moment. To Scott, he wondered, "Will the American Negro stand up under the terrible shell fire of this war as he has always stood under rifle fire and thus prove his superiority, spiritually and intellectually, to all the black men of Africa and Asia, who have failed under these conditions?" He shook off all doubt, thinking of the "hosts of colored men who must come after us. I wish I had a brigade, yes, a division or a corps of them. We'd make history and plant the hob-nailed boots of the 'Heavy Ethiopian Foot' in the Kaiser's face all right."[12]

16

"There Was Nothing between the German Army and Paris Except My Regiment"

As Bastille Day crept closer, General Henri Gouraud of the French Fourth Army, the gimpy-legged, one-armed hero of the Gallipoli Campaign, had set a trap to lure the Germans out into the open so they could be blown to bits. After the Boche attacked and chased retreating French and American soldiers, now fighting alongside his men—and that included the Rainbow Division—a counterstroke would annihilate the charging, strung out, unprotected enemy line. For each battalion of the 369th Regiment, a token force would be in the front-line trenches— no more than thirty men and one officer for each battalion—awaiting the German attack. In the Third Battalion, that sacrificial honor went to Capt. Hamilton Fish's K Company. He warned his father, "My company will be in the first position to resist the tremendous concentration against us and I do not believe there is chance of any of us surviving the first rush. I am proud to be trusted with such a post of honor and have the greatest confidence in my own men to do their duty to the end." He asked his father that "in case I am killed to be brave and remember that one could not wish a better way to die than for a righteous cause and ones country."[1]

The regiment's orders were, according to Capt. Arthur Little, to "coax the enemy to make the final assault upon our trenches in as heavy strength as possible." As the Allies feigned retreat, the Germans were certain to follow. And then the French artillery would hit them with a box barrage, encircling the Germans in a death trap. Machine gunners would add to the deadly counterattack.

"If not wholly destroyed," Little believed, "they would be almost sure to be so terrifically smashed as to render them practically certain of defeat."[2]

The Allied commander-in-chief, Ferdinand Foch, expected attacks on two fronts. The Germans would hit Flanders in the north and the Champagne sector in the south. He figured the first strike would be Champagne. "In order to play this double game effectively," he stated, "all the French units available had to be concentrated between the Oise and the Argonne. Rested and filled up to strength, they constituted, with the addition of some American and British divisions, an imposing mass of thirty-eight infantry divisions and six cavalry divisions. This was enough to meet the requirements of our defensive front in Champagne and of our offensive operations in the Soissons region."[3]

Throughout June and into the first days of July, the Americans were part of the nail-biting waiting game—waiting for the German assault. Nightly shelling harassed the New Yorkers. Influenza struck, too, afflicting 40 percent of the men in the regiment. Nerves frayed. Sgt. Noble Sissle felt an "air of tenseness that seemed to show that trouble brooded of a greater magnitude than we had witnessed in our section of the front."[4]

"All through the month of June," Little wrote, "the shelling of both of our sectors became dirtier and dirtier, the use of gas more and more frequent."[5]

Nevertheless, German raids across no-man's-land brought individual valor to a few men. Cpl. Frank Harden of Goshen stopped one raid with a small detachment of riflemen, plunking away at the darting foe until they had fallen back. For his heroics, he received the Croix de Guerre.

In the village of Maffrecourt, around which the three battalions were now encamped, a corner of a small churchyard had been set aside for soldiers who were killed or died of disease, most notably of influenza. Many of the men buried there were noncommissioned officers, and the regiment got to calling their section of the cemetery "Sergeant's Hill."

Capt. Napoleon Marshall had recently returned from gas school. His assignment as gas officer was of the "highest importance," he thought. Every night, all night long, he patrolled the forests near the trenches with an orderly—on alert for gas, ready to warn the men asleep in their huts and dugouts. His judgment "involved several factors: the distinction between solid shells and shrapnel and gas shells and direction and velocity of the wind. Gas shells make a wobbling sound as they travel thru the air, spinning over and over. The sharp whistle of the solid shell and the lazy whiz-bang of shrapnel were quickly distinguishable."

Marshall saw how constant shelling and the endless waiting had begun to affect the regiment's mood. He wrote, "The morale of the boys was slowly but visibly seeping."[6] In some cases, soldiers sneaked out of the trenches and went AWOL to distant villages. The artillery fire had proven too much for them. In a letter home, Marshall tried to capture the bombardment's awfulness. "All last night the cannonading was terrific and convulsing, the pen recoils from a description of the indescribable," he wrote. "Such noises and cataclysms can only be suggested, leaving the rest to the imagination. I do not know yet what toll it has taken of the lives of our brave men, for the action which lulled this morning is soon to resume."[7]

He reported that because too many men went absent without leave the commanding general of the Sixteenth Division had threatened to pull the Americans out of the line if they did not stay in the trenches. The general further threatened to send them back to St. Nazaire or elsewhere as laborers.

Sgt. Maj. "Plum" Cheatham remarked about the suspect courage of the "chaps" in a letter to his brother. "There's a popular saying among them, having referred to the day that might come when Fritzie penetrates us in force. That safety first flight is called 'making up a train.' There is a very comical sergeant who never takes to his dugout during avion raids or bombardments—he explains it this way, 'Too much bother fooling wif them dugouts: When the train starts I wants to ketch de cow ketcher!'"[8]

Hayward was now seeing the harmful consequences of the wholesale dumping of untrained draftees into the 369th that later caused him to complain to General Pershing. In one incident, Pfc. Horace Pippin, standing guard, spotted two men sneaking away. He ordered them to halt. When they didn't he shot one and captured the other. After turning him over to the officer of the day, he never saw the soldier again. Forced to do something quickly, Hayward appointed his new gas officer as acting provost marshal and ordered the appropriately named captain to clean up the mess.

For his new assignment that would take him into the surrounding villages where the miscreants were hiding, Marshall was given a beautiful, fleet-footed sorrel horse. His talent as a judge impressed Little. "I have never seen a better Summary Court Officer," he stated.[9]

Marshall went right to work. "Corralling the A.W.O.L.'s in the towns and on the roads and ordering them to report to their commanding officers I soon had discipline restored," he recorded. "I shall always remember the complete obedience which the boys of the 'Fighting Fifteenth' gave me. The regiment retained its place in the line and vindicated the hopes and aspirations of its officers.[10]

But the "cannonading" went on. A shell shrieked into a corral. Sixty horses were cut down. A stable sergeant lost his life. Dying along with him were Marshall's beautiful sorrel and a powerful bay owned by Fish.

"That meant difficulties in transportation of supplies in the immediate future," Little lamented, "and real hunger to come."[11]

Lt. James Europe did not allow the waiting game to get on his nerves. Suffering from eye trouble, perhaps from a German gas bomb, he was pulled out of the trenches and placed in the little hospital outside of Maffrecourt to rest. There he composed tunes inspired by life at the front as he had experienced it.

Resting in the same hospital, Sergeant Major Cheatham notified his brother of the musician's work. "Jim Europe is hors de combat. As a result of defective eyesight. This may not prove a permanent ailment and he may be back *en ligne* before this reaches you. I've been sick-listed myself and we both been *au repos* for a couple of weeks. Jim is capitalizing his time by composing war songs that have really got the needed punch. He ought to cash in heavily on his return."[12]

Before Europe had been sent to the hospital, he had brought with him to the support trench a small folding organ. In the evenings he played the organ and soldiers sang, and their songs wafted out across no-man's-land. An officer suggested he write a song about home "so far away." He wrote a melody that he called "Everything Reminds Me of You."

When he was relieved from trench duty, Europe found a "quaint" piano owned by a French family living in Maffrecourt who had no use for it. He borrowed the piano and had it lugged into the farmhouse where he was billeted. From the window, he had a panoramic view of rolling fields of yellow flowers and golden wheat and, as far as the eye could see, great swaths of red poppy and stands of poplar trees. Sissle remembered the "pure blue of the sun-lit heavens [that] seemed to descend to kiss the earth." He and Europe sat by the piano and started to write, first putting words to "Everything Reminds Me of You."

> In the blue of the skies, I see the blue of your eyes,
> In the thrilling song of a bird, your voice is heard,
> It thrills me, stills me, with love anguish fills me,

I find the white fleur-de-lis an emblem of your purity,
And as the bees kiss the vine, I feel your lips
   Touching mine,
The breath of the rose your perfumed tresses disclose,
   Everything reminds me of you,
   Everything reminds me of you!

The duo composed several other tunes, too. "I've an Observation Tower of My Own" played off the idea that, like actual observation posts such as the one Henry Johnson and Needham Roberts had manned a month earlier, a lover could secretly watch over his gal:

In my observatoire, I'm always looking at you,
Night and day, whether near or far away,
I see every little thing you do.
I'm a spy, Miss Butterfly, and I don't deny, you know why,
So be on the level, you charming little devil,
For I've an observation tower of my own.

They also wrote a song entitled "Trench Trot."

It was after collaborating with Sissle that Europe went back to commanding his machine-gun company. Here, according to Sissle, he suffered mildly from the gas poisoning that landed him in the little hospital with Sergeant Major Cheatham. More than likely, Europe had the flu. Sissle remembered that when he hurried off to visit Europe in the hospital ward, he heard the horrible sound of soldiers who had inhaled mustard gas. A bad dose meant open sores, blindness, scorched lungs, and, in many cases, death. Inside the ward, the pathetic victims burned into Sissle's mind. He saw eyes that were just "bleeding scabs," and, because their nasal passages had been seared, their gasp for "breath resembled the sound of the croak of the frogs that you hear at night passing down the country road."

Sissle found Europe sitting up in bed, hacking to beat the band. He was happy to see Sissle and couldn't wait to show him a new song he had just written. He called it "On Patrol in No Man's Land." When Sissle heard the tune, he at first didn't realize that here was a "masterpiece of jazz description—a soldier's experience in no-man's-land."

There's a minenwerfer coming,
Look out! (bang!)
Hear that roar! (bang!) There's one more! (bang!)
Stand fast! There's a Very light.
Don't gasp, or they will find you all right,
Don't start to bombing with those hand grenades (rat-a-tat-tat),

There's a machine gun! Holy spades!
Alert! Gas! Put on your mask!
Adjust it correctly and hurry up fast.
Drop! There's a rocket for the Boche Barrage,
Down! Hug the ground close as you can,
Don't stand! Creep and crawl, follow me, that's all.
What do you hear, nothing near.
Don't fear, all's clear,
That's the life of a stroll
When you take a patrol out in No Man's land
Ain't life great out in No Man's Land.[13]

After he left the hospital, Sissle was unaware that he and his friend would not see each other again until the war was over. Europe was shipped to a hospital in Paris. When he got out of the hospital, he stayed in Paris on leave. By the end of July Sissle had a chance for a commission. He was sent to a school for new officers and, after earning his second lieutenant's bars, was reassigned to the 370th Infantry, the old Eighth Illinois National Guard. But before he went off to school, Sissle had one more musical duty to perform for the 369th.

On the Fourth of July, the regimental band was ordered to Châlons-sur-Marne, headquarters of the French Fourth Army. The band set out by train to the city, not too distant from Maffrecourt. General Henri Gouraud had planned a gala Independence Day celebration for his French and American troops on the eve of what everyone felt would be the deciding battle of the Great War.

The Fourth was a bright, sun-filled day. Drum Major Sissle and Bandmaster Eugene Mikell led the sixty-plus-member band and the K Company quartet through the streets of Châlons, a city of almost forty thousand people, "playing some of our American marches and popular songs." U.S. flags fluttered along the route in honor of Independence Day. Then there was a concert in the city park, the first time an American band had played there. Sissle was again struck by the look of great sorrow and strain that showed on the faces of the French citizens. "It was quite a pleasure to see the effect that our music had upon these poor war-weary people."

Next to the train station the French had erected a platform and set up seats for five hundred people. Red Cross nurses, doctors, and ambulance drivers—the largest number of U.S. citizens the band had performed in front of, other than soldiers—mingled in the audience with French citizens. Several French generals were present, except the charismatic Gouraud. But he was on the way. Meanwhile, for those already there, the band began the concert.

"And my, how they did enjoy those good old American tunes and syncopated melodies, the quartette's [sic] singing and the boys' dancing," Sissle recalled. "Their faces were illumined with smiles and wreathed with happiness."

The concert was interrupted by an airplane duel. The band wanted to duck off the stage, but stayed rooted to the platform because none of the audience moved an inch. They watched the aerial combat until the French pilot shot down his German foe. The concert then resumed.

Gouraud arrived late. Sissle remembered seeing the "limping form of the little warrior as he came striding down the hill, laden with dust."[14] He briefly addressed the crowd. What Gouraud said was not taken down by Sissle, but earlier in the day he had given an interview to the *New York Times* correspondent Walter Duranty. "We are ready for whatever may come," the general had been quoted. "If the enemy should launch a big attack on this sector they will not pass. All of us, Americans and French alike, realize what it means to have been given the holding of the road to Paris. We will not fail in our trust."[15]

After his speech, Gouraud turned to the band and requested to hear the old plantation melodies and especially the drummers, Stephen and Herbert Wright. His last request, according to Sissle, was for the drum major to sing "Joan of Arc." The effect of the song and of Sissle's wonderful voice mesmerized the one-armed hero.

> Though his eyes seemed to be dimmed with tears, yet there flashed a light from them that literally burned with all the fire and courage for which this great warrior was known. It was quite noticeable that each time, as he stood and listened to the plaintive melody and the touching story of this number, he would be gazing into the skies as though there he saw the very likeness of Joan of Arc, and her mighty hosts that had been previously gathered on the battlefields of France to challenge the hostile foe that France might live and enjoy her freedom.

When Sissle finished, Gouraud stood motionless for a time as if "there was unfolding to him from the skies above some plan, some inspiration that he had the faith to believe would enable him to play an important part in turning back the mighty host that was threatening to devastate his native land."[16]

Three days later, Gouraud issued a proclamation to the "French and American Soldiers of the IVth Army." He ordered that it be read to "all men of all units." In it, he warned of the coming German attack, but said that his army was ready for a defensive battle, that his army had been powerfully reinforced—an "invincible fortress" prepared for a terrible bombardment—and that the "assault will be fierce, in a cloud of dust, of smoke and of gas." To all his men, he said: "In your breast beat brave and strong hearts of free men. Nobody will look back, nobody will fall back one step. Everybody will have only one thought: Kill, Kill many until they have enough of it. And it is why your General tells you: That assault, you will break it and it will be a beautiful day."[17]

Little remembered that when Gouraud's words were read, it had a "splendid effect upon the moral of the 4th Army."

Yet for days afterward, the feared assault never came. "Day after day wore on, and alarm after alarm proved to be false," Little wrote. "Everybody grew to be not only tired physically, with the strain of almost continuous duty, but bored and worn out mentally."[18]

In a 13 July dispatch, *New York Times* correspondent Edwin L. James reported: "There is one topic of conversation and speculation all along the allied line, and it is this—What has happened to the German drive?"[19]

Bastille Day passed quietly. The French provided bottles of champagne—one for every four soldiers—to celebrate their country's national holiday. Soldiers in the trenches and in the support line toasted Gouraud. "To our great general. God bless him!"[20] Back in America, churches paid tribute to France. The Stars and Stripes flew next to the Tricolor and organs beat out "The Star-Spangled Banner" and then the "Marseillaise." In Harlem, the old Fifteenth's first chaplain, the Rev. William H. Brooks, addressed one of his largest congregations in a long time at St. Mark's M. E. Church, declaring that there was no power greater than God's love and that the world must be governed by love, not physical power.

Still the Germans stayed put, even though there were reports that forty-four divisions had massed along the Somme and Aisne Rivers. Perhaps Field Marshal Paul von Hindenburg was biding his time, building his army even bigger. There was an eerie quietness along that part of the western front.

In a letter home, Cpt. Napoleon Marshall fretted. "We are preparing for an infantry attack."

"May God be with us."[21]

The quiet ended just after midnight, Sunday, 14 July, as the last moments of Bastille Day, 1918, faded into memory. Fierce artillery fire poured across the Marne River, thumping Allied positions along a fifty-mile front. Before daylight, the Germans attacked across the river, from north of Châlons in the Champagne province westward beyond

Château-Thierry. They pushed eight kilometers south and west, over-running deserted front-line trenches. The only obstacle that stood between the Germans and Paris was Gouraud's army, and it patiently waited to hit back.

As German shells first fell on the sector held by the 369th, the New Yorkers ducked their heads and longed for the bombardment to end. Yet the German aim was deadly. Five men were killed. Four soldiers in K Company, which had the honor of holding the front-line trenches, were obliterated by a blast. Fish described what happened. "My company was holding the first line position the night of the 15th, and if the boches had attacked in force we would have all been sacrificed. It was not a pleasant anticipation to go through for the successive nights, but luckily for us the boches did not attack in force and contended themselves with smothering us with shells. My company lost three men killed, six wounded and four badly gassed. The men conducted themselves bravely."[22]

The dead from K Company amounted to four. They were Cpl. Morris Link of Mount Vernon, Pvt. Fletcher Battle, twenty years old of 72 West 99th Street, both original volunteers of the old Fifteenth; and Pvts. Perry King of Pennsylvania and Marshall Scott, a draftee from West Virginia. It was Marshall's gruesome job to identify the dead soldiers. Along with a report to Fish he sent a watch and fragments of a book, asking if the captain could identify their owners. "Enclosed is a watch that was found on the body of one of the five men killed in action Sunday night. Two of the bodies were wrecked beyond recognition, upon the bodies the enclosed watch was found. Kindly determine if this watch was the property of Pvt. Marshall Scott." Fish later confirmed that it was Scott's watch. Marshall added that after going over the remains of another body, which had no identification tags, "A close examination of the pockets of the deceased revealed the fragments of a book which we are enclosing."[23] The deceased was Corporal Link, thirty-five. His younger brother, Oscar, survived the war. Link and Battles posthumously received the French war cross.

The bombardment ended by four-thirty. Fish was surprised that losses were so light. "The shell fire was awful," he explained. Now the Rattlers waited for the enemy to come hurtling toward them and, when they were out in the open, to mow them down. But rather than taking part in the planned counterattack, they were ordered to move three miles to the west to reinforce the French 161st Division, which was under severe attack. The sudden move meant a permanent transfer from General Gallais's Sixteenth Division to General Lebouc's 161st Division.

"We were shifted to the west to positions less than a mile from the front line," wrote Fish, "and we are ready in case of a big attack."[24]

Hayward felt that by the time his regiment had completed the shift, "[o]ur officers and men were tired almost to the point of utter exhaustion; they had been hours without food or water; nevertheless they executed this order, moved into and occupied their assigned positions and took up the combat cheerfully and without complaint."[25]

Here Lieutenant Shaw and his squad of machine gunners met a German charge head on while shells dropped all around them. An Associated Press (AP) reporter wrote that the exploding shells did not allow the lieutenant to stand up. Shaw, who had only recently crowed to his mother about his machine-gun training and how being the regimental machine-gun officer would be "a good safe job," had effectively camouflaged his two automatic weapons so the enemy marauders failed to spot them as they came tearing toward the trenches. When his men opened up a withering line of fire, the Germans faltered and fell back. Shaw's two guns fired more than five thousand rounds. Because he could not stand, Shaw rolled from one gun to another to direct the fire.

Not so Pvt. Howard Gaillard and Sgt. Robert Collins. As the Germans tried to regroup, Gaillard climbed atop the parapet. "And while enemy bullets were flying around him," the AP reported, "fired his rapid-fire piece from the hip, first at one group and then at the other."[26]

Collins ignored the return fire and falling shells and also jumped out of the trench, firing his rifle. The Germans were at point-blank range, and he cut them down. Later, he claimed he had left the safety of his trench because he didn't want to miss seeing the firefight.

Afterward, he said, "I thought their shells had messed us up a good deal. But man you should have seen what we done to them. Say, when our machine guns got through with 'em they looked like a bunch of Swiss cheeses."[27]

For his action, Shaw was promoted to captain and later received the Croix de Guerre. He wrote to his mother about the promotion. He had not yet heard about the Croix de Guerre. "I suppose it was on account of the night my two guns stopped a German raid of some size for we were personally congratulated by the French general and mentioned by the French to General Headquarters of the A.E.F." He added, "As you will probably see by now the big battle is on but the French are certainly giving them hell, aided by the Americans. We are in reserve so don't worry. This is the last battle and it will be a big victory."[28]

On 18 July, the *Times* ran a front-page story about the battle, comparing it to an "ultra-Wagnerian accompaniment of forked and sheet lightning and rolling thunder, with intermittent rain showers."

The 369th, now with the French 161st Division, took part in the counterattack. In the midst of the fighting, word reached Hayward that the Germans had been pushed back. Losses were heavy. After two days, the battle was over. The *Times* reported that "On long stretches of the front the wide fields are littered with German corpses, a horrible spectacle." The correspondent stated that "[T]hough heavily outnumbered, the army of Champagne has broken as formidable an onslaught as any allied army can have to meet, and it faces the future with high confidence born of such a test."[29]

Ferdinand Foch was now bristling with confidence. "On July 17th the Germans had been reduced to impotence," he wrote. "On the 18th the guns of the Allies were in turn to make their thunder heard."[30]

A bulletin from regimental headquarters by acting adjutant, 1st Lt. Roger Whittlesey, recapped the battle. It stated that the German attack had been designed to be the greatest of the war, that the Hun had planned to take Reims, Châlons, and Espernay, "thus straightening out their line, and then press on to Paris." But the attack failed.

East of Reims, on the line we had selected as our battle-line, we met and stopped them short everywhere. We have now retaken almost all of our former first line, which was evacuated before the attack, and are proceeding to take the rest. The enemy losses in the attack were heavy; we have taken many prisoners whose morale is very low. . . . The Germans who crossed the Marne have been forced to retire to the North bank, and not a German is now South of that point. . . . Of our own IVth Army, it is said that had it not been for the remarkable and heroic resistance of this Army, who met and stopped the enemy everywhere, the Commander in Chief would not have been able to dispose of his reserves to make the wonderful counteroffensive. General Gouraud, in the order of the Day, congratulates every man of the Army for their splendid resistance.[31]

Hayward was ecstatic about the performance of his men. Later he recollected with some braggadocio about the battle, "The first thing I knew there was nothing between the German army and Paris except my regiment. But that was fair enough—because there was nothing between us and Berlin except the German army. There were the Germans and there was Paris. They tried pretty hard to get by, but they never did. No German every got into a trench with my regiment who didn't stay there or go back with the brand of my boys on them."[32]

For Gotham's troops, their part in the counteroffensive was just beginning. Their new role was to relieve one regiment plus a battalion of Moroccans and, fighting within the 161st Division, push the Germans steadily back. Day after day. Their battle cry still remained, "God damn, le's go!"

By 21 July the regiment had at last taken over a front-line sector between Butte de Mesnil and Main de Massiges. But it seemed odd that instead of battling eastward toward the Rhine, they seemed to be inching west.

"Jokes were beginning to be exchanged about bumping into Paris for breakfast,"[33] remarked Little, recently promoted from captain to major.

Fish didn't want to breakfast in Paris with the 369th. He wanted a transfer. He still hoped his letter to General Hershey of the Seventy-eighth Division would reap results. To his father, he noted, "I hope to get my permission within ten days and expect to arrange a transfer . . . to the 78th Division."[34] In a letter to a family friend he wrote, "I hope to get my permission on Aug. 1st or as soon as this battle has become stabilized."[35]

For Fish and the 369th, there would be no stabilization. At least not the way Fish figured. Every day the French Fourth Army pushed the Germans back. In fact, the whole western front trembled with the Allies forcing the Germans back to a last stand at the Hindenburg Line, a brilliantly fortified defensive bulwark that stretched from the Alps to the North Sea.

For the New Yorkers, the push against the Germans was constant, with no letup, no chance for relief back to some rest area such as Aix-les-Bains, no dodging the endless artillery fire nor lethal gas bombs nor raiding parties, no getting by without any casualties. One bloody day blended into another. Among the severely wounded was Henry Johnson's brother-in-law, Pvt. Charles Jackson. Jackson, who lived in the same Albany house as Johnson when they enlisted together, had his right leg shot off.

In one chunk of a front line, Little and his men came across the bodies of twenty Germans lying at their posts. "These bodies we buried in excavations made in the sides of the trenches," he wrote. "In that sector it was impossible for a soldier to step out of a trench to seek, for any purpose, open ground between the arteries of communication, without drawing fire."[36]

Sgt. "Spats" Davis described to Arthur, his brother back in Harlem, how tired the men were—not just from the daily grind of pushing the Germans backward, but from all the shelling, too:

In the mornings, most of the valleys we went through in those days were full of gas and smoke from exploding shells or from the previous night's bombardment. The sickly sweet odor still smites my nostrils with a little effort of imagination. The air then was tinged a deep greyish blue, and from the top of the hill, you could barely distinguish men moving through the haze below. Inhaling these fumes and noxious gasses, as all of us did at one time or another, no doubt contributed to this inordinate capacity for deepest slumber.

In some cases, soldiers fell asleep while out in no-man's-land, cuddling close to the gaseous ground—sleeping hard enough to snore. "When we halted for a moment," Davis said, "or laid down on the ground to form an ambush, [men] would fall instantly asleep and even start snoring, to the anger and jeopardy of everyone in the party. To wake them was often fraught with possible calamity as to let them continue snoring."[37]

An AP report commented on sleeping soldiers. "Let the average soldier halt and be forced to lie down for a time and he goes to sleep almost immediately, unless he is forcibly kept awake. The leaders of at least one regiment have had to adopt a plan whereby all the members of a patrol, when they lie down, join hands with the white officer at one end. He keeps the squad awake by pressing the hand of the man next to him, who repeats the pressure to his right or left hand, receives an answering pressure as evidence that his companions are awake."[38]

Working his way across a swamp, Pfc. Pippin, who had enlisted in Goshen, remembered "shells droping every where, yet we were advancing sloley. I were in shell holes that were smoking, and they were hot, the machine guns were in trees as well as in bushes and in houses and any thing they could get a machine gun in. . . . The snipers were thick also. I seen a machine gun nest and I got him." Pippin, who wanted so much to be an artist, also picked off a sniper hiding in a tree. "I'm a good shot and I seen him. Then the swamp were safe to cross."[39]

By the first week of August, according to Hayward's calculation, the 369th had been "continuously under fire every day for about one hundred and thirty days."[40] During that time, the men proved their valor beyond a doubt. From 15 July to 31 July, the regiment suffered fourteen killed and fifty-one wounded.

Little's heart, he said, "had become hardened by the loss of human life [and that] I had become accustomed to the reports and the sights of men of God suffering and dying from wounds inflicted by other men of God."[41]

But near the end of July no officer had yet been killed. That changed on the 31st.

2nd Lt. Archibald Worsham, a Missourian, was assigned to the regiment on the 27th. In just a few days he had impressed Capt. Frederick Cobb of White Plains, who confided to Little that the young officer showed much promise. On the night of 30–31 July, he led a reconnaissance patrol into a swamp awash with German machine gunners. In the early morning he found the enemy and attacked. He was shot down and died with several of his men. His body was brought back and placed in a stable. Worsham was buried at the cemetery in Romagne, the eventual final resting place of 147 members of the 369th.

"The world-famed rag-time band of the 15th Heavy Foot played softly and solemnly that day," Little recalled, "and the colored soldiers, gathered bareheaded about the grave, sang with exquisite sweetness and fervor."[42]

Two weeks later, the 369th almost lost another officer—but this time as a prisoner. On the night of 17–18 August, 1st Lt. Gorman Jones, the Alabama transfer who survived a torpedoed troopship while on his way to France, and five of his men were pinned down in a trench by a box barrage. Along with the shrapnel flying from the exploding shells, the doughboys had donned their gas masks because the Germans were dumping gas canisters in their midst. Jones, according to war correspondent Herbert Corey, was not "on the best terms with the colored privates of his platoon. It was merely a difference in manner, for in Alabama race relationships differ from those of New York. But this difference had departed. Latterly, Jones and his platoon were on better terms for each had discovered the fighting blood of the other."[43]

When the shelling ended, Jones peered into the darkness. The moment he reached for a flare cartridge, a German leaped out of the darkness and onto his back, his hands around his throat.

"Silenz!" he hissed through clenched teeth. "Silenz!"

Jones and his handful of doughboys found themselves surrounded by at least seventeen Germans. They discovered two more large groups of them. Their only chance of survival was to throw down their weapons and surrender. As they were prodded back toward enemy lines at the end of a bayonet, they were about to become the 369th's first prisoners of war.

The Germans led Jones and his party past a listening post, unnoticed in the dark of night. Inside crouched Sgt. William Butler, a native of Salisbury, Maryland, who had enlisted in the old Fifteenth back in 1916. Once described as "a slight, good-natured colored youth who until a few years ago was a jack-of-all trades in a little Maryland town,"[44] Butler watched his men in the grip of the enemy with no possible way of escape. His blood boiled.

"Look out, you bush Germans! I'm comin!" Butler growled. He bolted out of his trench, his French Chauchaut automatic rifle cocked.

"Don't fire, Butler!" yelled Jones, afraid the Germans would kill them all.

"Not yet Sir, but soon!"

The Germans wheeled about. Seeing only the threatening shadow of Butler in the gloom, they feared an ambush, that all around them hid bloodthirsty Americans. The moment they took their eyes off their prisoners, Jones cracked the nearest guard in the jaw and his men lit out like greyhounds for the safety of their own lines. When Jones sailed past Butler on a dead run, he screamed, "Now let 'em have it, Sergeant!"

Butler opened up, blasting away at the Germans with his Chauchaut. Instead of standing fast, the slight sergeant single-handedly charged the platoon, bounding over no-man's-land "a-roaring and fogging, through the darkness with his automatic, and nobody knows how many Germans

Sgt. William Butler receives the Distinguished Service Cross from Colonel Hayward. Maj. Lorillard Spencer looks on. Butler won the medal by charging a group of Germans that were taking American prisoners behind the lines. Butler saved all of the prisoners and killed several of their German captors. MILES EDUCATIONAL FILMS

he killed."[45] One account claimed he killed ten. Another listed five. He rushed up to an enemy trench, dropping hand grenades on top of the frightened enemy. He even ripped open one German's stomach with a knife. He wounded many more, including a lieutenant. He carried the injured officer back to his own lines as a prisoner. But the officer died.

"Sgt. Butler . . . attacked with such fury, determination and effectiveness of fire," praised Hayward in a report to AEF headquarters, "as to kill certainly four enlisted men, putting the rest to flight and wounding the officer." Hayward added:

> It is interesting to note the report of this raid captured by us in a German dugout during the subsequent September attack. Butler is described as an "enemy group in over-whelming numbers" and the statement is made owing to the superiority of the rescuing party and the "blut lustige" (blood-thirstiness) of the black men, supposed to be French Negroes wearing English style helmets, the prisoners had to be abandoned. The report ends with the statement that eight men, including Lieut. Schmidt failed to return to the German lines.[46]

In the shelling before Butler's one-man melee, Lieutenant Jones suffered shrapnel wounds to his leg. As a medic wrapped up the wound, he advised the Alabamian, "Jonesie, we'll have to evacuate for that."

"You go to hell," Jones answered. "I'm going to stay with the outfit. They're fighting men."[47]

The *Afro-American* of Baltimore trumpeted Butler's heroics. With a headline reading, "Trenton Has Nothing on Salisbury," the following article stated, "Trenton, New Jersey, may have her Needham Roberts, but it takes Salisbury, Maryland, to produce a William Butler. Roberts had his comrade, Henry Johnson, to help him in repulsing a raiding party of Germans, but Butler took care of a German lieutenant and a squad of Boches all by himself."[48]

A later article in the *Afro-American* called the K Company sergeant "Maryland's Greatest Hero."[49]

For his action, Butler earned the American Distinguished Service Cross and Croix de Guerre.

But Hayward's men would soon learn that, because of the color of their skin, the Medal of Honor was not for them.

17

"Lieutenant, You Shot Me!
You Shot a Good Man!"

The day after Sgt. William Butler's exploits, the 369th Regiment was pulled from the front line and sent to train outside of Châlons where it was finally to become part of the all-black Ninety-third United States Division. The other regiments were the 370th, formerly the Eighth Illinois; the 371st, the only regiment in the division that filled its ranks with draftees; and the 372nd. As it turned out, the New Yorkers never joined those other regiments. The Ninety-third Division never functioned as a true division—only on paper.

Twenty days after settling down for training exercises—first at a camp at Les Maigneux and then at a camp at St. Oeun—and even after cleaning up the barracks for the arrival of the 370th at one of the camps, the Rattlers were on the move again. This time, they were assigned permanently to the French 161st Division, relieving the 115th ème Régiment d'Infantrie that had been split up and dispersed among other French regiments already in the line.

But the nearly three weeks that Col. William Hayward's men spent at Les Maigneux and St. Oeun proved useful, at least according to the colonel.

"Our stay at St. Oeun of a few days was valuable in that it gave us a slight opportunity to practice maneuvers by battalions," he said, "and work out a few simple terrain exercises which practice we found very useful in the subsequent attack of September 26th, even though at this point we were without even our French instructors."[1]

It was here that the 369th lost all of its African-American officers. An order by General John S. Pershing decreed that all black regiments should either be commanded by all white officers or all black officers— a backhanded form of segregation from old Black Jack himself. The only black officers remaining were chaplains Benjamin Robeson and Thomas Wallace.

Capt. Charles Fillmore, the founder of the old Fifteenth, and Lts. George Lacy and Lincoln Reid were transferred to the 370th Regiment. Capt. Napoleon Marshall went over to the 365th. Even Lt. James Europe, still recuperating in Paris, was sent packing. However, it didn't take Hayward long to get him back. After all, the band that he and Europe had recruited and paid for needed its inspirational and creative leader.

The 369th also lost a number of enlisted men who were sent off to officers' training school. Foremost were Sgt. Maj. Henry Cheatham and Sgt. Noble Sissle, Europe's Boswellian friend. Cheatham and Sissle wound up together in the 370th. Yet Sgt. Maj. Benedict Cheeseman, whom Cheatham had urged his father to help get into officers' school, never went anywhere. He stayed with the 369th.

Remembering his appointment as a second lieutenant, Sissle wrote "there must have been at least fifteen other officers of whom were originally sergeants at the 369th who had become members of the 370th."[2]

Before Fillmore left for the 370th, Major Arthur Little cited the "Handsome Major" from Ohio for "conspicuous bravery and devotion to duty." Little had been struck by Fillmore's "marked calmness and courage and persistency" during the counterstroke against the Germans in mid-July. "In forming the groups to go forward to relieve French groups, the Captain performed the duties not only of captain, but of lieutenant, sergeant and corporal, as well. He demonstrated fine leadership and set an inspiring example."[3]

Now, with the departure of Fillmore, Marshall, Lacy, and Reid, Hayward's regiment was commanded solely by white officers. The arrival of fresh officers, like Leon Cadore, the Brooklyn Dodger hurler; George Franklin Shiels, the Medal of Honor winner; and George Robb, a Kansas Republican who voted for Wilson only because the President promised to keep America out of the war, took some pressure off the veteran officers, some of whom had been around since early 1916, and had, like Hamilton Fish, been grousing to get out of the 369th.

Another of the recent transfers was Emmett Cochran, a second lieu-

Noble Sissle soon after he was commissioned as a second lieutenant. FROM *REMINISCING WITH SISSLE AND BLAKE*

tenant formerly with the Fifty-fourth Infantry. A native of Georgia, Cochran was living in Montgomery, Alabama, when he went off to officers' school. He was twenty-five. Whether he was a racist is not known, but his behavior on 21 August brought back in a heartbeat the unpleasant memories of the Alabama troops training at Camp Mills in the fall of 1917.

And champagne was to blame.

Colonel Hayward liked to boast that drunkenness was never a problem with his men. He claimed there were only six cases of drunkenness the whole time his regiment was in France. The 369th, he asserted, had "one of the lowest, if not the lowest, percentages of venereal disease or drunkenness in the A. E. F."[4]

Yet among the French troops, drinking champagne and wine was common, even in the trenches, and it was only natural that they shared the beverage with their American compatriots. 1st Lt. Robb from Salina, Kansas, a teetotaler all his life, got to liking the wine that soon filled one of his canteens instead of water. "Our biggest problem was the wine," Fish recalled. "The Poilu gets a canteen full of red wine every day, never water; but he's accustomed to it. He'd been sipping wine all his life, so he'd usually have it last all day. Not our men—they'd drink the whole darn thing in about fifteen minutes."[5]

"Champagne flows like water," Cheatham had written to his brother before he went off to be an officer in another regiment.

And of course some of the guards got wet. One came into a room where I was, just as a fellow was saying, "I'm more peaceful than [William Jennings] Bryan, and when I parade down 5th Ave. I'm not going to have no gun in my hand—I'm going to have a little dove of peace sitting calmly on my shoulder." And at this juncture a guard swaggered in—automatic hanging low, and "champagne" pronunciation. "To hell with the Kaiser," he yells. "I can lick a dozen like him!" And the other chap calmly remarked, "An' I'm going to vote the *prohibition* ticket, too, if it makes you feel that way."[6]

It was drunken guards of F Company on provost duty at the village of Dommartin-la-Planchette who were at the root of what happened a few days after Lieutenant Cochran joined the regiment.

F Company had a reputation as the toughest outfit in the 369th. The officers and enlisted men were mostly from Brooklyn, or from one of the other towns on Long Island. Company commander, Capt. John Holley Clark Jr., hailed from Flushing, where his father was the high school principal. Before the war, Clark had proven to be a hard-nosed attorney, a Hayward associate. But even his own enlisted men were a handful. If they didn't like certain orders or the way they were treated, they turned obstinate—or threatening. Rumor had it that if a sergeant issued an unwanted order, he'd get shot. When Cochran joined the regiment he was told about "Sergeant's Row."

"If there was a shot fired [in the regiment] and you didn't know where the shot came from, someone would turn to another and say, 'What was that sergeant's name?' and things like that," Cochran later stated. "Also, they claim that a sergeant would perhaps reprimand in the daytime and the next morning he would be found shot."[7]

On 21 August, Maj. Lorillard Spencer posted provost guards in nearby villages around Camp Les Maigneux, looking for soldiers absent without leave, drunk, or disorderly. The guards' orders were to stop all traffic entering the villages and examine passes. Spencer dispatched a detail of five men from F Company to Dommartin, directing them to halt and check all soldiers, officers included, as they entered the village. He put Sgt. Thomas Emanuel in charge. The other men on guard duty were Cpl. Elmer Perry and Pvts. Charles James, Roy Shields, and Walter Whittaker. The entire squad had enlisted in the old Fifteenth and sailed to France aboard the *Pocahontas*. They had taken part in the recent counteroffensive. No matter the reputation of their company, they were men to be trusted.

Private Whittaker, married and from Freeport, Long Island, was a "pretty quiet fellow," according to Sergeant Emanuel. "I never seen him drunk. I don't know when he was drinking and when he was sober because he was the same all the time from his looks." Whittaker never gave his captain any trouble, although Clark stated that he'd get "unusually loud in time of stress, payday, something like that. He would be one of the men who would go A.W.O.L., and get drunk like the rest of them."[8]

In Dommartin the detail had been given a bottle of champagne by a French soldier. Private Shields, who lived on Utica Avenue in Brooklyn, downed most of the bottle's contents and got drunk. The bottle more than likely was passed around among the provost guard. The men got a little loud, maybe too loud. Emanuel placed Shields under house arrest and took away his rifle. Whittaker slung Shield's rifle over his own shoulder. He now carried two rifles. Both were unloaded. In fact, none of the rifles carried by the detail were loaded. Under his arm Whittaker clutched a box of writing paper. Perhaps he intended to write a letter to his wife, Georgiana.

A white officer in the village, not a member of the 369th, warned Spencer that his guard detail was drunk and rioting. Spencer called for Cochran and ordered the lieutenant from M Company to take a squad of men and ride by ambulance cart to Dommartin and arrest Emanuel's entire guard detail.

"From the information I had," Spencer said, "they [Emanuel's detail] were probably pretty rough and I told him [Cochran] to use every means to get them and not allow them to disgrace the regiment any further."

Cochran strapped on an automatic pistol and then picked several men from F Company to accompany him to the village. Pvt. Percy Parker drove the horse-drawn cart with the officer by his side on the wooden seat. Five or six other privates sat in the back of the cart. Before they left, Spencer stopped the cart and, according to Parker, said, "There's some fellows up there [in Dommartin] who are drunk. I want you to bring them back. I don't want you to carry any arms with you. I don't think you will have any trouble, but if you do, get you a club and club them good alongside of the head."

Parker knew Whittaker, and expected no trouble from him. Like Emanuel he remembered him as "a pretty quiet fellow."

When the cart approached the village, Cochran told Parker to keep going. Sergeant Emanuel, seeing the cart loaded with soldiers from his own company, stepped into the middle of the road and raised his hand, ordering Parker to stop. Cochran nudged his driver not to slow down. Whittaker, standing off to the side with two rifles slung over his shoulders and the box of writing paper still tucked under one arm, also hollered for Parker to halt. Because the cart kept moving, he ran out into the road and grabbed the reins of the horse.

"Leave that horse alone!" Cochran shouted. "Let 'em go!"

Whittaker then tried to bring the animal to a standstill.

"Turn that horse loose!" Cochran barked again.

Drawing his automatic he leaped off the cart. Whittaker found himself staring into the barrel of Cochran's side arm. He unslung one of the rifles and placed the unloaded weapon on the ground. He then slipped the other rifle off. Not a word had been exchanged between the two men, officer and private. Even at the moment, Emanuel and Whittaker had no idea why Cochran was there and why his pistol was drawn. Then, as Whittaker crouched over—either to put the second unloaded rifle on the ground or to take aim at Cochran—the lieutenant shot him in the stomach. The bullet ripped through the private's body, came out his back, and then got caught in his pants. The sudden impact failed to knock him off his feet. He just stood there looking into Cochran's eyes.

"Well, Lieutenant," he said, "you have shot me. I was carrying out my orders, and you have shot a good man."

He stood for almost four minutes and then finally sank to his knees. "Boys," he gasped, "if I die tell all the people a good man is gone." He pitched forward onto his face, arms outstretched.

"Nobody move!" commanded Cochran. "I'll kill anyone who moves!"

For almost twenty minutes, not a soul stirred. At last, Cochran explained why he had been sent to the village and that everyone was under arrest. He at last ordered them to carry Whittaker to a dressing station. The wounded soldier was brought to a French station, and there he died.

Whittaker's body was sent back to Freeport. Lieutenant Cochran was court-martialed for murder. The trial lasted two days. No officer of the court was a member of the 369th Infantry. The prosecuting officer argued, "The duty incumbent upon an officer to take every care of the enlisted men under his command is all the greater when, as in the present case, they are of another race, of a race which had not had the advantages of ours, against misuse of power."

Cochran, who had heard the stories of how the enlisted men shot their own sergeants, said to the court that one of the reasons he fired at Whittaker was because "these men were all from F Company."

The judge advocate cited, in part, that "practically all the witnesses who were eye-witnesses of the shooting were colored soldiers, members of the 369th Infantry, and their story as to what happened is very unsatisfactory." The court found Cochran innocent, stating that the native of Georgia "from the evidence, justified in believing that at the time the accused fired the fatal shot, he thought his own life in danger. The acquittal is therefore approved. Lieut. Cochran will be released from arrest."[9]

Twenty years after killing Private Whittaker, ex-lieutenant Emmett Cochran, while living in Shreveport, Louisiana, killed himself in a hotel room with a single gunshot wound to the head.

In the days after Whittaker's death, orders arrived sending the 369th on a secret mission. "Tense excitement prevailed," Little recollected.

For ten days or more, rumors had been going the rounds of a great American offensive to be launched at the St. Mihiel salient, with final objective Metz. This mysterious order confirmed in many minds the conclusion which had been jumped at a week before, when our entire regiment had been withdrawn from sector, to the effect that our days with the French were drawing to a close—that we were to be returned to the American Army, made part of an American division, and go into a victory drive under American generals.[10]

18

"Shell-Shocked, Gassed, Sunk to the Verge of Delirium"

If the men of the 369th thought they were off to join Pershing's American Expeditionary Forces, they were wrong. They were still part of the 161st Division in Gen. Henry Gouraud's French Fourth Army.

Nevertheless, over the next few weeks, the men began a long, secretive journey that placed them opposite the heavily fortified Hindenburg Line. From the Alps to the North Sea, Allied troops had begun massing along the entire length of the famous line, ready for a final assault on the German armies.

Allied commander-in-chief Ferdinand Foch planned a series of attacks, spread over four days, that he hoped would dislodge the Germans and bring the war to an end before another harsh winter set in. The first attack was set for 26 September, when French and American forces would pound that section of the Hindenburg Line between the Suippe and Meuse Rivers. On 27 September, the British First and Third armies would hit the Germans entrenched near Cambrai. A day later, in Flanders, troops commanded by the Belgian king would strike between the North Sea and Lys. Finally, on 29 September, the British Fourth Army, which included New York's Twenty-seventh Division, would launch its attack toward Busigny and the St. Quentin Canal Tunnel.

For the assault on the 26th, Foch assigned Gen. John J. Pershing's new American First Army to the sector between the Meuse and the Argonne, a rugged chunk of land that would prove difficult to punch through. On that day, he chose Gouraud's French Fourth Army to move against the enemy between the Aisne and Suippe Rivers—for those attacking soldiers, another bad slice of real estate.

A key target was the major rail-supply line at Mézières, about fifty miles to the north on the Meuse River. At Grandpré, thirty-five miles south of Mézières, Gouraud's *poilus* would meet up with Pershing's doughboys and they would fight their way north. The French were to dislodge the Germans from the small villages along the way, forcing them west of the Meuse (for the 369th that meant the towns of Ripont, Sechault, and Challerange), while the Americans were to clear the Germans out of the Argonne forest and across the Meuse.

The scheme's success depended on lightning speed. There had to be no delay. Gouraud's and Pershing's armies had to break through—"ruptur[ing] the line of resistance . . . uninterruptedly to as great a depth as possible," Foch wrote on 25 September. "For this reason, halts in the development of the action must be avoided. This applies especially to the advance of the American Army between the Meuse and the French Fourth Army."

He added,

> The American Army therefore must endeavor before all else to press its advantage as far and as promptly as possible in the direction of Buzancy.
>
> The French Fourth Army is to cover the American Army by an advance towards the Aisne near Rethel, and this must be executed with similar speed, resolution and initiative. The Fourth Army must in all cases endeavour to maintain liaison with the American Army, but under no circumstances must it slow up the march of the latter, which remains the deciding factor.[1]

The 369th made its move toward the Hindenburg Line in the stealth of night. Squeezed into 150 French trucks, the New Yorkers were divided by battalion into four sections. They rolled northeast in single file. The road they were on was choked with military traffic. Their truck drivers were Senegalese soldiers. A French captain, or "train master," was in charge of each battalion. The commanders of the battalions were now Maj. Arthur Little, still leading the First, Capt. Frederick Cobb of White Plains at the head of the Second, and Maj. Lorillard Spencer, back from school, reassigned to the Third. As they rumbled through the night, their destination remained a mystery. Finally, the convoy stopped, but the trip was far from over. The men formed up and headed off on a march of thirty kilometers over an unpaved, ancient Roman road, straight and level, the dirt hard-packed as macadam.

The regiment stopped for two weeks, moved into the trenches, endured more shelling and skirmishes with the enemy, and then continued its journey northeast. It finally arrived at the village of Somme Bionne. It was here that Col. William Hayward found out that he and his boys were not about to be a part of any Pershing army; not the First nor the Second. They were to remain with Lebouc's French 161st Division, alongside a Moroccan regiment.

And it was at Somme Bionne that Hayward was first informed of the impending attack on the Hindenburg Line.

"We were told that the Army Gouraud was about to attack from Rheims to the Argonne at the same time that General Pershing's army attacked east of the Argonne," he later wrote. "That the joint objective was Grandpre where a union was to be affected between the two armies with such rapidity as to cut off and capture the entire German forces south of that point." He was told that after heavy bombardment the French Fourth Army would attack head-on along the entire front—a series of several charges that, according to Gouraud, would eat up six to ten kilometers a clip. The 369th would send two battalions into the line, alongside four French battalions. A third battalion would be held in reserve. These six front-line battalions would then take part in the first assault wave on the German defenses. "It was all made very clear," Hayward noted, "and no difficulty was experienced by the commanding officer of the 369th U.S. Infantry or his officers in grasping the plan in all its minutiae, notwithstanding the difference in language."[2]

With the plan of attack now known, Little gathered the men of the First Battalion on a hillside. Sgt. Hannibal Davis recalled how Little, talking to them like a father to his sons, told them "that a million men would go over the top with us when we went and the barrages and fighting would surpass anything we had ever seen. Then he told us the story of Marshal Ney [the French commander under Napoleon], whose knees shook during battle, but whose brave heart held him firm to his duty."

On the night of 24–25 September, the New Yorkers took their position at the start line, awaiting the coming fight. They had to pass down roads jammed with soldiers, French and Moroccan—"all moving up with us to the jumping off place," Davis recollected. "We at last came to rest somewhere—heaven only knows where—in the inky darkness, and sank down to rest and wait for the barrage."[3] Each soldier carried a *musette* bag slung over his shoulder, filled with iron rations, sardines, hard bread, and chocolate. They lugged cartridges, grenades, wire cutters, and two canteens of water. Their gas masks were placed at the alert position, across their chests.

The commander of tough F Company, Second Battalion, Capt. John Holley Clark Jr., who always carried little books of great literature with him on the battlefield, jotted in his diary of 25 September, "It's only a few hours off now, and it's a little solemn and nervous for all we can do. . . . It's going to be a big thing and the Frenchmen tell us there may be little to bother us after our artillery gets through. But I'm of little faith when it comes to stories of Fritz's not having much to offer in the way of resistance. I expect lots, and we'll be lucky if we aren't bumped off."[4]

Chaplain Benjamin Robeson remembered how the "boys'. . . nerves were tingling with the tension of the hour. The great adventure stared them in the face, the supreme sacrifice waited their coming on the hills beyond."[5]

At regimental headquarters, Hayward wrote: "So we waited and counted the minutes which crawled by, made our prayers, nibbled chocolate, looked at certain photographs, yawned, stretched and tried to be cheerful and absolutely normal and unconcerned."[6]

Two officers were missing when the 369th first dropped down into the trenches. They were both from K Company in Spencer's Third Battalion that had once again been assigned a dangerous role in the attack. Capt. Hamilton Fish had been sent to school in Langres. 1st Lt. Samuel Shethar, one of the old Seventh Regiment regulars who had joined the Fifteenth, was stuck in a hospital with influenza. Fish rushed back from Langres to join his company, puffing into the line just hours before the assault. Shethar slipped out of the hospital as an AWOL and also made it back in time for the fight.

"At eleven o'clock [P.M.] the great guns spoke," wrote Little, whose First Battalion was now held in reserve while the Second and Third were concealed in dugouts and tunnels in front of the Germans. "The Battle of the Meuse-Argonne was on!"[7]

The French bombardment roared for six hours and twenty-five minutes. It sounded like the "roll of a titanic drum, explosion so thick upon explosion that no separate sound could be distinguished." During the night, an American war correspondent stood atop a hill close to a "radiant" General Gouraud. "As far as the eye could see the northern sky was split up with flashes that winked out continuously along the whole line," he reported. "Nearly all were the sudden broad glare of French 'departures.' But now and then a tiny triangle of light marked the explosion

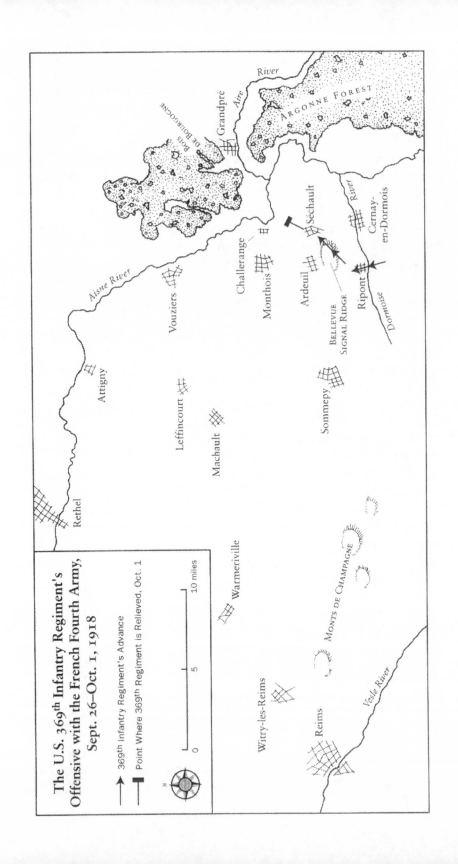

The U.S. 369th Infantry Regiment's
Offensive with the French Fourth Army,
Sept. 26–Oct. 1, 1918

369th Infantry Regiment's Advance

Point Where 369th Regiment is Relieved, Oct. 1

0   5   10 miles

of a German 'arrival.'" One of the French shells struck a distant ammunition dump. For hours afterward a "crimson glow" rose high above the horizon. In comparison to the French, the German counterbarrage was meek, he wrote.[8]

"The whole sky was lit up as though by one prolonged flash," Davis remembered. He recalled the drizzle and the midnight sky before the artillery, black and dismal, pressing down. And when the bombardment began, "the earth quivered under the dreadful shocks and even the air seemed to shake."[9]

Hayward compared it to the "Great White Way." The French shells passing close enough overhead so that he felt their vibration in his hair, sounded to him like "tens of thousands of the noisy birds, big and little, every one delivering himself of a hundred 'whews' and 'shishes' as he was on his way. They seemed not more than two feet above us. I wanted to stick my cane up and touch them."[10]

To the east of the French Fourth Army, Pershing's First Army thundered to life. "We of course never heard the American artillery," the colonel noted.[11]

A moment before the opening fire, K Company Cpl. Horace Pippin thought of home. "i could see it right in front of me. i wonder if i will see it agan. Then i thought of a litter [letter]. If i could only pull a litter from one of my pockets that came from home how happy i would be. But could i do it? No. For i had not seen a litter for some time. . . . Now i longed for a wird from home."

Pippin lit up his last cigarette and passed it around to the men in his squad. They wrapped themselves tightly in their blankets against the cold, damp night waiting for "zero hour" when they would charge across no-man's-land. None of them had overcoats to keep them warm.

One of the soldiers hunched close to Pippin dozed off and dreamt that he saw his mother, and she called to him to come home to her. He started going to her and then awoke with a start and found himself in the underground dugout. "I see he took it hard, but just at that time a shell came near the dug-out then there were no more rest for us that night."[12]

"How long was Dante in hell?" Hayward wondered. "We were in twelve days."[13]

"Just a snatch of sleep," Clark wrote in his diary on the 26th, "and we were out and over."[14]

The Rattlers jumped from their dugouts and trenches, and charged at a "merely quiet military walk"[15] through a dense mist toward a "high hill held by the Germans."[16] The sky had cleared during the night and by mid-morning the sun burned off the low-lying fog. Yet, as the entire French army surged forward, they met little resistance. The Germans had pulled back, perhaps trying to outfox Gouraud by applying the same tactics he had used months earlier in the Champagne counteroffensive. Watching the cheering *poilus* as they attacked, Walter Duranty of the *Times* saw that "the enemy has tried to refuse battle along the whole front."[17]

Little was stunned. The New Yorkers swept between two supposed strongholds for two thousand yards. By ten in the morning it seemed as if the Germans had been routed. "The first and second objectives had been taken with astonishing despatch," he observed, "and prisoners estimated at 18,000 were already in the hands of our division, and marching to the rear."[18]

Clark noted in his diary: "It has been pie so far."

Darting forward over "the most horribly torn up ground I have ever seen," Clark was struck by the absence of the enemy. "I guess the Germans got out before the storm hit."

Around two in the afternoon, he halted his men and allowed them to nap. "My men are sleeping quietly enough now and I've had a nice little nap myself as there has been a lull in the proceedings, but Fritz has a lot of his machine-guns on the next hill, and the bullets sing over us quite regularly. It's a pleasant sound, like the chirp of a bird."[19]

Davis believed that the all-night barrage had "absolutely obliterated all traces of the enemy's front line trenches."

> Where there had been a trench seven or more feet deep, there now existed hardly an impression in the earth; where there had been an impassable barrier of barbed wire, snarled as only the Germans and the devil know how to arrange it, there was now only a few occasional strands of wire protruding or laying on the ground here and there; where there had been a grove of trees, now only a few gaunt, seared spars pointed heavenward.[20]

Even Hayward was surprised there had been little opposition. The first German lines he saw had been annihilated.

Spencer's Third Battalion moved swiftly over the mucky, pockmarked ground. Then it cautiously approached the narrow Dormoise River at a point where it opened up into a tangled, machine-gun infested swamp. The Americans named the mire "Ripont Swamp" in honor of the town nearby. Here, at last, the waiting Germans fought back like wolves.

Was this the trap set by the enemy, similar to the one Gouraud had successfully set months earlier? Intense machine-gun fire whipped into Spencer's men. For a moment the line wavered.

Spencer, heavyset, bespectacled, walked calmly in front of his battalion as they crossed the river. As the Germans poured lead Spencer's way, his poise heartened the battalion—even as six bullets ripped apart his leg. In the confusion that followed, he was lost in the swamp. Lieutenant Shethar, still suffering from influenza, searched for him. When he found the wounded major, he lugged the big man back to a dressing station amid a storm of machine-gun bullets. His helmet was shot off, but he had saved his commander. For his action, Shethar earned the American Distinguished Service Cross.

Yet Spencer's wounding angered Capt. Lewis Shaw of the battalion machine-gun company. "Larry Spencer, the ass, was hit the first day needlessly."

Maybe so, but by inspiring his men, Spencer also received the Distinguished Service Cross.

With Spencer out of action, Hayward had three officers he felt could lead Third Battalion. Captains Shaw, Fish, or David L'Esperance, an attorney from Pelham who had flunked out of Princeton. To Fish's disappointment, the colonel tapped L'Esperance as the battalion's new commander.

In his machine-gun company, Shaw saw that Capt. Ed Walton suffered bullet wounds to the leg that put him out of action. 2nd Lt. John Richards took a shot in the face. "Poor McKenzie [John S. Mckensie] was killed. I had to go without officers after that."[21]

No sooner had these men under Shaw's command been wounded than he gulped too much gas. He had to be withdrawn from the battlefield. With so many officers now falling, the enlisted men turned to their noncoms for leadership.

Unfortunately, a number of the untrained draftees who had never been in combat until that day, snuck away from the fighting—heading back behind the line to safety and then as far away from the war as they dared go.

Cobb's Second Battalion, traveling over high, hilly, forested land on the regiment's right flank, ran into more Germans. Here resistance stiffened, too. Casualties mounted.

One of the wounded was Pvt. William Scott of 19 East 134th Street. A machine gunner, Scott remembered how the Rattlers were "going through the Germans like hell." He was with a platoon that stormed a trench. Fifteen Germans charged out. One of them tackled Scott. He grabbed the Harlem resident's rifle and smashed out his teeth out. The two grappled and fell to the ground. When they got back up, with Scott's mouth a red blur of blood, the Hun stabbed him in the shoulder with a bayonet. The blade missed penetrating the skin, but ripped open Scott's uniform.

"It didn't cut me, but it felt cold, and I thought it about time to end the argument," he later regaled a newspaper reporter. "So I got my bolo knife. And believe me, when I got my strokes in, there wasn't much of that German gentlemen left."[22]

Cobb's battalion worked its way over the Dormoise River on three narrow, wobbly footbridges. The men traveled single file. Shells splashed down around them. Geysers of water boiled up like cauldrons from hell, drenching the soldiers. Whenever a man lost his footing and tumbled into the river, the others roared—their laughter drowned out by the bigger roar of artillery.

With field glasses pressed to his eyes, Little watched from a safe distance the battalion crossing the river. "Many of the men behaved as if they were out on a lark, playing a game of 'Follow my leader,'" he wrote.

The Third Battalion had already fought its way over the river, and now the men of the Second Battalion joined L'Esperance's men. On the north bank, a series of steep hills and ridges, known as "Bellevue Ridge" and "Bellevue Signal," rose up. Here Little noticed the Germans waiting. And when the battalions started up the long incline where beyond stretched a great plain to the north, the "music of the artillery and machine guns broke out."[23]

Recalled Clark, "Fritz began to get in his deadly work and it got worse and worse till it couldn't get any worse." He explained that the Germans had found their mark. "Fritz could see us quite plainly, had the range exactly of every place we got into, and had no difficulty placing machine guns and field artillery where they'd do the most good."

Whenever a barrage died down, he said, medics got busy patching up the wounded in F Company or "just putting a tag on when that was all there was to do."

Pinned down in the bottom of a shallow trench, the men got as low as possible to the damp, gassy ground and spent the night "while the German artillery played on us and the machine gun bullets chirped over us like a great many birds."[24]

Cobb ordered the entire battalion to take refuge for the night. He planned to resume the advance in the early hours of the morning.

While Cobb's battalion had fought its way across the Dormoise River, on the morning of the 27th, Little's First Battalion, held in reserve, moved out for the first time. "We found about ten or twelve dead bodies of 2nd Battalion men," the major recalled. "The Germans had discovered Captain Cobb's command the afternoon before, and had shelled them out of their reversed trenches."[25]

The First Battalion reached its first position without incident. The fighting had moved far forward, still beyond the reach of the reserve unit. For Davis, "there was nothing more exciting than trailing along in single file and picking up souvenirs. Even so, we lost men every now and then from the enemy's desperate shelling or by machine gun bullets coming from somewhere or other up front."[26]

French field guns pushed forward with Little's men. Teams of four horses each strained as they pulled the heavy guns through shell holes and trenches and over barbed wire and the pitted, sticky, rough ground. Behind the guns, *poilus* leaned their backs into the big wheels. Whips cracked, and men swore in French.

Close to the banks of the Dormoise River, Little's men picked out the noise of a fight up ahead, and rushing to the top of a trench, they "waved and shouted in excited interest as they would have done at home at a ball game."[27]

What they were soon witnessing were pieces of the Second and Third Battalions in the midst of fighting their way across the river and into Ripont Swamp. Boche shells and machine gun bullets skipped across the stream, reminding Hayward of a hailstorm on the water's surface.

While Germans zeroed in on the Americans at the edge of the Dormoise, they picked out Little's Battalion standing and cheering on the parapet of the trench and let them have it, too. Their bombs hit with deadly accuracy. The New Yorkers raced along the top of the trench, praying they could dodge the incoming shells. Davis remembered, "[w]alking around a hill and into such a fire zone. Of course no one needed any orders to take cover. Those that didn't get down automatically were knocked down, by bullets, and I sailed pell-mell into a shell hole with another lad." After landing in the shell hole, Davis shook the lad to see if he was okay. When he pulled his hand away it was covered in blood. The soldier was dead.[28]

Across the Dormoise, as they shot their way through the Ripont Swamp, the men of K Company, Third Battalion, came under a blistering defense. Fish ordered Pvt. Elmer McCowan to serve as a messenger and to carry reports back to the battalion so that its new commander, L'Esperance, knew how the company was faring.

Grabbing the first message, McCowan, one of the original volunteers of the old Fifteenth who had lived with his mother Mattie Johnson at 268 West 131st Street before enlisting, headed on his first roundtrip through a hell storm of machine-gun fire. He negotiated that trip without getting shot, although the "Germans pumped machine gun bullets at me all the way." Fish handed him another message. As McCowan darted off, Fish yelled, "And bring me back a cup of coffee."

Recalled McCowan, "I had some time ducking those German bullets. Those bullets seemed very sociable, but I didn't care to meet up with them, so I kept traveling on high gear." The private again made it without a scratch. After he handed over his message, he scrounged up a tin can and filled it with coffee. With the can in his hand, he started back. This time, "it seemed the whole war turned on me." Bullets winged him. One passed through his pants' leg and "it made me hop, step and jump pretty lively." Spying a shell hole, he dove in, hitting the bottom hard. Somehow he had not yet spilt a drop of coffee. When he figured it was clear enough, he sprang out of the hole like a jackrabbit. A bullet dinged into the can, springing a leak. He plugged it up with his finger and then held the can aloft so the Germans could see it. One marksman found his antics not funny and plunked the can, opening up another leak. McCowan plugged that one with another finger and started off again.

Now the Germans were truly mad and fired away. The New Yorker's clothes were riddled, but not one bullet had touched his body. The can was also riddled, and he cupped both hands around it to keep the coffee from pouring out. He kept jumping into and out of shell holes. Then he made it to his own trenches, stumbled, and spilled all the coffee.

A half-hour later, McCowan was in front of the fighting, dressing wounded comrades and carrying the badly wounded back to the relative safety of the K Company trenches. Gas bubbled up from the swamp, and McCowan inhaled the fumes. But even when ordered to a dressing station, he refused to go.

A corporal in his company, Elmer Earl of Goshen, one of Fish's original upstate recruits, went out with McCowan to tend to the wounded. "We came to the edge of a swamp," he later recollected, "when enemy machine guns opened fire. It was so bad that of the fifty-eight of us who went into a particular strip, only eight came out without being killed or wounded." Earl made numerous forays into the thick of the fighting and carried back at least a dozen men.

For their action, Corporal Earl and Private McCowan earned the American Distinguished Service Cross.[29]

However, one of their K Company comrades they could not help that day was Cpl. Horace Pippin, Earl's Goshen neighbor.

One reason was that Pippin had fallen in with I Company. He was starved, having had nothing to eat for several days. He remembered how strong were the German lines, the thickets and trees swarming with machine gunners and snipers, and how shells dropped everywhere. "Yet we were advancing slowly," he said. He and another soldier moved from shell hole to shell hole, each earthen pit hot and filled with smoke. Harassed by a sniper, the two doughboys decided to split up. Pippin picked out a shell hole a few yards away, and made for it on the run. The sniper pulled off three quick shots. The first bullet caught Pippin in the neck. The second hit him in the shoulder. The third went through his right arm, making it useless. He toppled down into the hole. The firing stopped for a moment and his comrade dropped down next to him. He said he had taken care of the sniper. They shook hands and his friend rolled away. Pippin never saw him again.

Another sniper soon started to bang away at Pippin's shell hole. Shells also came close, showering him with dirt and debris. Bleeding, unable to plug up his wounds, unable to move, the Goshen resident spent the night and all the next morning alone in the pit. By afternoon a French soldier appeared along the edge of the crater. He looked down at Pippin and started to say something. The German sniper shot him. The bullet crashed through the back of his head and blew out his face.

"He sank on me," Pippin put down in his memoirs. "I seen him coming on but I could not move. I were just that weeke, so I hat to take him."

Pippin's will to survive was strong. With his good hand, the left, he freed the dead *poilu's* canteen and drank his water. He got to his bread, too, and ate it. To his surprise he discovered the Frenchman had coffee. Using his left hand he got to the coffee and drank some of it. He felt strong enough to get up. But still he could not move, could not push the body away from him. He stayed locked in a grisly embrace the rest of the day and into the night. It started to rain. Water rushed into the crater. Pippin struggled ever harder to get the dead man off him. But at last he had no more strength or energy. He felt faint, and soon fell asleep.

Sometime in the night he was found. "Two boys came and I woke up," he wrote. "They took the French man off me and then took me out of the shell hole for some distance where there were more wounded. . . . I layed out there for some time in the rain, waiting for my turn to be taken down the road to the ambulance."[30]

Pippin's ordeal was a nightmare that lasted all his life. The only way he could exorcise those demons that haunted him was to turn to painting. By the time he died in 1946 he was universally recognized as one of America's foremost folk artists even though he had lost the use of his right arm.

At four-thirty on 27 September, with the French on either side of them, the men of the Second Battalion, now safely across the Dormoise, started forward again. The Germans had pulled back, but on "Bellevue Ridge" and "Bellevue Signal," the heights that loomed over the river, they had left manned machine guns. Bullets poured down from the hill, whining into Cobb's boys.

Clark's company crawled up to the crest of another hill. "As the gray dawn broke we could see from where we lay in the grass the Germans coolly walking from gun to gun, sending out death and destruction by the minute." Clark, 2nd Lt. Oliver Parish, and twenty men were strung out in a line. They believed they were hidden from the Germans. But all of a sudden, the guns turned on them. 1st Sgt. George Williams of Brooklyn took a bullet. Next to him Pvt. Hesse Holland, a draftee from Texas, was fatally struck. "Poor little H. H. . . . gave a gasp and a groan and one after another the whole line was hit."[31]

Clark led his men off the hill. On the way down, Parish's orderly, Pvt. Willie Thompson of 40 South Oxford Street in Brooklyn, got hit in the hand when he and the lieutenant tried to scramble through a patch of barbed wire. Parish bound up the wound and took off down the hill. "We made it thru the fire of two machine guns and when I looked around Willie was not with me. Later I found out he was hit in the wire. He was fine young fellow and had a lot of nerve."[32]

The company took refuge in a shell hole and, according to their commander, the tough boys from Brooklyn "fought with great coolness for about fifteen minutes with rifle and automatic rifle against the machine guns, but the odds were too great." Everytime one of his men exposed a shoulder to fire his weapon he took a slug. Then Clark, described as always cool with a steady head, spotted more Germans circling around to his right, to open up enfilading fire. He knew his shell hole would soon be "good for nothing."

A French officer ordered a retreat, and the Second Battalion pulled back. Clark's riddled company slumped down into a gully only to be greeted by another storm of lead. They cleared out of the deadly spot and sprinted over the crest of hill, where for the moment they were out of the line of fire. They were right back where they had started. Wounded and dying men were scattered about. Clark collected fifteen able-bodied men and rounded up more men from two other decimated platoons.[33]

A sergeant in Cobb's battalion, regarded by Sgt. Davis as "particularly salty, hardheaded and tough-souled," wandered into a detachment of the First Battalion. Davis saw that he was crying tears of anger. Soldiers bunched around him. In his anguish he said that he had lost twenty men in his platoon, and all that had been left were himself, a lieutenant, and four privates. Soon the lieutenant and three of the privates went down. A moment later, the remaining private was killed. Now the sergeant wanted help to go back and save any of his men who might still be alive. Three men, carrying two stretchers, followed the sergeant back to the scene of the bloodbath. There, as they worked on the wounded, a German shell hit them, killing everyone—including the weeping sergeant.

In fact, a shell almost killed Davis. All he remembered was that something had hit him and he fell into a crater of muddy water. As he clawed himself up out the hole "there was a noise in my head like [the zooming of a] tuning fork."[34]

The survivors of the Second Battalion now had to wait through another night for yet another advance against the enemy.

Little, by this time, had begun to catch up to Cobb and L'Esperance. His men advanced easily. Casualties were light. "Being third wave in a movement . . . is a curious kind of position to be in. You get a lot of fire, but you don't get any chance to return fire." In the late afternoon, he realized that both battalions in front of him had been stopped. The day's fighting was winding down. "There was nothing but the desultory firing of artillery, punctuated very rarely with the rat tat tat tat tat of a machine gun."

He also found out that casualties in the first two days had been heavy. When he came across 1st Lt. Roger Whittlesey, the acting adjutant, he was told, "The 2nd Battalion was shot to hell in the dark early this morning, trying to take the ridge at Bellevue Signal."[35]

Back at the regimental field hospital, Maj. G. Franklin Shiels and 1st Lt. Willis Keenan were overwhelmed by the number of casualties brought to them—Americans and French alike. The two doctors and their aides, aprons soaked in blood, worked furiously to save as many men as they could. According to a report, with shells exploding close enough to be extremely bothersome, they handled between three and four hundred wounded on a single day.

The dead were placed side by side, as Davis described, "like so many sacks of oats." He remembered seeing the bodies and then Shiels coming out from under the dressing-station tent. "Our Major Doctor stood by and pointed them out to us as object lessons of 'what happens to damn fools who don't have the sense enough to take advantage of cover during an attack.'" Davis observed that the men who were wounded, the worst were the most patient. "Being close to death, they found a dignity and poise beyond the rest of us. . . . I cannot help but feel that many of the dead I saw simply bled to death while awaiting medical attention."[36]

The battle was far from over, and up ahead, past the northern slope of "Bellevue Ridge" and "Bellevue Signal," the land flattened out into "the most wonderful valley and plain dotted with towns, lakes, chateaux and farms."[37] Giant oak trees grew in abundance in the valley, "so huge," Davis remembered them, "they must have been hundreds of years old."[38] The 369th Infantry's objective was to relieve two French regiments and capture Sechault, to Clark, "a weird and eerie town."[39] Beyond Sechault it was to cross over a plain and through another forest called Les Petits Rosiers to the village of Challerange, a key railroad junction used by the German army and there take a farm. When these objectives had been completed, the regiment was to dig in and await new orders.

The 29th of September was a perfect day for a fight. The sky was cloudless, the air cool. Little's First Battalion, held in reserve since the 26th, had been given the honor of leading the assault on Sechault. Cobb's Second and L'Esperance's Third Battalions followed. All three trooped down off the northern ridges above the Dormoise River and moved on toward Sechault. Little set up a relay chain between himself and Hayward. He put Davis in charge. Runners were set two hundred yards apart. The runners were boys from the south, draftees who only three months earlier had been hoeing corn or picking cotton. Davis pointed out that he had to keep checking on them.

As Little's men descended the ridges and worked their way across the valley under bombardment, they discovered on the outskirts of Sechault a lost and cut-up company from the 372nd Infantry, one of the regiments that made up the so-called Ninety-third Division. The 372nd was fighting with the French 157th Division. According to Hayward, its K Company had "wandered far afield from its zone of advance and had been stopped outside the town by the machine gun fire from within."[40] Little attached the company to his own battalion—"a welcome reinforcement to us that night."[41]

A mile southeast of Sechault, a knob of ground, about three hundred feet high, shielded Cobb's Second Battalion from German artillery. The captain placed most of his men in skirmish formation on the protected side of the knob. Clark lined up his makeshift company on the east side of a road leading into Sechault. Here they were exposed to shellfire and were suffering casualties, so he wished Cobb would hurry up and order them forward.

"I finally became so anxious about our inaction," he wrote in his diary, "which if continued, would have proved fatal."[42]

Clark left his men and ran back to see Cobb. As he approached the battalion commander's post, an uneasy feeling crept over him. At that moment a German shell hit the protected side of the knob. When it burst, Clark saw Cobb fall. "I rushed to him, felt his pulse, found that he was dead." A piece of the exploding shell tore off the back part of Cobb's head. Clark and another soldier lifted their dead commander to the side of the road. There Clark crossed Cobb's arms over his chest and closed his eyes.

When Fish heard that Cobb had fallen, he left his company and worked his way to the hillside. "There was Cobb's body and one of his lieutenants, standing there with a blank stare in his eyes. I tried to talk to him, but he just kept looking into nowhere." Fish ordered the lieutenant to the rear, but the officer declined, saying he wanted to stay with his captain. Fish ordered him again to the rear. Instead of obeying, the lieutenant pulled out his pistol. That frightened Fish. But then, the soldier collapsed to the ground. Fish recalled that he was out like a light. "That poor fellow had given everything he had. There was nothing left."[43]

But for Clark there was no time to mourn the loss of his friend from the old Seventh Regiment. He hurried back to his company, placed Second Lieutenant Oliver Parish in charge. He then took command of the Second Battalion and ordered it forward toward Sechault, over a mile of countryside now heavily bombarded by the Germans.

"I have never seen so terrifying a barrage," Clark confessed, "and I wonder how any of us got through. But the men and officers behaved splendidly."[44]

As Clark's men moved closer to the town, Little's men, "in broad daylight, under heavy fire, and with less than ten casualties," relieved the two French regiments. At fifteen-minute intervals, Companies B, C, already famous because of Henry Johnson and Needham Roberts, and D, with 1st Lt. Lieutenant George Robb, the Kansas teetotaler who had picked up a taste for French wine, dropped down a sharp hill thick with foliage, formed a skirmish line, and advanced on Sechault. B Company took the southwest side, D Company, the northeast, and C Company, the center.

At the edge of Sechault, D Company cleared a squad of machine gunners from a brick house. During the firefight, one of the machine gunners nailed Lieutenant Robb. One bullet shattered his pistol, another knocked off his helmet, a third went through his canteen, filled with wine, and punched a hole in his side. He went down. His side burned, mostly from the wine oozing into his wound. Robb passed out for a moment. When he came to, he was ordered back to a dressing station. Instead, according to Little, "he used his first-aid packet for a bandage and refused evacuation." He stayed out of action for forty-five minutes and then hobbled after his men.

Before sweeping into the narrow, cobbled streets, the companies took cover for a moment in a ditch that ran along the very boundary of the town. As they huddled up, a German airplane buzzed them, the pilot operating a machine gun. The airplane swooped low enough that the Rattlers could see the pilot's face. When the pilot quit harassing Little's men, they piled out of the ditch and moved into Sechault.

Little then sent a message to Hayward's headquarters. It was now 5 P.M. "The town is filled with M. G. snipers," he scribbled. "We are cleaning slowly, but surely. Cannot tell you how soon we can go forward. Shall we halt when too dark to see?"

After sending the message, the major spied a troop of black soldiers coming toward him, working their way down a hill. He had no idea at first who they were. Then Capt. Eric Winston of H Company, Second Battalion, the national squash champion, ran up to him. Tears streamed down his face. Gasping and sobbing, he blurted, "Cobb's been killed!" He let Little know that Clark had now taken over command of the battalion and got it off the hill, where it was being shelled to pieces.

When Clark reached Little, all that was left of his battalion were about 150 men, not even the size of one company.

Even though this force had been terribly thinned out, Little was glad to see them. A report had reached him that the Germans were about to mount a counterattack. Although it was late afternoon and dusk had settled over the land, he ordered Clark to mop up Sechault.[45]

Clark's weary and battered Second Battalion moved out. "German machine gunners [were] sniping through all open spaces," he put down in his diary, "while German lights lit up the outskirts. . . . We were nervous about a counterattack." Because it was dark, the battalion holed up for the night in the ditch outside Sechault. Three machine guns were posted in a barn. Here Clark and his men waited, preparing to "make a last stand."

The counterattack never came. But in the early morning, the Germans shelled the Americans, "a most violent bombardment," Clark noted. It lasted until almost noon. More casualties piled up. Advance was impossible until the shelling stopped. At about noon the German guns went quiet. The Second Battalion and a company from the First Battalion at last entered the town, "a masterly flank movement executed by Capt. [Aaron] Bates of B Co. The machine guns just north of the town were dislodged." Using bayonets and grenades flung through open doors and cellar windows, Clark's men swept the streets and old stone houses of any enemy left behind. By seven the captain reported that Sechault was clear.

Second Battalion was then relieved and sent for a rest. Surviving officers and men were "dog tired, hungry and dirty," Clark wrote. "So exhausting had it been that, though we had had only a few casualties among the officers, I came out with only two beside myself; the rest [of the battalion was] simply shell-shocked, gassed, sunk to the verge of delirium."[46]

After Sechault had been taken, Little walked out in the open in a stupor. He needed to pull himself together. "What have I done this afternoon?" he wondered. "Lost half my battalion—driven hundreds of innocent men to their death." Then, as much a relief to himself as to his surviving officers, he joined them in a deserted stone house. They sat together in darkness: Capt. Seth MacClinton, clad in a private's coat, 1st Lt. George Seibel, 2nd Lt. Ernest McNish, and the wounded George Robb.

In the gloom, Little could tell that Robb still suffered "from his wounds and [was] quite weak; but he persistently refused to quit. He would be all right when the time for his relief should come, and he would be all right for the fight to come in the morning, too. He was just resting, that was all."[47]

The speed that Foch had called for in the Meuse-Argonne Offensive had not happened. Pershing's First Army, although gobbling up large tracts of the forest at first, was now bogged down, and that slowed Gouraud's Fourth Army struggling on his left flank. Further up the Hindenburg Line, Field Marshal Douglas Haig's British Fourth Army had gotten through, but at a gruesome cost. On the 29th, New York's 107th Infantry, made up mostly of old Seventh Regiment National Guardsmen from Manhattan's "silk stocking" district, where a number of the officers of the 369th had first served, charged the center of the line in front of the

St. Quentin Canal Tunnel. The 107th, attached to the British, was decimated, losing more men killed on a single day of fighting than any other regiment in U.S. history.

The biggest criticism hurled at the Americans fighting up and down the Hindenburg Line was that they were too inexperienced. For example, the 107th had been in actual combat only two weeks before it was ordered to charge the St. Quentin Canal Tunnel. Hayward complained that his troops had not been as effective as French troops, that they were "less skillful and suffered greater losses." The reason was simple enough—it was "practically their first war of movement and they had no previous training for such a contingency, except building railroads and dams at St. Nazaire."[48]

Now on the morning of 30 September, with three days of bloody, bitter fighting behind them, the weary men of the 369th Infantry had to cover fifteen hundred meters of open plain and tangled woods, known as Les Petits Rosier, scarred by trenches and craters, to capture a farm and hold the town of Challerange and the railroad junction there. The trenches and craters and woods in front were filled with Germans.

Accompanying the Rattlers in the advance were to be, on the left flank, the French 162nd Regiment and on the right, the French 163rd.

To do the job, Hayward counted on the bravery of his three battered battalions—all terribly undermanned. The strongest was Little's First Battalion. It consisted of three hundred men and nine officers. The Second, under Clark, had a hundred men and three officers. And L'Esperance's Third Battalion was down to 137 men and seven officers. The First and Third were consolidated to form a single combat unit, with Little in command and Clark second. What was left of the Third was held in reserve.

The men and officers spent a miserable, edgy night inside Sechault and in the trenches just outside of town. Their only comfort was the YMCA's Matt Bullock. "Every morning, as the cannon were belching, men falling and bullets whizzing, over the hill came a human form," Chaplain Robeson recalled. "On his back were strapped ten or more cartons of cigarettes, cigars and even the old reliable chew. On he came, now and then dropping for shelter. Men wondered why he came into the region of death. When twilight wrapped the hills in its shadows, back came the same form empty handed, weary but game. His coming and going stopped when there was no regiment to serve."[49] Before the war, Bullock had been the first African American to serve as a head coach at a predominately white college—coaching football at the University of Massachusetts.

Sometime around three in the morning, an unidentified patrol from the French 163rd Infantry unexpectedly emerged out of the darkness. The Americans fired on the men, killing one and wounding three. As the hours crept on, a messenger sprinted up to Little with news that the Germans were about to attack.

Men were kicked awake, with one officer cynically calling, "All out for Custer's last stand!"

Not a single soldier bolted—or caught the "train" out.

Instead, described Little, "The boys from Harlem . . . loosened their knives in their sheaths."[50]

No attack came. Rather, the Germans shelled Sechault. The French artillery, which was supposed to hammer away at the enemy, was silent. The French 163rd slipped past the Americans and moved off toward the woods. At 8:23 A.M. the 369th left Sechault. On the left, there was little resistance. But on the right, C and D companies encountered nests of machine gunners. Lieutenant Robb, already wounded, was hit again. He refused to abandon his company. Under Captain Bates, the nests were cleared out. He reported that more than twenty Germans had fled.

By 1 P.M. the 369th moved into Les Petits Rosiers. The woods were bristling with machine gunners and snipers. Little realized that getting through the woods was impossible without artillery support. He ordered his men out and called for the French to blast away. His men formed a line by a stream in front of the woods and waited.

As D Company stepped out of the woods, a German spotter plane flew by. A moment later, a shell hit the company command post. 1st Lt. George Seibel, company commander, and 2nd Lt. Ernest McNish were killed, as were several enlisted men. Shrapnel struck Lieutenant Robb. Three times within twenty-four hours the Kansan had been wounded. Each time he refused to leave his post. This time, although weakening from loss of blood, he took command of the company and organized its withdrawal. Then he witnessed Lieutenant Parish getting machine-gunned in the arm. He crawled over to the officer, leading a medic. They bound up Parish's arm, and he was taken to a first-aid station. At last Robb felt he had better get patched up. But now he was unable to leave the field of battle under his own power. He was placed on a litter and carried past Little. For a moment the stretcher bearers stopped. Little looked down at Robb.

"Lieutenant," he said, "you are a man after my own heart, and you have enough guts for ten men."[51]

Robb thought it the highest compliment ever given him—even higher

First Lt. George S. Robb, the only soldier from the 369th Regiment to win the Medal of Honor. Robb won the medal for refusing to leave his company until they reached safety despite being wounded three times during the attack on German lines near Sechault and Les Petits Rosiers, France, September 29–30, 1918. It has been argued that sergeants Henry Johnson and William Butler certainly deserved the Medal of Honor as well but were denied it because of the color of their skin.

KANSAS STATE HISTORICAL SOCIETY

than the Medal of Honor that he later received for his actions on the 29th and 30th.

Meanwhile, Little sent 1st Lt. Hal Landon with a message to Hayward. In it he warned that what was left of the regiment had better not reenter the woods without artillery bombardment first. Otherwise, he wrote, "The 15th N. Y. will be a memory."

At the last moment, word came back that a French regiment was on its way to relieve the 369th. At 1 A.M. on 1 October, the *poilus* arrived in the trenches in front of Les Petits Rosiers, allowing the doughboys to withdraw.

Going over the battlefield a few days later, Hayward saw the dead scattered everywhere. "I noticed," he wrote, "that our men and the French when killed generally cuddled in a heap. The Boche, however, was all sprawled out. Maybe because we were always attacking and most of the time crouched down. Both our dead and theirs looked like stuffed figures of wax, except those mutilated by shells."[52]

One of Hayward's lost platoons, led by 1st Lt. Charles S. Dean of Morristown, New Jersey, was found four days after the attack. The platoon was strung out in "perfect alignment, with faces toward the enemy and with bodies hanging on [barbed] wire, all present—none to be accounted for—all present—dead!"[53]

Between 25 September and 3 October, the 369th Infantry, which went into battle with twenty-four hundred men, lost nine officers and 135 enlisted men. Close to one thousand others were wounded, suffering from gunshots, gas, concussions, and shell shock. About six hundred men, who were not wounded seriously, retired from the battlefield rather than advance. Of that number, three hundred were formed into a provisional battalion and, forced by officers and noncommissioned officers, continued fighting. A dozen or more soldiers died of disease—mostly from pneumonia or influenza.[54]

The Rattlers moved up into the Vosges mountains as replacements poured in. The regiment was becoming less a New York outfit as soldiers came from the South and Midwest.

By 6 October, its fighting days were, for the most part, over.

Davis sank down on his raincoat and for the first time since the drive started, took off his boots. A luxury, he sighed. "My toes looked like toes, alright enough, but not like my old familiar toes." He placed his helmet between his feet and fell asleep.[55]

From a hospital bed, the gassed Capt. Lewis Shaw assured his mother that although "the present battle in the Champagne is still raging, everything is Jake by me."[56]

Fish, who for months had been yammering to his father that he wanted a transfer, wrote instead, "I am very glad now that I joined the reg't and took part in the offensive."[57]

And Clark admitted in his diary,

> Above all the horror of these days of battle, stands out my pride in my men and in their heroism. Where I bade them go they went, to their death too often, but with a heroic glad willingness that makes up for the rest. They were my men—the men I worked with and nursed and brought up as a father would his children, never knowing what glories they had undisclosed within them.[58]

In honor of the gallantry and comradeship of the 369 ème Régiment d'Infantrie U.S., which they had started calling "Hell Fighters," the

French felt these black American troops ought to lead the Allies to the Rhine River. Like a medieval army of knights and foot soldiers, their colors snapping in the autumn wind, Hayward's men came down out of the Vosges on the morning of 17 November. The war had been over for six days, and for the first time in four years, there was silence along the western front. The Hell Fighters marched across a plain to the left bank of the great river. Here the regiment occupied the villages of Blodelsheim, Belgau, and Fessenheim, a nine-kilometer stretch along the banks of the Rhine, while before them, remnants of a beaten and cowed German army fled across the river.

Astride a horse, with officers and men of the Headquarters Company arrayed behind him, Hayward rode down to the Rhine. What was going through his mind and the minds of all the men of the old Fifteenth New York has been lost. Perhaps they relished the fact that they had been in combat for 191 days, longer than any other American regiment in the war and that their casualties in the Champagne province from 8 April to 1 October were among the highest of any American regiment in the region. Although the Ninety-third Division did not officially fight as a division, its casualties were exceeded by only one other division, the Second. Even the storied Rainbow Division suffered fewer casualties.[59] Perhaps Hayward's men relished the fact that they had never lost a foot of ground nor had one of their own ever been taken prisoner. Or perhaps they thought back to those uncertain days of 1916 and 1917 when the regiment was just born: training with no armory, but in a theater, a storefront, or street corner; drilling with brooms, laughed at, scorned, rejected; ridiculed as Hayward's "tin soldiers."

Back then, you see, black was not a color of the rainbow.

Hayward slipped from his horse's saddle and, bending down, scooped up a handful of water. In front of his Harlem Hell Fighters—so all those orphans of Uncle Sam could see—he drank from the river. They were the first American combat troops to the Rhine. They would be the first to return home, too. And in the years and decades to come, they would fight in World War II, Korea, Vietnam, and Desert Storm.

New York now had its black National Guard Regiment, and these men of color would be orphans no more.

EPILOGUE

All Suns Had Gone Down

On the south side of the huge Victory Arch that spanned New York's elegant Fifth Avenue at Madison Square, erected to honor America's war heroes, men of the 369th Infantry Regiment—the Hell Fighters—were assembled for a welcome-home parade that would take them up the avenue and into Harlem. It was a mild winter day, 17 February 1919, and one million New Yorkers had turned out to witness the first homecoming of American combat troops from the battlefields of the western front. As they had done almost seven years earlier, when for the first time the Clef Club orchestra had performed before a racially mixed crowd at Carnegie Hall, Gotham's citizens were once again putting aside their differences to greet their African-American heroes.

There was feeling within the black community that from now on life was going to be different. Like their white counterparts, black soldiers had fought and died to make the world safe for democracy overseas. Now, back home, they expected the same rights and privileges.

1st Lt. James Europe, who had composed "Strength of a Nation," the hymn to the state's first regiment of black National Guardsmen, long before it was the old Fifteenth, expected it be so. He even counted on it. The director of the regimental band had admitted as much in a letter written from France to Eubie Blake. "As sure as God made man," Europe

New Yorkers wait to greet their returning war heroes, February 17, 1919.

wrote, "I will be on top and so far on top that it will be impossible to pull me down."[1] For the moment, it seemed he was right. After all, the entire United States wanted to hear his band's syncopated, ragtime airs that had rocked all of France from the Atlantic Ocean to the Alps. But first there was the welcome parade. Next an American tour. Maybe a worldwide tour. Then he could work on his lifelong dream—organizing a true National Negro Symphony Orchestra.

His friend Noble Sissle had similar feelings as he got ready to watch the parade. No longer the drum major of the 369th, he, too, had written Blake from France, soon after he had been commissioned a second lieutenant.

"Well old boy hang on then we will be able to knock them cold after the war. It will be over soon. Jim and I have P_____ [the military censor had deleted the city, probably Paris] by the balls in a bigger way than anyone you know."[2]

Sissle, who had been transferred to the 370th, made it back to New York in time for the parade. Because he was no longer with his old regiment, a bittersweet feeling filled his heart. The band was his band as much as anyone's—except maybe Europe's. He had played a big part in its creation, had been nursemaid to the Puerto Rican recruits, and, although sick as a dog, had been one of its stars as it barnstormed through

France from St. Nazaire to the doughboy rest area at Aix-les-Bains. His singing had made a French general weep. Now he was no longer its drum major, only a spectator.

Flags flew everywhere. And none were more proudly flying than Old Glory and the regimental colors, both brought back from France. Pinned to each one on the upper left-hand corner was the Croix de Guerre, awarded to all the men of the 369th by General LeBouc of the French 161st Division.

The heroes of the parade were Colonel William Hayward, Sergeant William Butler, the wounded like Lorillard Spencer, David L'Esperance, the one-legged Charles Jackson, and his brother-in-law, Sgt. Henry Johnson, all riding in cars. Standing up in the back of an open convertible, the revered Johnson waved heartily to the crowd. A few months earlier, a con artist had gone around Brooklyn claiming to be him. He got free meals, money, and a hero's adulation. Now New Yorkers could hurrah the genuine thing. The crowd loudly cheered Europe's band, of course, led by drum major Sgt. Gillard Thompson, the ex-Buffalo soldier.

Europe did not march in front of his men. He let Thompson do that. He stayed on the left side, next to the cornet players. As the band passed the reviewing stand in front of the Union League Club, where a huge sign read, "Welcome Home To Our Boys From Over Seas," he smartly turned eyes right and saluted.

Behind the band, Major Arthur Little's First Battalion tramped, fifteen men abreast, their rifles against left shoulders, bayonets fixed. "Every bayonet was shining just like the highest polished steel," observed Sissle. "Every rifle was as dustless as though it had been resting in an air-tight case. Trousers were creased, coats pressed and helmets shined as though they had never been covered with the white clay of the Champagne mountains."[3]

Arthur Davis, unable to serve in the war, but who had in the regiment two brothers—one of them "Spats"—and a brother-in-law, remembered how each soldier tried to be stone-faced as they trod along. The reason, he thought, was that each one "had come through having laid his life on the line, survived and had triumphed over ridicule, deception, ostracism and belittlement." Sharing the sentiments of Europe and Sissle, he later wrote, "This parade was a beginning of a new era that would open many new doors of hope for the black man."[4]

To the people of Harlem, Chaplain Benjamin Robeson wrote:

The battle is over, the victory won, and civilization saved. . . . How proud you were of them and their deeds. They had written into the book of history a chapter even time will not efface—the Fighting

Fifteenth. You saw the flag as it waved proudly bearing a Croix de Guerre; you embraced the immortal Johnson, who stands without peer; you watched the resolute step of Sergeant Butler, who breathes the air of fame; you saw others whose names were written on the banner of the daring and exceptionally brave. . . . You know their deeds.[5]

The soldiers' stoicism changed when they reached 110th Street, crossed over to Lenox Avenue, and stepped into Harlem.

The band broke into a Harlem favorite, "Here Comes Your Daddy Now." At that moment, mothers, wives, sweethearts, and sisters ran up to their loved ones in uniform, wrapped their arms around them and paraded right along. Recalled Little, "For the final mile or more . . . about every fourth soldier of the ranks had a girl upon his arm—and we marched through Harlem singing and laughing."[6]

The band also played "Whose Been There While I've Been Gone," and that tune, according to Sissle, "brought a spirit of revelry over the gathered multitude and turned the homecoming into one of happiness, at the same time not losing any of the patriotic spirit." The men "shuffled along " and "no police power could hold the people back."[7]

The Harlem Hell Fighters were home.

A few days after the parade, in Camp Upton where the doughboys had gone to be mustered out of the service, Europe announced that his Hell Fighter's Band had scheduled a ten-week tour of the United States. They would hit eighteen cities, from New York to Boston and west as far as St. Louis, back through Pittsburgh and Philadelphia, and return to Boston for a final three-day engagement. The tour would begin in mid-March and end in mid-May at Mechanics Hall. In Boston, there were plans for Europe and Gov. Calvin Coolidge to place a wreath at the memorial honoring the state's black Civil War regiment, the Fifty-fourth Massachusetts Infantry.

The tour was just the beginning. Europe and his music were back, ready to pick up where he had left off. As he told Blake, he was going to be so far on top that it would be impossible to pull him down.

With the band playing in packed auditoriums, concert halls, theaters, and even a mosque in every place they stopped, there was nothing that could get in his way now. Mechanics Hall was no different than Philadelphia, Chicago, Detroit, or St. Louis. Americans could not get enough of his jazz music.

The Pullman train carrying the large band and a quartet called the Harmony Kings left Philadelphia late on Friday, 8 May. After an overnight trip rolling northeast, the weary musicians reached Boston at seven the following morning. Europe had caught a cold. In fact, a number of the band members were sick. Although the deadly worldwide influenza epidemic had by this time begun to run its course, every day, newspapers still carried an obituary or two of someone or other who had died. Whatever was wrong with Europe it was bad enough for him to seek a physician once they reached Boston.

When the band members arrived at Mechanics Hall at noon to set up for the matinee, it was raining, and the wind that blew off Boston Harbor was cold and raw. It was a dismal day for other reasons, too. Besides being sick, the musicians were downcast like the weather because the gig in Boston marked their final concert as the 369th U.S. Infantry Regimental Band. As they set up for the last time, Europe was nowhere to be seen.

The stage manager showed Sissle to the dressing room that was set close to the stage. Sissle and Europe always shared dressing rooms on the road. Its size reminded Sissle of a large, drab committee room. It contained a plain eight-foot-long library table and several chairs. His and Europe's wardrobe trunks were shoved along the walls. At around two, Europe showed up, still ill. He said to Sissle that the physician had explained to him that if he didn't take care of himself, his cold could turn into pneumonia and then he'd be hospitalized.

Mechanics Hall was not an ideal building for anyone who was sick. "A very cold and barn-like auditorium," Sissle reported.

Nevertheless, the band, with Europe directing, made it through the matinee performance. Because of the weather, the audience was sparse. Rain pounded on the roof. The evening performance started off as poorly as the matinee. The rain refused to let up. Theatergoers chose to stay home where it was warm and cozy, especially those who knew the draftiness of Mechanics Hall.

"When the opening number was played," Sissle recalled, "there were quite a few empty seats noticeable throughout the auditorium—a condition quite unknown to our other engagements."

The tour was ending on a downbeat. Europe was in a sour mood. The weather, his sickness, and, according to his standards, hardly anybody was there.

And the two drummers, Stephen and Herbert Wright, were acting strangely. Herbert was getting up during a number and walking off the stage. Sissle, waiting in the wings for the end of the first set, went up to him and asked him if he was ill. The drummer replied that he was not. But Sissle, who had spent the past two years with him and knew his quirks, saw that he was in a "very sulky and nasty mood." According to Sissle, Wright began to complain about the way Europe treated him. If something went wrong, it was always his fault. Never Stephen's. "I work hard," he said, "and Steve never does anything right and he makes mistakes and then Lieutenant Europe looks back in the drummer section and commences to frowning at me."

Wright then went back on stage to finish his number. Sissle retired to the dressing room. When the set was over, Europe walked into the dressing room, followed by the so-called Wright brothers. Herbert Wright's drum still hung from his neck by a strap. Europe admonished both drummers about giving him a hard time when he was sick and for leaving the stage while the band was still playing. At that time, Roland Hayes, the famous tenor, and three of the Harmony Kings, Horace Berry, Harold Browning, and Exodus Drayton entered the dressing room.

An uneasy feeling came over Sissle, and he whispered to Wright that he better leave. He felt that the orphan from South Carolina was working himself into a rage. Wright got up and left, but he had hardly walked out when, according to Sissle, he barged back in, tore off his drum and hurled it into the corner, all the time screaming, "I'll kill anybody that takes advantage of me! Jim Europe, I'll kill you!"

Wright was sure that he had heard Europe say to him that he "didn't care a damn." With that, Wright said, "I threw my drum down and said 'I was through.'"

Wright's fist was balled up, holding a knife. No one in the room moved a muscle, except Europe and Wright. Europe picked up a chair and put the table between himself and the drummer, "a menacing dwarf," Sissle described him, "as he stood there in his distorted position, crouching as a ferocious animal preparing to lunge upon its victim."

Wright saw that Jim had "seized a chair and swung it back over his head. I then pulled out my pocket knife and held it out at arms length as a warning."

Everyone in the room yelled for Europe to knock the knife from Wright's hand, but nobody moved to help him. Not even his friend Sissle. They were too stunned, "paralyzed," Sissle said, "with humiliation and astonishment." The bandleader put down the chair and, as Wright claimed, "reached across the table that was between us to give me a push and ran into the knife." What Sissle recalled was Wright hurdling over the chair like a panther. "As he came through the air, Europe clasped his body and whirled it away from him, but as the demon had made up his mind to carry out his murderous attack with a back-hand blow, he made a wild swing of his knife, brought it down in the direction of Jim Europe's face."

No one knew then, but Wright himself, that the knife had punctured Jim's jugular vein. Sissle finally acted. He grabbed Wright and forced the drummer from the dressing room, saying, "What's the matter with you?"

Before he got an answer, one of the Harmony Kings yelped, "Sissle, come in at once! Herbert stabbed Lieutenant Europe!"

Back in the dressing room, Sissle saw Europe tugging at his stiff military collar, trying to unbutton it. The moment he unfastened the collar "a stream of blood spurted from a small wound." A towel was wrapped around his throat to "keep the precious blood in." He was carried by ambulance to the nearest hospital. Wright was taken into police custody. No one in the audience knew what had just happened backstage.

As Europe was being wheeled out, he said to Sissle to make sure that the band was at the Statehouse by nine the next morning for the ceremony at the memorial to Robert Gould Shaw and the Fifty-fourth Massachusetts Infantry. "I am going to the hospital, and I will have my wound dressed and I will be at the Common in the morning in time to conduct the band."[8]

That night in the hospital, Lt. James Europe died. He was thirty-nine years old. His dream of a "National Negro Symphony Orchestra" died with him, and America lost one of its greatest composers. Perhaps more than any other soldier, more than Col. William Hayward or Maj.

Funeral procession for James Reese Europe, murdered in 1919 by an enraged member of his band. Drum Major Gillard Thompson is on the far left of the funeral cortege. GILLARD THOMPSON, JR.

Arthur Little or Capts. Charles Fillmore and Hamilton Fish Jr. or Sgt. Henry Johnson, Jim Europe had been the heart and soul of the 369th Infantry—the Harlem Hell Fighters.

As Europe lay dead in a hospital in Boston, back in his cherished Harlem, the "Father of the Blues," W. C. Handy, fell into a fit of depression. Handy, who had composed "Memphis Blues," had no idea why he felt so low and was unable to sleep. At one in the morning he left his apartment and walked the sidewalks of New York. He boarded a subway, the Seventh Avenue Express, and rode it from one end of the line to the other. Back and forth. Back and forth. Even the rumble of the subway disturbed him.

> It was ghostly like the rumble of train wheels out of the past. What trains? What past? For me life had been filled with melancholy journeys, filled with trains rumbling through the night. . . . Always in the rumble of trains there had been the echoes of something sweetly sad, something lost perhaps. Sometimes they had inspired musical thoughts. . . . But tonight no music came. I heard only the click-click of wheels and felt only a numbness and foreboding.

Handy finally left the subway and walked up the stairs, blinking into the sun. It was broad daylight and he heard newsboys on street corners hollering, "Extra! Extra! All about the murder of Jim Europe! Extra!"

Overhead, the sun shone brightly. To Handy, "The new day promised peace. But all suns had gone down for Jim Europe, and Harlem didn't seem the same."[9]

NOTES

PROLOGUE

1. David Mannes, *Music Is My Faith* (New York: W.W. Norton & Co., 1938), 217.
2. Allon Schoener, *Harlem on My Mind: Black America 1900–1968* (New York: New York Press, 1995), 27.
3. Tom Fletcher, *100 Years of the Negro in Show Business* (New York: Burdge & Company, 1954), 258.
4. Mannes, *Music Is My Faith*, 217.
5. Natalie Curtis, "Black Singers and Players," *The Musical Quarterly* 5, 1919, 503.
6. Will Marion Cook, "A Hell of a Life," unpublished autobiography written in Asheville, N.C., 1937, 2.
7. Nobel Sissle, *Memoirs of Lieutenant "Jim" Europe,* manuscript held by the Library of Congress NAACP Records, Group II, Box 156, 22–23.
8. Fletcher, *100 Years,* 258.
9. New York *Evening Journal,* 1 May 1912, 24.
10. Schoener, *Harlem on My Mind,* 26–27.
11. Al Rose, *Eubie Blake* (New York: Schirmer Books, 1979), 59.
12. Sissle, *Memoirs,* 17.
13. Schoener, *Harlem on My Mind,* 26.
14. Sissle, *Memoirs,* 23.

15. Fletcher, *100 Years,* 259.
16. Mannes, *Music Is My Faith,* 218.
17. Sissle, *Memoirs,* 20.
18. Mannes, *Music Is My Faith,* 218.
19. Schoener, *Harlem on My Mind,* 26.
20. New York *Age,* 9 May 1912, 6.
21. Mannes, *Music Is My Faith,* 218–219.
22. "Concert of Negro Music," program, 2 May 1912, Carnegie Hall.
23. Curtis, "Black Singers and Players," 504.

CHAPTER 1

1. Cleveland *Gazette* 15 (13), 30 October 1897. The Ohio Historical Society, *The African-American Experience in Ohio,* 1850–1920.
2. *Gazette* 15 (41), 14 May 1898.
3. *Gazette* 15 (24), 15 January 1898.
4. Charles W. Fillmore to George A. Myers, nd, George A. Myers Papers, The Ohio Historical Society, *The African-American Experience in Ohio,* 1850–1920. Many of Fillmore's letters were undated.
5. Fillmore to Myers, nd.
6. *Gazette* 15 (39), 30 April 1898.
7. Fillmore to Myers, nd.
8. *Gazette* 15 (46), 18 June 1898.
9. *New York Times,* 6 February 1911, 3.
10. Ibid., 1 October 1915.
11. Ibid., 6 February 1911, 3.
12. Ibid., 8 February 1911, 3.
13. State of New York, Assembly Bill 1628, 19 April 1911.
14. *New York Times,* 13 July 1911, 8.
15. *Age,* 20 July 1911, 1.
16. Ibid., 26 July 1911, 1.
17. Ibid., 26 October 1911, 7.
18. Ibid., 1.
19. Ibid., 2 November 1911, 1.
20. Ibid., 9 November 1911, 1.
21. State of New York, Assembly Bill 157, 18 January 1912.
22. *Age,* 16 November 1911, 1.
23. Ibid., 23 November 1911, 1.
24. *New York Times,* 13 February 1912.
25. O'Ryan, John F., oral history, The Reminiscences of John F. O'Ryan, Oral History Collection, Columbia University, 16.
26. Ibid., 16–17.
27. *New York Times,* 5 October 1912, 3.
28. John A. Dix, *Public Papers of John A. Dix, Governor* (Albany, N.Y.: J. B. Lyon Company, 1912), 403–406.

29. Ibid., 406.
30. William Sulzer, *Public Papers of William Sulzer, Governor* (Albany, N.Y.: J. B. Lyon Company, 1914), 503.
31. *New York Legislative Record and Index* (Albany, N.Y.: The Legislative Index Publishing Company, 1 January to 2 June 1913), 409.
32. Edgar L. Murlin, *The New York Red Book* (Albany, N.Y.: J. B. Lyon Company, 1913), 40.
33. Ibid., 44.
34. Hamilton Fish, *Memoir of an American Patriot* (Washington, D. C.: Regnery Gateway, 1991), 20.
35. Murlin, *The New York Red Book,* 40.
36. *Age,* 19 December 1912, 4.
37. George W. Blake, *Sulzer's Short Speeches* (New York: J. S. Ogilivie Publishing Company, 1912), 42–43.
38. *New York Times,* 4 June 1913, 2.
39. *Age,* 12 June 1913, 4.

CHAPTER 2
1. *New York Times,* 18 October 1913, 1.
2. Fish, *Memoir of an American Patriot,* 20.
3. *New York Times,* 15 December 1924, 2.
4. Ibid., 18 October 1913, 3.
5. Ibid., 15 December 1924, 2.
6. Oswald Garrison Villard memo to W. E. B. Du Bois, 15 May 1913.
7. *Age,* 14 May 1914, 1.
8. Louis W. Stotesbury to Arthur W. Little, 4 November 1936.
9. Oswald Garrison Villard to Major Charles Young, 2 August 1913.
10. Friedrich Katz, *The Life and Times of Pancho Villa* (Stanford, Calif.: Stanford University Press, 1998), 7.
11. Ibid., 553.
12. Ibid., 553–555.
13. *New York Times,* 19 June 1916, 1.
14. Interview with Stephen Spencer, son of Lorillard Spencer, 15 October 2001.
15. Stotesbury to Little, 4 November 1936.
16. Arthur W. Little, *From Harlem to the Rhine* (New York: Covici, Friede, Publishers, 1936), 111–112.
17. Spencer interview, 15 October 2001.
18. *New York Times,* 7 April 1916.
19. *Age,* 1 June 1916, 1.
20. Ibid.
21. John F. O'Ryan, *The Story of the 27th Division* (New York: Wynkoop, Hallenbeck, Crawford, 1921), 573.
22. *Age,* 13 April 1916, 4.
23. Ibid., 30 March 1916, 1.

CHAPTER 3

1. Little, *From Harlem to the Rhine,* ix.
2. From a poster provided by Stephen Spencer, son of Lorillard Spencer.
3. Henry Berry, *Make the Kaiser Dance* (Garden City, N.Y.: Doubleday & Company, 1978), 415.
4. *Age,* 29 June 1916, 1.
5. Little, *From Harlem to the Rhine,* 113.
6. *Age,* 30 June 1916, 1.
7. Ibid., 6 July 1916, 1.
8. Brooklyn *Eagle,* 16 September 1917, 7.
9. *Age,* 6 July 1916, 1.
10. Most of the biographical material on Spottswood Poles has been complied by baseball historian and musician Fred (Fredrico) Brillhart, who has spent years studying the life of the "Black Ty Cobb."
11. James A. Riley, ed., *The Biographical Encyclopedia of the Negro Baseball Leagues* (New York: Carroll Graf, nd), 631.
12. Little, *From Harlem to the Rhine,* 115.
13. *The New Yorker,* 6 July 1981, 67.
14. *Age,* 15 June 1916, 6.
15. James Weldon Johnson, *Along This Way* (New York: Thè Viking Press, 1993), 176.
16. Captain Michael J. Reagor, 1882, "Herman J. Koehler: The Father of West Point Physical Education," *Assembly,* January 1993, 16.
17. *Age,* 13 July 1916, 1.
18. Little, *From Harlem to the Rhine,* 116.
19. *Age,* 27 July 1916, 1.
20. Ibid., 2.
21. Ibid., 1.
22. Ibid., 16 November 1916, 1.

CHAPTER 4

1. *Age,* 5 July 1917, 7.
2. Captain Napoleon B. Marshall, *The Providential Armistice: A Volunteer's Story* (Washington, D.C.: Liberty League, 1930), 3.
3. M. Grant Lucas, president of the MU-So-Lit Club of Washington, D.C., to Mrs. Hattie Gibbs Marshall, 14 June 1933. Moorland Spingarn Research Center, Howard University, Washington, D.C.
4. Little, *From Harlem to the Rhine,* 27.
5. Sissle, *Memoirs,* 34–37. In his memoirs, Noble Sissle paints a vivid picture about why James Europe enlisted in the Fifteenth Regiment. Although it certainly contains Sissle's own biased perspective, it carries a strong ring of authenticity.
6. Ibid., 37.
7. Reid Badger, *A Life in Ragtime: A Biography of James Reese Europe* (New York: Oxford University Press, 1995), 20.

8. Irving Lewis Allen, *The City in Slang: New York Life and Popular Speech* (New York: Oxford University Press, 1993), 179.
9. James Weldon Johnson, *Black Manhattan* (New York: Arno Press and The New York Times, 1968), 119.
10. Ibid., 120.
11. Fletcher, *100 Years*, 251–252.
12. Noble Sissle, "Show Business," *Age*, 23 October 1948.
13. Sissle, *Memoirs*, 16.
14. Sissle, "Show Business," *Age*, 9 October 1948, 6.
15. Sissle, *Memoirs*, 10–11.
16. Fletcher, *100 Years*, 251.
17. Sissle, *Memoirs*, 12–13.
18. *New York Times*, 10 March 1928, 8.
19. John W. Love to Noble Sissle, 28 January 1920, included in Sissle's *Memoirs*, 14.
20. Sissle, "Show Business," *Age*, 24 September 1948, 6.
21. Fletcher, *100 Years*, 252.
22. Johnson, *Black Manhattan*, 123.
23. Ibid.
24. Sissle, *Memoirs*, 27.
25. Fletcher, *100 Years*, 252.
26. Rose, *Eubie Blake*, 58–59.
27. Sissle, "Show Business," *Age*, 9 October 1948, 6.
28. Rose, *Eubie Blake*, 59.
29. A sampling of advertising copy from the *New York Times*, Sunday, 15 March 1914.
30. New York *Tribune*, "Negro Composer on Race's Music," 22 November 1914.
31. Badger, *A Life in Ragtime*, 86.
32. Irene Castle, *Castles in the Air* (Garden City, N.Y.: Doubleday & Company, 1958), 113.
33. *New York Times*, 27 May 1915.
34. Castle, *Castles in the Air*, 114.
35. Ibid., 85.
36. Ibid., 113–115.
37. New York *Evening Post*, "Negro's Place in Music," 13 March 1914.
38. Sissle, "Show Business," *Age*, 23 October 1948, 7. Although Sissle claimed in his column that he was writing about the arrival of a typical "Southland Troubadour," his account is so vivid that I believe he was writing from his own firsthand experience.
39. Robert Kimball and William Bolcom, *Reminiscing with Sissle and Blake* (New York: Viking Press, 1973), 34.
40. Sissle, "Show Business," *Age*, 23 October 1948, 7.
41. Sissle, "Show Business," *Age*, 9 October 1948, 7.
42. Rose, *Eubie Blake*, 55–57.
43. New York *Tribune*, "Negro Composer," 22 November 1914.

CHAPTER 5

1. Iver Bernstein, *The New York City Draft Riots: Their Significance for the American Society and Politics in the Age of the Civil War* (New York: Oxford University Press, 1990), 55.
2. Ibid.
3. Edwin G. Burrows and Mile Wallace, *Gotham: A History of New York City to 1898* (New York: Oxford University Press, 1999), 890.
4. Joseph T. Glatthaar, *Forged in Battle: The Civil War Alliance of Black Soldiers and White Officers* (New York: Meridian, 1991), 140–141.
5. Burrows and Wallace, *Gotham,* 895.
6. Ibid., 897.
7. Bernstein, *Draft Riots,* 57.
8. Burrows and Wallace, *Gotham,* 888.
9. Benjamin Quarles, *The Negro in the Civil War* (New York: A Da Capo Paperback, 1991), 190.
10. Ibid., 191.
11. Bernstein, *Draft Riots,* 67.
12. *New York Times,* undated (1864).
13. Sissle, *Memoirs,* 39.
14. *Age,* 2 October 1916, 7.
15. New York *Sun,* 5 October 1916, 1–2.
16. Ann Charters, *Nobody: The Story of Bert Williams* (New York: Macmillan, 1970), 184.
17. *New York Times,* 2 October 1916.
18. Charters, *Nobody,* 184.
19. Fletcher, *100 Years,* 249.
20. Little, *From Harlem to the Rhine,* 117–118.
21. *Seventh Regiment Gazette,* September 1916, 379.
22. *Public Papers of Charles Seymour Whitman, Governor: 1916* (Albany, N.Y.: J. B. Lyon Company, 1916), 882–883.
23. Little, *From Harlem to the Rhine,* 184.
24. *Age,* 5 October 1916, 4.
25. Little, *From Harlem to the Rhine,* 184.

CHAPTER 6

1. Sissle, *Memoirs,* 44.
2. Little, *From Harlem to the Rhine,* 119–120.
3. Sissle, *Memoirs,* 44.
4. Little, *From Harlem to the Rhine,* 116.
5. *Age,* 26 October 1916, 6.
6. Ibid., 19 April 1917, 1.
7. *New York Times,* 18 January 1925, 28.
8. Little, *From Harlem to the Rhine,* 120.
9. Sissle, *Memoirs,* 45.

10. Vivian Perlis interview with Eubie Blake, New Haven, Conn.: *Yale American Music Series,* January 1972, 15–16.
11. Little, *From Harlem to the Rhine,* 120–121.
12. *Age,* 19 April 1917, 1.
13. *Sissle,* Memoirs, 47.
14. Little, *From Harlem to the Rhine,* 121–122. (Frank DeBroit's name is spelled several different ways. I chose to use "DeBroit.")
15. John Chilton, *A Jazz Nursery: The Story of the Jenkins' Orphanage Bands* (London: Bloomsbury Book Shop, 1980), 24.
16. Sissle, *Memoirs,* 73–74.
17. Herbert Wright's biographical background was obtained from the records of the Superior Court for Suffolk County, Massachusetts.
18. The account of Europe's illness and departure to Puerto Rico appears in Sissle's *Memoirs.*
19. Ruth Glasser, *My Music Is My Flag: Puerto Rican Musicians and Their New York Communities, 1917–1940* (Berkeley: University of California Press, 1995), 55, 57.
20. Sissle, *Memoirs,* 53.
21. Glasser, *My Music,* 31.
22. Sissle, *Memoirs,* 53–54.
23. *Age,* 21 June 1917.
24. Ibid., 28 June 1917, 6.
25. Sissle, *Memoirs,* 64.
26. *Age,* 28 June 1917, 6.
27. Sissle, *Memoirs,* 65.
28. *Age,* 28 June 1917, 6.
29. Sissle, *Memoirs,* 65.
30. Ibid., 14–15.
31. Love to Sissle, 28 January 1920, included in *Memoirs.*

CHAPTER 7
1. Johnson, *Black Manhattan,* 232–233.
2. Sissle, *Memoirs,* 52.
3. Marshall, *The Providential Armistice,* 12.
4. *Age,* 12 April 1917, 4.
5. Ibid., 18 April 1917, 4.
6. Little, *From Harlem to the Rhine,* 1.
7. *Age,* 19 April 1917, 1.
8. Stephen L. Harris, *Duty, Honor, Privilege: New York's Silk Stocking Regiment and the Breaking of the Hindenburg Line* (Washington, D.C.: Brassey's, Inc., 2001), 28–29.
9. Little, *From Harlem to the Rhine,* 1.
10. Ibid., 3.
11. The characterizations of Arthur Little are contained in letters to him from former officers of the 369th Infantry: John H. Clark Jr., 3 July 1936, and

Harold M. Landon, 14 July 1936. The letters are part of a scrapbook Little kept that is still in his family.

12. Allison Danzig, *The Racquet Game* (New York: Macmillan, 1930).

13. Hamilton Fish's account of how he joined the Fifteenth is described in at least three publications. Henry Berry's *Make the Kaiser Dance,* Garden City: Doubleday & Company, 1978; his autobiography, *Hamilton Fish: Memoir of an American Patriot;* and an interview with Jon Guttman that appeared in the October 1991 issue of *Military History.*

14. Orange County *Times-Press,* 1 May 1917, 1.

15. Ibid., 24 April 1917, 5.

16. Horace Pippin, *Horace Pippin, 1888–1946, Notebooks,* c. 1920, Washington, D.C.: Archives of American Art, The Smithsonian Institution, filmed January 1972. In many cases, Pippin's spelling is phonetic.

17. Ibid., 1.

18. Albany *Evening Journal,* 14 April 1917, 1.

19. Little, *From Harlem to the Rhine,* 364.

20. *Age,* 1 June 1918, 1. Account of Needham Roberts enlisting in the Fifteenth Regiment is credited to his brother, William Roberts.

21. Sissle, *Memoirs,* 72.

22. Brooklyn *Daily Eagle,* 25 October 1917, 17.

23. Arthur P. Davis, *Here and There with the Rattlers* (Detroit: Harlo Press, 1979), 22.

24. Ibid., 23–24.

25. *Age,* 2 May 1912, 1.

26. *New York Times,* 30 November 1906, 6.

27. Ibid., 2 June 1923, 1.

28. Clement Richardson, *The National Cyclopedia of the Colored Race* (Montgomery, Ala.: National Publishing Company, 1919), 223.

29. *Age,* 2 June 1923, 1.

30. Ibid., 26 April 1917, 1.

31. Charles Fillmore to Joel Spingarn, 18 March 1917. F-154, Box 95-5, Manuscripts, Archives and Rare Books Division, Schomburg Center for Research in Black Culture, The New York Public Library, Astor, Lenox and Tilden Foundations.

CHAPTER 8

1. *New York Times,* 3 July 1917, 1.

2. *The Crisis,* September 1917, 14 (5), 221.

3. *Age,* 12 July 1917, 1.

4. New York *Tribune,* 27 May 1917, 18.

5. Ibid., 27 May 1917, 18.

6. Ibid.

7. *New York Times,* 28 May 1917, 17.

8. *Tribune,* 28 May 1917.
9. *Age,* 5 July 1917, 9.
10. Ibid., 6 July 1917, 9.
11. Noble Sissle, *Happy in Hell,* undated monograph, 2. Literary and Scholarly Typescript Collection, Manuscripts, Archives and Rare Books Division, Schomburg Center for Research in Black Culture, The New York Public Library, Astor, Lenox and Tilden Foundations.
12. *Age,* 15 July 1917, 7.
13. Little, *From Harlem to the Rhine,* 14.
14. *Age,* 19 July 1917, 1.
15. Little, *From Harlem to the Rhine,* 31.
16. Ibid., 35.
17. Sissle, *Memoirs,* 73–74.
18. Hayward to Adjutant General of the Army, 23 June 1920, 4.
19. *The Crisis,* September 1917, 14 (5), 241.
20. *New York Tribune,* 29 July 1917.
21. *The Crisis,* February 1918, 15 (3), 184.
22. Robert V. Haynes, *A Night of Violence: The Houston Riot of 1917* (Baton Rouge: Louisiana State University Press, 1976), 74. Haynes's account of the Houston riot is one of the best. For both quotes, Haynes cites the 21 August 1917 testimony of Sgt. William Nesbitt and a 5 September 1917 statement by Lt. William Chaffin.
23. William H. Amerine, *Alabama's Own in France* (New York: Eaton & Gettinger, 1919), 55–56.
24. *Age,* 18 October 1917, 6.
25. *The Call,* 18 September 1917, 2.
26. Brooklyn *Daily Eagle,* 15 October 1917, 3, and *Age,* 18 October 1917, 1.

CHAPTER 9
1. Little, *From Harlem to the Rhine,* 47.
2. *New York Times,* 31 August 1917, 3.
3. Ibid.
4. Speech of Hon. Samuel J. Nicholls, in the House of Representatives, 23 April 1917 (Spartanburg County Public Library), 5.
5. Spartanburg *Weekly Herald,* 1 August 1917, 4.
6. Samuel J. Nicholls to Secretary of War Newton Baker, 21 August 1917. Duke University, Samuel J. Nicholls Papers, Box 7.
7. *New York Times,* 31 August 1917, 4.
8. Ibid., 17 September 1917.
9. New York *Tribune,* 7 October 1917.
10. Spartanburg *Weekly Herald,* 31 August 1917, 4.
11. Spartanburg *Weekly Herald,* 1 September 1917, 4.
12. Capt. Charles Fillmore, B Company, to Headquarters, 15th Regiment, 23 August 1917 and 24 August 1917, respectively. National Archives and

Records Administration (NARA), Modern Military Records Branch, College Park, Maryland.

13. Sgt. H. C. Smith, B Company, to Col. Fillmore, 21 August 1917. National Archives and Records Administration.

14. Little, *From Harlem to the Rhine,* 46.

15. Causes of death are from Brigadier General J. Leslie Kincaid's *Roll of Honor: Citizens of the State of New York who Died while in the Service of the United States during the World War* (Albany, N.Y.: J. B. Lyon Company, 1922).

16. Brooklyn *Eagle,* 13 September 1917, 1.

17. Ibid.

18. *New York Times,* 14 September 1917, 3.

19. Brooklyn *Eagle,* 13 September 1917, 1.

20. Little, *From Harlem to the Rhine,* 47.

21. Berry, *Make the Kaiser Dance,* 416.

22. Hamilton Fish Jr. to Franklin Roosevelt, 4 October 1917, on file at the New York State Library, Albany, N.Y.

23. Fish, *Memoir of an American Patriot,* 28.

24. *Brooklyn Eagle,* 12 October 1917, 3.

25. *Age,* 18 October 1917, 1.

26. Little, *From Harlem to the Rhine,* 54–55.

27. *Age,* 18 October 1917, 1.

28. Fish, *Memoir of an American Patriot,* 26.

29. Little, *From Harlem to the Rhine,* 56.

30. Brooklyn *Eagle,* 18 October 1917.

31. Little, *From Harlem to the Rhine,* 55.

32. *Sissle,* Memoirs, 77.

33. Little, *From Harlem to the Rhine,* 58. I make the assumption that the soldier who was thrown into the gutter was, indeed, Henry Johnson. Little described him as the "boy . . . who, a few months later, was to prove against German raiding patrols that he was not afraid to fight."

34. Arthur E. Barbeau and Florette Henri, *The Unknown Soldiers: African-American Troops in World War I* (New York: Da Capo Press, 1996), 73. Little also mentions Marshall's being thrown off the trolley, but does not use the words "dirty nigger." See p. 57 in *From Harlem to the Rhine.*

35. Little, *From Harlem to the Rhine,* 59.

36. Ibid., 60–61.

37. Ibid., 59–63. The only account of this incident is by Little. As far as I know, no corroborative evidence has yet been found to back it up, although it more than likely took place. Thus, it deserves to be retold. None of the soldiers, it appears, were disciplined.

38. New York *Tribune,* 20 October 1917, 7.

39. Brooklyn *Eagle,* 25 October 1917, 8.

40. *Tribune,* 21 October 1917, 8.

41. *Eagle,* 22 October 1917, 8.

42. Sissle, *Happy in Hell,* 2.

43. Sissle, *Memoirs,* 78–82.

44. Little, *From Harlem to the Rhine,* 67–68.

45. Sissle, *Memoirs,* 82.

46. Little, *From Harlem to the Rhine,* 69.

47. Lewis Shaw, letter to his mother, nd. Lewis E. Shaw Papers, courtesy of the New York Historical Society.

48. Emmett Scott, "Critical Situations in the Camps," in *The American Negro in the World War* (Chicago: Homewood, 1919). Reprinted as *Scott's Official History of the American Negro in the World War* (New York: Arno Press and the *New York Times,* 1969).

49. Little, *From Harlem to the Rhine,* 70.

50. Scott, "Critical Situations in the Camps."

51. Ibid.

52. Hamilton Fish Jr. to his father, 23 October 1917, New York State Library, Albany, N. Y.

53. Sissle, *Memoirs,* 85.

54. Berry, *Make the Kaiser Dance,* 416.

55. Little, *From Harlem to the Rhine,* 71.

56. Berry, *Make the Kaiser Dance,* 416.

57. Albert M. and A. Churchill Ettinger, *A Doughboy with the Fighting 69th* (New York: Pocket Books, 1993), 9.

58. Center for American History, the University of Texas, Austin. The Center is a repository for newspaper articles clipped and collected from the vast Hearst Empire, as well as many non-Hearst newspapers, including the *New York Times.* Most of the articles are, unfortunately, undated.

59. Amerine, *Alabama's Own,* 56.

60. *A Pictorial History of the Negro in the Great World War, 1917–1918* (New York: Touissant Pictorial Company, 1919), 22.

61. Ettinger and Ettinger, *Doughboy,* 9.

62. Brooklyn *Eagle,* 24 October 1917.

63. Berry, *Make the Kaiser Dance,* 416.

64. Ettinger and Ettinger, *Doughboy,* 9.

65. Berry, *Make the Kaiser Dance,* 417.

66. *New York Times,* 28 October 1917, 28.

67. Berry, *Make the Kaiser Dance,* 417.

CHAPTER 10

1. Little, *From Harlem to the Rhine,* 75.

2. Sissle, *Memoirs,* 84–86.

3. Little, *From Harlem to the Rhine,* 76.

4. Fish to his father, 23 October 1917.

5. Shaw to his mother, 12 November 1917.

6. Report on the *USS Pocohontas* (*sic*) to Joint Board of Survey #1, 19 December 1919, National Archives and Records Administration.
7. Little, *From Harlem to the Rhine*, 77–78.
8. Sissle, *Memoirs*, 85.
9. Ranulf Compton, diary, 12 November 1917. Property of his granddaughter, Nathalie Compton Logan.
10. Little, *From Harlem to the Rhine*, 79.
11. *A Pictorial History of the Negro in the Great World War*, 22. Matthews's account indicates that the Third Battalion was in Camp Merritt before the first sailing of the *Pocahontas*, but I believe he was mistaken because after the troopship broke down, the entire regiment was stationed there until repairs had been made.
12. Compton, diary, 30 November 1917.
13. *A Pictorial History*, 22.
14. Little, *From Harlem to the Rhine*, 80.
15. Compton, diary, 5 December 1917.
16. Shaw to his mother, 3 December 1917.
17. *A Pictorial History*, 22.
18. Compton, diary, 6 December 1917.
19. William Hayward, quoted in *The Literary Digest*, 10 May 1919, 63–64.
20. Hayes, *A Night of Violence*, 1–5.
21. Shaw to his mother, 10 December 1917.
22. Compton, diary, 6 December 1917.
23. Little, *From Harlem to the Rhine*, 87.
24. Sissle, *Memoirs*, 87.
25. Compton, diary, 13 December 1917.
26. *New York Times*, 14 December 1917, 1.
27. Little, *From Harlem to the Rhine*, 88.
28. Sissle, *Memoirs*, 85.
29. Little, *Harlem to the Rhine*, 88.
30. Compton, diary, 14 December 1917.
31. Sissle, *Memoirs*, 88.
32. Compton, diary, 14 December 1917.
33. Sissle, *Memoirs*, 90.
34. Marshall, *The Providential Armistice*, 3.
35. Fish to Franklin D. Roosevelt, 1 January 1918, New York State Library, Albany.
36. Little, *From Harlem to the Rhine*, 90–91.
37. Marshall, *The Providential Armistice*, 3.
38. Sissle, *Memoirs*, 92.
39. Davis, *Here and There with the Rattlers*, 42.
40. Compton, diary, 25 December 1917.
41. Shaw to his mother, 28 December 1917.
42. Sissle, *Memoirs*, 93.

43. Fish, *Memoir of an American Patriot,* 28.
44. Compton, diary, 17–19 December 1917.
45. Sissle, *Memoirs,* 94–95.
46. Ibid., 95–96.
47. Compton, diary, "Xmas," 25 December 1918.
48. Shaw to his mother, 28 December 1917.
49. Scott, "Record of 'The Old Fifteenth,'" in *The American Negro in the World War.*
50. Fish, *Memoir of an American Patriot,* 28.
51. Shaw to his mother, 28 December 1917.
52. Little, *From Harlem to the Rhine,* 96.
53. Fish, *Memoir of an American Patriot,* 28.
54. Horace Pippin, *Notebooks.*
55. Sissle, *Memoirs,* 99–107.

CHAPTER 11

1. Sissle, *Memoirs,* 77.
2. *A Pictorial History,* 23.
3. William Hayward to R. D. Lillibridge, in the *New York Times,* 7 February 1918, 9.
4. Little, *From Harlem to the Rhine,* 98–99.
5. Compton, diary, 1 January 1918.
6. *A Pictorial History,* 23.
7. Sissle, *Memoirs,* 77–78.
8. General John J. Pershing, *My Experiences in the First World War,* I (1931; reprint, New York: Da Capo Press, 1995), 90.
9. Ibid., vol. 2, 228.
10. Berry, *Make the Kaiser Dance,* 418.
11. Brooklyn *Eagle,* 24 June 1917, 4.
12. *New York Times Magazine,* 23 June 1918, 10.
13. Fish letter to his father, nd.
14. William Hayward to Adjutant General of the Army, 23 June 1920.
15. Little, *From Harlem to the Rhine,* 99.
16. Compton, diary, 22–26 January 1918.
17. Fish to his father, 13 January 1918.
18. Shaw to his mother, 11 January 1917. (Obviously, Shaw misdated this letter. It was written in 1918.)
19. Sissle, *Memoirs,* 79.
20. Marshall, *The Providential Armistice,* 4.
21. Lorillard Spencer, quoted in the *Age,* 14 December 1918, 1.
22. From interviews conducted in the 1970s by William Miles for his film, *Men of Bronze.*
23. Sissle, *Memoirs,* 79–81.
24. Pippin, *Notebooks,* 4.

25. Fish to his father, nd.
26. Shaw to his mother, 11 January 1918.
27. Compton, diary, 15 January 1918.
28. Fish to "Tante," 30 January 1918.
29. *New York Times,* 19 December 1917, 9.
30. Ibid., 28 April 1918, IV, 8.
31. Winthrop Ames to Noble Sissle, 10 February 1920, included in Sissle, *Memoirs,* 124–125.
32. Sissle, *Memoirs,* 82.
33. Fish to his father, 13 January 1918.
34. Little, *From Harlem to the Rhine,* 99–100.

CHAPTER 12

1. James G. Harbord, *The American Army in France, 1917–1919* (Boston: Little, Brown and Company, 1936), 475.
2. *New York Times,* 18 April 1918, 20.
3. "Vacations de Luxe for American Soldiers in France," *Outlook,* 14 September 1918, 14–16.
4. Sissle, *Memoirs,* 84–85.
5. The account of the concert is taken from both Little's *From Harlem to the Rhine,* 126–128, and Sissle's *Memoirs,* 86–88, which is actually from an account that he wrote for the St. Louis *Post-Dispatch,* 10 June 1918.
6. Sissle, *Memoirs,* 88.
7. Little, *From Harlem to the Rhine,* 128–129.
8. Winthrop Ames to Noble Sissle, 10 February 1920, included in *Memoirs,* 124–129.
9. Ibid., 127–128.
10. *New York Times,* 18 February 1918, 3.
11. Sissle, *Memoirs,* 128.
12. Little, *From Harlem to the Rhine,* 137.
13. From the *369th Regimental Report* (condensed), 14 March 1919. National Archives and Records Administration.
14. *The Afro American* (Baltimore), 22 March 1918, 1.
15. Little, *From Harlem to the Rhine.* 138.
16. Ibid.
17. Morris J. MacGregor and Bernard C. Nalty, *Blacks in the United States Armed Forces: Basic Documents,* vol. IV, *Segregation Entrenched, 1917–1940* (Wilmington, Del.: Scholarly Resources, Inc.), 91.

CHAPTER 13

1. Little, *From Harlem to the Rhine,* 143.
2. Ibid., 145–146.
3. Berry, *Make the Kaiser Dance,* 418.
4. Sissle, *Happy in Hell,* title page.

5. Scott, "Record of 'The Old Fifteenth,'" in *The American Negro in the World War.*

6. Joe Lunn, *Memoirs of the Maelstrom: A Senegalese Oral History of the First World War* (Portsmouth, N.H.: Heinemann, 1999), 46–47.

7. Charles John Balesi, *From Adversaries to Comrades-in-Arms: West Africans and the French Military, 1885–1918* (Waltham, Mass.: Crossroads Press, 1979), 99.

8. Lunn, *Memoirs of the Maelstrom,* 142–143.

9. Report from General Gallais, 10 April 1918. Musée de L'Armée Hotel National des Invalides, Paris.

10. Sissle, *Memoirs,* 134.

11. Berry, *Make the Kaiser Dance,* 419.

12. Little, *From Harlem to the Rhine,* 148.

13. Davis, *Here and There,* 42.

14. Confidential Report from the 369th U. S. Infantry to Historical Division, American Expeditionary Force, 7 January 1919. National Archives and Records Administration.

15. Ibid.

16. Hamilton Fish to his father, 1 May 1918.

17. Scott, "Record of 'The Old Fifteenth,'" in *The American Negro in the World War.*

18. Hamilton Fish to his father. Date crossed out by censors.

19. Little, *From Harlem to the Rhine,* 183–188.

20. *Age,* 25 May, 1918, 2.

21. Ibid., 1 June 1918, 1.

22. Little, *From Harlem to the Rhine,* 147.

23. Ibid., 160.

24. Compton, diary, March–April, 1918.

25. Shaw to his mother, 2, 10 April 1918.

26. Marshall, *The Providential Armistice,* 4.

27. Hayward Report to Adjutant General of the Army, 23 June 1919, 7. National Archives and Records Administration.

28. Fish, 1 May 1918.

29. Ibid., 1 May 1918.

30. Little, *From Harlem to the Rhine,* 163.

31. Fish, 1 May 1918.

32. Little, *From Harlem to the Rhine,* 165–174.

33. Kimball and Bolcom, *Reminiscing with Sissle and Blake,* 66.

34. *New York Times,* 1 May 1918, 1.

35. Sissle, *Memoirs,* 155–164.

CHAPTER 14

1. *Age,* 11 May 1918, 1.

2. Lester Walton to Herbert Bayard Swope, 24 May 1918. Woodrow Wilson Papers, Sterling Library, Yale University.

3. "Irvin Cobb on the Negro Solider," *Age,* 31 August 1918, 4.
4. Irvin S. Cobb, *The Glory of the Coming* (New York: George H. Doran Company, 1918), 283.
5. *The Literary Digest,* 15 June 1918, 43–47.
6. Ibid.
7. Cobb, *The Glory of the Coming,* 292–297.
8. *The Literary Digest,* 15 June 1918, 43–47.
9. *Age,* 1 March 1919, 5.
10. Little, *From Harlem to the Rhine,* 192–199. Little's account, described as "The Battle of Henry Johnson," differs somewhat from several newspaper accounts, including that of Martin Green of the New York *Evening World* as well Johnson's own telling. But they all are essentially the same.
11. Cobb, *The Glory of the Coming,* 295.
12. *The Literary Digest,* 15 June 1918, 43–47.
13. *Age,* 25 May 1918, 1.
14. Ibid.
15. Cobb, *The Glory of the Coming,* 295.
16. *Age,* 31 August 1918, 4.
17. Ibid., 25 May 1918, 2.
18. Washington *Bee,* 14 September 1918, 1.
19. Lester Walton to Hon. Joseph Tumulty, Secretary to President Wilson, 12 June 1918. Sterling Library, Yale University.
20. *New York Times,* 27 July 1918, 7.
21. *Age,* 3 August 1918, 4.
22. Ibid., 28 July 1918, 1.

CHAPTER 15

1. *Age,* 15 May 1918, 1.
2. Memorandum from General Gallais to the commanding general, French VIII Corps, 19 May 1918. Musée de L'Armée Hotel National des Invalides, Paris.
3. Col. William Hayward to the Commander-in-Chief, G.H.Q., AEF, 9 October 1918. National Archives and Records Administration.
4. Scott, "Record of 'The Old Fifteenth,'" in *The American Negro in the World War.*
5. Brig. Gen. Lytle Brown, War Department, Memorandum (WPD 8142-172) for the Chief of Staff, 5 July 1918. Military History Institute, Carlisle, Penn.
6. Hamilton Fish to Gen. Mark Hershey, Seventy-eighth Division, 2 July 1918. National Archives and Records Administration.
7. Maj. Edwin Dayton to Capt. Hamilton Fish, 24 May 1918. Hamilton Fish Papers, New York State Library, Albany, N.Y.
8. Henry Plummer Cheatham to his father, 30 May 1918. Henry Plummer Cheatham Collection, 1892–1940, Manuscripts, Archives and Rare Books Division, Schomburg Center for Research in Black Culture, New York Public Library, Astor, Lenox and Tilden Foundations.

9. Cheatham to his brother, Chas. Cheatham, 30 May 1918. Schomburg Center for Research in Black Culture, New York Public Library.
10. Paul Robeson, *Here I Stand* (Boston: Beacon Press, 1958), 1–23.
11. Lewis Shaw to his mother, 6 May 1918. New York Historical Society.
12. Scott, "Record of 'The Old Fifteenth,'" in *The American Negro in the World War.*

CHAPTER 16
1. Hamilton Fish to his father, 8 July 1918.
2. Little, *From Harlem to the Rhine,* 214.
3. Ferdinand Foch, *The Memoirs of Marshall Foch,* Translated by Col. T. Bentley Mott (Garden City, N.Y.: Double, Doran and Company, 1931), 354.
4. Sissle, *Memoirs,* 174.
5. Little, *From Harlem to the Rhine,* 212.
6. Marshall, *The Providential Armistice,* 5.
7. Philadelphia *Tribune,* 17 August 1918, 1.
8. Cheatham to his brother, 30 May 1918.
9. Little, *From Harlem to the Rhine,* 29.
10. Marshall, *The Providential Armistice,* 5.
11. Little, *From Harlem to the Rhine,* 227.
12. Cheatham to his brother, 28 June 1918.
13. Sissle, *Memoirs,* 165–168.
14. Ibid., 173–180.
15. *New York Times,* 5 July 1918, 3.
16. Sissle, *Memoirs,* 180–181.
17. General Henri Gouraud Order 6641/3, 7 July 1918. National Archives and Records Administration.
18. Little, *From Harlem to the Rhine,* 220.
19. *New York Times,* 14 July 1918, 1.
20. Little, *From Harlem to the Rhine,* 222.
21. Philadelphia *Tribune,* 17 August 1918, 1.
22. *New York Times,* 20 August 1918.
23. Napoleon Marshall memorandum to Hamilton Fish, 18 July 1918. National Archives and Records Administration.
24. Fish to his father, 18 July 1918.
25. William Hayward, report to Assistant Chief of Staff, 7 January 1919, 4. National Archives and Records Administration.
26. Center for American History, University of Texas, Austin (See note 58, Chapter 9).
27. *New York Times,* 13 August 1918, 5.
28. Lewis Shaw to his mother, 18 July 1918.
29. *New York Times,* 18 July 1918, 1.
30. Foch, *The Memoirs of Marshall Foch,* 360.
31. Bulletin, 369th Headquarters, 20 July 1918. National Archives and Records Administration.

32. Center for American History, University of Texas, unidentified undated newspaper article.
33. Little, *From Harlem to the Rhine,* 226.
34. Hamilton Fish to his father, 18 July 1918.
35. Fish letter to "Virginia," 21 July 1918.
36. William Hayward report to Assistant Chief of Staff, 7 January 1919. National Archives and Records Administration.
37. Davis, *Here and There with the Rattlers,* 52–53.
38. Cleveland *Advocate,* 12 October 1918, 1.
39. Pippin, *Notebooks.*
40. Scott, "Record of 'The Old Fifteenth,'" in *The American Negro in the World War.*
41. Little, *From Harlem to the Rhine,* 248.
42. Ibid., 250.
43. Baltimore *Afro-American,* 11 October 1918.
44. *New York Times,* 28 April 1919.
45. Baltimore *Afro-American,* 11 October 1918.
46. William Hayward report to Assistant Chief of Staff, 7 January 1919, 5.
47. Baltimore *Afro-American,* 11 October 1918.
48. Ibid., 17 January 1919, 4.
49. Ibid., 30 August 1918, 1.

CHAPTER 17

1. William Hayward report to Assistant Chief of Staff, 7 January 1919, 5.
2. Sissle, *Memoirs,* 185.
3. Little, *From Harlem to the Rhine,* 239–240.
4. Hayward to the Adjutant General of the Army, 23 June 1920, 15. National Archives and Records Administration.
5. Berry, *Make the Kaiser Dance,* 419.
6. Cheatham to his brother, 30 May 1918.
7. Record of the Trial by General Court Martial of 2nd Lieut. Emmett Cochran, 369th Infantry, 29 November 1918, 108. National Archives and Records Administration.
8. Ibid., 97.
9. Ibid., Ruling from Judge Advocate's, 25 October 1918, 1–3.
10. Little, *From Harlem to the Rhine,* 253.

CHAPTER 18

1. Foch, *The Memoirs of Marshall Foch,* 408–410.
2. William Hayward report to Assistant Chief of Staff, 7 January 1919, 7. National Archives and Records Administration.
3. Davis, *Here and There,* 53–54.
4. John Holley Clark Jr., diary, 25 September 1918. Courtesy of the Clark family.

5. *Age,* 29 March 1919, 1.
6. *The Negro in the Great War,* 27.
7. Little, *From Harlem to the Rhine,* 269.
8. *New York Times,* 27 September 1918, 1.
9. Davis, *Here and There,* 54.
10. *The Negro in the Great War,* 26.
11. William Hayward report to Assistant Chief of Staff, 7 January 1919, 8.
12. Pippin, *Notebooks.* Pippin's notebook is difficult to read as it is rambling, without proper dates, and filled with phonetic spellings. There is no record of his wounds, although he was obviously severely wounded. I have taken the liberty of quoting from his work at points where I believe he was at the time he entered his thoughts on paper.
13. *The Negro in the Great War,* 27.
14. Clark, diary, 26 September 1918.
15. *Princeton Packet* (nd). Seeley G. Mudd Manuscript Library, Princeton University.
16. Davis, *Here and There,* 53.
17. *New York Times,* 27 September 1918, 1.
18. Little, *From Harlem to the Rhine,* 270.
19. Clark, diary, 26 September 1918.
20. Davis, *Here and There,* 55–56.
21. Shaw to his mother, 4 October 1918.
22. *Age,* 8 February 1919, 2.
23. Little, *From Harlem to the Rhine,* 273.
24. *Princeton Packet,* nd.
25. Little, *From Harlem to the Rhine,* 271.
26. Davis, *Here and There,* 57.
27. Little, *From Harlem to the Rhine,* 272.
28. Davis, *Here and There,* 57.
29. The accounts of McCowan's and Earl's heroism are in Scott, "Record of the 'Fifteenth'" in *The American Negro in the World War.*
30. Pippin, *Notebooks,* 50–56.
31. Clark, diary, 4 October 1918.
32. Oliver Parish to Arthur Little, 19 September 1936. From the Little family scrapbook.
33. Clark, diary, 4 October 1918.
34. Davis, *Here and There,* 64.
35. Little, *From Harlem to the Rhine,* 274.
36. Davis, *Here and There,* 64.
37. *The Negro in the Great War,* 27.
38. Davis, *Here and There,* 59.
39. Clark, diary, 4 October 1918.
40. Hayward report to Assistant Chief of Staff, 7 January 1919, 9.
41. Little, *From Harlem to the Rhine,* 290.

42. Clark, diary, 4 October 1918
43. Berry, *Make the Kaiser Dance*, 423.
44. Clark, diary, 4 October 1918.
45. Little, *From Harlem to the Rhine*, 286–288.
46. Clark, diary, 4 October 1918, and the Princeton Packet, nd.
47. Little, *From Harlem to the Rhine*, 293–294.
48. William Hayward report to Assistant Chief of Staff, 7 January 1919, 10.
49. *Age*, 29 March 1919. 1
50. Little, *From Harlem to the Rhine*, 297.
51. George Robb to Arthur Little, 27 November 1936. Little family scrapbooks.
52. *The Negro in the Great War*, 27.
53. Little, *From Harlem to the Rhine*, 311.
54. Although the actual number of casualties varies from source to source, I relied on Peter J. Linder, one of the foremost authorities on World War I casualties, Kincaid's *Roll of Honor* (see bibliography) that lists New Yorkers killed in the Great War, and the richly detailed *American Armies and Battlefields in Europe*, American Battle Monuments Commission, U.S. Government Printing Office, 1938, 369.
55. Davis, *Here and There*, 78.
56. Lewis Shaw to his mother, 9 October 1918.
57. Hamilton Fish to his father, 10 October 1918.
58. Clark, diary, 4 October 1918.
59. *American Armies and Battlefields in Europe*, 369.

EPILOGUE
1. Kimball and Bolcom, *Reminiscing with Sissle and Blake*, 66.
2. Ibid., 69.
3. Sissle, *Memoirs*, 191.
4. Davis, *Here and There*, 84.
5. *Age*, 29 March 1919, 1.
6. Little, *From Harlem to the Rhine*, 362.
7. Sissle, *Memoirs*, 195.
8. The account of Europe's death is taken from Sissle's *Memoirs*, 223–234, and the records of the Superior Court for Suffolk County, Massachusetts.
9. W. C. Handy, *Father of the Blues* (New York: Da Capo Press, 1991), 228–229.

BIBLIOGRAPHY

Allen, Irving Lewis. *The City in Slang: New York Life and Popular Speech.* New York: Oxford University Press, 1993.

Amerine, William H. *Alabama's Own in France.* New York: Eaton & Gettinger, 1919.

Anderson, Jervis. *This Was Harlem.* New York: Farrar, Straus Giroux, 1982.

Aptheker, Herbert, comp. & ed. *Writings by W.E.B. Du Bois in Periodicals Edited by Others.* Millwood, N.Y.: Kraus-Thomson Organization Limited, 1982.

American Armies and Battlefields in Europe, American Battle Monuments Commission, U.S. Government Printing Office, 1938.

Ayres, Leonard P. *The War with Germany: A Statistical Summary.* Washington, D.C.: Government Printing Office, 1919.

Badger, Reid. *A Life in Ragtime: A Biography of James Reese Europe.* New York: Oxford University Press, 1995.

Balesi, Charles John. *From Adversaries to Comrades-in-Arms: West Africans and the French Military, 1885–1918.* Waltham, Mass.: Crossroads Press, 1979.

Barbeau, Arthur E., and Florette Henri. *The Unknown Soldiers: African American Troops in World War I.* New York: Da Capo Press (reprint), 1996.

Berlin, Ira, Joseph P. Reidy, and Leslie S. Rowland, eds. *Freedom's Soldiers: The Black Military Experience in the Civil War.* Cambridge: Cambridge University Press, 1998.

Bernstein, Iver. *The New York City Draft Riots: Their Significance for American Society and Politics in the Age of the Civil War.* New York: Oxford University Press, 1990.

Berry, Henry. *Make the Kaiser Dance.* Garden City, N.Y.: Doubleday & Company, 1978.

Blake, George W. *Sulzer's Short Speeches.* New York: J. S. Ogilivie Publishing Company, 1912.

Broun, Heywood. *Our Army at the Front.* New York: Charles Scribner's Sons, 1919.

Brown, Lloyd L. *The Young Paul Robeson: "On My Journey Now."* Boulder, Colo.: Westview Press, 1997.

Bullard, Robert Lee. *Personalities and Reminiscences of the War.* New York: Doubleday, Page and Company, 1925.

Burrows, Edwin G., and Mike Wallace. *Gotham: A History of New York City to 1898.* New York: Oxford University Press, 1999.

Castle, Irene. *Castles in the Air.* Garden City, N.Y.: Doubleday & Co., 1958.

Charters, Ann. *Nobody: The Story of Bert Williams.* New York: Macmillan, 1970. Originally published: Garden City, N.Y.: Doubleday, 1962.

Charters, Samuel B., and Leonard Kunstadt. *Jazz: A History of the New York Scene.* New York: Da Capo Press (reprint), 1981.

Chilton, John. *A Jazz Nursery: The Story of the Jenkins' Orphanage Bands.* London: Bloomsbury Book Shop, 1980.

Clayton, Anthony. *France, Soldiers and Africa.* London: Brassey's Defence Publishers, 1988.

Cobb, Irvin S. *The Glory of the Coming.* New York: George H. Doran Company, 1918.

Cook, Will Marion. *A Hell of a Life.* Unpublished autobiography, Moorland Spingarn Research Center at Howard University, Washington, D.C.

Cooke, James J. *The Rainbow Division in the Great War.* Westport, Conn.: Praeger Publishers, 1994.

Cornish, Dudley Taylor. *The Sable Arm: Black Troops in the Union Army, 1861–1865.* Lawrence: University of Kansas Press, 1987.

Danzig, Allison. *The Racquet Game.* New York: Macmillan, 1930.

Davis, Arthur P. *Here and There with the Rattlers.* Detroit: Harlo Press, 1979.

Dix, John A. *Public Papers of John A. Dix, Governor.* Albany, N.Y.: J. B. Lyon, 1912.

Duberman, Martin Bauml. *Paul Robeson.* New York: Alfred A. Knopf, 1988.

Ettinger, Albert M., and A. Churchill. *A Doughboy with the Fighting 69th.* New York: Pocket Books (A Division of Simon and Schuster), 1993.

Farwell, Byron, *Over There: The United States in The Great War, 1917–1918.* New York: W. W. Norton & Co., 1999.

Fish, Hamilton. *Hamilton Fish: Memoir of an American Patriot.* Washington, D.C.: Regnery Gateway, 1991.

Fletcher, Tom. *100 Years of the Negro in Show Business.* New York: Burdge & Company, 1954.

Foch, Ferdinand. *The Memoirs of Marshall Foch.* Trans. Col. T. Bentley Mott. Garden City, N.Y.: Doubleday, Doran and Company, 1931.

Foster, Vernon. *Spartanburg: Facts, Reminiscenses, Folklore.* Spartanburg, S.C.: The Reprint Company, 1998.

Glasser, Ruth. *My Music Is My Flag: Puerto Rican Musicians and Their New York Communities, 1917–1940.* Berkeley: University of California Press, 1995.

Glatthaar, Joseph T. *Forged in Battle: The Civil War Alliance of Black Soldiers and White Officers.* New York: Meridian Press, 1991.

Goldhurst, Richard. *Pipe Clay and Drill: John J. Pershing: The Classic American Soldier.* New York: Reader's Digest Press, 1977.

Handy, W. C. *Father of the Blues.* New York: Da Capo Press (reprint), 1991. Originally published: New York: MacMillan, 1944.

Harris, Stephen L. *Duty, Honor, Privilege: New York's Silk Stocking Regiment and the Breaking of the Hindenburg Line.* Washington, D.C.: Brassey's Inc., 2001.

Haynes, Robert V. *A Night of Violence: The Houston Riot of 1917.* Baton Rouge: Louisiana State University Press, 1976.

Hicks, Luther C. *Great Black Hoosier Americans.* Shelbyville, Ind.: Shelby County Library, 1977.

Hunton, Addie W., and M. Kathryn Johnson. *Two Colored Women with the American Expeditionary Forces.* New York: G. K. Hall & Co., 1997.

Irwin, Will, Earl Chapin, and Joseph Hotchkiss. *A History of the Union League Club of New York City.* New York: Dodd, Mead & Co, 1952.

Johnson, James Weldon. *Along This Way.* New York: The Viking Press, 1933.

———. *Black Manhattan.* New York: Arno Press and the *New York Times,* 1968.

Katz, Friedrich. *The Life and Times of Pancho Villa.* Stanford, Calif.: Stanford University Press, 1998.

Kimball, Robert, and William Bolcom. *Reminiscing with Sissle and Blake.* New York: Viking Press, 1973.

Kincaid, Brig. Gen. J. Leslie. *Roll of Honor: Citizens of the State of New York Who Died while in the Service of the United States during the World War.* Albany, N.Y.: J. B. Lyon Company, 1922.

Lewis, David Levering. *W.E.B. Du Bois: Biography of a Race, 1868–1919.* New York: Henry Holt & Company, 1993.

Little, Arthur W. *From Harlem to the Rhine.* New York: Covici, Friede, 1936.

Lunn, Joe. *Memoirs of the Maelstrom: A Senegalese Oral History of the First World War.* Portsmouth, N.H.: Heinemann, 1999.

Mannes, David. *Music Is My Faith.* New York: W.W. Norton & Company, 1938.

Marshall, Captain Napoleon B. *The Providential Armistice: A Volunteer's Story.* Washington, D.C.: Liberty League, 1930.

McGee, Chap. Lt. John B. *History of Base Section Number I* [St. Nazaire]. From June 22, 1917 to February 1, 1919, Part 1.

MacGregor, Morris J., and Bernard C. Nalty. *Blacks in the United States Armed Forces: Basic Documents, Vol. IV, Segregation Entrenched, 1917–1940.* Wilmington, Del.: Scholarly Resources, Inc.

Murlin, Edgar L. *The New York Red Book.* Albany, N.Y.: J. B. Lyon Company, 1913.

Neuman, Fred G. *Irvin S. Cobb.* Paducah, Ky.: Young Printing, 1924.

———. *Irvin S. Cobb: His Life and Letters.* Emaus, Penn.: Rodale Press, 1938.

O'Ryan, Maj. Gen. John F. *The Story of the 27th Division.* New York: Wynkoop, Hallenbeck, Crawford, 1921.

Percy, William Alexander. *Lanterns on the Levee: Recollections of a Planter's Son.* New York: Alfred A. Knopf, 1975.

Pershing, Gen. John J. *My Experiences in the First World War.* New York: Da Capo (Reprint) Press, 1995.

A Pictorial History of the Negro in the Great World War, 1917–1918. New York: Touissant Pictorial Co., Inc., 1919. Originally published: New York: Stokes, 1931.

Pippin, Horace. *Horace Pippin, 1888–1946, Notebooks, c. 1920.* Washington, D.C.: Archives of American Art, Smithsonian Institution, filmed January 1972.

Quarles, Benjamin. *The Negro in the Civil War.* New York: A Da Capo (reprint), 1989. Originally published: Boston: Little, Brown, 1953.

Richardson, Clement. *The National Cyclopedia of the Colored Race.* Montgomery, Ala.: National Publishing Company, 1919.

Riley, James A., ed. *The Biographical Encyclopedia of the Negro Baseball Leagues.* New York: Carroll Graf, n.d.

Robeson, Paul. *Here I Stand.* Boston: Beacon Press, 1973.

Robeson, Paul, Jr. *The Undiscovered Paul Robeson: An Artist's Journey, 1898–1939.* New York: John Wiley & Sons, 2001.

Rose, Al. *Eubie Blake.* New York: Schirmer Books, 1979.

Schiedt, Duncan. *The Jazz State of Indiana.* Indianapolis: Indiana State Library, 1971.

Schoener, Allon, ed. *Harlem on My Mind: Black America, 1900–1968.* New York: The New Press, 1995. (Originally published by Random House, 1968.)

Scott, Emmett. *The American Negro in the World War.* Chicago: Homewood, 1919. Reprinted as *Scott's Official History of the American Negro in the World War.* New York: Arno Press and the *New York Times,* 1969.

Sissle, Noble. "Memoirs of Lieutenant 'Jim' Europe," unpublished manuscript held by the Library of Congress.

Smith, Eric Ledell. *Bert Williams: A Biography of the Pioneer Black Comedian.* Jefferson, N.C.: McFarland & Company, Inc., 1992.

Stearns, Michael, and Jean Stearns. *Jazz Dance: The Story of American Vernacular Dance.* New York: The Macmillan Co., 1968.

Sulzer, William. *Public Papers of William Sulzer, Governor.* Albany, N.Y.: J. B. Company, 1914.

Whitman, Charles Seymour. *Public Papers of Charles Seymour Whitman, Governor.* Albany, N.Y.: J. B. Lyon Company, 1916.

ARTICLES, INTERVIEWS, ORAL HISTORIES

Confidential Report from the 369th U. S. Infantry to Historical Division, American Expeditionary Force, 7 January 1919. National Archives and Records Administration.

"How Drafted Men Live." *New York Times,* 16 September 1917.

"100 Years of Dedicated Service: 1886–1986, The J. F. Floyd Mortuary." Spartanburg, S.C.: The J. F. Floyd Mortuary, 1986.

"Negro's Place in Music." New York *Evening Post,* 13 March 1914.

"Saint Nazaire Built on American Plan, Getting Ready for U.S. Trade after War." Brooklyn *Eagle,* 24 June 1917.

"Two Frenchmen Visit U.S. Base in France." *New York Times,* 23 June 1918.

"We Have the Regiment." New York *Age,* 12 June 1913.

"Yaphank Camp: First Description in Detail." *New York Times,* 12 August 1917.

Burlin, Natalie Curtis. "Negro Music at Birth." *The Musical Quarterly.* 1, Janaury 1919.

Curtis, Natalie. "Black Singers and Players." *The Musical Quarterly* 5, 1919.

Cutler, Elliott C., Jr. "Master of the Sword." *Assembly,* December 1980.

Fordham, Damon. "Spartanburg, South Carolina: One City, Two Incidents." *The Avery Review,* Spring 1999.

Guttman, Jon. "Regiment's Pride." *Military History,* October 1991.

Kennett, Lee. "The Camp Wadsworth Affair." *Fifty Years of the South Atlantic Quarterly,* 1975.

New York Legislative Record and Index. Albany, N.Y.: The Legislative Publishing Company, 1 January to 2 June 1913.

Nicholls, Hon. Samuel J. Speech in the House of Representatives, 23 April 1917.

O'Ryan, John F. The Reminiscences of John F. O'Ryan. The Oral History Collection, Columbia University.

Perlis, Vivian, interview with Eubie Blake, New Haven, Conn. *Yale American Music Series,* January 1972.

Reagor, Capt. Michael J. "Herman J. Koehler: The Father of West Point Physical Education." *Assembly,* January 1993.

Williams, Bert. "The Comic Side of Trouble." *The American Magazine* 85 (1), January 1918, 33.

INDEX

THE AUTHOR

Stephen L. Harris is the author of *Duty, Honor, Privilege: New York's Silk Stocking Regiment and the Breaking of the Hindenburg Line.* He and his wife Sue live in Weybridge, Vermont.

Rod Paschall is the editor of *Military History Quarterly* and the author of *The Defeat of Imperial Germany, 1917–1918.*